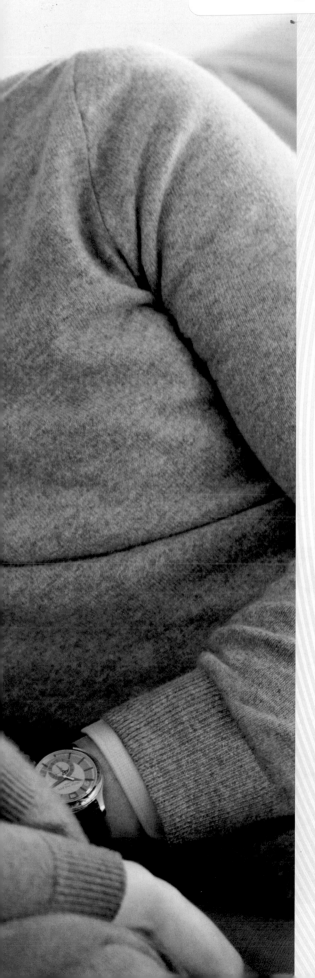

PATEK PHILIPPE
GENEVE

Begin your own tradition.

You never actually own
a Patek Philippe.

You merely take care of it for
the next generation.

Annual Calendar Ref. 5205G

THE ORIGINAL ANNUAL OF THE WORLD'S FINEST WRISTWATCHES

First published in the United States in 2015 by

TOURBILLON INTERNATIONAL
A MODERN LUXURY COMPANY

11 West 25th Street, 8th Floor
New York, NY 10010
Tel: +1 (212) 627-7732   Fax +1 (312) 274-8418
www.modernluxury.com/watches

Caroline Childers
PUBLISHER

Michel Jeannot
EDITOR IN CHIEF

Lew Dickey
CHIEF EXECUTIVE OFFICER

Michael Dickey
PRESIDENT

John Dickey
EXECUTIVE VICE PRESIDENT AND CO-CHIEF OPERATING OFFICER

Jon Pinch
EXECUTIVE VICE PRESIDENT AND CO-CHIEF OPERATING OFFICER

JP Hannan
CHIEF FINANCIAL OFFICER

Richard Denning
GENERAL COUNSEL

In association with **RIZZOLI** INTERNATIONAL PUBLICATIONS, INC.

300 Park Avenue South, New York, NY 10010

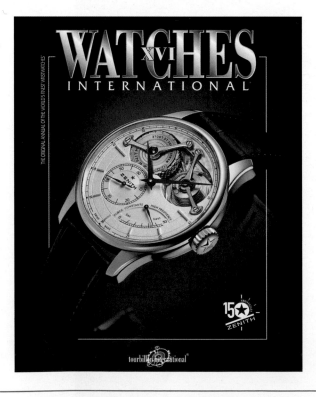

Breguet

Depuis 1775

Breguet, the innovator.
Invention of the shock-protection device, 1790

Inspired by "subscription watches", the Tradition 7027BR model daringly symbolizes the Breguet art of watchmaking through a subtle play on transparency effects and an eminent contemporary architectural design. It highlights one of Breguet's most important inventions, the *pare-chute*, designed to protect the balance pivots in case of impact, it was the forerunner of all modern shock-absorbing devices. History is still being written...

arije

RICHARD MILLE

A RACING MACHINE ON THE WRIST

www.richardmille.com

CALIBER EXTRA FLAT
TOURBILLON RM 017

From the first sundial...

One would have been hard pressed, upon the invention of the first sundial, to imagine that the artistry of the measure of time would one day surpass by leaps and bounds the importance of the very time being measured.

But such is the restless brilliance of the human mind—to seek the endless possibilities of the how, to find the question as fascinating as the answer, to capture the elusive spirit of elegance.

Each passing year presents new daring visions of creativity, and in turn the world's finest watchmakers challenge themselves, and one another, to discover new horizons in a field as rooted in the fabric of the Renaissance as in today's constant global scientific revolutions.

Ageless refinement and relentless reinvention stand side by side, to the awe of horologic enthusiasts and connoisseurs. Page after page, Watches International embraces the past, present and future of the noble art form. United in a single forum, timekeeping luminaries map the vast landscape of their field, each revealing a unique voice as they present the passing of time. While every timepiece shares a constant at the heart of its conception, each tells a story full of nuances and subtleties that bring to the passing second an undeniable individuality.

That first sundial's cast shadow did much more than illustrate time's journey through the day; it gave birth to an art that grows more varied and expressive with each striking demonstration.

Like the time whose passing it so inventively makes visible, haute horology does anything but stand still.

Michael Dickey

Villeret Collection

IB
1735
BLANCPAIN
MANUFACTURE DE HAUTE HORLOGERIE

cellini

Whether you're a seasoned collector or thinking about purchasing your first fine timepiece, Cellini Jewelers will tempt you with a carefully curated collection of watches from the world's finest brands.

Widely regarded as an horological tastemaker for nearly 40 years, Cellini's flair for breaking international brands into the American market is unparalleled. Both of its Manhattan boutiques were early to carry watches by A. Lange & Söhne, Greubel Forsey, Franck Muller and Hublot long before their popularity soared among collectors. Today the independent jeweler continues to be an influential launching pad for brands like De Bethune, HYT and Ludovic Ballouard.

Last year, Cellini added no less than four brands: Arnold & Son, Clerc, Urwerk and Waltham. The latter is the extraordinary American brand that helped revolutionize the watch industry in the 19th century. Re-launched in 2014, Waltham's Swiss-made timepieces are sporty interpretations of the brand's historic aeronautical clocks, including the cockpit timekeeper that accompanied Charles Lindbergh as he completed the first non-stop transatlantic flight in 1927.

For its modern re-launch, Waltham unveiled the Aeronaval collection, which consists of three models: Waltham XA, Waltham CDI and Waltham ETC. "The history of Waltham is truly incredible and not really well known. I was blown away when I started learning more about what they've done and where they've been—from its precise railroad pocket watches to its expeditions to the poles," says Cellini President Leon Adams.

Whether the brand is just starting out like Waltham, or an instantly recognizable icon like Jaeger-LeCoultre, Adams considers it a point of pride to carry a company's entire collection. That incredible depth creates an unparalleled experience that resonates deeply with people who are passionate about watches. What Cellini does best, Adams says, is use that range to help someone find the right watch. He explains, "If you like a particular complication or style, we line up models from several brands so you can weigh your options and judge for yourself what looks and feels right. You can't find that anywhere else, especially a mono-brand boutique."

▲ **BLACK GOLD OPAL EARRINGS**
Pink spinel adds a modern flair to these eye-catching opal and brown diamond drop earrings.

▲ **BLACK GOLD OPAL RING**
Black gold mirrors the antique feel of this opal ring with brown diamonds.

◄ **WALTHAM XA**
The Waltham XA takes its design cues from the clock Charles Lindbergh used in the Spirit of St. Louis.

MADISON AVENUE BOUTIQUE

HOTEL WALDORF-ASTORIA BOUTIQUE

SPARKLING PERSONALITY

But Cellini is known for more than just watches. Its boutiques are also ranked among Manhattan's finest jewelers. The company's impeccably high standards are reflected in everything from unrivaled selection and superior quality to the attentive experts who are ready to guide you through Cellini's glamorous universe.

From classic to contemporary, and subtle to stunning, the jewelry at Cellini encompasses a wide range of styles. Within this exquisite exhibition of glittering luxury, you'll find diamonds in every hue, impressive strands of pearls and magnificent emeralds, rubies and sapphires in one-of-a-kind, handmade settings. "We strive to create a world where the only limit is your imagination," Adams says.

To stay ahead of changing tastes, the collection evolves constantly, adding rare and unique pieces from around the world. For instance, as the popularity of black gold has exploded, Cellini has stayed at the forefront by seeking out the most innovative the designs. The wide cuff bracelet and opal jewelry featured here underscore black gold's inexhaustible versatility.

Cellini also introduced a range of jewelry creations that provide a colorful counterpoint to black gold's dark beauty. Each piece plays with perception by using transparent gemstones to add striking depth to the intricate patterns below. Built from the bottom up, most of the elaborate metalwork and gem setting is topped by faceted quartz, amethyst or topaz for a look that is guaranteed to spark its share of conversations.

Whether it's fine jewelry or collectible timepieces, Cellini is the place to see what's next.

**DOUBLE TOURBILLON 30°
TECHNIQUE BI-COLOR**
(Greubel Forsey)

**HYDROSCAPH H1
CHRONOMETER**
(Clerc)

DB28 MAXICHRONO
(De Bethune)

Hotel Waldorf-Astoria
301 Park Avenue at 50th Street
New York • NY 10022
212-751-9824

509 Madison Avenue at 53rd Street
New York • NY 10022
212-888-0505

800-CELLINI
www.CelliniJewelers.com

▲ **PINK AMETHYST NECKLACE**
White diamonds, pink sapphires and pink tourmalines
are set underneath faceted pink amethyst, crafted in
18-karat rose gold.

▶ **BLUE TOPAZ EARRINGS**
Faceted blue topaz earring accompanied by aquamarines
and blue and black sapphires, set in 18-karat white and
black gold.

▼ **BLACKENED BLACK GOLD MESH CUFF**
18-karat gold provides contrast for the brilliant white
diamonds in this bracelet.

▲ **ARNOLD & SON DSTB**
A true-beat seconds mechanism
is exposed on the dial side of
Arnold & Son's limited edition DSTB.

AUTHORIZED RETAILER

A. LANGE & SÖHNE	HYT
ARNOLD & SON	IWC
AUDEMARS PIGUET	JAEGER-LECOULTRE
BELL & ROSS	LUDOVIC BALLOUARD
BVLGARI	MAÎTRES DU TEMPS
CARTIER	PARMIGIANI
CHOPARD	PIAGET
CLERC	RICHARD MILLE
DE BETHUNE	ROGER DUBUIS
FRANCK MULLER	ULYSSE NARDIN
GIRARD-PERREGAUX	URWERK
GIULIANO MAZZUOLI	VACHERON CONSTANTIN
GREUBEL FORSEY	WALTHAM
H. MOSER & CIE	ZENITH
HUBLOT	

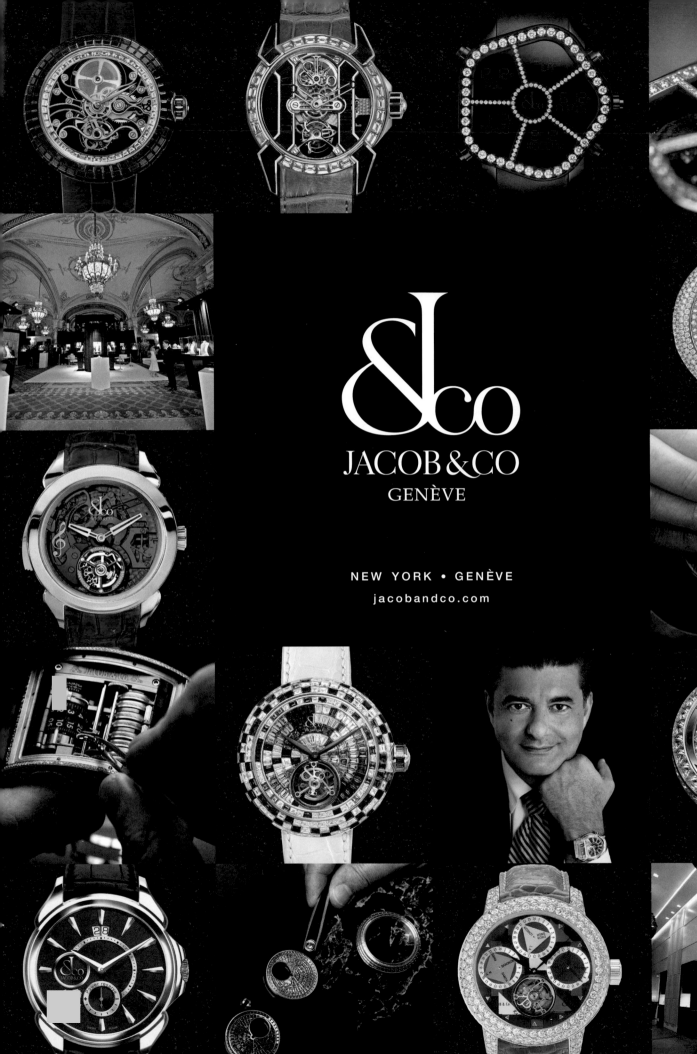

Creative DNA

Imagine for a moment that Picasso, Monet and Matisse came back to us in the 21st century. Inspired by a world full of new philosophies and inventions, their brushstrokes would surely stand out from one another's! Their artistic voices would emanate from the canvas with the same distinct, generation-defining personality. To switch fields—no modern work by Shakespeare could ever be confused with one by a contemporary Jane Austen.

Haute horology is no exception to this phenomenon. Like all artists, watchmakers imbue each of their varied creations with an unmistakable touch of their creative DNA. As they evolve from one generation to the next, inspired by ever-changing trends and innovations, master horologers use each timepiece to express their individuality. As watchmaking continues to defy the limits of what seems possible, each manufacture conquers contemporary challenges while preserving an artistic voice that sets it apart from the others: from the shape of its cases, to the signature style of its hands, numerals or dial layout, among other idiosyncrasies.

It is thus no wonder that many timepieces are passed down from generation to generation as heirlooms that connect families through the ages. Magnificent capsules, where an artist's unique vision collides with the Zeitgeist, watches are bound to their predecessors by a genetic code that remains constant, no matter how insistently time presses on.

Caroline Childers

HERMÈS
PARIS

HERMÈS. TIME REINVENTED.

DRESSAGE L'HEURE MASQUÉE

HERMÈS IMBUES TIME WITH A RESOLUTELY HEDONISTIC TOUCH BY PROVIDING A SPACE OF INFINITE FREEDOM.
THE DRESSAGE L'HEURE MASQUÉE WATCH KEEPS THE HOURS HAND HIDDEN BENEATH THE MINUTES HAND,
MAKING ITS APPEARANCE ONLY WITH A DELIBERATE PRESS ON THE CROWN-INTEGRATED PUSHBUTTON. THE FLEETING
APPARITION OF THE PLAYFUL HAND VANISHES AS SOON AS THE PRESSURE IS RELEASED. THIS DELIGHTFUL
GREAT ESCAPE FROM DAILY ROUTINE IS ENTIRELY CONCEIVED AND CONSTRUCTED BY THE MANUFACTURE HERMÈS,
AND ORCHESTRATED BY THE SELF-WINDING H1925 MOVEMENT, EQUIPPED WITH AN EXCLUSIVE PATENTED MECHANISM.

1.800.441.4488 - Hermes.com

⬤arije

PARIS
50 RUE PIERRE CHARRON   +33 (0)1 47 20 72 40
30 AVENUE GEORGE V   +33 (0)1 49 52 98 88
3 RUE DE CASTIGLIONE   +33 (0)1 42 60 37 77

CANNES
50 BOULEVARD DE LA CROISETTE +33 (0)4 93 68 47 73

SAINT-JEAN-CAP-FERRAT
GRAND-HOTEL DU CAP-FERRAT +33 (0)4 93 76 50 24

LONDON
165 SLOANE STREET +44 (0)20 7752 0246

Within the everyday world we think we know, we occasionally find pockets of something extraordinary. These places act as a refuge from the outside world, where cares are left at the door and the interior is devoted to a standard of luxury and care unknown anywhere else. Arije is one of those refuges.

With boutique-salons in Cannes, London and Paris, Arije creates worlds within worlds for the watch and jewelry lover who wishes to admire stunning jewels and groundbreaking timepieces within an atmosphere of understated elegance. The refined décor sets the tone of cosmopolitan savoir-faire and hospitality.

The sophisticated members of Arije's multilingual staff are experts in watches and jewelry, as able to discuss carat weight and stunning design as they are the new mechanical triumphs produced each year by such brands as Rolex, Cartier, Vacheron Constantin, Breguet and Guy Ellia. Arije's close relationships with the most prestigious brands in haute horology means that its boutique-salons often offer exclusive limited editions or the very first pieces in highly anticipated collections. Always au courant with the latest developments in horology, Arije has recently added Jacob & Co. and Christophe Claret to its unparalleled selection of watches and jewelry.

1. **OCTO FINISSIMO TOURBILLON**
   —the world's thinnest tourbillon
   (Bulgari)

2. **ROTONDE DE CARTIER ASTROCALENDAIRE**
   (Cartier)

3. **CIRCLE "LA PETITE"**
   (Guy Ellia)

4. **PORTUGUESE SIDÉRALE SCAFUSIA**
   (IWC)

5. **TRI-AXIAL TOURBILLON**
   (Girard-Perregaux)

The flagship boutique-salon of Arije's highly restricted circle, on rue Pierre Charron, has distilled the essence of Arije in Paris's Golden Triangle since 1980. Warm and convivial, it offers more than 30 of the world's most sought-after watch and jewelry brands. Two other stores in Paris on avenue George V and rue de Castiglione (between Place Vendôme and the Jardin des Tuileries in the most elegant area of Paris) add their own perspectives on Arije's vision of luxury. The welcoming ambience of golden light and subtle refinement also pervades the locations in London, Cannes and Saint-Jean-Cap-Ferrat.

6. HOMMAGE DOUBLE FLYING TOURBILLON
(Roger Dubuis)

7. SKELETON TOURBILLON PERPETUAL CALENDAR
(Breguet)

8. PATRIMONY ULTRA-PLATE CALIBRE 1731
(Vacheron Constantin)

9. ROYAL OAK CHRONOGRAPH
(Audemars Piguet)

10. COSMOGRAPH DAYTONA
(Rolex)

9.

10.

TO BREAK THE RULES,
YOU MUST FIRST MASTER
THEM.

THE VALLÉE DE JOUX. FOR MILLENNIA A HARSH,
UNYIELDING ENVIRONMENT; AND SINCE 1875 THE
HOME OF AUDEMARS PIGUET, IN THE VILLAGE OF LE
BRASSUS. THE EARLY WATCHMAKERS WERE
SHAPED HERE, IN AWE OF THE FORCE OF NATURE
YET DRIVEN TO MASTER ITS MYSTERIES THROUGH
THE COMPLEX MECHANICS OF THEIR CRAFT. STILL
TODAY THIS PIONEERING SPIRIT INSPIRES US TO
CONSTANTLY CHALLENGE THE CONVENTIONS OF
FINE WATCHMAKING.

AUDEMARS PIGUET

Le Brassus

MILLENARY
MINUTE
REPEATER

IN PINK GOLD,
WHITE ENAMEL DIAL.

An Extraordinary Industry

With the arrival of "smart" watches, is haute horology on the way out? Though the question is surely a worthy one, it is posed in the wrong terms. First of all, traditional horology and smart watches have very little to do with each other. And even if smart watches undoubtedly have a bright future ahead, Swiss horology will not be the industry most threatened by them.

However, since the release of the first smart watches, certain observers have predicted horology's demise. To this day, nothing has come of their dire forecasts. This was explained away with the addendum that we would have to wait for Apple to enter the arena to be sure of traditional watchmaking's disappearance. In the meantime, some are panicking, while others patiently, calmly wait for the arrival of new actors in the technological watch market.

Of course, watchmakers have not always been able to foresee the cataclysms that awaited them. But will they really undergo the same catastrophe that befell them with the arrival of quartz movements in the early 1980s? Even without clairvoyant powers, we can confidently say that this will not be the case. Let's look at a few numbers, while keeping in mind that Swiss watchmaking is a very small part of the industry as a whole. Swiss haute horology represents less than 1% of global watch production (but almost half of its dollar value). Swiss artisans craft in limited quantities mechanical artworks that inspire awe and tell time almost as an afterthought; elsewhere, factories produce hundreds of millions of watches at a time that display the time and other practical information. By the numbers, that gives us 10 million timepieces produced every year in Switzerland—besides the 20 million from Swatch—against... 1.2 billion watches produced elsewhere, almost 700 million of which are made in China! Against which of those two categories is Apple more likely to be a serious competitor?

That being said, the battle for the wrist is definitely on. But why not imagine the peaceful coexistence of these two very different worlds, or even both of them on the same wrist? Some traditional horologers are preparing themselves for such a case. In any case, the makers of high-end timepieces have a lot of resources upon which to draw. Their watches reveal mechanical genius and inspire dreams and emotion. This is precisely what we are presenting to you in this edition, describing brand by brand the values and genes of an extraordinary industry.

Michel Jeannot

PATRIMONY
PERPETUAL CALENDAR

VACHERON CONSTANTIN
Manufacture Horlogère. Genève, depuis 1755.

PIAGET

PERFECTION IN LIFE

WATCHES XVI INTERNATIONAL®

THE ORIGINAL ANNUAL OF THE WORLD'S FINEST WRISTWATCHES

TOURBILLON INTERNATIONAL
A MODERN LUXURY COMPANY
ADMINISTRATION, ADVERTISING SALES, EDITORIAL, BOOK SALES

11 West 25th Street, 8th Floor • New York, NY 10010
Tel: +1 (212) 627-7732   Fax: +1 (312) 274-8418

Caroline Childers
PUBLISHER

Michel Jeannot
EDITOR IN CHIEF

EDITORS	Elise Nussbaum
	Julie Singer
ART DIRECTOR	Mutsumi Hyuga
CONTRIBUTING EDITOR	Samson Crouhy
JUNIOR ASSISTANT EDITOR	Amber Ruiz
TRANSLATIONS	Susan Jacquet
VICE PRESIDENT OF OPERATIONS	Sean Bertram
DIRECTOR OF PRODUCTION & CREATIVE SERVICES	Erin Quinn
PRODUCTION MANAGER	Tim Maxwell
DIRECTOR OF INFORMATION TECHNOLOGY	Scott Brookman
NATIONAL DISTRIBUTION MANAGER	Hector Galvez
SALES ADMINISTRATOR	Ralph Gago

WEB DISTRIBUTION

www.modernluxury.com/watches

PHOTOGRAPHY
Photographic Archives
Property of Tourbillon International, a Modern Luxury Company

MODERN LUXURY

Lew Dickey
CHIEF EXECUTIVE OFFICER

Michael Dickey
PRESIDENT

EXECUTIVE VICE PRESIDENT AND CO-CHIEF OPERATING OFFICER	John Dickey
EXECUTIVE VICE PRESIDENT AND CO-CHIEF OPERATING OFFICER	Jon Pinch
CHIEF FINANCIAL OFFICER	JP Hannan
GENERAL COUNSEL	Richard Denning

Our quest for perfection.
PanoMaticInverse

Glashütte
ORIGINAL

MADEMOISELLE
PRIVÉ

Unique, the finely hand embroidered dials by the Maison Lesage offer an invitation to voyage through the intimate world of Gabrielle Chanel. Fine pearls, gold paillons and gold coated silk threads combine Métiers d'Art excellence and the refinement of Haute Couture. 18K yellow gold set with 60 diamonds (~1 carat).

THE CHANEL MOMENT

L'INSTANT
CHANEL

HUBLOT

THE ART OF FUSION

10 YEARS OF THE BIG BANG

HUBLOT

AN ENGINEERING LEGEND

In April 2005, Hublot introduced the Big Bang, **THE ICONIC DESIGN THAT WOULD REDEFINE WATCHMAKING FOR THE 21ST CENTURY**. The epitome of Hublot's Art of Fusion, the Big Bang collection builds a complete aesthetic upon an immediately recognizable foundation: the simple yet compelling form of the Big Bang case. Mr. Jean-Claude Biver, now Chairman of Hublot & President of the Watch Division, LVMH Group, and Ricardo Guadalupe, CEO of Hublot, created the Big Bang collection, which soon became Hublot's icon.

Hublot's passion for mechanical artistry makes for a natural partnership with Ferrari, a legendary name in the automotive world. The watchmaker has designed several models that draw inspiration from Ferrari's mechanical sophistication and sleek styling. The brand has also debuted numerous watchmaking innovations into this partnership, including the UNICO manufacture movement, patented quick release straps, and Magic Gold, the world's first highly scratch resistant version of this noble metal. Jean-Claude Biver elaborates: "It's an extraordinary fusion of the fine watchmaking craftsmanship held by Hublot and the exceptional Italian industrial achievement held by Ferrari, and an eternal pursuit for transcendent quality and innovation."

▲ **BIG BANG FERRARI KING GOLD**

2005

First Big Bang 301

2006

Ice Bang

Bigger Bang Tourbillon

2

▲ Jean-Claude Biver & Edwin Fenech, President of Ferrari North America.

▲ Ricardo Guadalupe & Ari Berger from Berger Joyeros (Hublot retailer in Mexico).

▲ **BIG BANG FERRARI CERAMIC CARBON**

◀ **BIG BANG FERRARI TITANIUM CARBON**

2007

Big Bang 1 Million

Big Bang Ayrton Senna Limited Edition

ATHLETIC POWERHOUSES

Over the last ten years, the brand has developed innovative alloys and high-tech materials with which to craft the collection, as well as ingenious ways to incorporate horological complications within the famous case. In its quest for excellence, Hublot has initiated partnerships with the most exceptional athletes on the planet, including the Los Angeles Lakers' Kobe Bryant, the Miami Heat's Dwyane Wade, the world's fastest man Usain Bolt, and soccer "god" Pelé.

The FIFA World Cup™ is the most-watched sports event in the world; a billion people tuned in for the final match in 2014. Hublot, the World Cup's Official Timekeeper, created the Big Bang UNICO Bi-Retrograde Chrono—quickly dubbed the Soccer Bang. With a color scheme that evokes the Brazilian flag, and chronograph counters specifically designed for soccer matches, the Soccer Bang epitomizes Hublot's commitment to the world of sport.

▲ Hublot provided the official time for the 2014 FIFA World Cup™.

▲ **BIG BANG UNICO BI-RETROGRADE CHRONO**

▲ Ricardo Guadalupe, Rihanna & Pelé

▲ Pelé & Ricardo Guadalupe with World Cup timer

2008

Big Bang Tutti Frutti

Bat Bang

2009

Big Bang Ceramic

Big Bang Earl Grey

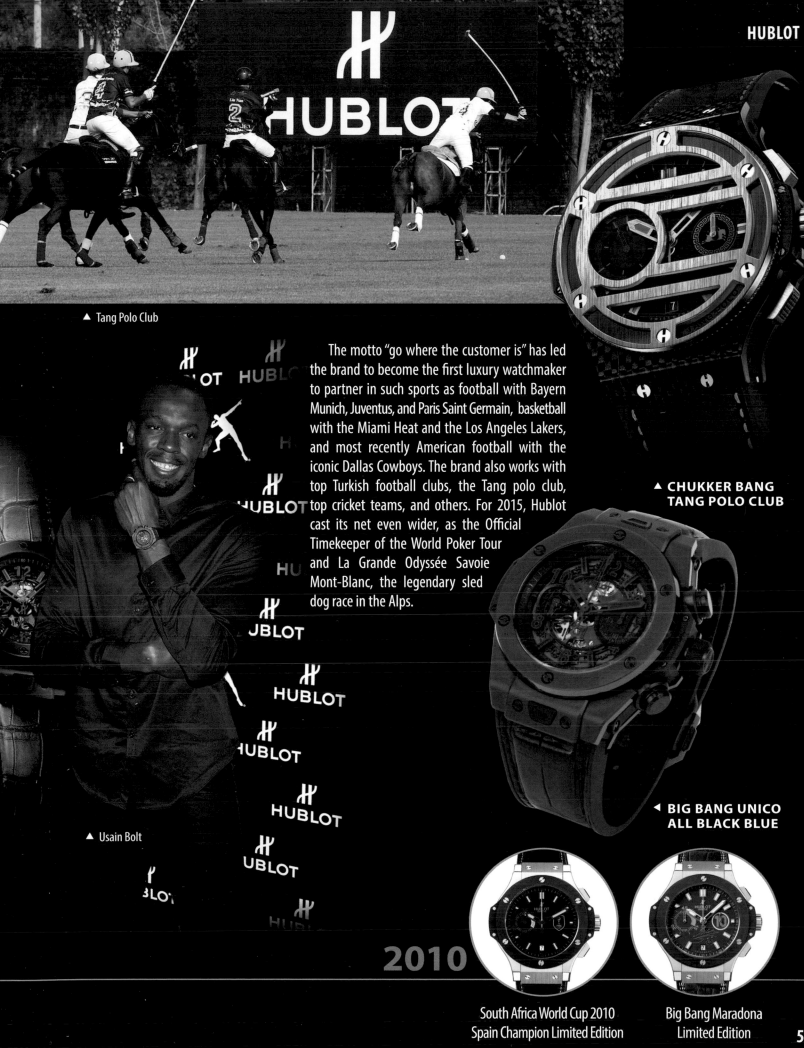

▲ Tang Polo Club

The motto "go where the customer is" has led the brand to become the first luxury watchmaker to partner in such sports as football with Bayern Munich, Juventus, and Paris Saint Germain, basketball with the Miami Heat and the Los Angeles Lakers, and most recently American football with the iconic Dallas Cowboys. The brand also works with top Turkish football clubs, the Tang polo club, top cricket teams, and others. For 2015, Hublot cast its net even wider, as the Official Timekeeper of the World Poker Tour and La Grande Odyssée Savoie Mont-Blanc, the legendary sled dog race in the Alps.

▲ Usain Bolt

▲ CHUKKER BANG
TANG POLO CLUB

◄ BIG BANG UNICO
ALL BLACK BLUE

2010

South Africa World Cup 2010
Spain Champion Limited Edition

Big Bang Maradona
Limited Edition

◄ **BIG BANG JEANS DIAMONDS**

▲ Gabrielle Union & Dwyane Wade

STYLE & SOPHISTICATION

In addition to the engineering exploits achieved within the Big Bang case, Hublot is constantly refining and experimenting with the Big Bang aesthetic. Already a style iconoclast with its first model—in steel and ceramic—the Big Bang has fearlessly pushed the visual boundaries of haute horology with such models as the Big Bang Leopard, Commando Bang Jungle and Big Bang Pop Art.

Stunning bejeweled models include the Tutti Frutti, Tutti Frutti Evolution, Boa Bang, Big Bang Jeans, Big Bang Shiny and a true series of masterpieces: Big Bang 1 Million, Big Bang 2 Million and Big Bang 5 Million.

▲ Jean-Claude Biver & Usain Bolt

▲ Ricardo Guadalupe & Kobe Bryant

▲ **BIG BANG TUTTI FRUTTI**   ▲ **BIG BANG POP ART**   ▲ **BIG BANG FLUO**

2011

2012

Big Bang Leopard   Big Bang Vendome Tourbillon

Big Bang Magic Gold Ferrari   Big Bang 5 Million

MATERIAL INNOVATION AND COMPLICATIONS

Just as its partners blend power and beauty, Hublot has worked tirelessly to develop new technologies for watch materials and complications, leading to the opening of a new Manufacture in 2015 that will double the brand's limited capacity.

Hublot's motto "The Art of Fusion" characterized the brash watchmaker from the start—Hublot was the first brand to combine gold and rubber in the same timepiece. In addition to the carbon fiber case that simplifies the resonant tones of the Big Bang Tourbillon Minute Repeater Carbon, Hublot has also pioneered the use of:

- Magic Gold (scratch-resistant gold)
- King Gold (gold alloy with 5% platinum)
- Colored ceramic
- Colored carbon fiber
- Osmium (most precious metal on Earth)
- Colorfast tinted glass

The Big Bang and Hublot's other collections more than hold their own in mechanical artistry: Hublot's watches house complicated movements and other technical innovations.

- UNICO award-winning in-house chronograph movement
- in-house minute repeaters (winning awards at SIHH 2014)
- in-house tourbillons
- quick-release straps
- longest power reserve (LaFerrari 50 day)

▲ **BIG BANG TOURBILLON MINUTE REPEATER CARBON**

▲ **BIG BANG FERRARI RED CERAMIC**

▲ **BIG BANG UNICO KING GOLD**

HUBLOT

▲ Hublot partnered with Depeche Mode to raise money for charity.

GIVING BACK

Hublot also focuses on its role as a philanthropic partner. Through its initiatives, auctions and special limited edition models, Hublot has raised money and awareness for the Womanity Foundation, diabetes research and amFAR. In Rio de Janeiro during the FIFA World Cup Brazil™, Ricardo Guadalupe, CEO of Hublot, joined Pelé in the Jacarezinho favela, to celebrate the brand's partnership with local architects and resident builders to realize a new soccer field for the children who live there.

At another recent event, Hublot teamed up with rock band Depeche Mode to benefit charity: water. Among other models, Hublot created the one-of-a-kind Big Bang Depeche Mode Steel, to be auctioned off with Depeche Mode memorabilia to raise money for the charity, which seeks to ensure a clean water supply in developing countries.

Guadalupe describes the brand's philosophy with heart: "With our success, we also care for one another. We are in the luxury business but we believe in giving back, specifically for the children."

▲ *top and bottom:*
Pelé & Ricardo Guadalupe celebrate a new soccer field with the children of the Jacarezinho favela.

▲ **BIG BANG DEPECHE MODE**

2013

Big Bang Carbon Bezel
Baguette Rubis

Big Bang Jeans

2014

Big Bang Pop Art

Classic Fusion Pelé

⊙Westime

▲ Westime Beverly Hills

From international timepiece collectors, to customers who are considering purchasing their first watch, Westime's four boutiques in Southern California cater to all by offering a broad and extensive selection of today's most desirable watches.

For nearly three decades, Westime has distinguished itself as the ultimate retail destination specializing in extraordinary watches. John Simonian, a third-generation watch expert with a passion for mechanical timepieces, founded Westime in 1987 when he opened the first boutique on Los Angeles's West Side. From its earliest days, Westime catered to a clientele that ranged from Hollywood celebrities and professional athletes, to the region's influential residents and international business travelers. Westime has since earned the return business of discriminating clients from around the globe.

Today, Westime's four locations reflect the iconic styles of their surrounding neighborhoods. Westime Beverly Hills is an intimate, multi-level boutique at the heart of the city's most glamorous shopping district. The boutique is located on Via Rodeo, a European-style shopping promenade that has emerged as a global destination for the finest watch, jewelry and accessory brands. High ceilings, marble flooring, contemporary furnishings, and showcases that feature champagne water-relief woodwork complement a pre-cisely edited selection of limited editions, high complications and even custom-made time-pieces created exclusively for Westime's clientele. Every member of Westime's affable, multi-lingual staff is dedicated to providing exceptional service—from explaining the specifics of complications, to hand-delivering a watch across the country.

Westime La Jolla is located north of San Diego in one of the country's most beautiful seaside communities. The light-filled store resides among charming shops, galleries and cafes on elegant Prospect Street, just steps from the Pacific Ocean. The boutique's gray slate flooring, natural wood and glass watch cases, and open floor plan invite customers to browse casually. The experienced Westime staff provides such special services as watch repairs and water resistance tests.

Westime Sunset is the largest boutique in the family. Its location on Sunset Boulevard in West Hollywood is near the chic restaurants and boutiques of Sunset Plaza and the legendary nightclubs of the Sunset Strip. The 6,600-square-foot Westime Sunset store reflects the bold buildings and signage of the neighborhood. Perforated and backlit metal panels wrap the asymmetrical façade, while a front wall of windows allows passersby to see the brightly lit scene inside. Asymmetrical angles and high-contrast materials including glass, Venetian plaster, steel, walnut and polished concrete create a gallery-like setting inside the two-story space. Custom corners for Audemars Piguet, Breitling, Omega, Zenith, Bulgari, and Buben & Zörweg enhance the shopping experience for fans of those popular brands.

◀ **ROYAL OAK OFFSHORE TITANIUM TOURBILLON CHRONOGRAPH**
(Audemars Piguet)

▲ Westime Malibu

▲ Westime Sunset

Last year, Westime opened its fourth boutique in Southern California, along Malibu's sun-drenched shores. Located within the open-air Malibu Country Mart, Westime Malibu joins such luxury lifestyle neighbors as Lanvin, Ralph Lauren, Calypso St. Barth and Mr. Chow. The boutique's décor complements Malibu's famously laid-back style of luxury. White-washed panels and sea-blue awnings frame Westime's oversize front windows. A cluster of Adirondack chairs provide the perfect spot for shoppers to take in the view of Westime's window displays while enjoying a rest in the sunshine. Inside the boutique, a sand and cream design scheme creates a serene backdrop for back-lit displays, as well as glass cases containing a tightly edited selection of watches and jewelry. Here customers can discover the collections of such prestigious brands as Audemars Piguet, Breitling, Franck Muller, Hublot, Shamballa Jewels and Zenith.

Westime is frequently noted as one of a dozen multi-brand retailers in the world that influences trends in the watchmaking industry. Led by John Simonian, his son Greg and daughter Jennifer, the company is dedicated to offering the most important creations from traditional watch brands, while also promoting the new guard in haute horology. Recent pieces available exclusively at Westime include Audemars Piguet's Royal Oak Offshore Titanium Tourbillon Chronograph limited edition, and Zenith's Pilot Type 20 Annual Calendar Tribute to Russell Westbrook. At Westime's boutiques, there is always something new to discover.

Westime also operates the Richard Mille Boutique Beverly Hills and Hublot Beverly Hills. The company is proud to support numerous charitable causes, including After-School All-Stars, Scripps and Special Olympics.

BRANDS CARRIED

AARON BASHA	H. MOSER & CIE.
AUDEMARS PIGUET	HUBLOT
BELL & ROSS	HYT
BLANCPAIN	JACOB & CO.
BREITLING	LONGINES
BRM	LOUIS MOINET
BUBEN & ZÖRWEG	LUDOVIC BALLOUARD
BULGARI	MAÎTRES DU TEMPS
CHOPARD	MB&F
CHRISTOPHE CLARET	MONTEGRAPPA
DE BETHUNE	NIXON
DEVON	OMEGA
DEWITT	PIERRE KUNZ
DIOR	REUGE
DÖTTLING	RICHARD MILLE
ERNST BENZ	ROLAND ITEN
FIONA KRUGER	RUDIS SYLVA
FRANCK MULLER	SHAMBALLA JEWELS
FREDERIQUE CONSTANT	SNYPER
GIRARD-PERREGAUX	TAG HEUER
GIULIANO MAZZUOLI	TISSOT
GLASHÜTTE ORIGINAL	UGO CALA
GREUBEL FORSEY	ULYSSE NARDIN
HAMILTON	URWERK
HARRY WINSTON	VERTU
HASSELBLAD	VISCONTI
HAUTLENCE	ZENITH

▲ **MAGNUM**
(Buben & Zorweg)

BEVERLY HILLS
254 North Rodeo Drive • Beverly Hills, CA 90210
T: 310-271-0000

LA JOLLA
1227 Prospect Street • La Jolla, CA 92037
T: 858-459-2222

MALIBU
3832 Cross Creek Road • Malibu, CA 90265
T: 310-456-2555

WEST HOLLYWOOD
8569 West Sunset Blvd. • West Hollywood, CA 90069
T: 310-289-0808

info@westime.com / www.westime.com

BIG BANG UNICO MAGIC GOLD
(Hublot)

FIFTY FATHOMS BATHYSCAPHE
(Blancpain)

RM 037 LADIES
(Richard Mille)

A WORLD OF WATCHES

WESTIME HAS DOMINATED THE CALIFORNIA WATCH SCENE since 1987, providing a home away from home for the world's most passionate horological enthusiasts. President Greg Simonian is thoroughly versed in watchmaking trends, classic complications and the secrets of matching each client with the perfect timepiece.

Westime has four locations (Rodeo Drive, Sunset Boulevard, Malibu and La Jolla). How do you divide your time among them?

Since my home and our corporate headquarters are also in the Beverly Hills area, I am between our Beverly Hills and Sunset Boulevard boutiques on a nearly daily basis. Malibu and La Jolla are farther afield, but—like our customers—I somehow find a reason to spend entire days working in those boutiques when the beach weather hits its peak!

Do you find the watch-buying culture is different in Los Angeles than in other regions? How so?

Yes, LA-based customers are not afraid to wear oversize watches, and many enjoy pairing sports watches with tailored attire, and classic watches with casual clothing. Those surprising pairings allow the watches to stand out!

How important do you find face-to-face conversations to be when helping a customer make a decision?

With the exception of our clients who have been working with the same Westime salesperson for many years and now enjoy the convenience of shopping with us via phone, email or even text message, the face-to-face factor is very important. And when they see me, the owner, personally standing behind each sale and working to ensure they shop with us for years in the future, it sets Westime apart from less personal points of sale that are part of large corporations.

"When (clients) see me, the owner, personally standing behind each sale and working to ensure they shop with us for years in the future, it sets Westime apart from less personal points of sale that are part of large corporations."

◄ **GREG SIMONIAN**

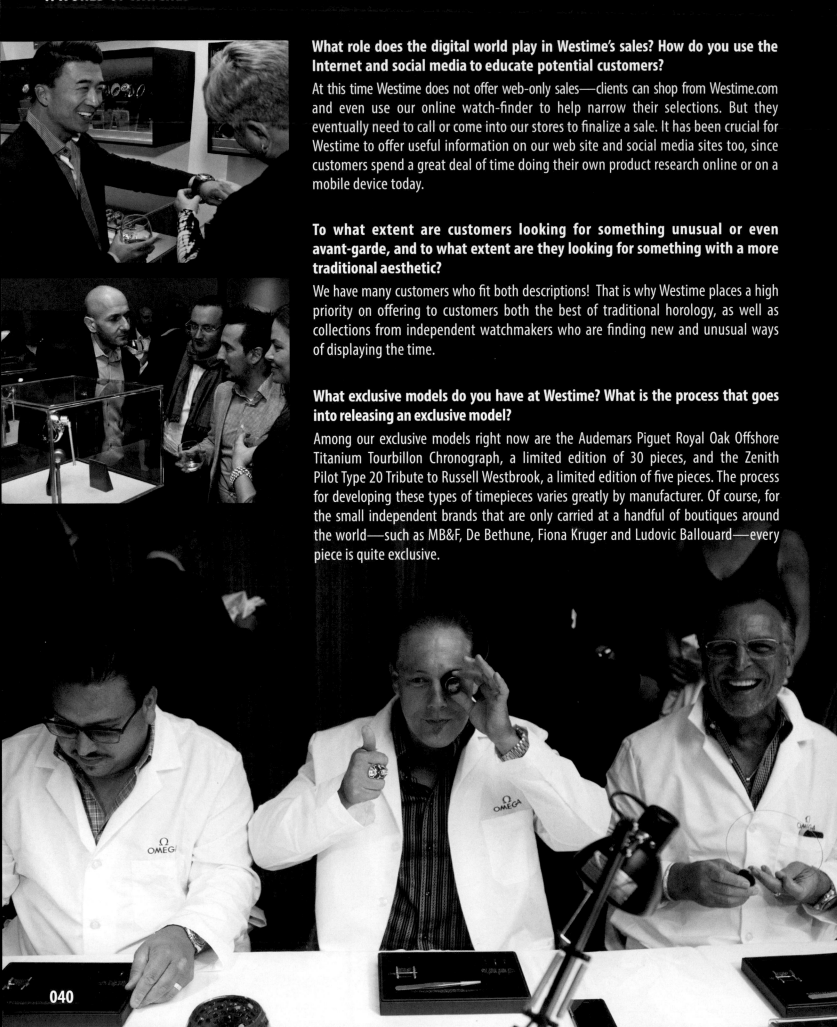

What role does the digital world play in Westime's sales? How do you use the Internet and social media to educate potential customers?

At this time Westime does not offer web-only sales—clients can shop from Westime.com and even use our online watch-finder to help narrow their selections. But they eventually need to call or come into our stores to finalize a sale. It has been crucial for Westime to offer useful information on our web site and social media sites too, since customers spend a great deal of time doing their own product research online or on a mobile device today.

To what extent are customers looking for something unusual or even avant-garde, and to what extent are they looking for something with a more traditional aesthetic?

We have many customers who fit both descriptions! That is why Westime places a high priority on offering to customers both the best of traditional horology, as well as collections from independent watchmakers who are finding new and unusual ways of displaying the time.

What exclusive models do you have at Westime? What is the process that goes into releasing an exclusive model?

Among our exclusive models right now are the Audemars Piguet Royal Oak Offshore Titanium Tourbillon Chronograph, a limited edition of 30 pieces, and the Zenith Pilot Type 20 Tribute to Russell Westbrook, a limited edition of five pieces. The process for developing these types of timepieces varies greatly by manufacturer. Of course, for the small independent brands that are only carried at a handful of boutiques around the world—such as MB&F, De Bethune, Fiona Kruger and Ludovic Ballouard—every piece is quite exclusive.

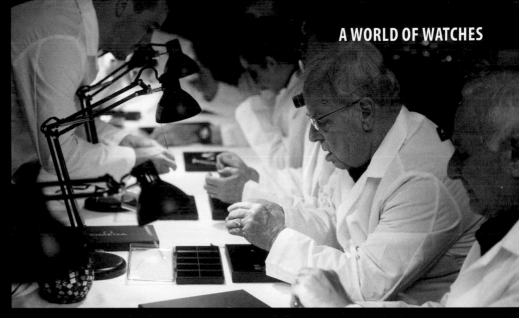

What is the role of site-specific events and dinners, parties, etc, at Westime?

There are many reasons to celebrate at Westime all year! We often host events, ranging from intimate dinners for a couple of clients with a master watchmaker, to watchmaking classes, to cocktail parties in our flagship store to celebrate the US launch of a new watch or the announcement of a celebrity brand ambassador for a line. These events are educational, but they also bring a brand to life for local clients.

What are the trends that you are noticing this year in the watchmaking world? What trends do you see as most exciting for the watch industry?

We will know more after the 2015 watch fairs, but already we are seeing evidence of new materials being used in watches, artistic detailing such as enamel and hand-painting, and the gradual scaling up of smaller watch models.

What new partnerships are you planning for 2015?

At the end of 2014, Westime partnered with Breitling to become the official timekeepers of the Los Angeles Clippers NBA team. So far, it has been a terrific alliance!

Does Westime have any plans for expansion?

We'll have a very active 2015, and that will include the relocation of our Beverly Hills boutique to a new space in the neighborhood.

[Summary]

CHAUMET

PARIS

Liens, la nouvelle Montre Chaumet

GUY ELLIA

PARIS
16 PLACE VENDÔME

CIRCLE « LA PETITE »

Dotée d'un boîtier ultra-plat de 45 ou 52 millimètres de diamètre pour 6 millimètres d'épaisseur pour la première et 7 millimètres pour l'autre, cette montre d'une extrême convexité épouse parfaitement le poignet de toutes les dames. Son boîtier se décline en or blanc, rose ou jaune avec lunette sertie ou entièrement serti. Son cadran au galbe parfait et à la finition poli-miroir ou satinée se définit au choix avec index en appliques, index sertis ou encore entièrement serti neige.

With an ultra-flat case of 45 or 52 millimetres in diameter and 6 millimetres thickness for the first and 7 millimeters for the other, this watch literally envelops women's wrist thanks to its impressive convexity. This case is available in white gold, rose gold and yellow gold, with a bezel set or full set. Its dial with a perfect curve and with a gold mirror or a gold matte aspect is available with simple markers, jewel-set markers or completely set.

[Web Site Directory]

ALPINA	www.alpina-watches.com		IWC	www.iwc.com
ARNOLD & SON	www.arnoldandson.com		JACOB & CO.	www.jacobandco.com
AUDEMARS PIGUET	www.audemarspiguet.com		JAEGER-LECOULTRE	www.jaeger-lecoultre.com
BEDAT & CO.	www.bedat.com		JAQUET DROZ	www.jaquet-droz.com
BLANCPAIN	www.blancpain.com		JEANRICHARD	www.jeanrichard.com
BOUCHERON	www.boucheron.com		LONGINES	www.longines.com
BREGUET	www.breguet.com		LOUIS MOINET	www.louismoinet.com
BVLGARI	www.bulgari.com		PARMIGIANI	www.parmigiani.ch
CARL F. BUCHERER	www.carl-f-bucherer.com		PATEK PHILIPPE	www.patek.com
CARTIER	www.cartier.com		PERRELET	www.perrelet.com
CHANEL	www.chanel.com		PIAGET	www.piaget.com
CHAUMET	www.chaumet.com		POIRAY	www.poiray.com
CHOPARD	www.chopard.com		RICHARD MILLE	www.richardmille.com
CHRISTOPHE CLARET	www.christopheclaret.com		ROGER DUBUIS	www.rogerdubuis.com
CORUM	www.corum.ch		ROLEX	www.rolex.com
DE BETHUNE	www.debethune.ch		TAG HEUER	www.tagheuer.com
DE GRISOGONO	www.degrisogono.com		VACHERON CONSTANTIN	www.vacheron-constantin.com
DIOR HORLOGERIE	www.dior.com		VULCAIN	www.vulcain-watches.ch
ERNST BENZ	www.ernstbenz.com		ZENITH	www.zenith-watches.com
FREDERIQUE CONSTANT	www.frederique-constant.com			
GIRARD-PERREGAUX	www.girard-perregaux.com		**RELATED SITES**	
GLASHÜTTE ORIGINAL	www.glashuette-original.com		BASELWORLD	www.baselworld.com
GUY ELLIA	www.guyellia.com		SIHH	www.sihh.org
HARRY WINSTON	www.harrywinston.com		**AUCTION HOUSES**	
HERMÈS	www.hermes.com		CHRISTIE'S	www.christies.com
HUBLOT	www.hublot.com		SOTHEBY'S	www.sothebys.com

CHAUMET

PARIS

Montre Attrape-moi… si tu m'aimes

Elegance is an attitude

Kate Winslet

Kate Winslet

Conquest Classic

Elegance is an attitude

Simon Baker

Conquest Classic Moonphase

Sascha Moeri
CEO of Carl F. Bucherer

AN INDEPENDENT SPIRIT

According to Sascha Moeri, CEO of Carl F. Bucherer, **THERE IS AN EVER-INCREASING DEMAND FOR MECHANICAL WATCHES AND PARTICULARLY FINELY CRAFTED SWISS MADE MODELS.** The Swiss brand, a family business since 1888, reinforced its independent standing in 2014 by acquiring new production facilities with the goal of increasing the volume of its own movement production, based on the CFB A1000 caliber, as well as realizing new technical developments. Spread between collections for women and men, the watchmaking creations from Carl F. Bucherer reflect the brand's mastery of traditional mechanical horology as well as high jewelry.

▲ **PATRAVI SCUBATEC**

How are Carl F. Bucherer collections structured?
Carl F. Bucherer provides a diverse portfolio that combines design with high-grade technology. There is a good balance between watches for ladies and gentlemen and each line does have a unique character. The PATRAVI line stands out with a sportive design. It is a great success all over the world. The classic MANERO line reflects the art of watchmaking in its most authentic form, with elegant timepieces. The ADAMAVI line is characterized by pure, timeless elegance and mechanical reliability, and the models of the ALACRIA line reveal our jewelers' craft. They are a tribute to feminine grace and beauty. We also launched a totally new collection for ladies, the PATHOS. It appeals with reliable mechanics and design: a delicate garland ornaments the case. Models equipped with mechanical movements are rarely to be found in the ladies' sector. Our ladies' watches are perfect examples of how we combine expertise in jewelry with the art of watchmaking.

Which Carl F. Bucherer watch would you choose as iconic?
In their own way, all Carl F. Bucherer watches perfectly embody our heritage and innovational spirit. You can see at one glance that they are examples of genuine craftsmanship. One of my personal favorites however is the PATRAVI TravelTec FourX. This timepiece is perfect for journeys, because it provides the possibility to preselect the direction you are traveling—East or West—and jump over time zones by just pressing one button. It is not only created for frequent flyers but also for anyone who communicates with the entire world.

Which were the most significant watches launched last year by Carl F. Bucherer?
We presented the diving watch PATRAVI ScubaTec. It does meet all functional and qualitative requirements of a high-performance sports watch and is perfect for every dive and water activity. We also launched the new PATHOS collection for women.

"Carl F. Bucherer's outlook for the future is very promising."

◄ SASCHA MOERI

Did Carl F. Bucherer have any surprises in 2014?

We've been doing extremely well, and sales have exceeded all our expectations. I am convinced that Carl F. Bucherer will remain on this successful path because we stand for values that are highly appreciated by our customers: tradition, independence and technological leadership.

Which are Carl F. Bucherer objectives in the future?

To continue our story of success, we have decided on assertive but measured expansion in our markets, which have grown steadily over the past few years. In terms of distribution, we focus on a successful and strong cooperation with selected partners in a worldwide network to reach more customers internationally. We are planning to open additional stores and points of sale in new markets, in Asia for instance. We would like to see the Carl F. Bucherer brand becoming more and more established all over the world.

How will your collections evolve?

Our objective is to produce exciting new models to strengthen our existing lines. And of course, we never stop striving after new, surprising developments that will be path-breaking for the watch industry. For example, we will further develop and refine our movements with peripheral rotor. They are based on our own patented in-house movement CFB A1000.

Will you further develop your production tools?

Our growth is limited only by production capacity. As a manufacturer of high-class watches, we don't strive for mass production, but want to uphold our extraordinary quality standards. However, we aspire to increase our sales figures and to achieve continuous sustainable growth. In 2009 we were selling approximately 6,000 pieces a year, and next year, the production volume will be up to 25,000 watches thanks to forward-looking changes in our company structure. For instance, we invested in the acquisition of the production site in Lengnau and plan to further expand it in the future. Thereby we will be able to produce and use more of our own in-house movements.

▲ **MANERO TOURBILLON LIMITED EDITION**

▶ **PATRAVI SCUBATEC**

Is there anything specific to the American market and customers?

The American market is a great example of the effective cooperation with our strong retail partners. Thanks to our large network, our strategy for building a stronger position in the U.S. market is already bearing fruit. In the USA, customers are very enthusiastic about our sportive, prominent watches like the PATRAVI TravelTec and the PATRAVI ScubaTec. But they also appreciate the values conveyed by our brand: the tradition of Swiss watchmaking is reflected in every timepiece of Carl F. Bucherer.

What does it mean to be an independent brand today?

To be independent is highly important for Carl F. Bucherer. While evolving as an independent brand, we also enjoy great support by our parent company Bucherer AG. Thus, we benefit from an over 125-year-long tradition as a premium watch and jewelry manufacturer, and are still family-owned in the third generation. Moreover, we are strengthening our independence by constant research and further development of our in-house movements. What also helps to consolidate the independence of the brand are strong production sites as well as our own broad retail network complemented with reliable distribution partners.

Has the watchmaking market been evolving for the last 10 years?

It is difficult to make general statements. But in the last 20 years, developments have shown that mechanical watches are becoming more and more popular. The share of mechanical watches is steadily growing. High-quality products are greatly appreciated, for example Swiss timepieces that ensure the highest watchmaking skills. Therefore, Carl F. Bucherer's outlook for the future is very promising.

What are your biggest challenges?

The achievement of our own manufacturing movement puts us in a strong position in the watch market. By expanding our production sites and our distribution network, we will consolidate the status of Carl F. Bucherer as an independent premium watch manufacturer that represents values like tradition, innovation and uncompromising quality standards.

◄ ADAMAVI

▲ ALACRIA DIVA

◄ PATHOS DIVA
HAUTE JOAILLERIE

CARL F. BUCHERER

FINE SWISS WATCHMAKING

Selected rose gold, precious titanium, extra-hard high-tech ceramic and tough natural rubber give time a new material form. Globetrotters will find that the Patravi TravelTec FourX brings them the perfect combination of luxury and high-tech. It displays three time zones at once and jumps across time zones at the touch of a button. With Carl F. Bucherer's engineering on a miniature scale, your journey through time can begin.

BOUND TO TRADITION – DRIVEN BY INNOVATION

"The DB 29 Maxichrono Tourbillon is as complex as it is marvelously simple."

▶ **PIERRE JACQUES**
CEO of De Bethune

Pierre Jacques

CEO of De Bethune

THE POWER OF THREE

IN 2014, DE BETHUNE WON TWO PRESTIGIOUS AWARDS FOR ITS DB 29 MAXICHRONO TOURBILLON: the "Chronograph Watch Prize" at the Grand Prix de l'Horlogerie de Genève (GPHG) and "Mejor Cronografo" at the Salon International Alta Relojería (SIAR). These new prizes—the titanium DB 28 had already won the "Aiguille d'or" at the GPHG three years previously—recognize the brand's blend of technical innovations and continuous aesthetic development. It is a wager that has paid off for this independent company, founded 13 years ago by David Zanetta, aesthete and collector, and Denis Flageollet, brilliant watchmaker/designer, and helmed today by Pierre Jacques, CEO.

How would you describe the double award-winning DB 29 Maxichrono Tourbillon?

This chronograph is simply superb! Simple, legible, beautiful, refined. It doesn't have several small counters for the seconds and minutes like a traditional chronograph, but rather five hands on the same central axis. That makes for an ultra-legible dial. In addition, a single pushbutton handles all the controls.

Of course, the simpler a watch appears, the more complex its mechanics actually are. We worked on the research and development behind this timepiece for seven years! It is the first chronograph of its kind. De Bethune has secured several patents for the mechanism. We developed an "absolute clutch" mechanism that gives rise to three semi-independent systems controlled by three interdependent column wheels. These facilitate the functioning of the different chronograph counters. It even measures longer intervals, up to 23 hours, 29 minutes, 59 seconds and nine tenths of a second. We have also filed a patent for the flat terminal curve of the balance spring, and have developed with this watch a true wrist-worn tourbillon in silicon and titanium. Thanks to these technological advances, we will be able to produce other calibers that are even more precise and high-performance.

The watch is still ultra-legible and very comfortable. The rose-gold case has a soft, rounded silhouette, emphasized by the characteristic cone-shaped De Bethune lugs. The double "officer-type" caseback opens using a monopusher button inserted into the crown at 3 o'clock. One can thus observe the chronograph movement and its splendid finishings, including the mirror-polished steel bridges. The DB 29 Maxichrono Tourbillon is exceptional; we will produce between just 10 and 20 pieces per year.

▶ **DB 29 MAXICHRONO TOURBILLON**

How do you delineate your collections?

We have two foundational collections. The DB 25 is more classical, with a round case and hollowed-out lugs. The DB 28 has more contemporary characteristics, with articulated lugs and titanium cases, but the same savoir-faire, notably for the finishings. We are also evolving and developing these collections. The DB 27 is the more accessible version of the DB 28. It has the same tilted lugs and titanium case, but with a different caliber, an automatic one.

De Bethune has its own style that pervades all of our models, without adhering to a fixed design code. You will often see cone-shaped lugs or moons in each line, or certain shapes of cases. For example, the DB 29 Maxichrono Tourbillon, which is very classical, uses a case from the DB 15. However, when we want to create something new, for example with the Dream Watch, we give ourselves complete freedom of action.

Do you have a watch that is emblematic of the brand?

Yes, we have several! First of all, the DB 25 QP, with its magnificent curved, guilloché dial, characteristic of De Bethune, and its moonphase. The DB 28 is also emblematic of our work and of our company. It is also the watch I wear; it is light, comfortable and sporty.

▲ DE BETHUNE'S AUBERSON FACILITIES

▼ DB 25 QP

What was most memorable for you about the year 2014?

2014 was a year of continuity for us. We presented many watches, notably the DB 29 Maxichrono Tourbillon, the DB 28 Maxichrono, the DB 28 Digitale, the Dream Watch, as well as a new perpetual calendar with the DB 25 QP. They all represent major technical as well as aesthetic innovations, such as the enameled dials. This result, the fruit of years of research, has garnered us a lot of recognition at the GPHG and SIAR for the DB 29 Maxichrono Tourbillon, as well as in Hong Kong with the Spiral magazine award for the Dream Watch 5.

What are De Bethune's goals for 2015?

We are keeping production low, around 400 watches, and we will continue to propose several new watches, including a DB 28, a first ever De Bethune World Time model, a chronograph and an extremely sophisticated grand complication model.

In terms of distribution, De Bethune is a niche brand; we know our clients and we know our markets. We sell part of our production ourselves. Our watches are also available in about 40 points of sale, mainly in Singapore, the United States and other places in Asia.

What does independence mean for De Bethune?

It does complicate some things, such as access to certain resources, financing or even visibility. These constraints are amply compensated for by total creative freedom. We produce our watches in a very fulfilling work environment.

What should an Independent brand look forward to in the next 10 years?

Will there be more or fewer independent brands? That will depend on economic fluctuations, but also on the ability of horology to remain an attractive option for the younger generations. Our grandparents collected pocket watches. Nobody uses those anymore. Even though most of my friends' children wear wristwatches at age 18, that doesn't mean that future generations will. The mechanical watch is not very useful, compared to the quartz watch, which counts extreme accuracy among its advantages. However, it is analogous to the world of cars. One may drive a Toyota Prius and continue to dream of a beautiful Lamborghini. Human beings are not perfectly rational creatures!

Are there more watchmaking connoisseurs these days?

There were already many connoisseurs at the beginning of the 2000s. They are still around, and new collectors are popping up, notably in emerging markets. The information is very readily available, and many clients are looking to understand and really know the watches they are buying.

▲ DREAM WATCH 5

▼ DB 28 DIGITALE

28
DB

CONTEMPORARY EXPRESSION OF WATCHMAKING ART

SPHERICAL MOON PHASE
SILICON/PLATINUM BALANCE WHEEL
TRIPLE PARE-CHUTE - SHOCK-ABSORBING SYSTEM
FLOATING LUGS

DE BETHUNE

L'ART HORLOGER AU XXIᴱ SIÈCLE

Ricardo Guadalupe
CEO of Hublot

EVOLUTION OF THE BIG BANG

IN 2015, HUBLOT CELEBRATES 10 YEARS OF ITS HIGHLY SUCCESSFUL FLAGSHIP COLLECTION, THE BIG BANG. Over the last decade, the brand has established its horological legitimacy, and it now equips the Big Bang UNICO (evolution of the Big Bang) with in-house movements, as well as the ultra-thin Classic Fusion. This year, Hublot will also enlarge its production capacities and enhance the Big Bang collection with a new house-made complication.

What does the Big Bang represent for Hublot?

The Big Bang made Hublot what it is today. This model singlehandedly revolutionized the brand. It is an "accelerated" adaptation of a famous classic Hublot watch from 1980—20 years of evolution condensed into one model. The Big Bang represents the essence of Hublot, which is the Art of Fusion in watchmaking, a blend of tradition and a vision of horology's future. It combines materials such as rubber, which we were the first to introduce in horology, with ceramic, Kevlar and many other materials.

The public identifies Hublot with the Big Bang. Is this an advantage or a disadvantage?

The Big Bang has brought us much success, and we have a lot to thank it for! It created a shock wave and allowed us to relaunch Hublot. The most prestigious watch brands are all identified with one iconic watch, an absolute reference that ensures their longevity. So Hublot has the Big Bang.

How do you respond to the allegations that the Big Bang resembles another well-known watch?

These accusations should have been made back in 1980, when Hublot released its first watch. With the Big Bang, we simply respected the design codes of that original watch. Like that other famous watch, it resembled a boat's porthole, so there were, of course, similarities between the two interpretations. Today, however, the Big Bang has earned its own reputation, and the comparison has faded.

"The Big Bang
revolutionized
Hublot."

◀ RICARDO GUADALUPE

In your opinion, which Big Bang model best represents the collection?

The All Black was created in 2006. Since then, we have presented a limited edition each year. Formerly, horology was focused on gray and gold. With the All Black model, we turned black into a high-end standard. We pushed the concept to extremes, with much success.

What is your favorite Big Bang?

The very first one, in steel and ceramic. This original version is also our best seller, even though we created it in 2004 and launched it in 2005, ten years ago! Eventually we will replace it with the Big Bang UNICO. It is the same model, but with our own movement.

How will you develop the Big Bang collection in the future?

Hublot will maintain our production output of about 40,000 watches per year, which is quite exclusive. To move toward the higher end, we will increase the horological value of our timepieces. That is why we will round out the collection with Big Bang models worth $50,000-$100,000 USD. Though we already offer tourbillons and minute repeaters, there are still several complications we don't do, such as perpetual or annual calendars, GMT indications or alarms. This year, we are presenting a perpetual calendar chronograph, with a UNICO base movement.

Could the Big Bang eventually run out of steam?

The key to success will be to continue its evolution, with new forms and functions. Just as Porsche has done with its 911 model! We have launched a second line, the Classic Fusion. We are also performing experiments in design and exploring new forms, such as the tonneau case. All these variations conserve Hublot's DNA. But the typical Hublot watch, such as the Big Bang or the Classic Fusion, will stay round.

How does the Classic Fusion relate to the Big Bang?

If the Big Bang was a shock wave, the Classic Fusion more faithfully reflects the Hublot of 1980. It has emerged within a trend toward classic, chic and elegant looks. It is more suited to the needs of a more traditional clientele. However, this Hublot interpretation of a classic watch maintains a strong brand identity. It has a rubber strap and uses ultra-thin movements with a high level of watchmaking sophistication. We believe that high-end watchmaking will survive through the value that it represents. That is why we emphasize our in-house movements and sometimes reveal them by choosing to omit the dial.

Hublot offers just two main collections and many limited series. Why is that?

The heart of our line, with a hundred different models, remains the same: watches in steel and ceramic, gold and ceramic or ceramic alone, released in several different sizes. At the same time, each year we offer new variations in limited editions, which suits the tastes of some of our clientele, who already own our basic models. This division also shows up in our points of sale, which offer a base of 30 to 60 watches and an assortment of limited series.

◄ BIG BANG UNICO

◄ CLASSIC FUSION

These limited series are notably a part of your partnership with Ferrari. How successful has this alliance been?

It has been a great success for both Ferrari and Hublot! We are partnered with the enormous prestige of Ferrari, a worldwide luxury reference. Before us, other watchmakers had not been able to make this collaboration work. We built the partnership from the ground up, based on a free exchange between the teams. Our objective, which we achieved, was to sell very high-end Hublot-Ferrari special editions to the owners of Ferrari automobiles! We are present at all the Ferrari events in the world—about 200 last year—from the smallest to the largest, such as the 60th anniversary of Ferrari in the USA, celebrated in Beverly Hills with a gathering of over 1,000 Ferraris. And every Ferrari representative has a Ferrari clock in the garage or showroom. Hublot is also present on the F1 car driven by Team Ferrari, which brings us some nice visibility. The five-year contract will be renewed.

Finally, Hublot has a new brand ambassador, Bar Refaeli. Which clientele are you targeting?

Bar Refaeli allows us to approach women in a brand-new way, with a photo shoot done by a famous Chinese photographer. Our goal is to sell 30% of our watches to women, as opposed to 25% today. Our creations, which are highly innovative, brightly colored and creative, appeal to women who already own classic watches and want some variety.

▶ **BIG BANG FERRARI**

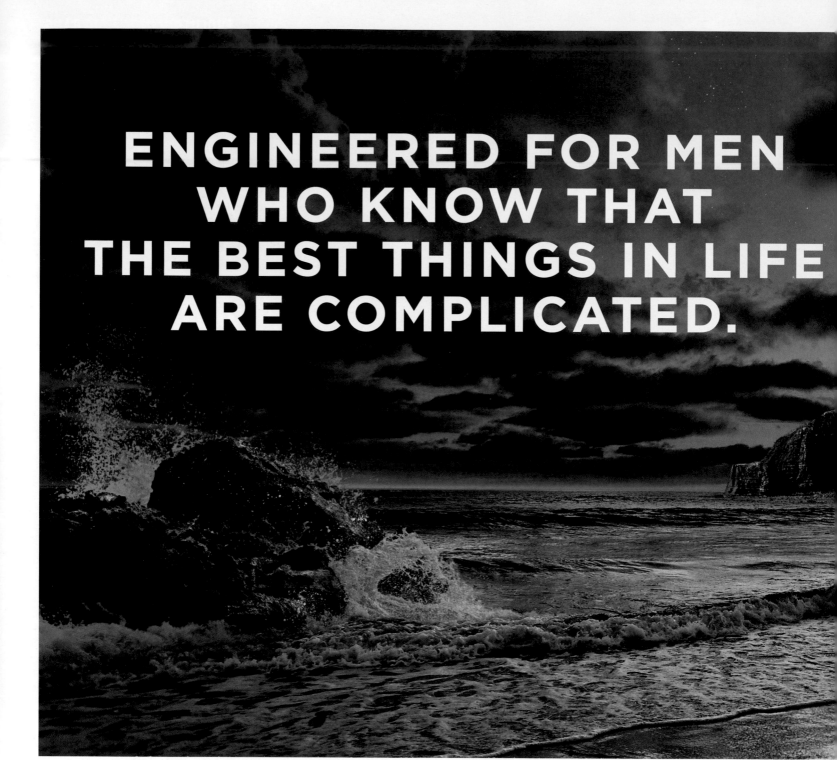

ENGINEERED FOR MEN WHO KNOW THAT THE BEST THINGS IN LIFE ARE COMPLICATED.

Portuguese Grande Complication. Ref. 3774: In every epoch, there are researchers, explorers and individuals of genius who are unable to resist the fascination of describing the indescribable, of making the incomprehensible comprehensible, and of giving substance to the supernal. These forward-looking thinkers still exist: today, they dedicate themselves to the development of sophisticated complications once deemed impossible. Highlights of their work can be found in the Portuguese Grande Complication, the flagship of the Portuguese family. It includes a mechanically programmed perpetual calendar, a perpetual moon phase display and a chronograph with hour, minute and seconds hands. The 79091 calibre's crowning glory, however, is a minute repeater that took no less than 50,000 hours to develop. Succumbing to its irresistible fascination, on the other hand, takes just a second. Want to bet? **IWC. ENGINEERED FOR MEN.**

"The El Primero Chronomaster 1969 sums up what Zenith stands for, both aesthetically and technically."

◀ **ALDO MAGADA**
New CEO of Zenith

Aldo Magada

CEO of Zenith

A STRONG CENTURY AND A HALF

ZENITH OPENED A NEW CHAPTER IN 2014, WITH THE ARRIVAL OF ALDO MAGADA AS CEO. In 2015, the watch manufacturer celebrates its 150th anniversary. Its new models continue the approach of refocusing the collections on three lines. The flagship collection is the legendary El Primero, equipped with its famous eponymous movement, which is accurate to one-tenth of a second. The El Primero Chronomaster 1969 model stands out as THE emblematic face of Zenith. The sporty Stratos and the classic Elite collections round out the brand's range. Zenith also continues to offer highly exclusive pieces, and even the option of creating personalized watches.

How would you define Zenith?
Above all, Zenith is defined by the high-frequency El Primero chronograph. It is the only series-produced chronograph of its kind on the market. Within the El Primero collection, Open represents the most recognizable, most important iteration of the concept. It's a very classic watch, but with a twist: the dial-side aperture that reveals the escapement.

Zenith has two other pillars: Stratos in the sport line and Elite for more refined models focused on hours, minutes and seconds. Elite replaces the former Captain collection. All the Captain chronographs will be integrated into the El Primero collection. So the Elite collection concentrates on three-handed models, with of course supplemental complications, such as the date, power reserve indication or moonphase. This kind of model is tremendously popular, particularly among women.

◄ **EL PRIMERO CHRONOMASTER 1969**

Which watch best represents Zenith?

The El Primero Chronomaster 1969! We would like it to be the face of Zenith on the market, as it clearly sums up what Zenith stands for, both aesthetically and technically. This iconic model brings together the historic colors of the first El Primero chronograph and Zenith's trademark dial-side aperture revealing the movement. The classic 42mm case suits men and women. The bezel is rather slim, providing a more comprehensive view of the dial, which we always finish with beautiful decorations. We are also improving the angles of the lugs, to make them even more comfortable for smaller wrists. We regard finishes and details as extremely important, even if they are not immediately visible.

How is the technical aspect of the El Primero Chronomaster 1969 representative of Zenith?

In 1969, Zenith presented the first integrated automatic chronograph movement. It is still the world's most precise series-produced mechanical movement, as its 36,000 vph frequency allows it to measure times to one tenth of a second! It has since become legendary, and powers all the El Primero Zenith chronographs. This proud lineage includes the El Primero Chronomaster 1969, released in 2012. It houses the El Primero 4061 caliber, a recent El Primero chronograph movement whose regulating organ has been moved to 10 o'clock so as to be visible through the dial aperture. This automatic caliber has been entirely designed, perfected and produced in-house. Its technical advantages include an over 50-hour power reserve and its lever and escape-wheel are made of silicon to ensure enhanced performance, especially in terms of longevity. Finally, it is water resistant to 100m.

What are you presenting at Baselworld this year?

Among various new models, we have a new, sporty Stratos watch, in the same spirit as its predecessors. In the Elite collection, we have a slightly larger men's model, with a diameter of 42mm. It is equipped with a new, automatic, three-hand Elite movement and it will be the base for future developments in the collection. In January, we also presented in Geneva a second Zenith Academy Christophe Colomb Hurricane Grand Voyage—an exceptional model.

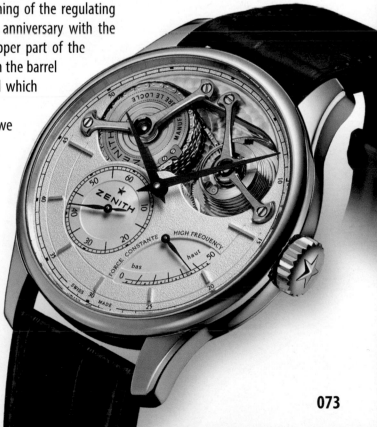

◀ The famous gyroscopic escapement developed by Zenith.

So you will continue to produce higher-end watches?

Absolutely! Even though our typical price point is between 9,000 and 12,000 Swiss francs, we will always create pieces of haute horology, particularly with the decorated El Primero cases.

When I see all the projects we have in the pipeline at the Manufacture, I know that we can serve a certain clientele in search of exclusive watches. We are building up our haute horology facilities with a dedicated workshop. Our clients can order bespoke, completely personalized watches. Someone who orders a watch in this way can communicate with and collaborate with a single watchmaker who will construct the entire watch, as well as providing service after the purchase.

What about research and development?

In terms of research in haute horology, the gyroscopic escapement on Zenith's Grand Voyage constitutes a real answer to a known problem. It is an intelligent and elegant solution that prevents gravity from exerting an undue influence on the functioning of the regulating organ. At the end of 2014, we opened the celebrations of our 150th anniversary with the Academy Georges Favre-Jacot, featuring a large aperture across the upper part of the dial providing a chance to observe the fusee-and-chain transmission with the barrel at 10:30, as well as the fusee around which the chain wraps itself and which appears at 1:30.

In terms of displays, we are headed toward more new features and we wish to create interesting and different experiences for the consumer.

▼ **ADADEMY GEORGES FAVRE-JACOT**

▲ Zenith Hurricane chain movement.

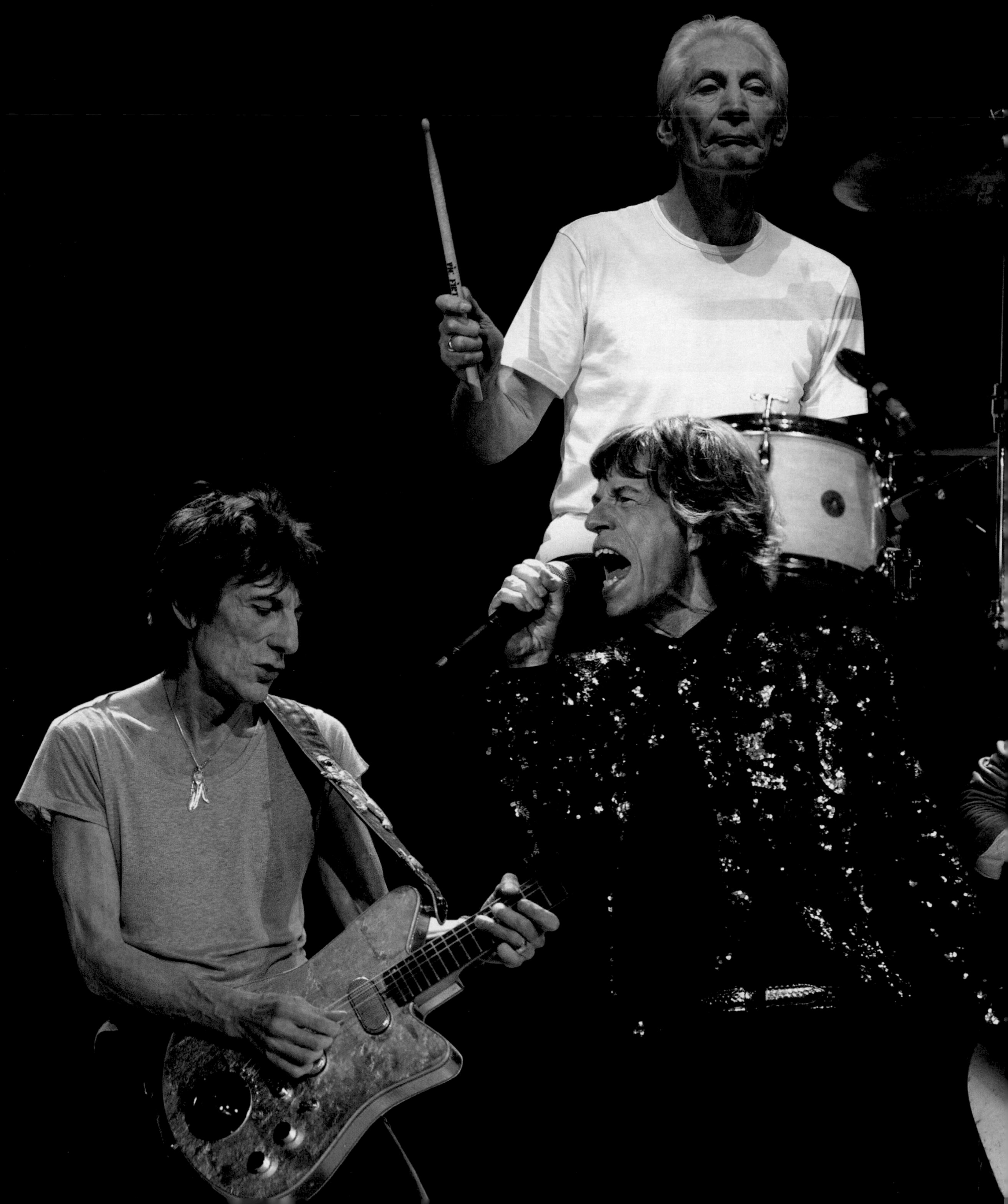

EL PRIMERO CHRONOMASTER 1969

TRIBUTE TO THE ROLLING STONES

ZENITH

SWISS WATCH MANUFACTURE

SINCE 1865

THE DNA OF HAUTE HOROLOGY

These days, it seems as though watch industry stakeholders no longer speak of history, tradition or even savoir-faire. These concepts are considered to be fragmented, partial and simplistic. Instead, today's watchmakers tend to use just one word when they describe their product lines: DNA. It is a term that is supposed to sum up the very essence of the brand and it harbors a good deal of symbolism that is well worth exploring.

The word "DNA" has been part of the watchmaker's vocabulary for several years now. It crept in at first, as if the speaker were newly unveiling carefully hidden mysteries. Now, however, it has become quite a common currency, spent whenever the speaker wants to lend an intellectual air to the proceedings. But what is it, really? We have known for many years about deoxyribonucleic acid (DNA), the molecule that encodes the genetic instructions of living organisms. By analogy, when we speak of watchmaking DNA, we mean that wristwatches also have a genome that provides a blueprint for their functioning. This genome, correctly decoded, relates to the very substance of the timepiece or the brand. It is a biological metaphor for a world of inanimate objects... But are they really inanimate? One thing is certain: watchmakers cultivate a climate of ambiguity on this topic. Let's hear what they have to say about DNA...

i. WATCHMAKING GROUPS

KERING

Formerly known as PPR, the French group Kering is a new arrival in the luxury world. This might explain its effort to establish itself by acquiring a portfolio of brands with a truly global reach. As of summer 2014, its latest acquisition was Ulysse Nardin, which joined Girard-Perregaux and JeanRichard.

▲ Reflet Large (Boucheron)

Boucheron

Founded in 1858, the jeweler Boucheron was the first to have set up shop in Paris's famous Place Vendôme at the turn of the 20th century. Jeweler to India's Maharajahs and other crowned heads, coveted by the stars of the new film industry, Boucheron made an early impression by anticipating the popularity of the neo-Gothic style, later embracing the values of naturalism and cementing its reputation with jewels inspired by pure Art Deco. An early arrival in the field of horology, the maison stood out with its 1947 Reflet model, in a rectangular gadrooned case, and has taken advantage of its collaboration with Girard-Perregaux to interpret the latter's Tourbillon with Three Gold Bridges in a haute jewelry register. With each creation, Boucheron conveys the same message: life is a celebration worthy of recognition by the best work the human hand can achieve. Jewelry is most assuredly part of this message.

▲ Epure Vitis Tourbillon and Diamonds (Boucheron)

Girard-Perregaux

With roots that go back to 1791, Girard-Perregaux can boast a solid tradition of mechanical watchmaking as its foundation. This tradition has a very literal embodiment in the company's Tourbillon with Three Gold Bridges, featuring a design patented in 1884 and which won the gold medal at the 1889 World's Fair in Paris. Girard-Perregaux was also the creator, in 1965, of one of the very first high-frequency mechanical movements to oscillate at 36,000 vph. Since the brand's revival in the 1980s and especially its integration into the Kering Group, Girard-Perregaux has demonstrated that it can still hold its own in the avant-garde of mechanical horology. This bet has paid off with two exceptional pieces presented over the last two years: the Constant Escapement, which presents a major innovation in the construction of the regulating organ, based on the physics principle of "buckling," and the Tri-Axial Tourbillon, an achievement that very few horologers have mastered. In terms of aesthetics, the Neo-Tourbillon with Three Gold Bridges consummates the quest for horological excellence that has led Girard-Perregaux to revive its noble origins.

▲ **Vintage 1945 Moonphases** (Girard-Perregaux)

◄ **Neo-Tourbillon** (Girard-Perregaux)

Ulysse Nardin

Since its creation in 1846, the history of Ulysse Nardin has been closely tied to innovation and chronometric precision. Given this history, it should come as no surprise that the brand's marine chronometers have equipped several armed forces since the beginning of the 20th century. When the brand was revived in the 1980s, these two obsessions emerged as characteristics of the brand. Recently, Ulysse Nardin has distinguished itself with a completely unprecedented series of astronomical watches. Simultaneously, the company is developing new manufacturing capabilities and engineering breakthroughs with silicon, a material that may lead to further advances in the future. In fact, at the dawn of the 21st century, Ulysse Nardin presented a concept watch that operated with an entirely lubricant-free movement.

▲ **Freak Diavolo** (Ulysse Nardin)

▶ **Imperiale Blue** (Ulysse Nardin)

ROGER DUBUIS

HORLOGER GENEVOIS

EXCALIBUR

**Exclusive RD01SQ Manufacture calibre
Skeleton Double Flying Tourbillon**

GENÈVE

**The only Manufacture to be 100% Poinçon de Genève certified.
The most demanding signature in fine watchmaking.**

LVMH

Over the years, LVMH has become a first-rate standard-bearer for watch-making and jewelry. The world's premier luxury company possesses a portfolio of highly complementary brands, among them the most respected jewelers on the planet.

Bvlgari

Originally from Greece, Sotirios Bulgaris opened his first workshop in Rome in 1884, Italianizing his name in the process. The maison would eventually become a veritable empire, extending its reach to the world of perfumes, accessories and luxury hotels. A famous jeweler, particularly esteemed for its jewelry sets, Bvlgari plunged into time measurement in the 1930s, first with feminine watches such as Tubogas and its essential descendent Serpenti, then with more masculine models such as the Bvlgari Bvlgari. The company acquired the brands Gérald Genta and Daniel Roth, affirming its status in the world of haute horology and using their capacities to present its own base caliber, the BVL 168. This progressive integration of horological specialties into the brand's larger mission has made Bvlgari a company with its own enviable reputation that does not hesitate to bring its elegant, daring, Italian style to the world of horological complexity. The result: Bvlgari has set records in ultra-thin watches with its Magsonic, a tourbillon watch with Westminster grand strike. Bvlgari's watches epitomize Swiss mechanical expertise at the service of Italian design.

◄ **Bvlgari Bvlgari** (Bvlgari)

▼ **Octo Finissimo Tourbillon** (Bvlgari)

Chaumet

Marie-Etienne Nitot, founder of Chaumet in 1780, became the official jeweler to Napoleon I, creating the jewels for the latter's marriage to Josephine (and then Marie-Louise), with skills that stemmed from his exceptional savoir-faire. Since that period, and despite some tumultuous times, Chaumet has never stopped upholding this tradition, carried over at a very early stage into the watchmaking world in collaboration with companies such as Patek Philippe or Jaeger-LeCoultre for movements. Chaumet has always preferred haute jewelry to haute horology, devoting its resources to the art of jewelers and craft masters so as to create the beautiful vessels for its timepieces. Its classic interpretations convey its approach to Parisian elegance.

▲ **Attrape-moi... si tu m'aimes**
(Chaumet)

▲ **Liens**
(Chaumet)

▲ **Dior VIII Montaigne**
(Dior Horlogerie)

Dior Horlogerie

The watchmaking branch of Dior made its debut in 2003 with the D de Dior, followed by Chiffre Rouge and the lines Dior Christal and Dior VIII. The name of the latter collection is far from coincidental—the numeral "8" is an important one in the world of Dior. It was on October 8, 1946 that Dior's first atelier was established, on Rue Montaigne in Paris's 8th arrondissement; in 2001, the fashion house opened its first jewelry and watch boutique at 8 Place Vendôme. This attachment demonstrates the brand's fidelity to the design codes of its founder. In terms of the company's timepieces, this fidelity expresses itself through a strong, distinctive aesthetic, based on Swiss horological techniques, featuring graceful curved lines inspired by the folds and pleats of Parisian haute couture.

▶ **Chiffre Rouge C03**
(Dior Horlogerie)

PATRIMONY

Circular perfection • Focusing on essentials • Harmonious proportions

Patrimony epitomises stylistic purity. Reflecting a deliberately minimalist aesthetic striking a fine balance between taut lines and soft curves, it asserts its personality through slender cases radiating an elegance inspired by the 1950s. Beneath the apparent simplicity, lies a wealth of sophistication.

The fine craftsmanship embodied in Patrimony bears the signature of the prestigious Hallmark of Geneva.

Patrimony retrograde day-date
18K 5N pink gold
Ø 42.5 mm
❦ Hallmark of Geneva
Caliber 2460 R31 R7, automatic
Retrograde hand-type day and date
86020/000R-9239

www.vacheron-constantin.com

VACHERON CONSTANTIN

Manufacture Horlogère. Genève, depuis 1755.

Hublot

Hublot is the third great success of Jean-Claude Biver, after Blancpain and Omega. Founded in 1980, the brand soon distinguished itself by the way it combined materials, particularly gold and rubber—a first in the watchmaking world. This approach, dubbed "The Art of Fusion" by Biver upon his arrival at the helm of the company in 2004, would revolutionize the industry. From success among the cognoscenti, Hublot would become a worldwide name. Thanks to Biver's PR genius, the brand began to appear in many different contexts, most notably sports and the arts. The bold, robust silhouettes of the watches also made an impact, enhanced by the use of new materials such as Magic Gold, a nearly unscratchable form of gold, and Hublonium, a brand-new alloy of magnesium and aluminum. These moves were matched by a solid mastery of mechanical watchmaking; the Hublot Manufacture stepped in to begin producing movements, notably the flyback chronograph Unico HUB 1240. The ability to create movements in-house has given free rein to the brand's watchmakers to design extraordinary pieces such as the Antikythera model, based on an ancient astronomical calculator found in the Aegean Sea.

▲ **Antikythera**
(Hublot)

◄ **Big Bang Unico Titanium Ceramic**
(Hublot)

DON'T CRACK UNDER PRESSURE

TAGHeuer

SWISS AVANT-GARDE SINCE 1860

TAG HEUER CARRERA CALIBRE 1887

By pushing you to the limit and breaking all boundaries, Formula 1 is more than just a physical challenge; it is a test of mental strength. Like TAG Heuer, you have to strive to be the best and never crack under pressure.

TAG Heuer

Member of the LVMH group since 1999, TAG Heuer's history is one of progressive industrial integration. Divided among four sites, the watch brand's production capacities now include creation of base movements (mainplate and bridges), dials and cases, as well as departments that handle assembly and research and development. This last department has already designed horological breakthroughs such as the V4, with a "motor" equipped with drive belts for energy transmission, and the Carrera MikroPendulum, the world's first watch with a regulating organ based on magnetic fields—a stunning break with centuries of tradition. The company's new strategy, developed by Jean-Claude Biver, emphasizes accessible price points and a renewed focus on its fundamentals. Having built a solid reputation on its longstanding commitment to the world of athletics, TAG Heuer has, throughout its history, created watches and time measurement instruments that are among the most precise in the world. The brand will continue to devote itself to that tradition.

▲ **Formula 1 Calibre 16**
(TAG Heuer)

◄ **Monaco Calibre 36**
(TAG Heuer)

THE THINNEST
TOURBILLON
MOVEMENT
IN THE WORLD

BVLGARI

OCTO

finissimo

TOURBILLON

«*Details make perfection, and perfection is not a detail*»
Leonardo da Vinci

de GRISOGONO

GENEVE

Zenith

Founded in 1865, Zenith is a watch manufacturer that belongs to the rare breed of Swiss brands capable of creating a timepiece from beginning to end. Among its collections are two exceptional movements: the famous 1969 El Primero, the first automatic-winding, mechanical chronograph to beat at 36,000 vph and measure time to one-tenth of a second, and the 1994 Elite movement, an ultra-thin caliber that oscillates at 28,800 vph. For many years, Zenith's rivals ordered parts from its manufacturing arm to outfit some of their own models, such as Rolex's Daytona or Cartier's Pasha. This practice has ended; Zenith now supplies its own models exclusively, especially since the brand has for several years now become associated with modern-day adventurers such as Felix Baumgartner, the first man to break the sound barrier in free fall. This has led to new territory for the brand to conquer, notably with its Pilot collection and models that emphasize Zenith's horological savoir-faire, such as the high-frequency Zenith Academy Christophe Colomb Hurricane, with a fusee-chain transmission and Gravity Control system inspired by marine chronometers.

▲ **El Primero Chronomaster 1969**
(Zenith)

▲ **Pilot Montre d'Aéronef Type 20** (Zenith)

RICHEMONT

Formerly known as PPR, the French group Kering is a new arrival in the luxury world. This might explain its effort to establish itself by acquiring a portfolio of brands with a truly global reach. As of summer 2014, its latest acquisition was Ulysse Nardin, which joined Girard-Perregaux and JeanRichard.

A. Lange & Söhne

Founded in 1845, A. Lange & Söhne was a well-known company before its Glashütte factory was bombed on the last day of World War II, then expropriated in 1948 under the regime of the German Democratic Republic. It would take the fall of the Berlin Wall in 1990 for Walter Lange, representative of the fourth generation of Germany's most famous watchmaking family, to reinstate the brand on a global level. Four years later, A. Lange & Söhne presented its first "new" timepiece, a Lange 1 equipped with large date, an unusual display at the time, and one that has become the brand's trademark. Since then, A. Lange & Söhne has dedicated itself to reviving the Saxon watchmaking tradition by way of classically designed watches and an impeccable mastery of grand complications. This approach culminated in the 2013 Grande Complication, equipped with a monopusher flyback chronograph, a perpetual calendar with moonphase, and a minute repeater with grand and small strike. It is powered by one of the forty-odd calibers developed and produced in-house by the brand since its rebirth in 1994.

▶ **Grand Complication**
(A. Lange & Söhne)

▶ **Lange Zeitwerk** (A. Lange & Söhne)

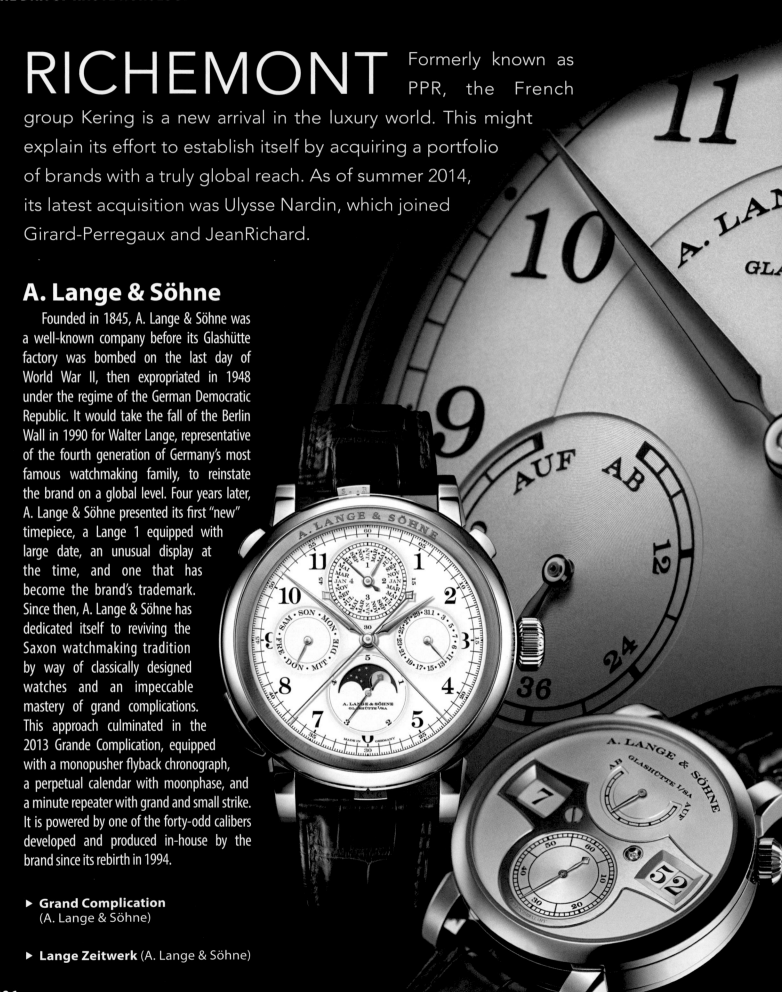

BRASIL

OFFICIAL WATCHMAKER

CONFEDERAÇAO BRASILEIRA DE FUTEBOL

PARMIGIANI

FLEURIER

KALPA DONNA
Steel
Quartz movement
Steel bracelet

Made in Switzerland

www.parmigiani.ch

Cartier

Though Cartier earned the nickname "Jeweler of Kings and King of Jewelers" shortly after its establishment by Lousi-François Cartier in 1847, it was also an early comer to horology. This was expressed through a series of iconic timepieces such as the Santos (1904), the Tortue (1912) or the Tank (1919), and more recent watches like the Pasha (1985) and the Ballon Bleu (2007). This penchant for time measurement has achieved more recognition with the recent creation of a department of haute horology. In about five years, it has created almost 20 original movements to drive collections displaying a rare degree of consistency in terms of both style and expertise. To underscore these efforts, Cartier has also presented two concept watches as of this writing—a collection of avant-garde technological advances that will endow current collections with higher precision and increased reliability.

▲ **Tank Française**
(Cartier)

▲ **Rotonde Astrorégulateur**
(Cartier)

CHRISTOPHE CLARET

Maestoso

TRADITIONAL PIVOTED DETENT ESCAPEMENT WITH CONSTANT FORCE

IWC Schaffhausen

It was an American, Florentine Ariosto Jones, who founded the International Watch Co in Schaffhausen, in 1868. Under his direction, the house built a solid reputation in complicated watches, while belonging to the group of pioneering watchmakers in the aeronautical sector. Long an independent company, IWC joined the Richemont Group in 2000, at the same time as Jaeger-LeCoultre and A. Lange & Söhne. Since then, the brand has targeted one clear objective: producing all of its watch components in-house. The goal is well on its way to becoming a reality, as almost 70% of the company's sales derive from its own movements, a number that was just a few percent a decade ago. Specializing in masculine watches with a lot of potential, IWC has also been innovative, particularly as one of the first horologers to use titanium and ceramic. The brand stands out for its highly distinctive collections, such as the "historical" lines Aquatimer, Ingenieur, Portofino, Da Vinci, Portuguese and Pilot. IWC keeps its watch lines fresh by revisiting each collection in turn every few years, redeveloping its lineup from top to bottom.

◄ **Portuguese Chronograph Classic** (IWC)

▼ **Big Pilot's Watch Perpetual Calendar Top Gun** (IWC)

PERRELET

1777

TURBINE PILOT

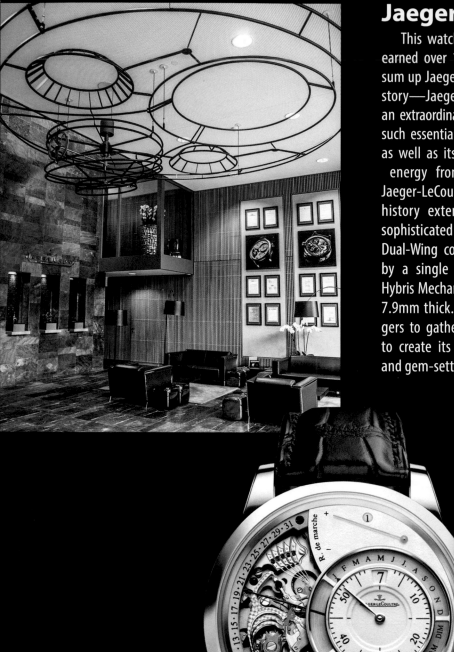

Jaeger-LeCoultre

This watch manufacturer has produced over 1,200 movements and earned over 100 patents. In a few short words, that description might sum up Jaeger-LeCoultre, founded in 1833. There is however more to the story—Jaeger-LeCoultre has distinguished itself over the decades by an extraordinary creativity in mechanical horology, with a resume that lists such essential pieces as the Reverso, the Duoplan, the Memovox Polaris as well as its famous Atmos clock featuring a movement that derives energy from changes in temperature and atmospheric pressure. Jaeger-LeCoultre is an essential part of watchmaking history. That history extends to the present, with numerous highly technically sophisticated constructions such as the spherical tourbillon, the Dual-Wing concept (composed of two independent mechanisms joined by a single regulating organ) or its extra-thin pieces such as the Hybris Mechanica 11 Répétition Minutes et Tourbillon Volant, which is just 7.9mm thick. Jaeger-LeCoultre is also one of the extremely rare horologers to gather under the same roof the 40-odd professions necessary to create its timepieces, including such "métiers d'art" as enameling and gem-setting.

Panerai

The founding myth of Panerai Is that of an Italian watchmaking brand established in 1860, specializing in instruments for the Italian Navy, which commissioned a series of watches built to resist the extreme conditions encountered by its combat swimmers. From the confidential production of this kind of watch, at that time equipped with Rolex movements, a legend was born. This legend was expertly maintained by the Richemont Group, which orchestrated the brand's comeback, with an unexpected helping hand from Sylvester Stallone, who loved Panerai's robust, indestructible style. Since then, the brand has remained remarkably faithful to its original collections: Luminor and Radiomir. It releases them in new models that are equipped with essentially in-house movements, following the watchmaker's aesthetic codes line for line.

◄ **Radiomir 1940**
(Panerai)

▼ **Luminor 1950**
Chrono Monopulsante
Left-Handed
8 Days Titanio
(Panerai)

Piaget

Founded in 1874 by Georges Edouard Piaget, the brand has earned a reputation in jewelry as well as horology. In the latter arena, Piaget relies upon completely integrated manufacturing facilities that have allowed it to dominate the universe of the ultra-thin, a timeless symbol of elegance. The brand's spectacular list of hits includes a double record: the world's thinnest automatic watch (5.25mm), and the thinnest manual-winding watch ever made, the Altiplano 900P, with a total thickness of 3.65mm. This double record is just part of a vast lineage. Piaget has operated in a state of continuous innovation since 1957's release of the 9P movement, just 2mm thick. Out of the watchmaker's 37 movements produced since that time, 25 are considered ultra-thin, and 14 of those hold the record for slimness in their respective categories.

▲ **FortyFive Perpetual Calendar**
(Piaget)

▲ **Altiplano 38 mm 900P**
(Piaget)

▲ **Classique Chronometer**
(Ralph Lauren)

▶ **Petite Link & Link**
(Ralph Lauren)

Ralph Lauren

Stemming from collaboration between Ralph Lauren and the Richemont Group, Ralph Lauren Watch & Jewelry Company presented its first watch collections in 2009. They embody the spirit of Ralph Lauren in their timeless glamour and luxury, as well as Swiss savoir-faire, with movements provided by Piaget and Jaeger-LeCoultre. This combination of design and mechanical expertise has thus given rise to expressive collections such as Stirrup, with equestrian roots, or Sporting, inspired by the automotive world, not to mention the Art Deco 867 model, a tribute to the creative euphoria of the Roaring Twenties.

▲ Métiers d'Art Fabuleux Ornements
(Vacheron Constantin)

Vacheron Constantin

"Do better if it is possible, and that is always possible"—this sentence, from an 1819 letter from François Constantin to Jacques-Barthélémy Vacheron, has become the credo of this watchmaker and lies at the very heart of technically sophisticated, precious haute horology. It is not coincidental that the brand has recently committed itself, body and soul, to the preservation of "métiers d'art" with its collection of the same name, as these "artistic professions" have become an essential element of this approach to time measurement. In this arena, Vacheron Constantin has all the pedigree and legitimacy one could desire. It is the oldest watch manufacture in the world that has remained in constant operation since its founding in 1755. This is expressed through strongly classical collections, including several, such as Historiques, Malte, Traditionnelle and Patrimony, that are inspired by the brand's models from the last century. It also comes out via the consummate art of mechanical horology, as is shown by the brand's many movements combining ingenuity, precision and respect for watchmaking tradition. Vacheron Constantin's most important pieces bear the Poinçon de Genève, the industry's most exclusive certification. The brand recently released the Astronomica, a manual-winding miniature marvel with 15 horological complications.

◄ Patrimony Contemporaine Date et Jour Rétrogradants
(Vacheron Constantin)

LOUIS MOINET

1806

20-SECOND TEMPOGRAPH

INVENTOR OF THE CHRONOGRAPH

Louis Moinet, Switzerland at +41 32 753 68 14, info@louismoinet.com

◄ **Villeret**
8 jours
(Blancpain)

SWATCH GROUP

The Swatch Group, the largest watch company in the world, is also the group that benefits from the largest palette of brands that covers the entire horological spectrum, from plastic Swatch and Flik Flak watches to the most sophisticated timepieces. Its incursion into the high-end reaches of the industry is relatively recent, but its 2013 acquisition of Harry Winston demonstrates that the sector continues to increase in importance.

▲ **Fifty Fathoms Automatique**
(Blancpain)

Blancpain

Watch lovers are quite familiar with the importance of Blancpain, first founded in 1735. From its creation of the first automatic-winding wristwatch (1926) to its manual-winding 13R0 base movement, with three barrels providing an eight-day power reserve, Blancpain's history is studded with exceptional pieces. Among these are: the Ladybird, equipped with the smallest round movement of its day (1956), the 1735, a timepiece that combines six previous complicated masterworks in one (1991), the Equation du Temps Marchante, the first wrist-worn equation of time (2004), or another world-first, the One-Minute Flying Carrousel (2008). Though Blancpain passed through a fallow period from 1950 to 1980, it has since undergone a renaissance, under the leadership of first Jean-Claude Biver and then the Swatch Group. The brand now has its own development unit and movement production department, formerly called the Manufacture Frédéric Piguet. It can also rely on iconic models such as the Fifty Fathoms, the first modern diving watch, which was originally released in 1953 and relaunched in 2007. Upon these foundations, Blancpain continues to cultivate its adventurous spirit with collections such as Léman or L-evolution, but it is most recognized and prized for the classic lines perfectly embodied in its Villeret collection.

Breguet

Abraham-Louis Breguet (1747-1823) needs no introduction. As one of the most creative watchmakers in history, he invented the tourbillon regulator (patented in 1801) and created the incredible Marie-Antoinette, a pocket watch integrating all the complications of the 18th century, which held onto its title as the most complicated watch in the world for over a century. Breguet has been a part of the Swatch group since 1999, under the direct, personal leadership of the late Nicolas G. Hayek. The brand is a blend of the purest classicism and a fundamental pioneering spirit, precisely following the blueprint laid out by the brand's founder in 1775. In other words, this watchmaking giant, with 200 patents to its name, never stops innovating, especially in the realms of high-frequency movements, the use of silicon in its highly sensitive calibers, and the introduction of magnetic components, such as its magnetic pivot, which is key to a stable, dynamic system that is self-correcting and self-centering. In this spirit, the company has completely verticalized its production, creating all components in-house.

▲ **Classique Tourbillon Extra-plat automatique** (Breguet)

▶ **Reine de Naples Jour/Nuit** (Breguet)

Harry Winston

Established in New York in 1932 by the man nicknamed "The King of Diamonds," Harry Winston first made a splash in horology in 1989, with its first collection: The Ultimate Timepieces. In 2007, the brand debuted its own manufacturing facility in Geneva, and it joined the Swatch Group in 2013. The year 2001 marked the beginning of Harry Winston's serious forays into haute horology, with its novel concept of the Opus series. The idea was to present an annual limited edition watch, a truly exceptional piece realized in partnership with one of the most talented watchmakers of the moment. In opposition to the watch world's often secretive culture when it comes to creators, Harry Winston has been completely transparent about each model's authorship—itself a guarantee of spectacular success. The brand first launched its Project Z line in 2004, a collection exclusively crafted in Zalium—Harry Winston's own alloy of aluminum and zirconium. This was followed by the Histoire du Tourbillon, which reinvented the eponymous complication upon a base of Greubel Forsey's work. The superlative technical sophistication of Harry Winston's timepieces matches that of its jewelry lines.

▲ **Premier Feathers**
(Harry Winston)

▲ **Opus Eleven**
(Harry Winston)

Jaquet Droz

Jaquet Droz was a peerless mechanical watchmaker, who largely earned his fame in 18th-century Europe through his humanoid automatons, of which the Writer and the Musician still survive today. The company he founded did not survive him, though its reputation was equally well-established in the watch world, thanks to trade with England and China. In 2000, the Swatch Group breathed new life into Jaquet Droz, producing models directly inspired by the automatons of yesteryear, such as The Bird Repeater, or stylistically refined pieces that emphasized traditional decorations such as painting on enamel, paillonnage or micro-sculptural techniques. The brand's trademark is the Grande Seconde, inspired by a Jaquet Droz pocket watch whose Grand Feu enamel dial features off-center, overlapping counters for the hours and the minutes.

◀ **The Bird Repeater**
(Jaquet Droz)

▲ **Grande Seconde Quantième**
(Jaquet Droz)

114

VULCAIN

MANUFACTURE DEPUIS 1858

The Watch for Presidents.

AVIATOR INSTRUMENT CHRONOGRAPH
Automatic movement, nickel coating, skeleton rotor
Hour, minute, seconds counter at 9, date window at 6
30-minute chronograph counter at 3, 12-hour counter at 6
www.vulcain-watches.com

Photo credit: © Christophe McДull

Manufacture des Montres Vulcain S.A. - Chemin des Tourelles 4 - 2400 Le Locle - Switzerland - Tel. +41 (0)32 930 80 10 - Fax +41 (0)32 930 80 19 - info@vulcain-watches.ch

Longines

Longines, which was founded in 1832, has the world's oldest registered trademark logo still in use in its original form. The brand built its reputation in aeronautics as well as the field of time measurement in athletics. It was indeed Longines that Charles Lindbergh, the first man to complete a solo, nonstop, trans-Atlantic flight (in 1927), commissioned to create the first hour angle watch with a bezel and rotating dial. It was also Longines that would create the first time measurement mechanism that could be automatically, electrically triggered. The brand has maintained this sporty yet technically sophisticated tradition, prizing elegance as a crucial aspect of its "attitude." In fact, Longines carries elegance with it to the four corners of the Earth, as it sponsors an increasing number of horse races around the world.

▲ **Conquest Heritage 1954-2014**
(Longines)

▲ **Prima Luna** (Longines)

◄ **Dark side of the moon**
(Omega)

Omega

To evoke Omega, one need only mention James Bond and the space race, two universes that respectively represent the watchmaker's flagship collections: Seamaster and Speedmaster Professional. However, Omega is clearly much more than that, with 160 years of history behind it and an illustrious role as quasi-official timekeeper of the Olympic Games. It is the only Swiss brand to have taken up the challenge of producing the co-axial escapement, invented by the brilliant George Daniels. This was an important technological advance for accuracy, and the brand is now entering a new phase with its latest-generation Master Co-Axial movements, which boast the distinction of complete imperviousness to magnetism.

► **Seamaster 300 Master Co-Axial**
(Omega)

28
DB

CONTEMPORARY EXPRESSION OF WATCHMAKING ART
SPHERICAL MOON PHASE
SILICON/PLATINUM BALANCE WHEEL
TRIPLE PARE-CHUTE - SHOCK-ABSORBING SYSTEM
FLOATING LUGS

GPHG
GRAND PRIX D'HORLOGERIE DE GENÈVE
— 2011 —
"Aiguille d'Or" Grand Prix

DE BETHUNE
L'ART HORLOGER AU XXIᵉ SIÈCLE

ii. INDEPENDENT COMPANIES

Not all of the most esteemed brands are part of a watchmaking group—far from it. Indeed, there are a number of privately owned watchmakers that prize their independence quite highly. One of these brands, Rolex, which belongs to the Hans Wilsdorf Foundation, is probably the biggest watchmaker in the world in terms of sales.

Audemars Piguet

With around 1,000 employees, Audemars Piguet, established in Brassus in 1875, holds the title of the oldest watch manufacturer in the world that remains in the hands of its founding families. This proof of independence has become a point of pride for the brand. Today, the descendants of Jules-Louis Audemars and Edward-Auguste Piguet head its board of directors. This exceptional longevity by no means implies an aging reputation—quite the opposite. Audemars Piguet has always been in the avant-garde of haute horology, throughout a history filled with exceptional timepieces. With an unquestioned expertise in the world of grand complications, most notably minute repeater watches, and its recent research into new materials, notably the house's specialty, forged carbon, Audemars Piguet has always deftly handled both tradition and innovation. The best proof of this is the Royal Oak. Criticized upon its launch in 1972, the Royal Oak—the first luxury sports watch in steel—has become one of the 20th century's most iconic timepieces.

▲ **Royal Oak Offshore Chronograph**
(Audemars Piguet)

▶ **Jules Audemars Metropolis**
(Audemars Piguet)

BOUCHERON

PARIS

REFLET

"The rebirth of an icon"

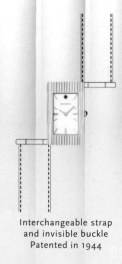

Interchangeable strap
and invisible buckle
Patented in 1944

boucheron.com

Chanel

The French fashion house entered the watch world in the late 1980s, with the creation of a watch department in La Chaux-de-Fonds, Switzerland. The first fruit of this development was the Première, whose silhouette was directly inspired by the shape of the Place Vendôme and the stopper of the famous Chanel Nº 5 perfume bottle. The Mademoiselle model, also immediately recognizable, followed. It was in the year 2000 that Chanel really made waves, with its launch of the J12, the model that would truly "democratize" the use of ceramic in watch cases. The J12 has been so successful that in just a decade and a half, it has become a case study, "the first iconic watch of the 21st century," as Chanel likes to describe it. Interpreted in several sizes and equipped with such horological complications as the tourbillon, dual time zone, and even a "mysterious" retrograde hour, the J12 is, for Chanel, the modern man's watch.

▲ **J12 Rétrograde Mystérieuse** (Chanel)

▲ **Première Tourbillon Volant** (Chanel)

Chopard

First established in 1860, and revived in 1963 by the Scheufele family, Chopard has been able to make its name in jewelry—as underscored by its spectacular creations for the Cannes Festival, of which it is a partner—as well as in watches. In the latter field, the brand has embarked on the long journey to becoming a complete watch manufacturer. The endeavor began with the Chopard Manufacture, devoted to the creation of L.U.C movements, high-end calibers that drive the brand's more technical pieces. Chopard then laid the foundation for an increased production capacity for base movements, pushing its independence one step further. This vertical integration, a twenty-year process in all, demonstrates the patience and the care that the brand brings to its collections, which are both classic and daring.

▲ **L.U.C 150 All-in-One**
(Chopard)

▲ **Happy Sport Medium Automatic**
(Chopard)

Hermès

Established in 1837 in Paris, Hermès produced its first watches in 1928, the prelude to a 50-year collaboration with Swiss watchmaking's most prestigious names. This stage in the brand's evolution was so successful that in 1978 the company founded La Montre Hermès in Bienne, Switzerland. This department went on to produce now-iconic Hermès timepieces such as the Arceau (1978), the Clipper (1981), the Cape Cod (1991), the Heure H (1997) and the Dressage (2003). This last piece, equipped with a movement from Vaucher Manufacture Fleurier, gave rise to the opportunity for Hermès to buy a stake in Vaucher in 2006, which it did in order to secure its supply of high-quality calibers. Since then, the brand has stood out for its creations such as Les Grandes Heures, Le Temps suspendu or L'Heure masquée, a poetic interpretation of time that conceals the highly complex mechanism within.

▲ **Cape Cod Tonneau** (Hermès)

▶ **Dressage l'Heure Masquée**
(Hermès)

▲ **Grandmaster Chime**
(Patek Philippe)

Patek Philippe

Patek Philippe celebrated its 175th anniversary in 2014. In the hands of the Stern family since 1932, this watch manufacturer is considered to belong to the very restricted ranks of historic haute horology brands. Patek Philippe stands out even in this circle, thanks to a strong capacity for innovation and a perfect mastery of the artisanal arts related to watch exteriors. Its reputation is so extraordinary that an international clientele has chosen the horologer to execute commissions for bespoke timepieces that reunite the greatest possible number of complications, for example, the 24 within the 1934 Henry Graves model, a world record at the time. It is no coincidence that Patek Philippe regularly elicits a furor in auction houses, with historical pieces that sell for six-figure sums. This sustained popularity is the basis for the brand's well-known advertising campaign that posits, "You never actually own a Patek Philippe. You merely look after it for the next generation."

▲ **Nautilus**
(Patek Philippe)

Rolex

Known the world over, Rolex is renowned in the watch industry for the quality and reliability of its products, and nothing will happen to damage this reputation—since the entire Rolex production is certified by the COSC. Founded by Hans Wilsdorf in 1905, the brand soon distinguished itself with its 1926 Oyster model, the first truly water resistant wristwatch, which would gain Rolex a foothold in the realm of diving. Over the decades, Rolex would thus expand its collections of timepieces considered to be true technological achievements, such as the 1953 Submariner, a model with bidirectional rotating bezel, helium valve and luminescent hands especially designed for deep dives. The Submariner would grace the wrist of James Bond for 12 years. This capacity for innovation has remained with Rolex, which can also pride itself on being one of the most integrated watch manufacturers in the industry.

▲ **Daytona Platinum** (Rolex)

◀ **Sea-Dweller Deepsea**
(Rolex)

iii. CONTEMPORARY CREATORS

Today's watch world is full of little gems: recently launched companies with an eccentric vision of horology, old names updated for the present day or brands living up to the name of their genius creator. Contemporary horology has everything to gain from this different approach to time measurement.

Bell & Ross

Founded in 1994 and belonging to the Wertheimer family (owners of Chanel), Bell & Ross lays claim to a Swiss tradition of military watches, essentially pilot's watches and watches tailored to extreme conditions. In this line, the brand has devoted itself to a minimalist design code in which each detail counts and function matters most of all. Bell & Ross watches are designed to be robust and technical, based on four fundamental principals: legibility, water resistance, precision and functionality. In recognition of these qualities, Bell & Ross has been named the official watch provider for many special missions or Army corps, such as the Space Lab, the French Air Force or the Groupe d'Intervention de la Gendarmerie nationale française.

▶ **BR126 Flyback** (Bell & Ross)

◀ **BR03-92 Heritage** (Bell & Ross)

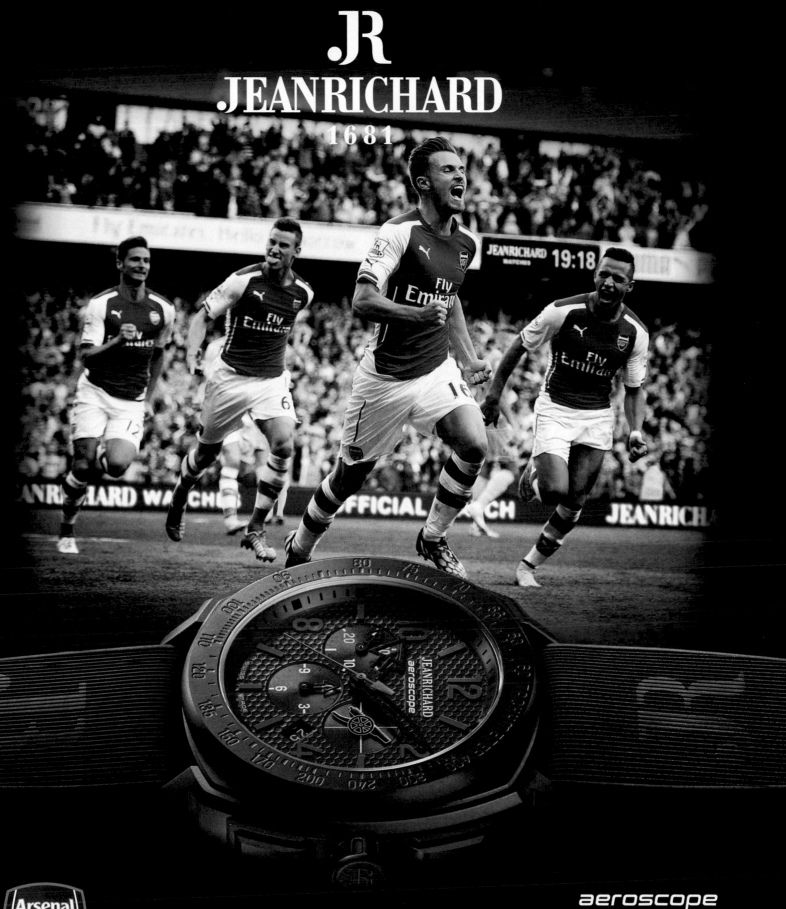

JR
JEANRICHARD
1681

aeroscope

OFFICIAL WATCH

Multi-layer sandblasted black DLC-coated titanium case. Titanium bezel engraved and filled with «Arsenal» red paintings. Swiss mechanical automatic movement. «Arsenal» red honeycomb stamped pattern dial. Rubber strap. Limited and numbered edition of 250 pieces.
jeanrichard.com – Follow **our** story **@JRwatches**

Bovet

The story of Bovet reaches back to 1822, with the company's creation by four brothers who would develop the business of exporting watches specially designed for the Chinese market. The models were sturdy, precise and particularly resistant to humidity. Practically absent from horology since the 1950s, the brand was relaunched in 1989, then acquired by Pascal Raffy in 2001, together with the Manufacture Dimier 1738. Since then, Bovet has perpetuated the brand's tradition of wristwatches with crown and bow positioned at 12 o'clock. Bovet has partnered with the famous Italian design firm Pininfarina to create a line of highly technical models.

▲ **Pininfarina Ottantadue** (Bovet)

▲ **Dimier Recital 8** (Bovet)

Carl F. Bucherer

It was in 1888 that Carl Friedrich Bucherer opened his first watch boutique in Lucerne, and in 1919 that he would launch a collection of watches bearing his name. Since then, the business, which is now owned by the third generation, has never stopped selling timepieces under its own brand. In 2007, the company entered the next phase, swelling the elite ranks of Swiss watch manufacturers by producing its own movement: the elegantly designed CFB A1000. Immediately recognizable, the movement is most notable for its peripheral oscillating weight. Over the years, useful functions have been added to this base movement, such as indications for the day of the week, large date or the power reserve. The harmonious balance of the collections is matched by the power of the Bucherer distribution network, one of the most important European watch retailers.

▶ **Manero PowerReserve** (Carl F. Bucherer)

▶ **Patravi ChronoGrade** (Carl F. Bucherer)

ARNOLD & SON
SINCE 1764

INSTRUMENT COLLECTION
DSTB

Hand-crafted in Switzerland

Caliber A&S6003: manufacture movement / *Haute Horlogerie* finishing: hand-chamfered bridges with polished edges, fine circular graining and *Côtes de Genève rayonnantes*, dial plate with large circular finishing, circular satin-finished wheels, blued screws / self-winding / power reserve over 50 h. **Functions:** hours, minutes, true beat seconds. **Case:** 18-carat red gold / diameter 43.5 mm. **www.arnoldandson.com**

▲ **Poker**
(Christophe Claret)

▶ **Margot**
(Christophe Claret)

Christophe Claret

Christophe Claret boasts a perfect mastery of grand complications, with a particular predilection for tourbillons and musical watches. It all started in Geneva, where a young watch lover studied at the Ecole d'horlogerie, then with a watchmaker who initiated him into the secrets of the profession. He started to buy, restore and resell complicated watches. At the 1987 Baselworld Fair, Claret garnered his first important commission, for minute repeater movements with animated jacks. The die was cast: in 1989, he created his own business in La Chaux-de-Fonds, later premiering several world-firsts in the heights of Le Locle, Switzerland. Christophe Claret has demonstrated year after year—and under his own name since 2009, that the tradition of extremely high-end, complicated watches, crafted in state-of-the-art facilities, deserves its reputation as a quasi-mythical segment of haute horology. His motto is, "In watchmaking, everything has been done and everything is still to be discovered." Evidence of the truth of this abounds in Christophe Claret's repertoire, from the incredible, playful, interactive, mechanical watches 21 Blackjack, Baccara and Poker to its complicated Margot ladies' watch.

Corum

Under the leadership of Antonio Calce, who became CEO in 2007, Corum, founded in 1955, has transformed the way it positions its collections. The brand now focuses on the sports watch market with its Admiral's Cup collection, and haute horology with the Bridge watches, which are powered by Corum's famous baguette movements, an incomparable horological achievement and a technical showcase for the brand. Acquired by Chinese business interests in 2013, the brand continues down this path, imbued on the one hand with seafaring adventurousness and on the other with extremely refined classicism.

◀ **Admiral's Cup
AC-One 45**
(Corum)

◀ **Ti-Bridge
Power Reserve**
(Corum)

de GRISOGONO

In 1993, Fawaz Gruosi, founder of de GRISOGONO, opened his first boutique in Geneva. Without a real commercial strategy, but gifted with an unparalleled flair for jewelry, he stood out from his very first creations. Little by little, the brand made a name for itself, thanks to the genius idea of using galuchat and black diamonds, which had both been ignored for decades. He showed the same daring spirit for watchmaking when he presented the brand's first timepiece in 2000, readily declaring his complete inexperience in the field. That first watch, called Instrumento Uno, set the tone for what was to come, as the brand entered the market at the high end. de GRISOGONO's other watch collections followed, each one more surprising than the last, such as the now-famous Occhio Meccanico, a minute repeater whose dial resembled the diaphragm of a camera. de GRISOGONO has never deviated from its consistent principles of disrupting the horological establishment with impressive pieces, iconoclastic in form but impeccable in mechanics.

▲ **Tondo by night**
(de GRISOGONO)

▲ **Otturatore**
(de GRISOGONO)

Greubel Forsey

The tourbillon is the star of any timepiece from Greubel Forsey, a company founded in 2001 whose research has resulted in three creations to date: the Double Tourbillon 30° (2004), the Quadruple Tourbillon (2005) and the Tourbillon 24 Secondes (2006). The complication has often been criticized for its anachronistic character, deemed to be not only superfluous but often burdensome as well. As a response, Greubel Forsey has performed experiments that prove the tourbillon's efficacy as a tool for increased precision. The brand also aspires to a refined, classical standard of beauty, with an almost obsessive attention to details and finishings. This approach explains Greubel Forsey's very limited production, with around 100 pieces per year. The watchmaker's latest triumph, the Art Piece One, is an artistic creation designed with the artist Willard Wigan, one of whose mirco-sculptures is integrated into the crown. The sculpture is visible thanks to a magnifying system that was specially developed for the watch, along with apertures designed to allow in natural light.

▶ **Art Piece 1**
(Greubel Forsey)

▶ **Quadruple Tourbillon à différentiel**
(Greubel Forsey)

Collection Ma Première et ses bracelets interchangeables

PARIS • GENEVA • TOKYO

WWW.POIRAY.COM

Hautlence

Until its 2012 acquisition by the MELB holding company of Georges-Henri Meylan, former director of Audemars Piguet, Hautlence was essentially one product. Today, after 10 years of existence and a rather tough period, the watchmaker clearly aspires to become a brand. To achieve this, it has introduced a new array of products, notably watches positioned as an affordable luxury. This involved no concessions, however, in terms of the technical sophistication of the timepieces, contemporary watches that won over former soccer player Eric Cantona, an avid collector of "street art" and a new ambassador/designer for the brand.

▲ **HL2**
(Hautlence)

▲ **INVICTUS Morphos**
(Hautlence)

H. Moser & Cie

The historical roots of this brand go back to 1828, when the watchmaker Heinrich Moser opened an establishment in Saint Petersburg. He met with such success that he launched his own brand, with production based in Le Locle. After continuing its operations into the 20th century, H. Moser & Cie did not survive the quartz crisis. It was relaunched in 2002 and soon acquired by MELB Holding, company of the former director of Audemars Piguet. Nevertheless, the spirit of the brand has remained the same, perfectly symbolized by the resolute classicism of its timepieces, discreetly powered by state-of-the-art movements. At H. Moser & Cie, whose in-house production capacities include movements and balance springs, elegant sobriety reigns supreme.

▲ **Mayu** (H. Moser & Cie)

▶ **Perpetual** (H. Moser & Cie)

Jacob & Co.

Located since 2004 on New York's 57th Street, near Central Park, Jacob Arabo started out by crafting jewelry with a penchant for platinum and diamonds. It was not long before famous entertainers and athletes indulged themselves and showed off their idiosyncratic personal style by flaunting his creations. The same unbridled creativity shows up in the watch collections of Jacob & Co., launched in 2002. Breaking completely with horology's established codes, in their design as well as the construction of their complications, the brand's watches cultivate an aesthetic that leaves nobody indifferent. In time Arabo, the "King of Bling," opened an atelier in Geneva, which works closely with watchmaking subcontractors to realize these incomparable pieces.

▲ **Time Traveler Epic SF 24** (Jacob & Co.)

▶ **Astronomia Tourbillon** (Jacob & Co.)

MB&F

Maximilian Büsser & Friends (MB&F) represents a new philosophy of time measurement that dates back to 2005. Instead of watchmakers' characteristic discretion, bordering on omerta, when it comes to revealing the provenance of their movements or components, MB&F practices complete transparency. In other words, under the leadership of its founder—whose fertile imagination leads to the creation of unheard-of timepieces—a group of the watch industry's most talented professionals collaborates on common creations, which take form as watches that have never previously been seen on a human wrist. And when it comes to rendering unto Caesar… MB&F creates an exhaustive list of all participants who helped realize these extra-terrestrial timepieces.

▲ **LM2**
(MB&F)

▶ **HM6**
(MB&F)

Movado

The creation of Movado in La Chaux-de-Fonds dates to 1881. Acquired by the North American Watch Corp. in 1983, the brand was to lend its name to the whole group starting in 1996. Movado has always stood out for the simple, refined design of its watches, a sober, Bauhaus-influenced aesthetic. The famous dial designed by Nathan George Horwitt, entirely black and featureless but for a single golden dot at 12 o'clock—representing the sun, that oldest time reference—earned Movado a place in the Design collection of New York's Museum of Modern Art. The Museum Watch sets the tone for the brand's collections, guided by an aesthetic vision of functionality.

▲ **Gravity**
(Movado)

▶ **Museum Sport**
(Movado)

Parmigiani

The Parmigiani brand was created in 1996, by a watchmaker who already had a reputation as a brilliant restorer of older timepieces. This new creative space gave him the freedom to follow his talent, and design pieces striking the perfect balance between moderation and excess, sobriety and baroque opulence. In addition to the brand's complicated, unusual collections, the Sandoz Family Foundation, Parmigiani's major shareholder, would construct a veritable watchmaking group around the brand, with companies that manufacture everything from the movement to the case and dial. Over the years, this entity has perfected its vertical integration. Parmigiani can thus operate totally independently, with the eccentric spirit that characterizes the brand's timepieces.

▲ **Bugatti Watch** (Parmigiani)

▲ **Kalpa XL Tourbillon Diamonds** (Parmigiani)

Richard Mille

After having directed the watch department at Matra (which was soon acquired by Seiko), then led Mauboussin's first forays into watchmaking, Richard Mille created his own company in 2001. The three founding principles of the Richard Mille brand are a perfect illustration of its timepieces: the best of watchmaking technique pushed to the extreme, the architectural aspect of watches conceived in three dimensions, and finishing done by hand. The radical, outstanding nature of Richard Mille's watches immediately earned the young brand a choice place in the world of haute horology. To confirm its success, Richard Mille has joined forces with the world of athletic elites, the "friends" for which the brand has developed specific watches, including complicated models, that resist the challenging conditions inherent to their respective sports. In short, Richard Mille watches are unparalleled, and the "simplest" among them is identifiable at a glance.

▲ **RM 56-02 Felipe Massa**
(Richard Mille)

◀ **RM 016**
(Richard Mille)

Ernst Benz

PRECISION INSTRUMENTS FOR TIMEKEEPING

CHRONOSCOPE | CHRONOCOMBAT
www.ernstbenz.com

Alpina
1883 GENEVE

INDEPENDENT FEMININITY

Long known for its luxury sport watches, **ALPINA EXTENDS ITS FORAY INTO WOMEN'S WATCHES** with the elegant Comtesse collection and a partnership with double Olympic Ski Champion Tina Maze.

Bound by a love of Alpine tradition, Maze and Alpina also share a particular set of principles that spell success in any endeavor, whether intellectual, athletic or horological. The perseverance and independence evidenced by the skier and the horologer make them stand out even in the most rarefied circles.

The Genevan watchmaker's Comtesse collection springs from the quintessential Alpine values of character, luxury and simplicity. The collection's subtle yet assertive aesthetic combines stylish elements to create a piece that is more than the sum of its parts. Alpina's AL-525 automatic movement, which boasts 26 jewels and 38-hour power reserve, drives all the models in the collection, which are housed in either a stainless steel or two-tone case (in stainless steel and a gold-plated or yellow PVD bezel). In any iteration, the case measures a chic 34mm in diameter and is water resistant to 5atm.

The versatile material used for the case and the three-link bracelet highlights the touches of luxury with which Alpina generously graces the Comtesse line. A mother-of-pearl dial serves as a refined backdrop for diamond or drop-shaped indexes between the Arabic numerals. The practical use of luminescent dots ensures that the wearer can tell time day or night. A yellow-gold or stainless steel bezel shine in unadorned versions or with a sparkling 48 diamonds set around the perimeter.

Winner of two gold medals at the 2014 Olympic Games in Sochi, Tina Maze shares many fundamental qualities with Alpina, which make her choice as brand ambassador an obvious one. Like the independent watchmaker, Maze struck out on her own and created a team with her coach, a decision that led to her triumph in Sochi. Her perseverance in the face of obstacles recalls the longevity of Alpina, which boasts a history stretching back 130 years. A shared affection for the Alpine region also clearly unites the Swiss watchmaker and Maze, one of today's best female skiers.

Alpina knows that in elite sports or elite horology, there are no shortcuts. From its in-house movement manufacturing—a proud tradition that began in 1883—to its invention of the modern sports watch in 1938, to its continued emphasis on innovation, athletics and style, Alpina is as eternal as the mountains that inspire it.

▶ **COMTESSE**
A chic two-tone version of the lady Comtesse sparkles with 48 diamonds on its Ø 34mm bezel.

A shared affection for the Alpine region clearly unites the Swiss watchmaker and Tina Maze, one of today's best female skiers.

◀ **TINA MAZE**
One of the world's best female skiers, Tina Maze is a natural fit for Alpina as brand ambassador.

ALPINA

ALPINER AUTOMATIC — REF. AL-525VGR4E6

Movement: automatic-winding AL-525 caliber; 38-hour power reserve; 26 jewels.
Functions: hours, minutes, seconds; date at 6.
Case: stainless steel; Ø 41.5mm; glass box sapphire crystal; caseback engraved with Alpine sunrise signal; water resistant to 5atm.
Dial: dark gray sunray with matte outer ring; rose-gold-plated hour markers and numerals; luminous dots.
Strap: light brown genuine alligator leather with off-white stitches.
Suggested price: $1,395

Also available: stainless steel and yellow PVD case with bi-color yellow central link PVD-coated metal bracelet (ref. AL-525S4E3B).

ALPINER CHRONOGRAPH — REF. AL-750SG4E6B

Movement: automatic-winding AL-750 caliber; 46-hour power reserve; 25 jewels.
Functions: hours, minutes, seconds; date at 6; chronograph: 12-hour counter at 6, 30-minute counter at 12, 60-second counter at 9; telemeter.
Case: stainless steel; Ø 41.5mm; glass box sapphire crystal; caseback engraved with Alpina sunrise symbol; water resistant to 5atm.
Dial: silver gray sunray with matte outer ring; dark gray counters, Arabic numerals and hour markers; luminous dots.
Bracelet: metal.

Suggested price: $2,850
Also available: stainless steel with black genuine leather strap with off-white stitches (ref. AL-750SG4E6).

ALPINER CHRONOGRAPH 4 — REF. AL-860S5AQ6B

Movement: automatic-winding AL-860 caliber; 46-hour power reserve; 30 jewels; anti-magnetic; ISO764 certified to 4,800 A/m; anti-shock.
Functions: hours, minutes; small seconds at 9; chronograph: 30-minute counter at 3, central chronograph seconds hand.
Case: stainless steel; Ø 44mm; bi-directional turning compass bezel; sapphire crystal; water resistant to 10atm.
Dial: silvered sunray with applied luminous hour markers; white luminous nickel hands.

Bracelet: metal.
Price: available upon request.
Also available: stainless steel with black alligator leather strap (ref. AL-860S5AQ6).

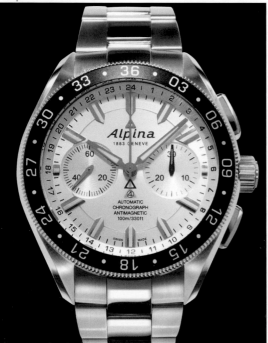

ALPINER GMT — REF. AL-550G5AQ6

Movement: automatic-winding AL-550 caliber; 38-hour power reserve; 26 jewels; anti-magnetic; ISO764 certified to 4,800A/m; anti-shock.
Functions: hours, minutes, seconds; date at 3; GMT.
Case: stainless steel; Ø 44mm; bi-directional compass bezel; sapphire crystal; water resistant to 10atm.
Dial: black sunray; applied luminous hour markers; white luminescent hands.
Strap: black alligator leather.
Suggested price: $2,495

Also available: stainless steel with silver sunray dial and applied luminescent hour markers on metal bracelet (ref. AL-550S5AQ6B).

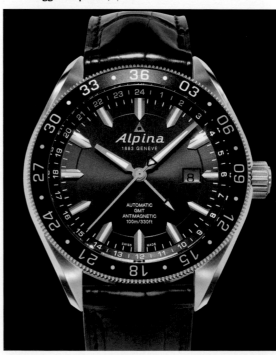

STARTIMER PILOT WORLDTIMER MANUFACTURE   REF. AL-718B4S6

Movement: automatic-winding AL-718 manufacture caliber; 42-hour power reserve; 26 jewels; perlage and circular Côtes de Genève decoration; PVD black coated Alpina rotor.
Functions: hours, minutes, seconds; date by hand adjustable via crown; worldtime (24 cities); day/night indicator; second time zone.
Case: brushed and polished stainless steel; Ø 44mm; convex sapphire crystal; transparent caseback; water resistant to 10atm.
Dial: black; luminescent hour markers and numerals; white luminescent hands.
Strap: black genuine leather; stainless steel folding buckle.
Note: delivered with special pilot gift box.
Suggested price: $3,995

STARTIMER PILOT AUTOMATIC CHRONOGRAPH   REF. AL-860GB4FBS6

Movement: automatic-winding AL-860 caliber; 46-hour power reserve; 30 jewels.
Functions: hours, minutes; small seconds at 9; chronograph: 30-minute counter at 3, central chronograph hand.
Case: stainless steel with black PVD coating; Ø 44mm; scratch-resistant sapphire crystal; transparent caseback; water resistant to 10atm.
Dial: gray sunray; applied hour markers and Arabic numerals.
Strap: soft black genuine leather.
Note: limited edition of 8,888 pieces.
Suggested price: $3,395
Also available: stainless steel with gray sunray dial (ref. AL-860GB4S6).

STARTIMER PILOT CHRONOGRAPH BIG DATE   REF. AL-372N4S6

Movement: quartz; AL-372 caliber; 48-month battery life; 13 jewels.
Functions: hours, minutes, seconds; large date at 6; chronograph: 12-hour at 2, 30-minute counter at 10, 60-second counter at 6.
Case: stainless steel; Ø 44mm; scratch-resistant sapphire crystal; screw-down caseback engraved with Cessna plane image; water resistant to 10atm.
Dial: petrol blue with white large minute markers; white hands with Alpina signature on seconds hand.
Strap: genuine leather.
Suggested price: $1,095
Also available: stainless steel with black PVD and green dial (ref. AL-372GR4FBS6).

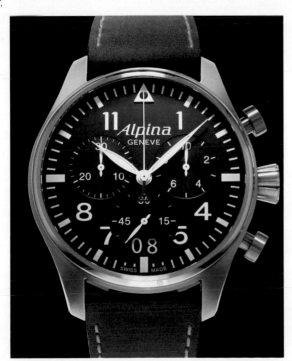

SEASTRONG DIVER 300   REF. AL-525LB4V36

Movement: automatic-winding AL-525 caliber; 38-hour power reserve; 26 jewels.
Functions: hours, minutes, seconds; date at 3; diving turning bezel.
Case: stainless steel; Ø 44mm; unidirectional black PVD polished diving bezel; scratch-resistant domed sapphire crystal; water resistant to 30atm.
Dial: black with white luminous hour markers and hands; red and white luminescent minute hand; seconds hand with red triangle.
Strap: black rubber.
Suggested price: $1,595
Also available: stainless steel with orange and white luminescent minute hand and metal bracelet (ref. AL-525LBO4V26B).

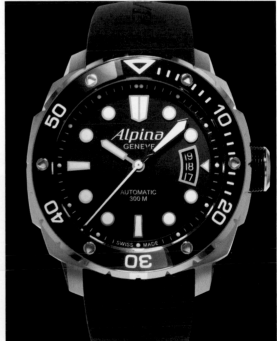

ARNOLD & SON

SINCE 1764

A PIONEERING SPIRIT

A giant of haute horology for 250 years, Arnold & Son honors its rich English heritage with two timepieces that **DRAW FROM THE GLORY OF THE PAST TO DAZZLE THE EYES AND MIND OF THE MOST MODERN OF WATCHMAKING CONNOISSEURS**.

John Arnold's momentous achievements in the field of marine chronometers are celebrated on the face of the manufacture's expressive DSTB. Named for its Dial-Side True-Beat seconds mechanism, the 43.5mm 18-karat red-gold timepiece grants a spectacular view of one of maritime exploration's most crucial complications. The true-beat module, ticking precisely once per second, allows for an exact reference point in the calculation of longitude at sea. Arnold & Son's dynamic exhibition of the mechanism's anchor-shaped lever pays further tribute to the navigators who used this horological innovation. Displayed alongside the lever on the upper-left quadrant of the multi-dimensional dial, the movement's wheels and golden bridges provide stunning contrast to the off-centered hours-and-minutes subdial at 4 o'clock. The DTSB showcases Arnold & Son's mastery of haute horology with a delicate yet powerful coexistence of understated clarity and exposed complexity. This vivid artistic stage, blending the elegant and the intricate, endows the watch with a captivating allure. The transparent caseback completes the effect by revealing the piece's 32-jewel movement's perfect finishes and rhodium-treated skeletonized oscillating weight. The DTSB is worn on a hand-stitched alligator leather strap.

◀ **DSTB**
Named for its dial-side demonstration of its true-beat seconds mechanism, this self-winding wristwatch celebrates John Arnold's distinguished contributions to the field of maritime horology.

The DTE presents two time zones on independent subdials, complemented by a double-tourbillon escapement with 18-karat red-gold bridges.

▲ **DTE**

The DTE revives the concept of double movements with stunning aplomb, using two barrels, two independent time zones and two tourbillons.

Arnold & Son's brilliant mixture of British elegance and Swiss watchmaking finesse represents a duality that has set the brand apart for two and a half centuries.

The DTE explores this duality in its stunning revival of the age-old tradition of "double movements." The 18-karat red-gold DTE, powered by a double-barrel hand-wound movement, presents its riveting architecture atop a Côtes de Genève backdrop. The timepiece presents two time zones on independent subdials, complemented by the exquisite sophistication of a double-tourbillon escapement with elevated 18-karat red-gold bridges. Positioned at 12 and 6 o'clock and displaying the hours and minutes against Roman or Arabic numerals, the DTE's two time zones operate independently of one another, each boasting their own gear train and tourbillon escapement. This meaningful autonomy permits the owner to set each to any of the planet's time zones, including those offset from GMT by the rare quarter- or half-hour increments. At 2 and 8 o'clock, the watch's crowns play off the linear symmetry of the dial.

HMS LADY   REF. 1PMMP.W01A.C114A

Movement: manual-winding A&S1101 caliber; Ø 23.7mm, thickness: 2.5mm; 42-hour power reserve; 17 jewels; 21,600 vph; Swiss escapement; decoration: golden treated with Haute Horlogerie finishing: manually hand-engraved bridges with English-style floral motif, blued screws.
Functions: hours, minutes; small seconds at 6.
Case: 4N rose gold; Ø 34mm, thickness: 7.19mm; set with 76 VVS diamonds (0.685 carat); crown engraved with Arnold & Son logo; transparent caseback; water resistant to 3atm.

Dial: cream; rose-gold hour markers.
Strap: honey hand-stitched alligator leather; 4N rose-gold buckle engraved with Arnold & Son logo.
Note: limited edition of 100 pieces.
Suggested price: $21,000
Also available: various strap colors; with or without diamond setting.

HMS1   REF. 1LCAW.S09A.C111W

Movement: manual-winding A&S1001 caliber; Ø 30mm, thickness: 2.7mm; 90-hour power reserve; 21 jewels; 21,600 vph; Swiss escapement; two barrels; decoration: nickel-silver movement, rhodium treated with Haute Horlogerie finishing, hand-chamfered bridges with polished edges, fine circular graining and Côtes de Genève rayonnantes, blued screws with bevelled and mirror-polished heads.
Functions: hours, minutes; small seconds at 6.
Case: white gold; Ø 40mm, thickness: 7.68mm; crown engraved with Arnold & Son logo; antireflective sapphire crystal; water resistant to 3atm.

Dial: silvery guilloché panier.
Strap: black alligator leather; white-gold buckle engraved with Arnold & Son logo.
Suggested price: $18,950
Also available: 4N rose gold (ref. 1LCAP. S10A.C111A).

HMS HORSES SET   REF. 1LCAP.W03A.C111A

Movement: manual-winding A&S1001 caliber; Ø 30mm, thickness: 2.7mm; 90-hour power reserve; 21 jewels; 21,600 vph; Swiss escapement; two barrels; decoration: nickel-silver movement, rhodium treated with Haute Horlogerie finishing: hand-chamfered bridges with polished edges, fine circular graining and Côtes de Genève rayonnantes, blued screws with bevelled and mirror-polished heads.
Functions: hours, minutes.
Case: 4N rose gold; Ø 40mm, thickness: 7.68mm; crown engraved with Arnold & Son logo; transparent caseback; water resistant to 3atm.

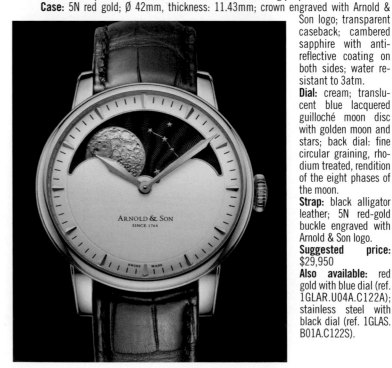

Dial: white lacquer; hand-finished miniature painting.
Strap: black alligator leather; 4N rose-gold buckle engraved with Arnold & Son logo.
Note: limited edition of 28 sets of two pieces as tribute to Chinese New Year.
Suggested price: $55,100 (for set of two watches).
Also available: black lacquer dial (ref. 1LCAP. B04A.C111A).

HM PERPETUAL MOON   REF. 1GLAR.I01A.C122A

Movement: manual-winding A&S1512 caliber; Ø 34mm, thickness: 5.35mm; 90-hour power reserve; 27 jewels; 21,600 vph; Swiss escapement; decoration: nickel-silver movement, rhodium treated with Haute Horlogerie finishing: manually chamfered bridges with polished edges, fine circular graining and Côtes de Genève rayonnantes, blued screws with polished and chamfered edges
Functions: hours, minutes; perpetual moonphase at 12: disc: Ø 29 mm, moon: Ø 11.2, second moonphase indication on caseback for time setting purposes.
Case: 5N red gold; Ø 42mm, thickness: 11.43mm; crown engraved with Arnold & Son logo; transparent caseback; cambered sapphire with anti-reflective coating on both sides; water resistant to 3atm.

Dial: cream; translucent blue lacquered guilloché moon disc with golden moon and stars; back dial: fine circular graining, rhodium treated, rendition of the eight phases of the moon.
Strap: black alligator leather; 5N red-gold buckle engraved with Arnold & Son logo.
Suggested price: $29,950
Also available: red gold with blue dial (ref. 1GLAR.U04A.C122A); stainless steel with black dial (ref. 1GLAS. B01A.C122S).

CTB   REF. 1CHAS.S02A.C121S

Movement: automatic-winding A&S7103 caliber; Ø 30.4mm, thickness: 8.5mm; 50-hour power reserve; 28,800 vph; column wheel; ceramic ball bearing; decoration: NAC gray treated with haute horlogerie finishing: hand-chamfered bridges and polished edges, fine circular graining and Côtes de Genève rayonnantes, circular satin-finished wheels, screws with beveled and mirror-polished heads, oscillating weight: skeletonized with brushed surfaces.
Functions: hours, minutes; true beat seconds; chronograph.
Case: stainless steel; Ø 44mm; cambered antireflective sapphire crystal; transparent caseback; water resistant to 3atm.
Dial: light gray and silvery opaline.
Strap: black hand-stitched alligator leather.
Suggested price: $27,750
Also available: red gold (ref. 1UTAR.S01A).

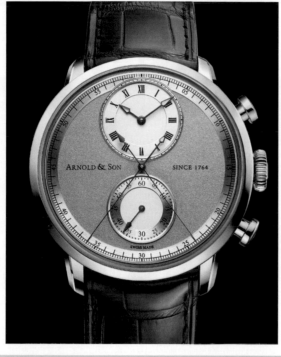

UTTE   REF. 1UTAR.S02A.C120A

Movement: manual-winding A&S8200 caliber; Ø 32mm, thickness: 2.97mm; 90-hour power reserve; 21,600 vph; Swiss escapement; decoration: nickel-silver movement, rhodium treated with Haute Horlogerie finishing: unique hand-engraved tourbillon bridge, hand-chamfered bridges with polished edges, fine circular graining and Côtes de Genève rayonnantes, circular satin-finished wheels with hand-chamfered and polished edges, blued screws with bevelled and mirror-polished heads; tourbillon cage: satin-finish with chamfered and polished edges..
Functions: off-centered hours, minutes at 12; tourbillon with small seconds at 6.
Case: red gold; Ø 42mm, thickness: 8.34mm; crown engraved with Arnold & Son logo; transparent caseback; cambered sapphire with antireflective coating on both sides, water resistant to 3atm.
Dial: silvery-white and silvery opaline.
Strap: brown hand-stitched alligator leather; red-gold buckle engraved with Arnold & Son logo.
Suggested price: $73,900
Also available: palladium (ref. 1UTAG.S04A.C121G).

DSTB   REF. 1ATAS.S02A.C121S

Movement: automatic-winding A&S6003 caliber; Ø 38mm, thickness: 7.39mm; 50-hour power reserve; 32 jewels; 28,800 vph; decoration: palladium treated with haute horlogerie finishing, hand-chamfered bridges and polished edges, fine circular graining and Côtes de Genève rayonnantes, dial plate NAC gray treated with large circular finishing, circular satin-finished wheels, blued screws with beveled and mirror-polished heads; true beat seconds bridges: rose-gold treated, satin-finished with hand-chamfered and polished edges; oscillating weight: rhodium treated, skeletonized with brushed surfaces.
Functions: off-centered hours, minutes at 4; true-beat seconds at 11.
Case: steel; Ø 43.5mm, thickness: 13.mm (without glace box); crown engraved with Arnold & Son logo; transparent caseback; water resistant to 3atm.
Dial: silvery-white opaline and gold circular brushed; sapphire seconds counter.
Strap: black hand-stitched alligator leather; steel buckle engraved with Arnold & Son logo.
Suggested price: $32,555
Also available: red gold (ref. 1ATAR.L01A.C120A).

DSTB   REF. 1ATAR.L01A.C120A

Movement: automatic-winding A&S6003 caliber; Ø 38mm, thickness: 7.39mm; 50-hour power reserve; 32 jewels; 28,800 vph; decoration: palladium treated with haute horlogerie finishing, hand-chamfered bridges and polished edges, fine circular graining and Côtes de Genève rayonnantes, dial plate NAC gray treated with large circular finishing, circular satin-finished wheels, blued screws with beveled and mirror-polished heads; true beat seconds bridges: rose-gold treated, satin-finished with hand-chamfered and polished edges; oscillating weight: rhodium treated, skeletonized with brushed surfaces.
Functions: off-centered hours, minutes; true beat seconds.
Case: 18K red gold; Ø 43.5mm; cambered antireflective sapphire crystal; transparent caseback; water resistant to 3atm.
Dial: white lacquered; domed sapphire; sapphire seconds counter.
Strap: black hand-stitched alligator leather.
Note: limited edition of 50 pieces for 250th anniversary.
Suggested price: $48,550.

AUDEMARS PIGUET

Le Brassus

KINGLY COMPLICATIONS

Swiss watchmaking legend Audemars Piguet launches **A CONCEPT TIMEPIECE** that significantly enhances the acoustic quality of horological chiming technology as well as two **ROYAL OAK OFFSHORE** models that enhance their ultra-rugged character with micro-mechanical artistry and spellbinding finishes.

In 2015, Audemars Piguet unveils a watch that is potentially the most sonically considered minute repeater of modern times: the Royal Oak Concept RD#1, a concept watch developed according to the principles of stringed instrument making. The Manufacture's concept watch program was launched in 2002 and this 2015 piece adds to Audemars Piguet's esteemed history of technological development. It is the result of over a century of innovation and a dedicated eight-year sound-research initiative. Audemars Piguet has conducted this program, initiated in 2006, in collaboration with the EPFL (Ecole Polytechnique Fédérale de Lausanne). Included were a musician who crafts stringed instruments, an academic consultant from the Geneva conservatory and a sound engineer. Each responded to the research program in different ways. The result? Royal Oak Concept RD#1 is not simply an academic exercise but a minute repeater watch that awakens sound. Today the sound research continues at a dedicated Acoustic Lab at the company's Le Brassus manufacture. With three patents pending, Audemars Piguet has applied the findings of this study to the Royal Oak Concept RD#1,

a concept timepiece that significantly enhances the acoustic quality of horological chiming technology and that achieves an unprecedented volume of sound transmission in a water resistant case.

Audemars Piguet, the family-owned Le Brassus Manufacture, is known for its exceptional horological concepts, its independent spirit and a desire to push the limits of engineering excellence. It has been creating concept pieces since 2002 but it has been experimenting with mechanical watch technology from its inception as a Manufacture in 1875. Now, the Manufacture's drive to explore acoustic quality in a mechanical chiming watch has resulted in a benchmark achievement: Royal Oak Concept RD#1 is the most sonically considered concept timepiece created by a Swiss Manufacture in the digital era. Defying the necessary restrictions of waterproofing, Royal Oak Concept RD#1 breaks the rules of chiming watches by mastering sound.

The Royal Oak Concept RD#1 is inspired by the technological quality of minute repeaters created during the pinnacle of steel gong technology during the period from 1920-1930—just before electricity became an everyday resource. At this time, the Le Brassus watchmakers were not only considering mechanical progression but also the acoustic quality and range of chiming watches. Hence, this era has long intrigued the company's in-house craftsmen, designers and archivists.

The same steel gong system that Audemars Piguet has used since the company was founded in 1875 is still at the heart of minute repeater technology today. The long steel strip that curves meticulously around the movement (the gong) is worked to super strength. It requires the time-honored skill of an experienced watchmaker so that when the gong is fully assembled, the sonic qualities of the steel are primed to achieve a harmonious tone. Filing the gongs is a meticulous task—if the steel is overworked, the tone of the chime is compromised.

The RD#1 is a significant development in Audemars Piguet's rich history of creating unique concepts. In 2015, the Le Brassus Manufacture has fully explored the potential of chiming sound, while never losing sight of the natural pleasure we derive from listening to it.

Royal Oak Concept RD#1 is not simply an academic exercise but a minute repeater watch that awakens sound.

ROYAL OAK OFFSHORE SELFWINDING TOURBILLON CHRONOGRAPH

The Royal Oak Offshore Selfwinding Tourbillon Chronograph complements its powerful visual allure with a level of sophistication and finesse worthy of the line's iconic status in haute horology. Protected by a case made of forged carbon, a popular material in the aerospace industry, and black ceramic, the 44mm timepiece exudes masculine indestructibility. Its self-winding caliber fittingly echoes this identity with a 335-component construction that builds off the manufacture's nearly century and a half of expertise. The exquisitely decorated movement, revealed in part through an aperture at 1 o'clock, powers the wristwatch with exceptional precision and efficiency. The timepiece's column-wheel chronograph ensures a smooth release of the central seconds hand upon the press of the ergonomic ceramic "start" pusher. An 85-part tourbillon, revealed via a 6 o'clock opening in the "Méga Tapisserie" dial, honors the modern personality of the watch with a blackened titanium bridge. A mechanical triumph such as the Caliber 2897, with variable-inertia balance, deserves a stage befitting its magnificence. The timepiece's caseback provides exactly that, thanks to the movement's integration of an optimized peripheral oscillating weight in 950 platinum. Along with reducing the thickness of the caliber and increasing its winding speed and efficiency, the peripheral construction provides an exceptional view of the hand-decorated movement's meticulously finished components.

ROYAL OAK OFFSHORE TOURBILLON CHRONOGRAPH

A masterful display of three-dimensional architecture and elegant sophistication, the Royal Oak Offshore Tourbillon Chronograph plays off the imposing quality of its robust 950-platinum and black ceramic case with a brilliant demonstration of contrast and geometry. The 44mm hand-wound timepiece, fitted with a torque-restricting crown system that prevents strain on the movement during winding, splendidly integrates the architecture of its caliber into an expressive blue dial. Symmetrical openings at 12 and 6 o'clock reveal the Caliber 2933's ingenious twin-barrel construction and emphasize a three-dimensional construction. Running in parallel using a superior locking system, the 338-part movement's barrels provide an exceptional power reserve of 10 days. The watch's tourbillon, visible at 9 o'clock beneath a black anodized-aluminum bridge, opposes the traditional display of the column-wheel chronograph's 30-minute counter at 3 o'clock, and further reinforces the timepiece's use of depth. The mechanical exhibition continues on the rear of the watch, where a sapphire crystal caseback allows for an unobstructed view of the movement's details, gears, bridges and intricate motifs. The Royal Oak Offshore Tourbillon Chronograph, a bold proclamation of Audemars Piguet's inspired mastery of haute horology, is worn on a blue rubber strap that adds the grace note to its harmony of sophistication, elegance and sporty masculinity.

▲ ROYAL OAK OFFSHORE TOURBILLON CHRONOGRAPH

The dial-side exhibition of a tourbillon and ingenious twin-barrel construction brings three-dimensional depth to this hand-wound platinum masterpiece with column-wheel chronograph.

◄ ROYAL OAK OFFSHORE SELFWINDING TOURBILLON CHRONOGRAPH

Revealed via apertures on the dial, this timepiece's spectacular caliber is revealed through the caseback thanks to the intelligent construction of an optimized peripheral oscillating weight.

AUDEMARS PIGUET

ROYAL OAK OFFSHORE CHRONOGRAPH   REF. 26470ST.00.A801CR.01

Movement: automatic-winding 3126/3840 caliber; 13¼ lines; Ø 29.92mm, thickness: 7.16mm; 55-hour power reserve; 365 components; 59 jewels; 21,600 vph.
Functions: hours, minutes; small seconds at 12; date at 3; chronograph: 12-hour counter at 6, 30-minute counter at 9, central chronograph seconds hand; tachometer.
Case: stainless steel; Ø 42mm; black ceramic screw-locked crown and pushbuttons; glareproof sapphire crystal and caseback; water resistant to 10atm.
Dial: ivory-toned with Mega Tapisserie pattern; brown Arabic numerals with luminescent coating; white-gold Royal Oak hands with luminescent coating; brown counters; brown inner bezel.
Strap: brown "Hornback" alligator leather; stainless steel pin buckle.
Suggested price: $26,000

ROYAL OAK OFFSHORE CHRONOGRAPH   REF. 26470ST.00.A027CA.01

Movement: automatic-winding 3126/3840 caliber; 13¼ lines; Ø 29.92mm, thickness: 7.16mm; 55-hour power reserve; 365 components; 59 jewels; 21,600 vph.
Functions: hours, minutes; small seconds at 12; date at 3; chronograph: 12-hour counter at 6, 30-minute counter at 9, central chronograph seconds hand; tachometer.
Case: stainless steel; Ø 42mm; black ceramic screw-locked crown and pushbuttons; glareproof sapphire crystal and caseback; water resistant to 10atm.
Dial: blue with Mega Tapisserie pattern; white Arabic numeral markers with luminescent coating; white-gold Royal Oak hands with luminescent coating; silver toned counters; blue inner bezel.
Strap: blue rubber; stainless steel pin buckle.
Suggested price: $25,600

ROYAL OAK OFFSHORE CHRONOGRAPH   REF. 26470ST.00.A101CR.01

Movement: automatic-winding 3126/3840 caliber; 13¼ lines; Ø 29.92mm, thickness: 7.16mm; 55-hour power reserve; 365 components; 59 jewels; 21,600 vph.
Functions: hours, minutes; small seconds at 12; date at 3; chronograph: 12-hour counter at 6, 30-minute counter at 9, central chronograph seconds hand; tachometer.
Case: stainless steel; Ø 42mm; black ceramic screw-locked crown and pushbuttons; glareproof sapphire crystal and caseback; water resistant to 10atm.
Dial: black with Mega Tapisserie pattern; white Arabic numerals with luminescent coating; white-gold Royal Oak hands with luminescent coating; black counters; black inner bezel.
Strap: black hand-stitched "Hornback" alligator leather; stainless steel pin buckle.
Suggested price: $26,000

ROYAL OAK OFFSHORE CHRONOGRAPH   REF. 26470ST.00.A104CR.01

Movement: automatic-winding 3126/3840 caliber; 13¼ lines; Ø 29.92mm, thickness: 7.16mm; 55-hour power reserve; 365 components; 59 jewels; 21,600 vph.
Functions: hours, minutes; small seconds at 12; date at 3; chronograph: 12-hour counter at 6, 30-minute counter at 9, central chronograph seconds hand; tachometer.
Case: stainless steel; Ø 42mm; black ceramic screw-locked crown and pushbuttons; glareproof sapphire crystal and caseback; water resistant to 10atm.
Dial: slate gray with Mega Tapisserie pattern; black Arabic numeral markers with luminescent coating; white-gold Royal Oak hands with luminescent coating; black counters; black inner bezel.
Strap: gray hand-stitched "Hornback" alligator leather; stainless steel pin buckle.
Suggested price: $26,000

ROYAL OAK OFFSHORE CHRONOGRAPH   REF. 26470OR.00.10000R.01

Movement: automatic-winding 3126/3840 caliber; 13¼ lines; Ø 29.92mm, thickness: 7.16mm; 55-hour power reserve; 365 components; 59 jewels; 21,600 vph.
Functions: hours, minutes; small seconds at 12; date at 3; chronograph: 12-hour counter at 6, 30-minute counter at 9, central chronograph seconds hand; tachometer.
Case: 18K pink gold; Ø 42mm; black ceramic screw-locked crown and pushbuttons; glareproof sapphire crystal and caseback; water resistant to 10atm.
Dial: pink gold-toned with Mega Tapisserie pattern; black Arabic numerals with luminescent coating; black counters; pink-gold Royal Oak hands with luminescent coating; black inner bezel.
Bracelet: 18K pink gold; AP folding clasp.
Suggested price: $69,200

ROYAL OAK OFFSHORE CHRONOGRAPH   REF. 26470OR.00.A002CR.01

Movement: automatic-winding 3126/3840 caliber; 13¼ lines; Ø 29.92mm, thickness: 7.16mm; 55-hour power reserve; 365 components; 59 jewels; 21,600 vph.
Functions: hours, minutes, small seconds at 12; date at 3; chronograph: 12-hour counter at 6, 30-minute counter at 9, central chronograph seconds hand; tachometer.
Case: 18K pink gold; Ø 42mm; black ceramic screw-locked crown and pushbuttons; glareproof sapphire crystal and caseback; water resistant to 10atm.
Dial: pink gold-toned with Mega Tapisserie pattern; black Arabic numerals with luminescent coating; black counters; pink-gold Royal Oak hands with luminescent coating; black inner bezel.
Strap: black hand-stitched "large square scale" alligator leather; 18K pink-gold pin buckle.
Suggested price: $40,700

ROYAL OAK OFFSHORE CHRONOGRAPH   REF. 26402CB.00.A010CA.01

Movement: automatic-winding 3126/3840 caliber; 13¼ lines; Ø 29.92mm, thickness: 7.16mm; 55-hour power reserve; 365 components; 59 jewels; 21,600 vph.
Functions: hours, minutes; small seconds at 12; date at 3; chronograph: 12-hour counter at 6, 30-minute counter at 9, central chronograph seconds hand; tachometer.
Case: white ceramic; Ø 44mm; white ceramic bezel; screw-locked crown and pushbuttons; titanium pushbutton guards and links; antireflective sapphire crystal; water resistant to 10atm.
Dial: light silver-tone; Mega Tapisserie pattern; blue counters; white-gold applied hour markers and Royal Oak hands with luminescent coating; blue inner bezel.
Strap: white rubber; titanium pin buckle.
Suggested price: $41,700

ROYAL OAK OFFSHORE DIVER   REF. 15707CB.00.A010CA.01

Movement: automatic-winding 3120 caliber; 11¾ lines; Ø 26.6mm, thickness: 4.26mm; 60-hour power reserve; 280 components; 40 jewels; 21,600 vph.
Functions: hours, minutes, seconds; date at 3; dive-time measurement.
Case: white ceramic; Ø 42mm; white ceramic bezel; screw-locked crown; titanium links; water resistant to 30atm.
Dial: light silver tone with Mega Tapisserie pattern; applied white-gold hour markers; light silver-toned rotating inner bezel with diving scale and zone from 60 to 15 minutes in blue.
Strap: white rubber; titanium pin buckle.
Suggested price: $23,900

AUDEMARS PIGUET

ROYAL OAK OFFSHORE DIVER   REF. 15707CE.00.A002CA.01

Movement: automatic-winding 3120 caliber; 11¾ lines; Ø 26.6mm, thickness: 4.26mm; 60-hour power reserve; 280 components; 40 jewels; 21,600 vph.
Functions: hours, minutes, seconds; date at 3; dive-time measurement.
Case: black ceramic; Ø 42mm; black ceramic bezel and screw-locked crown; titanium links; glareproof sapphire crystal; water resistant to 30atm.
Dial: black; Mega Tapisserie pattern; blackened white-gold hour markers and Royal Oak hands (orange minute hand) with luminescent coating; black rotating inner bezel with diving scale and zone from 60 to 15 minutes in orange.

Strap: black rubber; titanium pin buckle.
Suggested price: $23,900

LADIES QUARTZ ROYAL OAK OFFSHORE   REF. 67540SK.ZZ.A010CA.01

Movement: quartz caliber 2714.
Functions: hours, minutes; date at 3.
Case: stainless steel; Ø 37mm; white rubber-clad bezel and crown; bezel set with 32 brilliant-cut diamonds (approx. 1.02 carats); glareproof sapphire crystal; water resistant to 5atm.
Dial: light silver-tone; Mega Tapisserie pattern in center; blackened gold applied hour markers and Royal Oak hands with luminescent coating.
Strap: white rubber; stainless steel pin buckle.

Suggested price: $16,000

LADIES QUARTZ ROYAL OAK OFFSHORE   REF. 675400K.ZZ.A010CA.01

Movement: quartz caliber 2714.
Functions: hours, minutes; date at 3.
Case: 18K pink gold; Ø 37mm; white rubber-clad bezel set with 32 brilliant-cut diamonds (approx. 1.02 carats); white rubber-clad crown; glareproof sapphire crystal; water resistant to 5atm.
Dial: light silver-tone; Mega Tapisserie pattern in center; pink-gold applied hour markers and Royal Oak hands with luminescent coating.
Strap: white rubber; 18K pink-gold pin buckle.

Suggested price: $31,300

ROYAL OAK OFFSHORE TOURBILLON CHRONOGRAPH   REF. 26550AU.00.A002CA.01

Movement: automatic-winding caliber 2897; Ø 35mm, thickness: 8.32mm; 65-hour power reserve; 335 components; 34 jewels; 21,600 vph; variable inertia balance with screws and balance spring with Philips terminal curve; finishing: all parts finely hand-decorated, bridges and mainplate rhodiumed, circular-grained, beadblasted and hand-drawn with file strokes, polished angles, beveled screw rims and slits; circular satin-brushed 950 platinum peripheral oscillating weight.
Functions: hours, minutes; small seconds at 9; chronograph: 30-minute counter at 3, central chronograph seconds hand; tourbillon at 6.

Case: forged carbon; Ø 44mm, thickness: 14mm; black ceramic bezel, crown and pushbuttons; titanium pushbutton guards; glareproof sapphire crystal caseback with Royal Oak Offshore engraving.
Dial: black; Mega Tapisserie pattern; black counters; gold applied hour markers; gold Royal Oak hands with luminescent coating; sapphire inner ring.
Strap: black rubber; titanium pin buckle.
Note: limited edition of 50 pieces.
Suggested price: $273,200

ROYAL OAK OFFSHORE TOURBILLON CHRONOGRAPH   REF. 26388PO.00.D027CA.01

Movement: manual-winding 2933 caliber.
Functions: hours, minutes; small seconds at 3; tourbillon at 9; chronograph: central seconds hand.
Case: 950 platinum; Ø 44mm; black ceramic bezel; black ceramic screw-locked crown and pushbuttons; glareproof sapphire crystal; water resistant to 10atm.
Dial: blue; openworked at 6, 9 and 12; silver-toned counter; Arabic numerals and white-gold Royal Oak hands with luminescent coating; blue inner bezel.
Strap: blue rubber; 950 platinum AP folding clasp.
Suggested price: $332,800

ROYAL OAK TOURBILLON CONCEPT GMT   REF. 26580IO.00.D010CA.01

Movement: manual-winding 2930 caliber.
Functions: hours, minutes; GMT, second time zone at 3; day/night indicator; tourbillon at 9.
Case: titanium; Ø 44mm; white ceramic bezel, screw-locked crown and pushbuttons; water resistant to 10atm.
Dial: openworked; white ceramic central bridge; white-gold Royal Oak hands with luminescent coating; black anodized aluminum tourbillon bridge.
Strap: white rubber; titanium AP folding clasp.
Suggested price: $214,200

LADIES SELFWINDING ROYAL OAK   REF. 15402OR.ZZ.D003CR.01

Movement: automatic-winding 3120 caliber; 11¾ lines; Ø 26.6mm, thickness: 4.26mm; 60-hour power reserve; 280 components; 40 jewels; 21,600 vph.
Functions: hours, minutes, seconds; date at 3.
Case: 18K pink gold; Ø 41mm; fully set with diamonds; screw-locked crown; glareproof sapphire crystal and caseback; water resistant to 5atm.
Dial: diamond pavé; pink-gold applied hour markers and Royal Oak hands with luminescent coating.
Strap: gray hand-stitched alligator leather with large square scales; 18K pink-gold AP folding clasp fully set with diamonds.
Note: 511 diamonds (approx. 4.16 carats).
Suggested price: $82,300

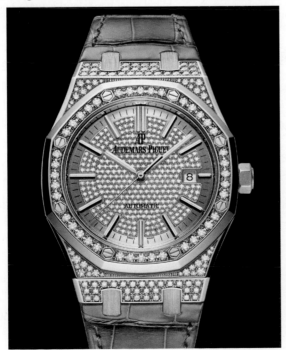

OPENWORKED EXTRA-THIN ROYAL OAK   REF. 15204OR.00.1240OR.01

Movement: automatic-winding caliber 5122.
Functions: hours, minutes; date at 3.
Case: 18K pink gold; Ø 39mm; glareproof sapphire crystal; water resistant to 5atm.
Dial: openworked slate gray; pink-gold applied hour markers and Royal Oak hands with luminescent coating.
Bracelet: 18K pink gold; AP folding clasp.
Suggested price: $85,800

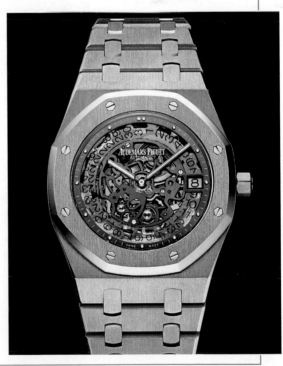

BEDAT & C°
GENEVE

REGAL & RADIANT

BEDAT & C° again showcases its **FEMININE ART DECO SENSIBILITIES** with a trio of timepieces that turn the lady's wrist into a shimmering stage of exquisite diamonds and daring, intricate décors.

One model, with reference number 384.060.S01, plays off the effortless fluidity of the brand's No3 collection with a dial-side arabesque that rises from the face as a superb complement to the bezel's generous setting of precious stones. The three-dimensional motif curves sensually throughout the brushed opaline dial, enlivened by the house's iconic "8" numeral, blooming flower at 7 o'clock, and six diamonds taking the place of the hour markers. Set into the slender bezel of the Art Deco creation's tonneau-shaped case, 49 additional diamonds bestow their dazzling radiance upon every millimeter of the face's flow of lines. This geometrically inclined beauty indicates the hours and minutes via two blued steel hands and is worn on a rolled-edge hand-stitched alligator strap.

The visual depth of the black mother-of-pearl dial on a timepiece with reference number 828.040.M04 sets a hypnotic tone of colorful nuances and gentle play of light that permeates the timepiece's entire design. Joining the bezel's and crown protector's 151 sparkling diamonds in illuminating each sinuous turn of the face's applied arabesque, six bejeweled hour markers, including one in the heart of the intricate flower at 7 o'clock, accentuate the vibrant luster of the mother-of-pearl backdrop. A white hand-stitched alligator strap perfectly complements the soft tones of the design and accentuates the high legibility of the three blued steel hands. Powered by a self-winding movement in line with BEDAT & C°'s strict "Swiss Certified Label of Origin" (A.O.S.C.®) standards, the 36.5mm wristwatch possesses a 42-hour power reserve.

▲ **384.060.S01**
This Art Deco-inspired timepiece boasts a bezel adorned with 49 diamonds, as well as an opaline dial that showcases six diamond markers and a three-dimensional arabesque.

▶ **828.040.M04**
A triple-A-grade black mother-of-pearl dial adds a soft yet rich backdrop to this ladies' diamond-set mechanical wristwatch.

A one-of-a-kind Grand Feu enamel dial resounds with the colorful energy of an emerald that plays off the lavish notes of the case's sumptuous gem-setting and architecture.

The Swiss master of feminine radiance goes all out on a show-stopping piece with reference number 887.550.E01. A staggering 271 diamonds invigorate the 18-karat palladium and white-gold case of the hand-wound wristwatch, creating a stunning juxtaposition of petals around the flower's magnificent center. A one-of-a-kind Grand Feu enamel dial, engraved by hand to exhibit the arabesque in its utmost grandeur, resounds with the colorful energy of an emerald at 7 o'clock, which joins five diamond hour markers in playing off the lavish notes of the case's sumptuous gem-setting and architecture. Fittingly, BEDAT & C° finishes the 38.5mm timepiece with a delightful twist of synergy between jewelry and haute horology: a rotating diamond at 6 o'clock joins two luminescent blued steel hands in bringing to life this masterpiece of graceful feminine opulence.

◀ **887.550.E01**

This extravagant yet tasteful masterpiece honors the delicacy of its Grand Feu enamel dial with a lavish setting of diamonds on the case's shimmering petals.

BEDAT & C°

NO. 1   REF. 118.030.109

Movement: automatic-winding ETA caliber 8¾ 2000.1; 42-hour power reserve; BEDAT & C° A.O.S.C.® certificate.
Functions: hours, minutes, seconds; date at 6.
Case: stainless steel; 34.3x40.5mm; inner bezel set with 49 diamonds; crown integrated with case middle; sapphire crystal caseback; water resistant to 5atm.
Dial: opalin guilloché; eight diamond hour markers; black Roman numerals at 12 and 4, BEDAT & C° logo 8 at 8.
Strap: rolled-edge, hand-stitched alligator leather; stainless steel folding buckle.

Note: approx. 1.347 carats.
Suggested price: $14,495

NO. 2   REF. 228.230.909

Movement: quartz ETA 7¾ M956.032; long-life battery; BEDAT & C° A.O.S.C.® certificate.
Functions: hours, minutes.
Case: stainless steel; Ø 36.5mm; double bezel: handmade stream pattern, set with 102 diamonds; antireflective sapphire crystal; water resistant to 5atm.
Dial: white mother-of-pearl; six diamond hour markers; black Roman numerals at 2, 4, 6 and 10, BEDAT & C° logo 8 at 8.
Strap: rolled-edge satin Charms; stainless steel folding buckle.
Note: approx. 1.739 carats.

Suggested price: $15,075

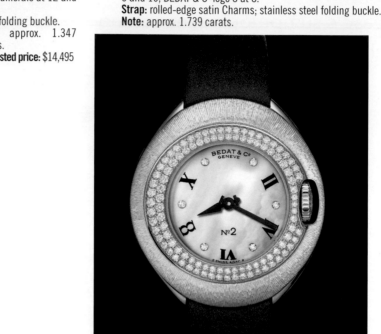

NO. 3   REF. 315.070.100

Movement: automatic-winding ETA caliber 11½ 2892A2; 42-hour power reserve; BEDAT & C° A.O.S.C.® certificate.
Functions: hours, minutes, seconds; date at 6.
Case: stainless steel; 33.5x38.7mm; bezel set with 71 diamonds; thumbtack crown; antireflective sapphire crystal caseback; water resistant to 5atm.
Dial: opalin guilloché; Roman numerals with BEDAT & C° logo 8 at 8; BEDAT & C° luminescent blued steel hands.
Strap: rolled-edge woven alligator leather; stainless steel folding buckle.

Note: approx. 2.058 carats.
Suggested price: $17,095

EXTRAVAGANZA   REF. 325.450.900

Movement: manual-winding personalized BEDAT & C° ETA caliber 10½ 7001; 42-hour power reserve; BEDAT & C° A.O.S.C.® certificate.
Functions: hours, minutes; unique rotating diamond at 6.
Case: 18K rose gold; 36x51.5mm; tonneau-shaped, waisted at 12 and 6; fully pavé with 312 diamonds; crown integrated within case middle; sapphire crystal caseback; water resistant to 5atm.
Dial: pearlized mother-of-pearl; reflector at 6; black Roman numerals with BEDAT & C° logo 8 at 8; BEDAT & C° blued steel hand; BEDAT & C° luminescent blued steel hand.

Strap: rolled-edge hand-stitched alligator leather; 18K rose-gold pin buckle set with 66 diamonds.
Note: approx. 6.064 carats.
Suggested price: $94,550

NO. 3   **REF. 384.061.600**

Movement: quartz ETA caliber 5½ 976.001; BEDAT & C° A.O.S.C.® certificate.
Functions: hours, minutes.
Case: stainless steel; 22.75x36.45mm; tonneau-shaped, waisted at 12 and 6; bezel set with 49 diamonds; thumbtack crown; sapphire crystal caseback; water resistant to 5atm.
Dial: opalin guilloché; black Roman numerals with BEDAT & C° logo 8 at 8; BEDAT & C° blued steel hands.
Bracelet: stainless steel "mille mailles"; stainless steel folding clasp.
Note: approx. 1.197 carats.
Suggested price: $11,095

NO. 8   **REF. 828.041.600**

Movement: automatic-winding ETA caliber 11½ 2892-A2; 42-hour power reserve; BEDAT & C° A.O.S.C.® certificate.
Functions: hours, minutes, seconds; date at 3.
Case: stainless steel; Ø 36.5mm; bezel and crown set with 151 diamonds; antireflective sapphire crystal; water resistant to 5atm.
Dial: opalin guilloché; black Roman numerals with BEDAT & C° logo 8 at 8; BEDAT & C° blued steel hands.
Bracelet: stainless steel "mille mailles"; stainless steel folding clasp.
Note: approx. 1.5 carats.
Suggested price: $15,750

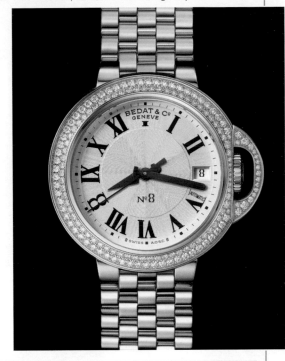

NO. 8   **REF. 832.440.980**

Movement: automatic-winding ETA caliber 11½ 28923; 42-hour power reserve; BEDAT & C° A.O.S.C.® certificate.
Functions: hours, minutes, seconds; date at 6; dual time.
Case: 18K rose gold; Ø 41.5mm; bezel and crown protector set with 166 diamonds; sapphire crystal caseback; water resistant to 5atm.
Dial: white mother-of-pearl circular zone and opalin guilloché central zone; six diamond hour markers; Roman numerals at 2, 4 and 10, BEDAT & C° logo 8 at 8.
Strap: rolled-edge hand-stitched alligator leather; 18K rose-gold cap with stainless steel folding buckle.
Note: approx. 1.99 carats.
Suggested price: $32,550

NO. 8   **REF. 838.060.909**

Movement: automatic-winding personalized BEDAT & C° ETA caliber 11½ 2892A2; 42-hour power reserve; in-house made BEDAT & C° logo "8" rotor; BEDAT & C° A.O.S.C.® certificate.
Functions: hours, minutes, seconds; date at 6.
Case: stainless steel; Ø 36.3mm; polish-finished bezel set with 47 diamonds; crown integrated within caseband; sapphire crystal caseback; water resistant to 5atm.
Dial: six diamond hour markers; black Roman numerals at 2, 4, 10 and 12, BEDAT & C° logo 8 at 8.
Strap: rolled-edge hand-stitched alligator leather; stainless steel folding buckle.
Note: approx. 1.206 carats.
Suggested price: $12,025

A vibrant juxtaposition to the Villeret 12-Day One-Minute Flying Tourbillon's otherwise understated aesthetic, the flying tourbillon is revealed in all its glory.

Blancpain's rich tradition of record-setting tourbillons has included the world's thinnest hand-wound flying tourbillon, as well as its first self-winding tourbillon with an 8-day power reserve. The horologer carries on the legacy with a tourbillon of extraordinary distinction. The Villeret 12-Day One-Minute Flying Tourbillon accomplishes a remarkable 12-day power reserve with just a single barrel. The timepiece is driven by the groundbreaking 242 caliber, which contains 243 components, including a balance spring and pallet-fork horns in silicon, within a thickness of a mere 6.1mm. The 42mm platinum timepiece, with a double-stepped case, showcases its spectacular centerpiece through a generous aperture at 12 o'clock in the Grand Feu enamel dial. A vibrant juxtaposition to the design's otherwise understated two-hand aesthetic, the flying tourbillon is revealed in all its glory, thanks to the absence of an upper bridge. The timepiece's sophistication does not end with this dial-side exhibition. Visible through a sapphire crystal caseback, the movement's numerous embellishments relate the manufacture's artistic expertise. The oscillating weight's entirely open-worked construction permits an optimal view of the caliber's meticulous decorations, such as the intricate hand-guilloché motifs of the bridges and power reserve disc.

▲ **VILLERET 12-DAY ONE-MINUTE FLYING TOURBILLON**
The understated refinement of a two-hand display sets the stage for the exhibition of this platinum timepiece's enlarged flying-tourbillon carriage.

BLANCPAIN

VILLERET TOURBILLON VOLANT UNE MINUTE 12 JOURS   REF. 66240-3431-55B

Movement: automatic-winding 242 caliber; Ø 30.6mm, thickness: 6.10mm; 288-hour power reserve; 243 components; 43 jewels; flying tourbillon.
Functions: hours, minutes; one-minute flying tourbillon at 12.
Case: platinum; Ø 42mm, thickness: 11.65mm; sapphire crystal caseback; water-resistant to 3atm.
Dial: white Grand Feu enamel.
Strap: black alligator leather.
Note: limited edition of 188 pieces.

Suggested price: $148,800
Also available: 18K red gold on brown alligator leather strap, limited edition of 188 pieces (ref. 66240-3631-55B).

VILLERET CARROUSEL VOLANT UNE MINUTE   REF. 66228-3442-55B

Movement: automatic-winding 228 caliber; Ø 26.2mm, thickness: 5.89mm; 120-hour power reserve; 209 components; 35 jewels.
Functions: hours, minutes; one-minute flying carrousel at 12.
Case: platinum; Ø 40mm, thickness: 11.8mm; sapphire crystal caseback; water resistant to 3atm.
Dial: stamped flinqué opaline.
Strap: black alligator leather.
Note: limited edition of 88 pieces.

Suggested price: $133,800
Also available: 18K red gold with stamped flinqué opaline dial and brown alligator leather strap (ref. 66228-3642-55B); 18K red gold with stamped flinqué opaline dial and 18K red-gold bracelet (ref. 66228-3642-MMB).

VILLERET 8 JOURS   REF. 6630-3631-55B

Movement: automatic-winding 1335 caliber; Ø 30.6mm, thickness: 5.65mm; 192-hour power reserve; 220 components; 35 jewels.
Functions: hours, minutes, seconds; date at 3.
Case: 18K red gold; Ø 42mm, thickness: 11.25mm; sapphire crystal caseback; water resistant to 3atm.
Dial: white cambered Grand Feu enamel.
Strap: brown alligator leather.
Suggested price: $28,900

Also available: 18K red gold with 18K red-gold bracelet (ref. 6630-3631-MMB); 18K white gold with black alligator leather strap (ref. 6630-1531-55B); 18K white gold with 18K white-gold bracelet (ref. 6630-1531-MMB).

VILLERET QUANTIEME PERPETUEL 8 JOURS   REF. 6659-3631-55B

Movement: automatic-winding 5939A caliber; Ø 32mm, thickness: 7.25mm; 192-hour power reserve; 379 components; 42 jewels; under-lug correctors.
Functions: hours, minutes; small seconds; perpetual calendar; moonphases; leap-year indication.
Case: 18K red gold; Ø 42mm, thickness: 13.5mm; sapphire crystal caseback; water resistant to 3atm.
Dial: white cambered Grand Feu enamel.
Strap: brown alligator leather.

Suggested price: $58,900
Also available: 18K red gold with 18k red-gold bracelet (ref. 6659-3631-MMB); platinum with black alligator strap, limited edition of 188 pieces (ref. 6659-3431-55B).

VILLERET CARROUSEL PHASES DE LUNE   REF. 6622L-3631-55B

Movement: automatic-winding 225L caliber; Ø 31.9mm, thickness: 6.86mm; 120-hour power reserve; 281 components; 40 jewels; under-lug correctors.
Functions: hours, minutes; one-minute flying carrousel at 12; calendar; moonphase.
Case: 18K red gold; Ø 42mm, thickness: 12.74mm; sapphire crystal caseback; water resistant to 3atm.
Dial: white cambered Grand Feu enamel.
Strap: brown alligator leather.
Suggested price: $129,600
Also available: platinum with black alligator leather strap, limited edition of 88 pieces (ref. 6622L-3431-55B).

VILLERET CHRONOGRAPHE FLYBACK PULSOMETRE   REF. 6680F-3631-55B

Movement: automatic-winding F385 caliber; Ø 31.8mm, thickness: 6.65mm; 50-hour power reserve; 322 components; 37 jewels; pulsometer.
Functions: hours, minutes; flyback chronograph, date at 6.
Case: 18K red gold; Ø 43.6 mm, thickness: 13.5mm; sapphire crystal caseback; water resistant to 3atm.
Dial: white cambered Grand Feu enamel.
Strap: brown alligator leather.
Suggested price: $31,600
Also available: 18K red gold with 18K red-gold bracelet (ref. 6680F-3631-MMB).

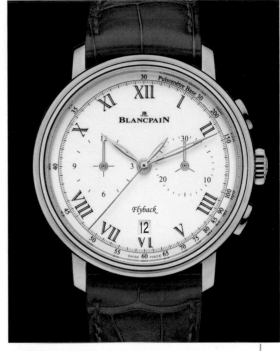

FIFTY FATHOMS BATHYSCAPHE CHRONOGRAPHE FLYBACK   REF. 5200-0130-NABA

Movement: automatic-winding F385 caliber; Ø 31.8mm, thickness: 6.65mm; 50-hour power reserve; 322 components; 37 jewels.
Functions: hours, minutes; small seconds at 6; date at 4:30; flyback chronograph.
Case: satin-brushed black ceramic; Ø 43.6mm, thickness: 15.25mm; sapphire crystal caseback; water-resistant to 30atm.
Dial: black.
Strap: black NATO strap.
Suggested price: $17,200
Also available: satin-brushed black ceramic on black canvas strap (ref. 5200-0130-B52A); satin-brushed steel on black NATO strap (ref. 5200-1110-NABA); satin-brushed steel on black canvas strap (ref. 5200-1110-B52A); satin brushed steel on steel bracelet (ref. 5200-1110-70B).

FIFTY FATHOMS BATHYSCAPHE   REF. 5000-1110-B52-A

Movement: automatic-winding 1315 caliber; Ø 30.6mm, thickness: 5.65mm; 120-hour power reserve; 227 components; 35 jewels.
Functions: hours, minutes, seconds; date at 4:30.
Case: satin-brushed steel; Ø 43mm, thickness: 13.4mm; water resistant to 30atm.
Dial: meteor gray.
Strap: black sail-canvas.
Suggested price: $10,500
Also available: satin-brushed steel with black NATO strap (ref. 5000-1110-NAB-A); satin-brushed steel with khaki green sail-canvas strap (ref. 5000-1110-K52-A); satin-brushed steel with khaki green NATO strap (ref. 5000-1110-NAB-A).

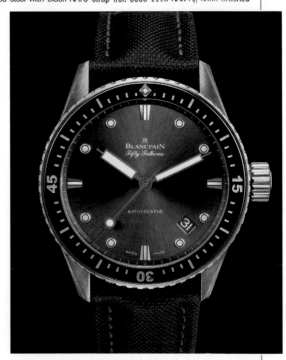

BLANCPAIN

VILLERET ULTRAPLATE   REF. 6651-1127-55B

Movement: automatic-winding 1151 caliber; Ø 27.4mm, thickness: 3.25mm; 100-hour power reserve; 210 components; 28 jewels.
Functions: hours, minutes, seconds; date at 3.
Case: stainless steel; Ø 40mm, thickness: 8.7mm; sapphire crystal caseback; water-resistant to 3atm.
Dial: white.
Strap: black alligator leather.
Suggested price: $9,800

Also available: stainless steel with steel bracelet (ref. 6651-1127-MMB); 18K red gold with brown alligator leather strap (ref. 6651-3642-55B); 18K red gold with 18K red-gold bracelet (ref. 6651-3642-MMB).

VILLERET QUANTIEME COMPLET   REF. 6654-1529-55B

Movement: automatic-winding 6654 caliber; Ø 32mm, thickness: 5.32mm; 72-hour power reserve; 321 components; 28 jewels.
Functions: hours, minutes, seconds; small seconds at 6; perpetual calendar: month and day at 12, date by hand; moonphase at 6.
Case: 18K white gold; Ø 40mm, thickness: 10.74mm; sapphire crystal caseback; water resistant to 3atm.
Dial: blue-lacquered flinqué.
Strap: blue alligator leather.

Suggested price: $25,700
Also available: stainless steel with white dial and stainless steel bracelet (ref. 6654-1127-MMB); 18K white gold with white dial and and black alligator leather strap (ref. 6654-1127-55B); 18K red gold with opaline dial and brown alligator leather strap (ref. 6654-3642-55B); 18K red gold with opaline dial and 18K red-gold bracelet (ref. 6654-3642-MMB).

VILLERET QUANTIEME COMPLET 8 JOURS   REF. 6639-3642-55B

Movement: automatic-winding 6639 caliber; Ø 32mm, thickness: 7.6mm; 192-hour power reserve; 303 components; 35 jewels.
Functions: hours, minutes; moonphase and small seconds at 6; secured calendar: day and month at 12, central date hand; under-lug correctors.
Case: 18K red gold; Ø 42mm, thickness: 13.07mm; sapphire crystal caseback; water resistant to 3atm.
Dial: opalin.
Strap: brown alligator leather.

Suggested price: $39,500
Also available: 18K red gold with 18K red-gold bracelet (ref. 6639-3642-MMB).

LE BRASSUS CARROUSEL REPETITION MINUTES CHRONOGRAPHE FLYBACK   REF. 2358-3631-55B

Movement: manual-winding 2358 caliber; Ø 32.8mm, thickness: 11.7mm; 65-hour power reserve; 546 components; 59 jewels.
Functions: hours, minutes; small seconds on the flying carrousel at 6; flyback chronograph: central 30-minute counter, central seconds hand; cathedral gong; secured movement.
Case: 18K red gold; Ø 45mm, thickness: 17.80mm; sapphire crystal caseback; water-resistant to 3atm.
Dial: white Grand Feu enamel.

Strap: brown alligator leather.
Suggested price: $449,600

WOMEN HEURE DECENTREE   REF. 3650A-3754-58B

Movement: automatic-winding 2663SR caliber; Ø 26.2mm, thickness: 4.45mm; 72-hour power reserve; 226 components; 34 jewels.
Functions: hours, minutes; retrograde small seconds at 6.
Case: 18K red gold; Ø 38.6mm, thickness: 10.3mm; set with diamonds (approx. one carat); crown set with diamond (approx. 0.09 carat); sapphire crystal caseback; water resistant to 3atm.
Dial: mother-of-pearl; set with diamonds (approx. 0.153 carat).
Strap: white ostrich leather.
Suggested price: $33,000
Also available: 18K white gold with blue mother-of-pearl dial (ref. 3650A-3554L-58B); stainless steel with white dial, approx. 1.153 carats (ref. 3650A-4528-55B).

WOMEN HEURE DECENTREE QUANTIEME RETROGRADE   REF. 3653-1954L-58B

Movement: automatic-winding 2650RL caliber; Ø 26.2mm, thickness: 5.37mm; 65-hour power reserve; 302 components; 32 jewels.
Functions: off-centered hour and minutes at 6; central date hand; moonphase at 12.
Case: 18K white gold; Ø 36mm, thickness: 10.75mm; set with diamonds (approx. 2 carats); water resistant to 3atm.
Dial: mother-of-pearl; set with diamonds (approx. 0.021 carat).
Strap: white ostrich leather.
Suggested price: $41,300
Also available: 18K red gold with mother-of-pearl dial set with diamonds and white alligator leather strap (ref. 3653-2954-58B).

WOMEN QUANTIEME COMPLET   REF. 3663A-4654-55B

Movement: automatic-winding 6763 caliber; Ø 27mm, thickness: 4.9mm; 100-hour power reserve; 262 components; 30 jewels.
Functions: hours, minutes; small seconds at 6; central date hand; day and month at 12; moonphase and small seconds at 6.
Case: stainless steel; Ø 35mm, thickness: 10.57mm; set with diamonds (approx. 1.92 carats); 35mm; thickness. 10.57mm, water resistant to 3atm.
Dial: mother-of-pearl; set with nine diamonds (approx. 0.025 carat).
Strap: white alligator leather.
Suggested price: $18,700
Also available: stainless steel with mother-of-pearl dial and steel bracelet (ref. 3663A-4654-71B); stainless steel with mother-of-pearl dial and steel bracelet with diamonds (ref. 3663A-4654-87B); stainless steel with blue mother-of-pearl dial and white alligator leather strap (ref. 3663-4654L-52B); stainless steel with blue mother-of-pearl dial and steel bracelet (ref. 3663-4645L-71B); stainless steel with blue mother-of-pearl dial and steel bracelet with diamonds (ref. 3663-4654L-87B); 18K red gold with mother-of-pearl dial and white alligator leather strap (ref. 3663-2954-55B); 18K red gold with mother-of-pearl dial and 18K red-gold bracelet (ref. 3663-2954-76B); 18K red gold with mother-of-pearl dial and 18K red-gold bracelet with diamonds (ref. 3663-2954-89B).

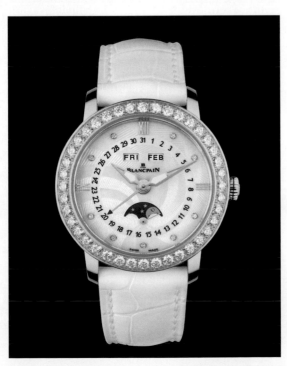

WOMEN CHRONOGRAPHE GRANDE DATE   REF. 3626-2954-58A

Movement: automatic-winding 26F8G caliber; Ø 25.6m, thickness: 7mm; 40-hour power reserve; 495 components; 44 jewels.
Functions: off-centered hours and minutes at 12; date at 6; chronograph: 12-hour counter at 9, 30-minute counter at 3, central seconds hand.
Case: 18K red gold; Ø 38.6mm, thickness: 13.1mm; set with 40 diamonds (approx. 2.105ct); water resistant to 3atm.
Dial: white mother-of-pearl with diamonds (approx. 0.13 carat).
Strap: white ostrich leather.
Suggested price: $43,900
Also available: 18K white gold with blue mother-of-pearl dial (ref. 3626-1954L-58A); stainless steel with blue mother-of-pearl dial (ref. 3626-4544L-64A).

BOUCHERON
PARIS

JOIE DE VIVRE

DRAWING INSPIRATION FROM MIDCENTURY DESIGN, CLASSIC ARTWORKS, THE BOUNTY OF NATURE AND THE HOUSE'S OWN HISTORY, Boucheron presents two collections that illuminate the link between watchmaking and fine jewelry.

Sleek gadroons dominate the aesthetic of the Reflet collection, creating a dramatic play of light that emphasizes the rectangular cases' vertical orientation. Reminiscent of rule-breaking "contemporary" art and design from the mid-20th century, these gadroons actually stem from a much deeper history, having long been a stylized calling card for Boucheron's pieces. The abstracted geometrical lines show up throughout the long history of the Place Vendôme jeweler, a history alluded to in the Reflet's "secret signature": a barely-there hologram on the watch's sapphire crystal depicts the Place Vendôme's iconic obelisk, surrounded by a frame that resembles this characteristic design element. This sure mark of authenticity pairs with another on the caseback, where an engraved declaration, "Je ne sonne que les heures heureuses," expresses the watchmaker's philosophy of noting only life's happiest moments.

Available in small (29.5x18mm), medium (35.5x21mm) and large (42x24mm) variations, the Reflet watches bear several of Boucheron's signature touches. The sapphire cabochon on the crown (to take only one example), is encircled by double gadroons (to take another one). Boucheron's commitment to seamless elegance extends the entire circumference of the wrist: the cleverly engineered buckle disappears into the strap.

Blurring the lines between watchmaking and fine jewelry even further, the Reflet Pompon interprets the clean lines of the collection using a palette of round and baguette-cut diamonds. The precious gems, set in white gold, not only frame the dial, but serve as the dial itself, adding to the piece's dazzling monochrome aesthetic. Diamonds make up the very strap upon which the watch is mounted, evoking the easy movement and soft texture of material used in haute couture. Completing the picture, a removable diamond-bedecked tassel swings from the clasp—another beloved Boucheron symbol.

Using the finesse of the goldsmith's art, Boucheron interprets the beauty of nature.

Boucheron moves from rectangular to circular cases, and from abstract geometrical inspiration to the organic beauty of nature, with its Épure d'Art collection. Using the finesse of the goldsmith's art and meticulous craftsmanship, Boucheron recreates the beauty of the nature, which may appear to be random but in fact follows certain invariable laws. The sweeping rush of the ocean dominates Vague de Lumière, which evokes the famous Hokusai print *The Great Wave off Kanagawa*. Polished hematite serves as a backdrop for over-powering waves of water and sea foam, depicted in round and baguette-cut diamonds and sculpted in relief upon the dial. A diamond-set bezel and sapphire-set crown sport Boucheron's trademark gadroons.

The Oursin model from the same collection reveals the underlying principles that govern both our notion of time and the growth of undersea creatures. The radial symmetry of the sea urchin guides the design of the dial, which is fully set with diamonds, sapphires and 18 cabochons covered in blue lacquer. These cabochons, and the diamond-set double gadroons that radiate from the center of the dial, take the place of more traditional hour markers. Sculpted in three dimensions, the gem-studded animal possesses a commanding physical presence on the dial, making a worthy addition to Boucheron's storied menagerie.

◄ **VAGUE DE LUMIÈRE**
Based on a famous Japanese wood-block print, Boucheron's Vague de Lumière captures the sea's power in light-filled diamonds.

◄ **OURSIN**
A creature of simple yet colorful beauty, the sea urchin has earned a place in Boucheron's menagerie, taking on diamonds, sapphires and lacquered cabochons in this 41mm timepiece.

◄ **REFLET**
Crafted in steel, yellow gold or pink gold, Boucheron's Reflet watches all exhibit an effortless elegance with design elements such as vertical gadroons that hearken back to the early days of the Parisian House.

◄ **REFLET POMPON**
Already a stunning work of diamond-set jewelry, the Reflet Pompon also includes a diamond tassel that can be worn dangling from the wristwatch's clasp, or integrated into a separate piece of jewelry.

BOUCHERON

EPURE OURSIN   REF. WA021417

Movement: automatic-winding Girard-Perregaux GP4000 caliber; 40-hour power reserve; 28,800 vph; 27 jewels; personalized finishing for Boucheron: Côtes de Genève crossed with alternating sand finishing, blue-tinted screws, openworked oscillating weight in the form of Boucheron's mark.
Functions: hours, minutes.
Case: polished 18K white gold; Ø 41mm, thickness: 11.9mm; bezel set with double gadroons; blue sapphire cabochon crown; domed antireflective sapphire crystal caseback engraved with "Je Ne Sonne Que Les Heures Heureuses" and consecutive number and limited edition; water resistant to 5atm.
Dial: full pavé; sea urchin treated in volume; made of six double gadroons set with white and gray diamonds and 18 cabochons in volume with three different sizes covered in blue lacquer; sea urchin paved and shaded with blue sapphires.
Strap: blue alligator leather with folded edge and invisible stitching; 18K white-gold pin buckle.
Note: 355 stones.
Price: available upon request.

EPURE VAGUE DE LUMIERE   REF. WA021416

Movement: automatic-winding Girard-Perregaux GP4000 caliber; 40-hour power reserve; 28,800 vph; 27 jewels; personalized finishing for Boucheron: Côtes de Genève crossed with alternating sand finishing, blue-tinted screws, openworked oscillating weight in the form of Boucheron's mark.
Functions: hours, minutes.
Case: polished 18K white gold; Ø 41mm, thickness: 11.9mm; set with diamonds (approx. 2.1 carats); blue sapphire cabochon crown; case side with double gadroons and beveled horns; domed antireflective sapphire crystal caseback engraved with "Je Ne Sonne Que Les Heures Heureuses" and consecutive number and limited edition; water resistant to 5atm.
Dial: polished hematite; white-gold sculpted wave with trough paved in baguette and round diamonds; stick-shaped hands faceted with matte and polished finishings.
Strap: gray alligator leather with folded edge and invisible stitching; 18K white-gold pin buckle.
Note: approx. 3.67 carats.
Price: available upon request.

AJOUREE ARONDA   REF. WA017312

Movement: quartz ETA E01 caliber.
Functions: hours, minutes.
Case: 18K white gold; interior: Ø 18mm, exterior: Ø 38mm; 214 diamonds (approx. 3.61 carats); antireflective sapphire crystal; 18K white-gold caseback with pushbutton for setting the time, engraved with "Boucheron," "Je Ne Sonne Que Les Heures Heureuses" and "Swiss Made."
Dial: gray mother-of-pearl; anthracite horizontal painted BOUCHERON logo at 12; silvered stick-shaped hands.
Strap: gray brushed satin; 18K white-gold pin buckle engraved with Boucheron logo.
Price: available upon request.

AJOUREE NURI   REF. WA07311

Movement: quartz ETA E01 caliber.
Functions: hours, minutes.
Case: 18K white gold; interior: Ø 18mm, exterior: Ø 38mm; 256 stones; antireflective sapphire crystal; 18K white-gold caseback with pushbutton for setting the time, engraved with "Boucheron," "Je Ne Sonne Que Les Heures Heureuses" and "Swiss Made."
Dial: pink mother-of-pearl; anthracite horizontal painted BOUCHERON logo at 12; silvered stick-shaped hands.
Strap: brushed satin; 18K white-gold pin buckle engraved with Boucheron logo.
Price: available upon request.

REFLET SMALL	REF. WA030501

Movement: quartz ETA 976.001 caliber; six jewels.
Functions: hours, minutes.
Case: polished steel; Ø 29.5x18mm, thickness: 6.45mm; bezel set with double vertical gadroons; blue sapphire cabochon crown; antireflective sapphire crystal on interior with secret signature in form of hologram bearing the Vendôme column; caseback engraved with "Boucheron," "Je Ne Sonne Que Les Heures Heureuses" and "Swiss Made"; water resistant to 3atm.
Dial: white lacquer; silver hour markers: Roman numerals at 12, 3, 6 and 9; silver BOUCHERON logo at 12; silvered stick-shaped hour and minute hands.
Strap: black patent calfskin.
Price: available upon request.

REFLET SMALL	REF. WA030505

Movement: quartz ETA 976.001 caliber; six jewels.
Functions: hours, minutes.
Case: polished steel; Ø 29.5x18mm, thickness: 6.45mm; bezel set with double gadroons and 32 diamonds; blue sapphire cabochon crown; antireflective sapphire crystal on interior with secret signature in form of hologram bearing the Vendôme column; caseback engraved with "Boucheron," "Je Ne Sonne Que Les Heures Heureuses" and "Swiss Made"; water resistant to 3atm.
Dial: silvered with vertical satiny gadroons; four diamond hour markers; silvered stick-shaped hands.
Strap: black patent calfskin.
Price: available upon request.

REFLET SMALL	REF. WA030507

Movement: quartz ETA 976.001 caliber; six jewels.
Functions: hours, minutes.
Case: polished 18K gold; Ø 29.5x18mm, thickness: 6.45mm; bezel set with double vertical gadroons; blue sapphire cabochon crown; antireflective sapphire crystal on interior with secret signature in form of hologram bearing the Vendôme column; caseback engraved with "Boucheron," "Je Ne Sonne Que Les Heures Heureuses" and "Swiss Made"; water resistant to 3atm.
Dial: golden with vertical satined gadroons; four diamond hour markers; golden stick-shaped hour and minute hands.
Strap: black patent calfskin.
Price: available upon request.

REFLET SMALL	REF. WA030508

Movement: quartz ETA 976.001 caliber; six jewels.
Functions: hours, minutes.
Case: polished 18K gold; Ø 29.5x18mm, thickness: 6.45mm; bezel set with double vertical gadroons and 32 diamonds; blue sapphire cabochon crown; antireflective sapphire crystal on interior with secret signature in form of hologram bearing the Vendôme column; caseback engraved with "Boucheron," "Je Ne Sonne Que Les Heures Heureuses" and "Swiss Made;" water resistant to 3atm.
Dial: golden with vertical satiny gadroons; four diamond hour markers; golden stick-shaped hour and minute hands.
Strap: black patent calfskin.
Price: available upon request.

BOUCHERON

REFLET MEDIUM — REF. WA030403

Movement: quartz ETA 976.001 caliber; six jewels.
Functions: hours, minutes.
Case: polished steel; Ø 35.5x21mm, thickness: 7.8mm; bezel set with double vertical gadroons; blue sapphire cabochon crown; antireflective sapphire crystal on interior with secret signature in form of hologram bearing the Vendôme column; caseback engraved with "Boucheron," "Je Ne Sonne Que Les Heures Heureuses" and "Swiss Made"; water resistant to 3atm.
Dial: silvered with vertical satined gadroons; silvered BOUCHERON logo at 12; silvered stick-shaped hour and minute hands.
Strap: black patent calfskin.
Price: available upon request.

REFLET MEDIUM — REF. WA030404

Movement: quartz ETA 976.001 caliber; six jewels.
Functions: hours, minutes.
Case: polished steel; Ø 35.5x21mm, thickness: 7.8mm; bezel set with double vertical gadroons; blue sapphire cabochon crown; antireflective sapphire crystal on interior with secret signature in form of hologram bearing the Vendôme column; caseback engraved with "Boucheron," "Je Ne Sonne Que Les Heures Heureuses" and "Swiss Made"; water resistant to 3atm.
Dial: silvered with vertical satined gadroons; four diamond hour markers silvered BOUCHERON logo at 12; silvered stick-shaped hour and minute hands.
Strap: black patent calfskin.
Price: available upon request.

REFLET MEDIUM — REF. WA030405

Movement: quartz ETA 976.001 caliber; six jewels.
Functions: hours, minutes.
Case: polished steel; Ø 35.5x21mm, thickness: 7.8mm; bezel set with double vertical gadroons and 36 diamonds; blue sapphire cabochon crown; antireflective sapphire crystal on interior with secret signature in form of hologram bearing the Vendôme column; caseback engraved with "Boucheron," "Je Ne Sonne Que Les Heures Heureuses" and "Swiss Made"; water resistant to 3atm.
Dial: silvered with vertical satined gadroons; four diamond hour markers; silvered BOUCHERON logo at 12; silvered stick-shaped hour and minute hands.
Strap: black patent calfskin.
Price: available upon request.

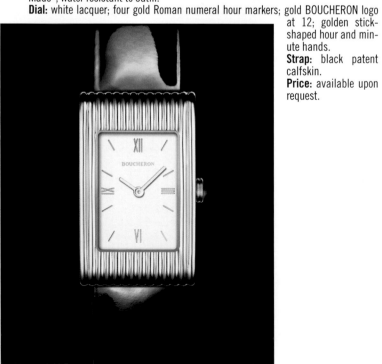

REFLET MEDIUM — REF. WA030406

Movement: quartz ETA 976.001 caliber; six jewels.
Functions: hours, minutes.
Case: 18K yellow gold; Ø 35.5x21mm, thickness: 7.8mm; bezel set with double vertical gadroons; blue sapphire cabochon crown; antireflective sapphire crystal on interior with secret signature in form of hologram bearing the Vendôme column; caseback engraved with "Boucheron," "Je Ne Sonne Que Les Heures Heureuses" and "Swiss Made"; water resistant to 3atm.
Dial: white lacquer; four gold Roman numeral hour markers; gold BOUCHERON logo at 12; golden stick-shaped hour and minute hands.
Strap: black patent calfskin.
Price: available upon request.

REFLET LARGE   REF. WA030301

Movement: automatic-winding ETA 2671 caliber; 38-hour power reserve; 28,800 vph; 25 jewels.
Functions: hours, minutes.
Case: polished steel; Ø 42x24mm, thickness: 7.68mm; bezel set with double vertical gadroons; blue sapphire cabochon crown; antireflective sapphire crystal on interior with secret signature in form of hologram bearing the Vendôme column; caseback engraved with "Boucheron," "Je Ne Sonne Que Les Heures Heureuses" and "Swiss Made"; water resistant to 3atm.
Dial: white lacquer; blue sapphire cabochon at 12; silvered hour markers, Roman numerals at 3, 6 and 9; silver BOUCHERON logo at 12; silvered stick-shaped hour and minute hands.
Strap: black alligator leather.
Price: available upon request.

REFLET LARGE   REF. WA030302

Movement: automatic-winding ETA 2671 caliber; 38-hour power reserve; 28,800 vph; 25 jewels.
Functions: hours, minutes.
Case: polished steel; Ø 42x24mm, thickness: 7.68mm; bezel set with double vertical gadroons; blue sapphire cabochon crown; antireflective sapphire crystal on interior with secret signature in form of hologram bearing the Vendôme column; caseback engraved with "Boucheron," "Je Ne Sonne Que Les Heures Heureuses" and "Swiss Made"; water resistant to 3atm.
Dial: anthracite; vertical satined finishing; polished hematite cabochon at 12; silvered BOUCHERON logo at 12; silver stick-shaped hour and minute hands.
Strap: gray alligator leather.
Price: available upon request.

REFLET LARGE   REF. WA030304

Movement: automatic-winding ETA 2671 caliber; 38-hour power reserve; 28,800 vph; 25 jewels.
Functions: hours, minutes.
Case: polished steel; Ø 42x24mm, thickness: 7.68mm; bezel set with double vertical gadroons and 36 diamonds; blue sapphire cabochon crown; antireflective sapphire crystal on interior with secret signature in form of hologram bearing the Vendôme column; caseback engraved with "Boucheron," "Je Ne Sonne Que Les Heures Heureuses" and "Swiss Made"; water resistant to 3atm.
Dial: silvered with vertical satin gadroons; blue sapphire cabochon at 12; three polished nail hour markers at 3, 6 and 9; silvered BOUCHERON logo at 12; silvered stick-shaped hour and minute hands.
Strap: black alligator leather.
Price: available upon request.

REFLET LARGE   REF. WA030305

Movement: automatic-winding ETA 2671 caliber; 38-hour power reserve; 28,800 vph; 25 jewels
Functions: hours, minutes.
Case: polished pink gold; Ø 42x24mm, thickness: 7.68mm; bezel set with double vertical gadroons; blue sapphire cabochon crown; antireflective sapphire crystal on interior with secret signature in form of hologram bearing the Vendôme column; caseback engraved with "Boucheron," "Je Ne Sonne Que Les Heures Heureuses" and "Swiss Made"; water resistant to 3atm.
Dial: white lacquer; blue sapphire cabochon at 12; silvered hour markers, Roman numerals at 3, 6 and 9; silver BOUCHERON logo at 12; silvered stick-shaped hour and minute hands.
Strap: black alligator leather.
Price: available upon request.

Breguet
Depuis 1775

CLASSIQUE CULTURE

Breguet bestows upon all its creations a 240-year horological history, most famously marked by its founder's invention of the tourbillon in 1801. **THE SWISS WATCHMAKER PRESENTS TWO TIMEPIECES THAT EPITOMIZE THE MANUFACTURE'S JOURNEY THROUGH TIME WITH A FUSION OF TIME-HONORED REFINEMENT AND CONTEMPORARY SOPHISTICATION**… and naturally, tourbillons.

Breguet's Classique Ultra-Thin Tourbillon is a rendezvous of technical innovation and of the best tradition has to offer, all within record-breaking dimensions. In a striking visual juxtaposition, the timepiece's silvered 18-karat gold dial echoes the ultra-contemporary tone of its platinum 42mm case, while displaying a tremendous respect for artisanal classic ng four individual guilloché patterns, all executed by hand. The watch's off-centered main attraction at 5 o'clock enliven this meticulous artistic demonstration. The 581DR caliber houses an off-centered tourbillon of which the lightened titanium carriage carries a Breguet balance with a silicon balance spring, as well as a specially developed escapement. A patented high-energy barrel provides an impressive 80-hour power reserve despite the movement's high frequency (28,800 vph) and wealth of mechanical sophistication. Breguet does not cease its quest for excellence there, endowing the 42-jewel movement with a bidirectional peripheral oscillating weight in platinum, thereby permitting an overall watch thickness of just 7mm, the thinnest for a self-winding tourbillon.

On the dial, two emblematic open-tipped blued-steel hands indicate the hours and minutes against a highly legible outer ring of Roman numerals, while the power reserve reads off it utmost clarity via a blued steel stem on a sector embellished with a guilloché chevron motif. A subtle blue sapphire in the middle of the tourbillon's bridge completes the harmonious interplay of vivid color against the silvered backdrop.

◀ CLASSIQUE ULTRA-THIN TOURBILLON

This timepiece boasts a patented titanium tourbillon carriage and owes its groundbreaking slenderness in part to a bidirectional platinum rotor mounted on the periphery of the self-winding caliber.

A masterpiece of haute horology in every sense of the word, the Classique Perpetual Calendar Tourbillon magnificently blends art and technical sophistication.

Breguet's Classique Perpetual Calendar Tourbillon honors its mechanical achievement with an architecture that plays on all three dimensions to maximize the space of its superbly decorated dial. Governing the upper half of the face, the watch's principal subdial, distinguished by its elevated chapter ring, is paired with the perpetual calendar's retrograde date indicator above a guilloché background in Clous de Paris. At 3 o'clock, the watch's month indicator, arranged in perfect symmetry with the instantaneous day counter on the left of the dial, contrasts the latter's guilloché wave motif with an openworked exhibition interrupted only by the central integration of a leap-year display. A one-minute tourbillon at 6 o'clock, mounted on a slight dome, accentuates the timepiece's multi-dimensional construction. This unusual setup is punctuated by a blued-steel triple small seconds hand that operates between the mechanism's chamfered bridge and the elevated hour-and-minute chapter ring. The visual enchantment continues on the back of the 41mm 18-karat rose-gold timepiece, where a sapphire crystal reveals the hand-wound 558QP2 caliber's engravings and delicate finishes.

A masterpiece of haute horology in every sense of the word, the Classique Perpetual Calendar Tourbillon showcases watchmaking's magnificent blend of art and technical sophistication.

▲ **CLASSIQUE PERPETUAL CALENDAR TOURBILLON**
A masterful display of three-dimensional architecture, this perpetual calendar ingeniously maximizes the use of space, thus providing a substantial exhibition of its one-minute tourbillon amidst a wealth of meaningful information.

CLASSIQUE TOURBILLON ULTRA-THIN   REF. 5377PT/12/9WU

Movement: automatic-winding Breguet caliber 581 DR; Ø 36mm, thickness: 3mm; 90-hour power reserve; 42 jewels; 28,800 vph; one-minute tourbillon in titanium cage; silicon hairspring; hubless peripheral rotor.
Functions: hours, minutes; small seconds on tourbillon at 5.
Case: platinum; Ø 42mm, thickness: 7mm; sapphire crystal; transparent caseback; water resistant to 3atm.
Dial: 18K gold, silvered and engine-turned in four different patterns; hour and minute counters with clou de Paris hobnail motif and barleycorn motif edge; tourbillon bridge set with blue sapphire.
Strap: reptile skin; double folding clasp.
Suggested price: $149,500
Also available: rose gold ($163,800).

CLASSIQUE GRANDE COMPLICATION TOURBILLON PERPETUAL CALENDAR   REF. 3797BR/1E/9WU

Movement: manual-winding Breguet caliber 5580QP2; Ø 37.09mm; 50-hour power reserve; 18,000 vph; one-minute tourbillon; Breguet spring; balance with gold weight screws.
Functions: off-centered hours, minutes at 12; small seconds on tourbillon at 6; perpetual calendar: retrograde date at 12, day at 9, month and leap year at 3.
Case: rose gold; Ø 41mm, thickness: 11.6mm; sapphire crystal; transparent caseback; water resistant to 3atm.
Dial: 18K gold, silvered and engine-turned in four different patterns; individually numbered and signed BREGUET; hours chapter with Roman numerals on sapphire disc; Breguet open-tipped hands in blued steel.
Strap: reptile skin; double folding clasp.
Suggested price: $164,900
Also available: platinum ($179,200).

CLASSIQUE GRANDE COMPLICATION SKELETON TOURBILLON PERPETUAL CALENDAR   REF. 3795BR/1E/9WU

Movement: manual-winding Breguet caliber 558PQ3; 14½ lines; 50-hour power reserve; 21 jewels; 2.5Hz; lateral lever escapement and balance with adjustment screws on a Breguet spring; adjusted in six positions.
Functions: off-centered hours, minutes at 12; small seconds on tourbillon at 6; perpetual calendar: retrograde date at 12, day at 9, month and leap year at 3.
Case: 18K rose gold; Ø 41mm; finely fluted caseband; welded lugs with screw bars; sapphire crystal caseback; water resistant to 3atm.
Dial: skeletonized in silvered 18K gold; individually numbered and signed BREGUET; Roman numeral hour markers; Breguet open-tipped hands in blued steel.
Strap: leather; triple-blade folding clasp.
Suggested price: $240,600
Also available: platinum ($254,900).

CLASSIQUE DAME   REF. 9068BB/12/976/DD00

Movement: automatic-winding Breguet caliber 591A; Ø 26mm, thickness: 3.15mm; 38-hour power reserve; 25 jewels; 28,800 vph; silicon lever escapement and hairspring.
Functions: hours, minutes; sweep seconds; date at 3.
Case: white gold; Ø 33.5mm.
Dial: silvered.
Strap: reptile skin; buckle.
Suggested price: $26,600

Also available: rose gold ($26,100).

REINE DE NAPLES DAY/NIGHT HIGH JEWELRY   REF. 8999BB/8D/874/DD0D

Movement: automatic-winding Breguet caliber 78CS; 57-hour power reserve; 45 jewels; 25,200 vph; silicon hairspring.
Functions: hours, minutes; day/night indication via rotating titanium disc.
Case: white gold; 34x42.05mm, thickness: 10.8mm; diamond-set bezel; diamond cabochon on crown; lugs set with 35 diamonds; sapphire crystal; transparent caseback.
Dial: diamond set.
Strap: satin; double folding clasp set with 26 diamonds.
Note: bezel and dial set with 73 diamonds.
Suggested price: $225,200

REINE DE NAPLES PRINCESS   REF. 8968BR/X1/986/0D0D

Movement: automatic-winding Breguet caliber 591C; Ø 26mm, thickness: 2.95mm; 38-hour power reserve; 25 jewels; 28,800 vpg; silicon anchor and lever escapement.
Functions: hours, minutes.
Case: rose gold; 34.95x43mm, thickness: 9.58mm; bezel set with 16 diamonds; diamond cabochon on crown; sapphire crystal; transparent caseback; water resistant to 3atm.
Dial: charcoal gray.
Strap: reptile skin; buckle set with 29 diamonds.
Suggested price: $28,200
Also available: silver-plated dial.

CLASSIQUE CHRONOMETRIE   REF. 7727BR/12/9WU

Movement: manual-winding 574DR caliber; 14 lines; 60-hour power reserve; 45 jewels; 10 Hz; numbered and signed BREGUET; double barrel; in-line Swiss silicon lever escapement; double silicon balance springs; magnetic pivots; adjusted in six positions.
Functions: hours, minutes; small seconds at 12; tenths of a second at 1; power reserve indicator at 5.
Case: 18K rose gold; Ø 41mm; finely fluted caseband; welded lugs with screw bars; sapphire crystal caseback; water resistant to 3atm.
Dial: 18K gold; silvered and engine-turned in six different patterns; individually numbered and signed BREGUET; Breguet polished steel open-tipped hands.
Strap: leather; triple-blade folding clasp.
Suggested price: $40,000
Also available: white gold ($40,500).

CLASSIQUE RESERVE DE MARCHE   REF. 5277BR/12/9V6

Movement: manual-winding 515DR caliber; 15¼ lines; 96-hour power reserve; 23 jewels; 4Hz; patented high-energy barrel; in-line Swiss lever escapement; silicon balance spring; adjusted in six positions.
Functions: hours, minutes; small seconds at 6; power reserve indicator at 1:30.
Case: 18K rose gold; Ø 38mm; finely fluted caseband; welded lugs with screw bars; sapphire crystal caseback; water resistant to 3atm.
Dial: 18K gold; silvered and engine-turned in hobnail pattern; individually numbered and signed BREGUET; Roman numeral hour markers; Breguet polished steel open-tipped hands.
Strap: leather.
Suggested price: $19,000
Also available: white gold ($19,500).

CLASSIQUE CHRONOGRAPH
REF. 5287BB/92.9ZV

Movement: manual-winding Breguet caliber 515 DR; Ø 34.4mm, thickness: 3.6mm; 96-hour power reserve; 23 jewels; 28,800 vph; silicon hairspring.
Functions: hours, minutes; subsidiary seconds; chronograph; tachometer.
Case: steel; Ø 38mm, thickness: 8mm; sapphire crystal; transparent caseback; water resistant to 3atm.
Dial: black.
Strap: reptile skin; buckle.
Suggested price: $50,200

Also available: light dial; rose gold ($49,700).

CLASSIQUE LA MUSICALE
REF. 7800BR/AA/9YV02

Movement: automatic-winding 901 caliber; 17¼ lines; 45-hour power reserve with sound, 55-hour power reserve when silent; 59 jewels; 4Hz; in-line Swiss lever escapement; silicon flat balance spring; adjusted in six positions.
Functions: hours, minutes, seconds; minute repeater.
Case: 18K rose gold; Ø 48mm; caseband engraved with musical score; welded lugs with screw bars; full caseback; water resistant to 3atm.
Dial: rotating; platinum-plated and engine turned; individually numbered and signed BREGUET; Roman numeral hour markers on flange; Breguet polished steel open-tipped hands; center rotates when music is activated; on/off indicator for sound in aperture between 9 and 10; power reserve indicator for music in aperture at 3.
Strap: leather.
Suggested price: $89,600

TYPE XXII
REF. 3880BR/Z2/9XV

Movement: automatic-winding 589F caliber; 13¾ lines; 40-hour power reserve; 27 jewels; 10Hz; numbered and signed BREGUET; BREGUET balance-wheel with regulating screws; silicon balance spring; adjusted in six positions.
Functions: hours, minutes; small seconds at 9; date at 6; second time zone indicator at 6; chronograph: 12-hour counter at 3, half-minute totalizer in center, central seconds hand on 30-second basis.
Case: 18K rose gold; Ø 44mm; finely fluted caseband; two-way rotating bezel with 60-minute scale; screw-down crown; round-ended horns; water resistant to 10atm.

Dial: brown; signed BREGUET; luminous hands and Arabic numeral hour markers; red chronograph hand.
Strap: leather.
Suggested price: $35,500
Also available: rose-gold bracelet ($55,500).

MARINE LADIES CHRONOGRAPH
REF. 8827ST/5W/986

Movement: automatic-winding 550 caliber; 10½ lines; 45-hour power reserve; 47 jewels; 3Hz; numbered and signed BREGUET: silicon inverted in-line Swiss lever escapement; flat silicon balance spring; adjusted in six positions.
Functions: hours, minutes; small seconds and date at 6; chronograph: 12-hour counter at 9, 30-minute counter at 3, central seconds hand.
Case: steel; Ø 34.6mm; finely fluted caseband; welded lugs with screw bars; sapphire crystal caseback; water resistant to 5atm.
Dial: white mother-of-pearl; individually signed and numbered BREGUET; Arabic numeral hour markers; Breguet polished-steel open-tipped hands.
Strap: turquoise leather.
Suggested price: $19,500
Also available: blue dial, rose gold ($60,800).

REINE DE NAPLES   REF. 8967ST/51/J50

Movement: automatic-winding Breguet caliber 591C; Ø 25.6mm, thickness: 2.95mm; 38-hour power reserve; 25 jewels; 28,800 vph; silicon anchor and lever escapement.
Functions: hours, minutes.
Case: stainless steel; 34.95x43mm, thickness: 9.58mm; sapphire cabochon on crown; sapphire crystal; transparent caseback.
Dial: mother-of-pearl.
Strap: reptile skin; double folding clasp.
Suggested price: $18,500
Also available: various dials.

HERITAGE CHRONOGRAPH   REF. 5400BB/12/9V6

Movement: automatic-winding 550 caliber; 10½ lines; 52-hour power reserve; 47 jewels; 3 Hz frequency; individually numbered and signed BREGUET; silicon inverted straight-line lever escapement and balance-spring; Breguet balance wheel.
Functions: hours, minutes; small seconds and date at 6; chronograph: 12-hour counter at 9, 30-minute counter at 3.
Case: 18K white gold; tonneau-shaped; fine fluting on the caseband; water resistant to 3atm.
Dial: 18K silvered gold; hand-engraved on a rose engine; individually numbered and signed BREGUET; chapter ring with Roman numerals; blued steel BREGUET hands; secret signature.
Strap: leather.
Suggested price: $44,100
Also available: pink gold ($43,000).

HERITAGE   REF. 8860BR/11/386

Movement: automatic-winding 586L caliber; Ø 13½ lines, thickness: 7 lines; 40-hour power reserve; 38 jewels; 3Hz; numbered and signed BREGUET; in-line lever escapement and flat balance-spring in silicon; adjusted in six positions.
Functions: hours, minutes; moonphase at 1.
Case: 18K rose gold; 35x25mm; curved tonneau with finely fluted caseband; water resistant to 3atm.
Dial: mother-of-pearl center, engine-turned by hand in flinqué alterné pattern; chapter ring in frosted silver-plating; individually numbered and signed BREGUET; hours chapter with Roman numerals; moonphase with rose-gilt moon; open-tipped BREGUET hands in polished steel.
Strap: woven leather.
Suggested price: $28,700
Also available: with diamonds ($33,300); white gold ($29,700); white gold set with diamonds ($54,800).

TRADITION GRANDE COMPLICATION   REF. 7047BR/G9/9ZU

Movement: manual-winding Breguet 569 caliber; 16 lines; 50-hour power reserve; 43 jewels; 2.5Hz; numbered and signed BREGUET; anthracite coating; power reserve indication on barrel drum; constant torque ensured throughout the running of the watch due to fusée and chain transmission; titanium upper bridge of the tourbillon carriage BREGUET type tourbillon bar; straight-line Swiss lever escapement; BREGUET titanium balance with four gold adjustment screws; BREGUET silicon balance spring.
Functions: off-centered hours and minutes; small seconds on the tourbillon at 1.
Case: 18K rose gold; Ø 41mm; finely fluted caseband; welded with rounded lugs; screw-secured spring bars; sapphire crystal caseback; water resistant to 3atm.
Dial: black-coated engine-turned 18K gold; individually numbered and signed BREGUET; chapter ring with Roman numerals; polished steel "moon" tip BREGUET hands.
Strap: alligator leather.
Suggested price: $175,600
Also available: yellow gold ($174,800); platinum ($189,700).

BVLGARI

SYMBOLS FOR ETERNITY

Driven by a passion for timeless symbolism and distinguished timekeeping, Italian horologer Bulgari presents four timepieces that capture **THE MAGNIFICENCE OF INSPIRED GEOMETRY, THE RADIANCE OF LIGHT AND THE COLOSSAL ACHIEVEMENT OF THE INFINITESIMAL**.

Like the sundials that first allowed our ancient predecessors to measure the passage of time throughout the day, Bulgari's LVCEA harnesses the mesmerizing beauty of light with passion and purity.

Housed in an 18-karat pink-gold case whose perfectly round figure symbolizes the circularity of past, present and future, the self-winding ladies' wristwatch illuminates its journey with a scintillating setting of 43 brilliant-cut diamonds on the bezel. The 33mm timepiece's black opaline dial sports guilloché soleil treatment, adding depth and dimension to its golden indexes and Roman numerals, as well as nodding to its solar inspiration. Driving the hours, minutes, running seconds and date, the hand-wound 21-jewel B77 caliber boasts a power reserve of 42 hours. Replenishing this power reserve is an act of aesthetic pleasure in and of itself: the 18-karat pink-gold crown is set with a diamond cabochon and surrounded by an audacious ring of pink synthetic corundum. A sapphire crystal caseback exhibits the 28,800 vph movement's delicate finishes. Finally, the 18-karat pink-gold bracelet, composed of numerous scales, ensures that light infuses, enriches and beautifies every moment.

▶ **LVCEA**

This homage to time and light is brought to the height of brilliance by a combination of luxurious 18-karat pink gold, 44 diamonds and a cabochon ring in pink synthetic corundum.

A Bulgari signature for nearly 75 years, the ancient symbol of the serpent embraces the arm of its wearer in an interplay of mythology and modern codes of design.

The seductive and sinuous elegance of the snake gracefully wraps itself around the woman's wrist with a Serpenti timepiece of irresistible decadence.

A signature of the Italian watchmaker for nearly three quarters of a century, the ancient symbol of the serpent embraces the arm of its wearer in an interplay of mythology and modern codes of design, of supple aesthetics and refined feminine strength. Echoing the contemporary lines of a free-flowing tubogas, the Serpenti's two-twirl 18-karat pink-gold bracelet is enlivened by an alternating pattern of red lacquer and 198 brilliant-cut diamonds. The intricately crafted coil thus guides the eyes of its admirer to the curved head of the majestic animal. There, a red-lacquer dial is home to two gold-plated hands indicating the hours and minutes against 12 indexes set with 33 more brilliant-cut gemstones.

Juxtaposing vibrant colors and precious materials in a fabulous declaration of Bulgari's finesse and imagination, the Serpenti adorns its owner's wrist with a show of elegant sensuality that comes to life with each precious second.

▲ **SERPENTI**

A configuration of 198 brilliant-cut diamonds and red-lacquer finishes brings to life the exquisite scales that make up this sinuous serpentine homage.

BVLGARI

Bulgari's 41.5mm Octo Velocissimo epitomizes the watchmaker's passion for geometric symbolism. The 18-karat pink-gold timepiece owes its elegant yet powerful masculine character to an emblematic shape particularly dear to the brand. Found throughout some of the crowning architectural achievements of humanity's numerous civilizations, the octagon, a dynamic fusion of circle and square, endows the self-winding wristwatch with an imposing sense of inherent balance. The polished black-lacquer dial displays a single number, the Arabic numeral "12," at the top of the face. Joining two skeletonized hour and minute hands at the center of the exhibition, a lean gold-plated stem hints at the sophistication of the heartbeat within. The 31-jewel BVL Calibre 328, oscillating at an impressive frequency of 36,000 vph and boasting a silicon escapement, drives a high-precision column-wheel chronograph whose 30-minute and 12-hour counters at 3 and 6 o'clock are complemented by a subtle date window between 4 and 5 o'clock and running-seconds module on the left of the dial. The Octo Velocissimo is worn on a black alligator strap with 18-karat pink-gold folding buckle, and allows its wearer a fascinating view of its intricately decorated movement through a transparent caseback.

The Octo Finissimo Tourbillon honors the age-old mysticism of the octagon with a mechanical foundation of equally historic distinction.

The groundbreaking platinum timepiece declares its triumph in micro-mechanical innovation with an exhibition at 6 o'clock of the world's thinnest-ever flying tourbillon. Measuring an astonishing 1.95mm in thickness, the record-setting hand-wound caliber makes no concessions in performance in its extraordinary quest for absolute refinement. An array of brilliant solutions permits the 249-component movement to achieve its slim dimensions while maximizing precision, performance and autonomy. From the integration of a peripherally driven ultra-thin ball-bearing mechanism, to the ingenious elimination of the regulator assembly, the meticulously decorated caliber, with variable-inertia balance and remarkable 55-hour power reserve, represents the breadth of Bulgari's virtuosity. Yet on the rich stage of its polished black-lacquer dial, the Octo Finissimo Tourbillon revels in profound simplicity. A single Arabic numeral and two openworked hands indicate the hours and minutes with understated sobriety, but beneath this understated façade beats an horological achievement of colossal proportions.

▲ OCTO FINISSIMO TOURBILLON

Beating at the heart of this platinum timepiece's refined codes of design is the world's thinnest-ever flying-tourbillon movement, visible at 6 o'clock through the black-lacquer dial.

◄ OCTO VELOCISSIMO

The elegant masculinity of this watch's octagonal case in 18-karat pink gold is matched by the excellence of a 36,000 vph column-wheel-chronograph caliber with silicon escapement.

BVLGARI

OCTO FINISSIMO — REF. 102028

Movement: manual-winding BVL 128 – FINISSIMO caliber; Ø 36.6mm, thickness: 2.23mm; 65-hour power reserve; 26 jewels; extra-thin.
Functions: hours, minutes; small seconds at 7:30; power reserve indication on case-back.
Case: brushed and polished platinum; Ø 40mm; platinum crown with ceramic insert; polished platinum caseback with sapphire crystal and engraving; water resistant to 3atm.
Dial: black polished and lacquered; painted rhodium-plated hour markers; faceted and skeletonized rhodium-plated hands.
Strap: integrated black semi-glossy alligator leather; platinum ardillon buckle.
Suggested price: $26,200

BULGARI BULGARI CANTENE — REF. 102037

Movement: quartz caliber B 046; Bulgari customized, decorated with Bulgari logo; seven jewels.
Functions: hours, minutes.
Case: 18K pink gold; Ø 31mm, thickness: 8.1mm; set with 43 brilliant-cut diamonds (approx. 1.18 carats); 18K pink-gold crown set with pink rubellite; antireflective sapphire crystal; engraved 18K pink-gold caseback; water resistant to 3atm.
Dial: mother-of-pearl, 12 diamond hour markers (approx. 0.13 carat).
Bracelet: 18K pink-gold chain; one twirl; set with 24 brilliant-cut diamonds (approx. 1.29 carats); three-blade deployant buckle.
Suggested price: $42,000

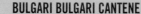

SERPENTI — REF. 102112

Movement: quartz caliber 8033; Bulgari customized, decorated with Côtes de Genève and Bulgari logo.
Functions: hours, minutes.
Case: polished 18K white gold; Ø 26mm, thickness: 8.25mm; set with six brilliant-cut diamonds (approx. 0.45 carats); antireflective sapphire crystal; satin-finished white-gold caseback with engraving; water resistant to 3atm.
Dial: black sapphire crystal; set with 33 diamonds (approx. 0.06 carat); rhodium-plated hands.
Bracelet: 18K white gold; two twirls; set with 198 brilliant-cut diamonds (approx. 6.31 carats) and 56 onyx.
Suggested price: $91,000

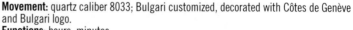

SERPENTI — REF. 102113

Movement: quartz caliber 8033; Bulgari customized, decorated with Côtes de Genève and Bulgari logo.
Functions: hours, minutes.
Case: polished 18K pink gold; Ø 26mm, thickness: 8.25mm; set with six brilliant-cut diamonds (approx. 0.45 carats); antireflective sapphire crystal; satin-finished pink-gold caseback with engraving; water resistant to 3atm.
Dial: red lacquer; set with 33 diamonds (approx. 0.06 carat); gold-plated hands.
Strap: 18K pink gold with red lacquer; two twirls; set with 198 brilliant-cut diamonds (approx. 6.31 carats).
Suggested price: $81,000

OCTO VELOCISSIMO   REF. 102115

Movement: automatic-winding BVL 328 – VELOCISSIMO caliber; Ø 30mm, thickness: 6.62mm; 50-hour power reserve; 31 jewels; 36,000 vph.
Functions: hours, minutes; small seconds at 9; date at 4:30; chronograph: 12-hour counter at 6, 30-minute counter at 3, central chronograph seconds hand.
Case: 18K pink gold; Ø 41.5mm, thickness: 13.07mm; screw-down 18K pink-gold crown with ceramic insert; antireflective sapphire crystal; brushed 18K pink-gold caseback with engraving; water resistant to 10atm.
Dial: black-lacquered polish; hand-applied pink-gold plated and polished hour markers; faceted and skeletonized pink-gold plated hands.
Strap: integrated black alligator leather; 18K pink-gold folding buckle.
Suggested price: $29,000

OCTO SOLOTEMPO   REF. 102119

Movement: automatic-winding BVL 191 – SOLOTEMPO caliber; Ø 25.6mm, thickness: 3.8mm; 42-hour power reserve; 26 jewels; 28,800 vph.
Functions: hours, minutes, seconds; date at 3.
Case: 18K pink gold; Ø 38mm, thickness: 10.35mm; screw-down 18K pink-gold crown with ceramic insert; antireflective sapphire crystal; 18K pink-gold caseback with engraving; water resistant to 10atm.
Dial: silver; hand-applied pink-gold-plated hour markers; faceted and skeletonized pink-gold-plated hands.
Strap: integrated brown alligator leather; 18K pink-gold folding buckle.
Suggested price: $22,200

SERPENTI   REF. 102128

Movement: quartz caliber 8033; Bulgari customized, decorated with Côtes de Genève and Bulgari logo; five jewels.
Functions: hours, minutes.
Case: 18K pink gold; Ø 35mm, thickness: 9mm; set with 38 brilliant-cut diamonds (approx. 0.29 carat); 18K pink-gold crown set with pink rubellite; antireflective sapphire crystal; polished 18K pink-gold caseback with engraving; water resistant to 3atm.
Dial: black lacquer; curved; gold-plated hour markers and Roman numerals at 12 and 6; gold-plated hands.
Bracelet: 18K pink gold; two twirls; set with 94 brilliant-cut diamonds (approx. 0.6 carat); black ceramic.
Suggested price: $30,600

OCTO TOURBILLON XT   REF. 102138

Movement: manual-winding caliber BVL 268; Ø 32.6mm, thickness: 1.95mm; 52-hour power reserve; 11 jewels; 21,600 vph; extra-thin flying tourbillon without bridges; entirely decorated by hand with Côtes de Genève finishing.
Functions: hours, minutes; tourbillon at 6.
Case: platinum; Ø 40mm, thickness: 5mm; 18K white-gold crown with black ceramic insert; antireflective sapphire crystal.
Dial: black lacquer; rhodium-plated hands.
Strap: black alligator leather; platinum ardillon buckle.
Suggested price: $138,000

BULGARI BULGARI CANTENE — REF. 102169

Movement: quartz caliber B 046; Bulgari customized, decorated with Bulgari logo; seven jewels.
Functions: hours, minutes.
Case: 18K pink gold; Ø 31mm, thickness: 8.11mm; set with 42 brilliant-cut diamonds (approx. 1.18 carats); antireflective sapphire crystal; polished 18K-gold caseback with engraving; water resistant to 3atm.
Dial: black lacquer; 12 diamond hour markers (approx. 0.13 carat); pink-gold-plated hands.

Bracelet: 18K pink gold; two twirls; 100 brilliant-cut diamonds (approx. 3.57 carats); 50 black onyx; three-blade deployant buckle.
Suggested price: $66,000

BULGARI BULGARI CANTENE — REF. 102170

Movement: quartz caliber B 046; Bulgari customized, decorated with Bulgari logo; seven jewels.
Functions: hours, minutes.
Case: polished 18K pink gold; Ø 31mm, thickness: 8.11mm; set with 42 brilliant-cut diamonds (approx. 1.18 carats); 18K pink-gold crown set with coral; antireflective sapphire crystal; 18K pink-gold polished caseback with engraving; water resistant to 3atm.
Dial: carnelian; set with 12 diamond hour markers; pink-gold-plated hands.

Bracelet: 18K pink gold; one twirl; set with 14 corals; three-blade deployant buckle.
Suggested price: $39,700

BULGARI BULGARI CANTENE — REF. 102171

Movement: quartz caliber B 046; Bulgari customized, decorated with Bulgari logo; seven jewels.
Functions: hours, minutes.
Case: polished 18K pink gold; Ø 31mm, thickness: 8.11mm; set with 42 brilliant-cut diamonds (approx. 1.18 carats); 18K pink-gold crown set with white mother-of-pearl; antireflective sapphire crystal; 18K pink-gold polished caseback with engraving; water resistant to 3atm.
Dial: white mother-of-pearl; set with 12 diamond hour markers (approx. 0.13 carat).

Bracelet: 18K pink gold; two twirls; set with 50 white mother-of-pearl segments; three-blade deployant buckle.
Suggested price: $55,000

LVCEA — REF. 102191

Movement: automatic-winding caliber B77; 42-hour power reserve; 21 jewels; 28,800 vph.
Functions: hours, minutes, seconds; date at 3.
Case: polished 18K pink gold; Ø 33mm, thickness: 9.87mm; set with 43 brilliant-cut diamonds (approx. 1.204 carats); 18K pink-gold crown set with pink synthetic corundum and diamond (approx. 0.025 carat); water resistant to 5atm.
Dial: black opaline; guilloché soleil treatment set with eleven diamond hour markers; date aperture; pink-gold-plated hands.
Bracelet: 18K pink gold; set with 117 diamonds (approx. 1.989 carats); three-blade deployant buckle and Bulgari logo.
Suggested price: $41,600

LVCEA   REF. 102194

Movement: quartz caliber B 046; seven jewels; Bulgari customized, decorated with Bulgari logo.
Functions: hours, minutes.
Case: polished steel and 18K pink gold; Ø 28mm, thickness: 7.18mm; 18K pink-gold crown with pink synthetic corundum and diamond; antireflective sapphire crystal; polished steel caseback with engraving.
Dial: white mother-of-pearl; set with 12 diamond hour markers; pink-gold-plated hands.
Bracelet: 18K pink gold and steel; three-blade deployant buckle with pushbuttons and Bulgari logo.
Suggested price: $9,400

LVCEA   REF. 102198

Movement: automatic-winding caliber B77; 42-hour power reserve; 21 jewels; 28,800 vph.
Functions: hours, minutes.
Case: polished steel and 18K pink gold; Ø 33mm, thickness: 9.87mm; 18K pink-gold crown with pink synthetic corundum and diamond; antireflective sapphire crystal; polished steel caseback with engraving.
Dial: white mother-of-pearl; set with 11 diamond hour markers; pink-gold-plated hands.
Bracelet: 18K pink gold and steel; three-blade deployant buckle with pushbuttons and Bulgari logo.
Suggested price: $10,900

SERPENTI   REF. 102202

Movement: quartz caliber 8033; Bulgari customized, decorated with logo; five jewels.
Functions: hours, minutes.
Case: 18K pink gold; Ø 35mm, thickness: 9mm; set with 38 brilliant-cut diamonds (approx. 0.29 carat); 18K pink-gold crown set with pink rubellite; antireflective sapphire crystal; 18K pink gold caseback with engraving; water resistant to 3atm.
Dial: white lacquer; curved; gold-plated hour markers and Roman numerals at 12 and 6; gold-plated hands.
Bracelet: 18K pink gold; one twirl; set with 58 brilliant-cut diamonds (approx. 0.37 carat); white ceramic.
Suggested price: $21,800

LVCEA   REF. 102260

Movement: automatic-winding caliber B77; 42-hour power reserve; 21 jewels; 28,800 vph; Bulgari customized, decorated with Bulgari logo.
Functions: hours, minutes, seconds; date at 3.
Case: polished steel and 18K pink gold; Ø 33mm, thickness: 9.87mm; set with 43 brilliant-cut diamonds (approx. 1.204 carats); 18K pink-gold crown with pink synthetic corundum and diamond; antireflective sapphire crystal; polished steel caseback with engraving
Dial: black opaline; guilloché soleil treatment; gold-plated Roman numerals 12 and 6; pink-gold-plated hands.
Bracelet: 18K pink gold and steel; three-blade deployant buckle with pushbuttons and Bulgari logo.
Suggested price: $35,000

BVLGARI

OCTO	REF. 102105	OCTO	REF. 102249

Movement: automatic-winding Solotempo caliber; Manufacture-made.
Functions: hours, minutes, seconds; date at 3.
Case: steel; Ø 38mm.
Dial: sapphire blue.
Bracelet: steel.
Price: available upon request.

Movement: automatic-winding Solotempo caliber; Manufacture-made.
Functions: hours, minutes, seconds; date at 3.
Case: steel; Ø 38mm.
Dial: sapphire blue dial.
Strap: blue alligator leather.
Price: available upon request.

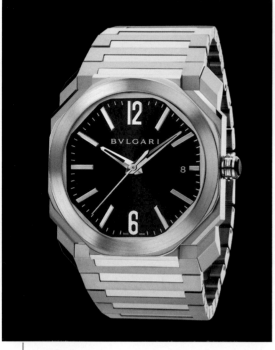

LVCEA	REF. 102328	LVCEA	REF. 102329

Movement: automatic-winding.
Functions: hours, minutes, seconds.
Case: 18K pink gold; Ø 33mm.
Dial: mother-of-pearl.
Strap: alligator leather.
Price: available upon request.

Movement: automatic-winding.
Functions: hours, minutes, seconds.
Case: 18K pink gold; Ø 33mm; bezel set with brilliant-cut diamonds.
Dial: mother-of-pearl; brilliant-cut diamond hour markers.
Strap: alligator leather.
Price: available upon request.

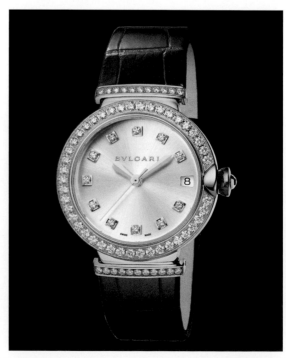

BULGARI BULGARI LADY — REF. 102374

Movement: quartz movement.
Functions: hours, minutes.
Case: steel; Ø 26mm; bezel set with brilliant-cut diamonds.
Dial: mother-of-pearl; brilliant-cut diamond hour markers.
Bracelet: steel.
Price: available upon request.

BULGARI BULGARI — REF. 102162

Movement: automatic-winding B77 caliber; 42-hour power reserve; 21 jewels; 28,800 vph; Bulgari customized; decorated with Bulgari logo.
Functions: hours, minutes.
Case: 18K pink gold (approx. 33g of gold); Ø 33mm, thickness: 7.65mm; set with 36 brilliant-cut diamonds (approx.1.44 carats); 18K pink-gold crown set with a pink rubellite; water resistant to 3atm.
Dial: aventurine; set with 10 diamond indexes (approx. 0.17 carat).
Strap: blue alligator leather; 18K pink-gold ardillon buckle (approx. 2.28g of gold).
Suggested price: $26,200

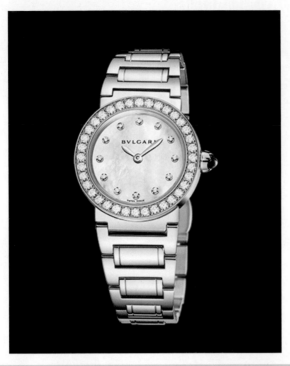

DIVA — REF. 102254

Movement: quartz.
Functions: hours, minutes.
Case: 18K white gold; Ø 39mm; polished and set with brilliant-cut diamonds and round-cut diamonds.
Dial: white mother-of-pearl.
Strap: satin; polished 18K white-gold three-blade deployant buckle and round clasp set with brilliant-cut diamonds.
Suggested price: $75,000

DIVA — REF. 102217

Movement: quartz.
Functions: hours, minutes
Case: 18K pink gold; Ø 39mm; polished and set with brilliant-cut diamonds, amethysts, rubellites and peridot beads.
Dial: white mother-of-pearl.
Strap: satin; polished 18K pink-gold three-blade deployant buckle and round clasp set with brilliant-cut diamonds.
Suggested price: $46,300

CARL F. BUCHERER

FINE SWISS WATCHMAKING

THE DRIVE TO DIVE

Drawing from a rich watchmaking tradition dating back to 1888, family-run horologer Carl F. Bucherer unveils three stunning and distinct timepieces, including the newest member of the illustrious Patravi series: a stylish, yet practical, diver's timepiece **BORN TO EXPLORE THE OCEAN'S FASCINATING MYSTERIES**.

The Patravi ScubaTec captures the elegance of functionality. The 44.6mm diver's timepiece exposes a mastery of contrast as the stainless steel case brings a vibrant energy to the watch's deep black dial and black-and-blue ceramic bezel. The COSC-certified wristwatch continues this sporty narrative inside as well as out. Powering the timepiece with precision, the self-winding CFB 1950.1 caliber animates a three-hand choreography of hours, minutes and seconds, in addition to date via an aperture at 3 o'clock. The Patravi ScubaTec belongs on the wrist of an oceanic adventurer. Safeguarding the movement's integrity in the grueling conditions of up to 500m below the surface, an automatic helium valve permits a safe escape of gases during both the diver's ascent and descent, while a sapphire crystal nearly 4mm thick protects the inner workings from the significant pressure of the event. The combination of a large dial, generous SuperLumiNova coating on all crucial indicators and anti-reflective coating on both sides of the sapphire crystal allows the wearer an optimal degree of visual clarity. This genuine and robust diving companion places its wearer's safety at the forefront of its design. The bezel, designed with two contrasting colors and large, bold Arabic numerals, can only rotate counterclockwise, so that any accidental alteration to its intended position will only shorten the owner's dive time. Back on land, the Patravi ScubaTec's spectacular three-dimensional graphic of two manta rays on the caseback summons up the ocean's submerged majesty.

▲ **PATRAVI SCUBATEC**

This authentic diver's timepiece with 38-hour power reserve is water resistant to 500m, boasting an automatic helium valve, robust case construction and manufacture self-winding movement.

The Pathos Diva's rose-gold halo enlivens the timepiece with subtle light interplay in three dimensions.

The Pathos Diva takes on elegant femininity with a radiance and luxury befitting its delicate design. Powered by the self-winding CFB 1963 caliber, the 34mm stainless steel and 18-karat rose-gold timepiece indicates the hours, minutes, seconds and date on a vivid white dial framed by a detailed 18-karat rose-gold aureole. The vibrant halo, extended to the side of the case in an expression of the design's dual-tone personality, enlivens the timepiece with subtle light interplay in three dimensions. The Pathos Diva makes of the feminine wrist a delightful stage for splendor, where lines, light and dynamic composition join forces with inebriating harmony.

On its complicated Manero Tourbillon model, the Lucerne watchmaker demonstrates exquisite craftsmanship and timeless sophistication. Piercing the timepiece's warm silver dial, the hand-wound CFB T1001 caliber's tourbillon exposes its deft construction through a generous aperture at 6 o'clock. The date, displayed by hand against 31 numerals on the periphery of the face, adds a unique twist of intelligent architecture in its preservation of the watch's unsaturated design and ease of legibility. The 188-piece limited edition timepiece is finished with a 24-hour indicator at 12 o'clock, while a tasteful arc at 9 o'clock reminds the wearer of the impressive 70-hour power reserve.

▲ PATHOS DIVA
An intricate 18-karat rose-gold aureole brings distinction and dimension to the delicate two-tone design of this self-winding lady's timepiece.

▼ MANERO TOURBILLON
Worn on a hand-stitched Louisiana alligator strap, this wristwatch boasts a peripheral hand-guided date display, 24-hour indicator, 70-hour power reserve and exposed tourbillon.

CARL F. BUCHERER

PATRAVI CHRONODATE — REF. 00.10624.08.33.21

Movement: automatic-winding CFB 1956 caliber; Ø 30mm, thickness: 7.3mm; 42-hour power reserve; 49 jewels.
Functions: hours, minutes; small seconds at 3; large date at 12; chronograph: 12-hour counter at 6, 30-minute counter at 9, central chronograph seconds hand.
Case: stainless steel; Ø 42mm, thickness: 14.1mm; screw-down crown; antireflective sapphire crystal; water resistant to 5atm.
Dial: black; eight polished hour markers.
Bracelet: stainless steel.

Suggested price: $6,900
Also available: stainless steel on strap ($6,300); various dial and strap color combinations.

PATRAVI EVOTEC DAYDATE — REF. 00.10625.13.33.21

Movement: automatic-winding CFB A1001 caliber; Ø 32mm, thickness: 6.3mm; 55-hour power reserve; 33 jewels; peripheral rotor; dynamic shock absorber (DSA); patented central dual adjusting system (CDAS), which requires adjustment only once.
Functions: hours, minutes; small seconds at 6; day at 9; large date at 11.
Case: stainless steel; 44x44.5mm, thickness: 14mm; rubber bezel; screw-down crown; antireflective sapphire crystal; sapphire crystal caseback.
Dial: black; twelve polished hour markers.
Bracelet: stainless steel.

Suggested price: $10,800
Also available: stainless steel on calfskin strap with stainless steel folding clasp ($9,900); 18K rose gold on calfskin strap ($33,900); various bezel, dial and strap options.

PATRAVI CALENDAR — REF. 00.10629.08.33.01

Movement: automatic-winding CFB A1004 caliber; Ø 32mm, thickness: 6.9mm; 55-hour power reserve; 33 jewels; peripheral rotor; patented dynamic shock absorber (DSA); patented central dual adjusting system (CDAS), which requires adjustment only once.
Functions: hours, minutes; small seconds at 6; perpetual calendar: day at 9, large date at 11, 53-week indicator.
Case: stainless steel; Ø 42.6mm, thickness: 12.85mm; screw-down crown; antireflective sapphire crystal; water resistant to 5atm.

Dial: black; twelve polished hour markers.
Strap: black calfskin leather; stainless steel folding clasp.
Suggested price: $10,300
Also available: stainless steel with silver dial on brown calfskin strap with stainless steel folding clasp ($10,300); stainless steel with silver dial on bracelet ($11,200); 18K rose gold on strap ($31,500).

PATRAVI T-GRAPH — REF. 00.10615.08.13.21

Movement: automatic-winding CFB 1960 caliber; Ø 30mm, thickness: 7.3mm; 42-hour power reserve; 47 jewels.
Functions: hours, minutes; small seconds at 3; large date at 12; chronograph: 30-minute counter at 9, central chronograph seconds hand; power reserve indicator at 6.
Case: stainless steel; 39x42mm, thickness: 13.8mm; screw-down crown; antireflective sapphire crystal; water resistant to 5atm.
Dial: silver; eight polished hour markers.
Bracelet: stainless steel.

Suggested price: $8,000
Also available: 18K rose-gold bracelet ($43,000); 18K rose gold with strap ($25,900); stainless steel with various dial and strap combinations ($7,500-$8,000).

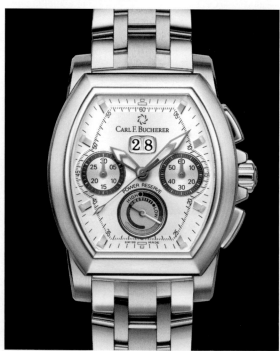

PATRAVI TRAVELTEC FOUR-X   REF. 00.10620.22.93.01

Movement: automatic-winding CFB 1901.1 caliber; Ø 28.6mm, thickness: 7.3mm; 42-hour power reserve; 39 jewels; COSC-certified chronometer.
Functions: hours, minutes; small seconds at 3; date at 4:30; chronograph: 12-hour counter at 6, 30-minute counter at 9, central chronograph seconds hand; three time zones.
Case: 18K rose gold; Ø 46.6mm, thickness: 15.5mm; ceramic bezel; screw-down crown; rubber pushbutton; titanium monopusher; antireflective sapphire crystal; water resistant to 5atm.
Dial: skeletonized; nine polished 18K rose-gold hour markers.
Strap: black rubber; 18K rose-gold pin buckle.
Note: limited edition of 125 pieces.
Suggested price: $52,900
Also available: palladium; titanium pin buckle ($52,900).

PATRAVI TRAVELGRAPH   REF. 00.10618.13.53.01

Movement: automatic-winding CFB 1901 caliber; Ø 28.6mm, thickness: 7.3mm; 42-hour power reserve; 39 jewels.
Functions: hours, minutes; small seconds at 3; date at 4:30; chronograph: 12-hour counter at 6, 30-minute counter at 9, central chronograph seconds hand; GMT, second time zone.
Case: stainless steel; Ø 42mm; rubber bidirectional rotating bezel; screw-down crown; antireflective sapphire crystal; water resistant to 5atm.
Dial: blue; nine polished hour markers.
Strap: blue calfskin; stainless steel folding clasp.
Suggested price: $7,300
Also available: stainless steel bracelet ($7,900); various dial, strap and bezel color combinations.

MANERO POWERRESERVE   REF. 00.10912.03.33.01

Movement: automatic-winding CFB A1011 manufacture caliber; Ø 32mm, thickness: 6.3mm; 55-hour power reserve; 33 jewels.
Functions: hours, minutes; small seconds at 6; perpetual calendar: day at 9, large date at 11, power reserve indication at 3.
Case: 18K rose gold; Ø 42.5mm, thickness: 12.54mm; screw-down crown; domed antireflective sapphire crystal; water resistant to 5atm.
Dial: black; twelve polished hour markers.
Strap: Louisiana alligator leather; 18K rose-gold pin-lock folding clasp.
Suggested price: $26,100
Also available: 18K rose gold with silver dial and strap; stainless steel bracelet ($11,700); stainless steel with strap ($11,000).

MANERO TOURBILLON   REF. 00.10918.03.33.01

Movement: manual-winding CFB T1001 caliber; Ø 41.8mm, thickness: 12.52mm.
Functions: hours, minutes; date via central hand; 24-hour indication at 12; tourbillon at 6; power reserve indicator at 9.
Case: 18K rose gold; Ø 41.8mm, thickness: 12.67mm; domed antireflective sapphire crystal; sapphire crystal caseback; water resistant to 3atm.
Dial: black; six 18K rose-gold polished hour markers.
Strap: black alligator leather; 18K rose-gold pin buckle.
Note: limited edition of 188 pieces.
Suggested price: $98,800
Also available: 18K rose gold; silver dial; brown alligator leather strap.

CARL F. BUCHERER

PATRAVI SCUBATEC   REF. 00.10632.24.53.01

Movement: automatic-winding CFB 1950.1 caliber; Ø 26.2mm, thickness: 4.6mm; 38-hour power reserve; 26 jewels; COSC-certified chronometer.
Functions: hours, minutes, seconds; date at 3.
Case: stainless steel and 18K rose gold; Ø 44.6mm, thickness: 13.45mm; stainless steel and ceramic bezel; screw-down crown; automatic helium valve; antireflective sapphire crystal; water resistant to 50atm.
Dial: blue; twelve luminous hour markers.
Strap: rubber; stainless steel folding diving clasp with extension system and comfort adjustment system.

Suggested price: $9,800
Also available: adjustable stainless steel bracelet with stainless steel diving clasp, various dial color combinations ($6,800); stainless steel on rubber strap with stainless steel diving clasp ($6,400); stainless steel and 18K rose-gold two tone on bracelet with various dial color combinations ($11,800).

MANERO CHRONOPERPETUAL   REF. 00.10907.03.13.01

Movement: automatic-winding CFB 1904 caliber; Ø 30mm, thickness: 7.6mm; 50-hour power reserve; 49 jewels.
Functions: hours, minutes; small seconds; flyback chronograph; perpetual calendar: day, date, month, leap year; moonphase.
Case: 18K rose gold; Ø 42.5mm, thickness: 14.3mm; tachometer on bezel; antireflective sapphire crystal; water resistant to 3atm.
Dial: silver; eight polished 18K rose-gold hour markers.
Strap: brown alligator leather; 18K rose-gold pin buckle.

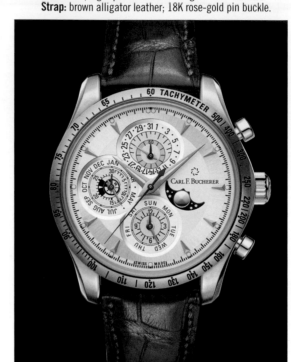

Note: limited edition of 100 pieces.
Suggested price: $52,600
Also available: 18K rose gold with black dial and black alligator leather strap with 18K rose-gold pin buckle ($52,600); stainless steel with alligator leather strap and stainless steel folding clasp ($33,000).

PATRAVI SCUBATEC   REF. 00.10632.24.23.21

Movement: automatic-winding CFB 1950.1 caliber; Ø 26.2mm, thickness: 4.6mm; 38-hour power reserve; 26 jewels; COSC-certified chronometer.
Functions: hours, minutes, seconds; date at 3.
Case: stainless steel and 18K rose gold; Ø 44.6mm, thickness: 13.45mm; stainless steel and ceramic bezel; screw-down crown; automatic helium valve; antireflective sapphire crystal; water resistant to 50atm.
Dial: white; twelve luminous hour markers.
Bracelet: 18K rose gold and stainless steel; stainless steel folding diving clasp with extension system and comfort adjustment system.

Suggested price: $11,800
Also available: adjustable stainless steel bracelet with stainless steel diving clasp, various dial color combinations ($6,800); stainless steel on rubber strap with stainless steel diving clasp ($6,400); stainless steel and 18K rose-gold two tone ceramic bezel on rubber strap with various dial color combinations ($9,800).

MANERO CENTRALCHRONO   REF. 00.10910.08.13.01

Movement: automatic-winding CFB 1967 caliber; Ø 30mm, thickness: 7.4mm; 44-hour power reserve; 47 jewels.
Functions: hours, minutes; small seconds; date at 6; chronograph: 60-second counter and central minute counter; day/night indicator.
Case: stainless steel; Ø 42.5mm, thickness: 14.24mm; antireflective sapphire crystal; water resistant to 3atm.
Dial: silver; nine polished hour markers.
Strap: brown alligator leather; stainless steel pin buckle.

Suggested price: $7,100
Also available: black dial on black alligator leather strap with stainless steel pin buckle; silver or black dial on stainless steel bracelet ($7,700).

PATRAVI TRAVELTEC GMT   REF. 00.10620.08.53.21

Movement: automatic-winding CFB 1901 caliber; Ø 28.6mm, thickness: 7.3mm; 42-hour power reserve; 39 jewels; COSC-certified chronometer.
Functions: hours, minutes; small seconds; date; chronograph; GMT, three time zones.
Case: stainless steel; Ø 46.6mm, thickness: 15.5mm; screw-down crown; stainless steel monopusher; antireflective sapphire crystal; water resistant to 5atm.
Dial: blue; nine polished hour markers.
Bracelet: stainless steel.
Suggested price: $11,400
Also available: stainless steel on strap ($10,900); 18K rose gold on strap ($44,000) or bracelet ($63,500); various dial and strap color combinations.

PATRAVI CHRONOGRADE   REF. 00.10623.03.93.01

Movement: automatic-winding CFB 1902 caliber; Ø 30mm, thickness: 7.3mm; 42-hour power reserve; 51 jewels.
Functions: hours, minutes, seconds; large date; flyback chronograph; retrograde indicator; annual calendar; bidirectional power reserve indicator.
Case: 18K rose gold; Ø 44.6mm, thickness: 14.1mm; screw-down crown; antireflective sapphire crystal; water resistant to 5atm.
Dial: black; seven 18K rose-gold polished hour markers.
Strap: alligator leather; 18K rose-gold pin buckle.
Suggested price: $33,900
Also available: 18K rose-gold bracelet ($53,000); stainless steel with calfskin strap ($10,900); stainless steel bracelet ($11,500); various dial and strap color combinations.

PATHOS DIVA   REF. 00.10580.08.25.31.01

Movement: automatic-winding CFB 1963 caliber; Ø 20mm, thickness: 4.8 mm; 38-hour power reserve; 25 jewels.
Functions: hours, minutes, seconds; date.
Case: stainless steel; Ø 34mm; thickness: 9.65mm; set with 54 diamonds (approx. 0.7 carat); antireflective sapphire crystal; water resistant to 3atm.
Dial: white; eleven polished hour markers.
Bracelet: stainless steel.
Suggested price: $10,000
Also available: various dial, metal and diamond combinations ($4,600- $14,300).

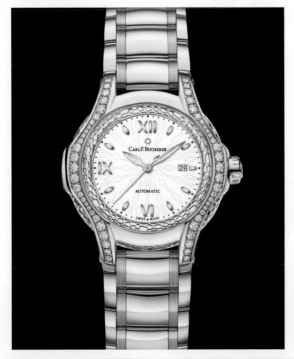

PATHOS DIVA   REF. 00.10580.07.23.21.02

Movement: automatic-winding CFB 1963 caliber; Ø 20mm, thickness: 4.8 mm; 38-hour power reserve; 25 jewels.
Functions: hours, minutes, seconds; date.
Case: stainless steel and 18K rose gold; Ø 34 mm, thickness: 9.65mm; antireflective sapphire crystal; water-resistant to 3atm.
Dial: white; nine polished 18K rose-gold hour markers.
Bracelet: stainless steel and 18K rose gold.
Suggested price: $9,000
Also available: various dial, metal and diamond combinations ($4,600-$14,300).

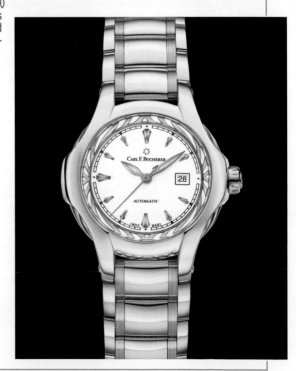

Cartier

COMPLETE CREATIVITY

As early as 1888, the first reference to wristwatches can be found in the Cartier archives. At around the same time, pocket and chatelaine watches were also popular, but for Louis Cartier, the future lay in wristwatches. It was the beginning of a long love story, and the stepping stone to the creation of many iconic models. Shaped watches, mystery watches, watches with complications: Tortue, Santos, Tank, Ballon Bleu de Cartier... These names refer to a certain shape, a winding crown, a "rail-track" minute circle, hands, and all keep Cartier time... Similar yet different, they are recognizable at first glance, reflecting a simple but stylish aesthetic, geometric but soft, always elegant, never fussy. This is the perfect equation that makes them either men's or women's watches, casual or sophisticated, depending on the time of day or the way in which they are worn. Their growing success bears witness to the fact that time is on their side. Today boasting more than 165 years of creativity and daring, Cartier possesses a unique status in the world of contemporary watchmaking.

Creative and legendary, *thanks to the continued prominence of Cartier's iconic watches.*

ROTONDE DE CARTIER GRANDE COMPLICATION SKELETON

A fascinating skeletonized architecture provides the perfect stage to showcase this hand-wound 950/1000 platinum timepiece. Joining the open-worked three-subdial exhibition of the 9406 MC Manufacture caliber's perpetual calendar, two revered complications showcase the superb finesse of their construction. While the timepiece's meticulously finished flying tourbillon dazzles at 12 o'clock, the caliber's minute repeater complements its sonorous performance with a revelation of its finely polished hammers on either side of the month counter at 6 o'clock. A blue sapphire cabochon on the platinum crown echoes the dial's vibrant color combination.

Creative and powerful, thanks to the modernity of Cartier's Fine Watchmaking Manufacture. A melting pot of craftsmanship and skills founded on the exceptional expertise of 170 crafts with men and women sharing the same unique passion and goal: the production of watches, the development of movements, and the application of jewelry techniques to the world of watchmaking.

ROTONDE DE CARTIER REVERSED TOURBILLON

A bold juxtaposition of clean lines and mechanical elements, this 18-karat white-gold wristwatch reverses conventional horological architecture to present its wearer with a riveting view of some of the movement's seldom-observed components. In doing so, the hand-wound timepiece exposes on the dial side a number of the 9458 MC Manufacture caliber's bridges and traditionally concealed elements against a backdrop that exudes a sense of geometric purity. Piercing the sunray motif of the luxurious 18-karat white-gold dial, the watch's flying tourbillon joins two blued steel hands in demonstrating the extensive technical mastery of the brand.

Creative and visionary, thanks to Cartier's pioneering and daring spirit—the starting point for its concept watches.

ROTONDE DE CARTIER ASTROTOURBILLON SKELETON

This 18-karat white-gold timepiece epitomizes Cartier's daring spirit of innovation with a unique presentation of one of haute horology's most celebrated complications. Performing a full orbit of the open dial every 60 seconds, the 9461 MC Manufacture caliber's ingenious astrotourbillon executes its own internal revolutions while rotating on a dynamic axis from the center of the movement. A sense of celestial weightlessness, achieved by the generous skeletonization of the design, allows for a fascinating view of the watch's primary attraction.

Creative and daring, thanks to Cartier's talent for innovation and research, which has given life to never-seen-before complications. Mysterious and skeleton watches figure among the finest examples of this concentration of expertise.

RONDE LOUIS CARTIER FILIGREE WATCH

Housed in a 42mm 18-karat yellow-gold case set with a row of brilliant-cut diamonds, this hand-wound timepiece's magnificent dial reveals two panthers brought to life with the painstaking ornamental art of filigree. The majestic animals, composed of 22-karat yellow gold, platinum and brilliant-cut diamonds, with eyes made of vivid emeralds, emanate powerful grace above a starry deep-blue sky, beneath the warmth of two apple-shaped 18-karat yellow-gold hands indicating the hours and minutes. This sumptuous masterpiece is driven by the hand-wound 430 MC Manufacture movement and is worn on a dark-blue alligator-skin strap adorned with brilliant-cut diamonds on the folding buckle.

Creative and inventive, as shown by the imagination and passion expressed in the creation of the Cartier d'Art collection. These watches, born from a blend of innovation and tradition, perpetuate forgotten crafts and expertise.

Creative and unique, due to Cartier's standing as "jeweler to kings and king of jewelers," as the creator of exceptional pieces.

PANTHÈRE CAPTIVE DE CARTIER WATCH

Under the watching eyes of a regal panther, this 18-karat rhodiumized-white-gold wristwatch adorns its display of the hours and minutes with an inspired display of scintillating luxury. Set with generous rows of brilliant-cut diamonds on everything from the dial and bezel to the bracelet, the 23mm timepiece boasts, at 12 o'clock, a diamond-set depiction of a panther's head, whose onyx nose and pear-shaped emerald eyes bring to the piece's shimmering opulence a touch of imperial beauty.

CLÉ DE CARTIER 35MM – NEW AESTHETIC

A row of brilliant-cut diamonds on its 18-karat rhodiumized-white-gold case sets a dazzling frame for a dial of decisive elegance and refined sobriety. Enlivened by the vibrant tone of an alligator-leather strap in shiny fuchsia pink, this self-winding 35mm wristwatch tastefully combines sunray and lacquered finishes to give its dial a sense of texture and dynamic geometry. At 6 o'clock, the 1847 MC Manufacture caliber's date aperture interrupts a sequence of large Roman numerals that ensure effortless reading of the hours, minutes and seconds. The timepiece is finished with an 18-karat rhodiumized-white-gold key set with a sapphire.

CARTIER

ROTONDE DE CARTIER GRANDE COMPLICATION SKELETON   REF. W1556251

Movement: manual-winding 9405 MC caliber; ultra-thin; 50-hour power reserve; certified Poinçon de Genève timepiece.
Functions: hours, minutes; minute repeater; flying tourbillon; perpetual calendar.
Case: 950/1000 platinum; Ø 45mm, thickness: 12.57mm; 950/1000 platinum crown set with blue cabochon sapphire crown; sapphire caseback; water resistant to 3atm.
Dial: double dial: outer ring forming railroad minute track, center forming counters; skeletonized; blued steel apple-shaped and hammer-shaped hands.
Strap: black alligator leather; 18K white-gold double adjustable buckle.

Note: limited edition of 50 numbered pieces.
Price: available upon request.

ROTONDE DE CARTIER REVERSED TOURBILLON   REF. W1556246

Movement: manual-winding 9458 caliber; 50-hour power reserve; certified Poinçon de Genève timepiece.
Functions: hours, minutes; tourbillon.
Case: 18K white gold; Ø 46mm; 18K white-gold beaded crown set with blue cabochon sapphire; sapphire caseback; water resistant to 3atm.
Dial: 18K white gold; blued steel sword-shaped hands.
Strap: black alligator leather; 18K white-gold double adjustable deployant buckle.
Note: limited edition of 100 numbered pieces.

Price: available upon request.

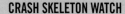

ROTONDE DE CARTIER ASTROTOURBILLON SKELETON   REF. W1556250

Movement: manual-winding 9461 MC caliber; 48-hour power reserve.
Functions: hours, minutes; astrotourbillon complication with rotation of cage in one minute.
Case: 18K white gold; Ø 47mm, thickness: 15.5mm; 18K white-gold beaded crown with sapphire cabochon; sapphire caseback; water resistant to 3atm.
Dial: skeletonized; blued steel sword-shaped hands.
Strap: black alligator leather; 18K white-gold double adjustment deployant buckle.
Note: limited edition of 100 numbered pieces.

Price: available upon request.

CRASH SKELETON WATCH   REF. W7200001

Movement: manual-winding 9618 caliber; 3-day power reserve.
Functions: hours, minutes.
Case: 950/1000 platinum; 28.2x45.3mm, thickness: 9.6mm; 950/1000 platinum beaded crown set with blue cabochon sapphire; sapphire caseback; water resistant to 3atm.
Dial: skeletonized; movement's bridges forming Roman numerals; blued steel sword-shaped hands.
Strap: black alligator leather; 18K white-gold double adjustable deployant buckle.

Note: limited edition of 67 numbered pieces.
Price: available upon request.

ROTONDE DE CARTIER   REF. W1556240

Movement: automatic-winding caliber 1904-FU MC; 48-hour power reserve.
Functions: hours, minutes; small seconds at 6; large date at 12; second time zone with retrograde display at 10; day/night indicator.
Case: 18K pink gold; Ø 42mm, thickness: 11.96mm; 18K pink-gold fluted crown set with cabochon sapphire; sapphire caseback; water resistant to 3atm.
Dial: silvered guilloché; blued steel hands.
Strap: brown alligator leather; 18K pink-gold double adjustable deployant buckle.
Price: available upon request.

ROTONDE DE CARTIER   REF. W1556369

Movement: manual-winding 9753 MC caliber; 40-hour power reserve.
Functions: hours, minutes; calendar at 12; power reserve indicator at 6.
Case: steel; Ø 40mm, thickness: 8.94mm; steel fluted crown set with synthetic cabochon-shaped spinel; water resistant to 3atm.
Dial: silvered guilloché; blued steel hands.
Strap: black alligator leather; steel double adjustable deployant buckle.
Price: available upon request.

CALIBRE DE CARTIER DIVER   REF. W2CA0004

Movement: automatic-winding caliber 1904-PS MC; 48-hour power reserve.
Functions: hours, minutes; small seconds at 6; date at 3.
Case: ADLC-coated steel; Ø 42mm, thickness: 11mm; ADLC-coated steel bezel with indicator in SuperLumiNova™ and 18K pink-gold ring; 18K pink-gold faceted crown set with faceted synthetic spinel.
Dial: black; partly snailed; hour markers in SuperLumiNova™; gilded steel sword shaped hands coated with SuperLumiNova™.
Strap: rubber; ADLC-coated steel ardillon buckle.
Price: available upon request.

CALIBRE DE CARTIER DIVER   REF. W2CA0006

Movement: automatic-winding caliber 1904-PS MC; 48-hour power reserve.
Functions: hours, minutes; small seconds at 6; date at 3.
Case: ADLC-coated steel; Ø 42mm, thickness: 11mm; ADLC-coated steel bezel with indicator in SuperLumiNova™; steel faceted crown set with faceted synthetic spinel.
Dial: black; partly snailed with indicators in SuperLumiNova™; steel sword-shaped hands coated with SuperLumiNova™.
Strap: rubber; ADLC-coated steel ardillon buckle.
Price: available upon request.

CARTIER

RONDE LOUIS CARTIER FILIGREE WATCH   REF. HPI00929

Movement: manual-winding 430 MC caliber; 40-hour power reserve.
Functions: hours, minutes.
Case: 18K yellow gold; Ø 42mm, thickness: 8mm; set with brilliant-cut diamonds; 18K yellow-gold beaded crown set with brilliant-cut diamond; water resistant to 3atm.
Dial: 18K yellow gold set with brilliant-cut diamonds; 22K yellow-gold and platinum filigree panther motif; emerald eyes; 18K yellow-gold apple-shaped hands.
Strap: dark blue alligator leather; 18K yellow-gold folding buckle set with brilliant-cut diamonds.

Note: limited edition of 20 numbered pieces.
Price: available upon request.

REVES DE PANTHERES WATCH   REF. HPI00930

Movement: manual-winding 9916 MC caliber; 48-hour power reserve.
Functions: day/night disc for hours; minutes hand.
Case: rhodiumized 18K white gold; Ø 42.75mm; set with brilliant-cut diamonds; rhodiumized 18K white-gold beaded crown set with brilliant-cut diamond.
Dial: rhodiumized 18K white gold set with brilliant-cut diamonds; rhodiumized 18K white-gold panthers with lacquer spots; blued steel sword-shaped hands.
Strap: dark blue alligator leather; rhodiumized 18K white-gold double adjustable deployant buckle set with brilliant-cut diamonds.

Note: numbered edition.
Price: available upon request.

ROTONDE DE CARTIER DAMASQUINAGE WATCH   REF. HPI00914

Movement: manual-winding 9601 MC caliber; 72-hour power reserve.
Functions: hours, minutes.
Case: 18K pink gold; Ø 42mm; 18K pink-gold beaded crown set with cabochon sapphire; water resistant to 3atm.
Dial: 18K white gold; 22K yellow-, pink- and white-gold damascene panther décor; lacquer nose and spots; onyx background; steel apple-shaped hands with yellow-gold finish.
Strap: brown alligator leather; 18K pink-gold double adjustable deployant buckle.

Note: limited edition of 50 numbered pieces.
Price: available upon request.

TORTUE STONE MOSAIC PANTHER DECOR WATCH   REF. HP100721

Movement: manual-winding 430 MC caliber; 40-hour power reserve.
Functions: hours, minutes.
Case: 18K pink gold; 43x34.2mm; set with brilliant-cut diamonds; 18K pink-gold octagonal crown set with brilliant-cut diamond; water resistant to 3atm.
Dial: 18K pink gold; stone mosaic panther décor with spots and nose in onyx mosaic and eyes in green stone mosaic; blued steel apple-shaped hands.
Strap: black alligator leather; 18K pink-gold double adjustable deployant buckle set with brilliant-cut diamonds.

Note: limited edition of 30 numbered pieces.
Price: available upon request.

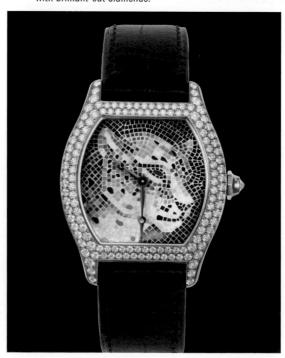

BALLON BLANC DE CARTIER 30MM REF. HPI00759

Movement: quartz; polished steel time-setting tool set with titanium cabochon.
Functions: hours, minutes.
Case: 18K pink gold; Ø 30.2mm, thickness: 8.46mm; brilliant-cut diamond at 4 (0.2 carat); water resistant to 3atm.
Dial: flinqué mother-of-pearl; blued steel sword-shaped hands.
Bracelet: 18K pink gold set with brilliant-cut diamonds.
Price: available upon request.

BALLON BLEU DE CARTIER 36MM REF. WE9005Z3

Movement: automatic-winding; 38-hour power reserve.
Functions: hours, minutes, seconds.
Case: 18K pink gold; Ø 36.6mm, thickness: 12.1mm; bezel set with brilliant-cut diamonds; 18K pink-gold fluted crown set with cabochon sapphire; water resistant to 3atm.
Dial: silvered opaline; guilloché and lacquered; blued steel sword-shaped hands.
Bracelet: 18K pink gold.
Price: available upon request.

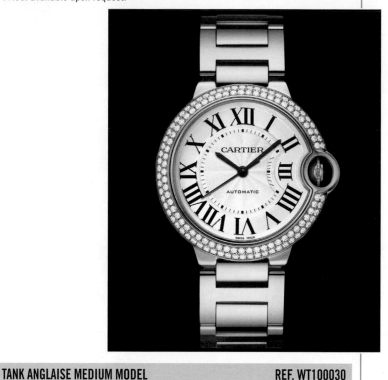

CLE DE CARTIER 31MM REF. WJCL0003

Movement: automatic-winding.
Functions: hours, minutes, seconds; date.
Case: 18K pink gold; Ø 31mm, thickness: 11.04mm; set with brilliant-cut diamonds; 18K pink-gold key set with a sapphire; water resistant to 3atm.
Dial: sunray finish and lacquer; blued steel sword-shaped hands.
Bracelet: 18K pink gold.
Price: available upon request.

TANK ANGLAISE MEDIUM MODEL REF. WT100030

Movement: automatic-winding; 38-hour power reserve.
Functions: hours, minutes.
Case: rhodiumized 18K white gold; 26.2x34.7mm, thickness: 7.1mm; set with brilliant-cut diamonds; rhodiumized 18K white-gold nonagonal crown set with brilliant-cut diamonds; water resistant to 3atm.
Dial: flinqué; silvered lacquered; blued steel sword-shaped hands.
Strap: shiny fuchsia alligator leather; 18K rhodiumized-white-gold double adjustable deployant buckle.
Price: available upon request.

CHANEL

IN FULL FLOWER

The history of CHANEL abounds with meaningful symbolism that extends all the way back to the origins of the famed Maison. Two exquisite models from its Mademoiselle Privé collection **INCORPORATE CHANEL'S PAST AND PRESENT** in technique, theme and guiding inspiration.

The collection's very name—Mademoiselle Privé—evokes both the timeless, feminine sense of style for which French women are known and the exclusive nature of true luxury. The words were emblazoned on the door of Gabrielle Chanel's Paris studio, marking the way to a realm in which unbridled creativity joined with expert craftsmanship to create a legend.

Among the comets, stars, lions and feathers that were so dear to Mademoiselle Chanel and which inspire the Mademoiselle Privé collection, one motif takes pride of place: her adored flower, the camellia. The sublime refinement and understated color of the blossom led to its role as a leitmotif within the Maison's designs, until the camellia became an undeniable symbol of Mademoiselle Chanel herself. The camellia-inspired timepieces use several time-honored horological techniques—gem-setting, enameling and engraving, to name a few—to depict the delicate bloom, and the collection's true brilliance lies in the way it uses the crafts of haute couture in two particular watches.

These floral flights of fancy offer an intimate glimpse inside the world of Mademoiselle Chanel.

In a stunning collaboration with famed embroidery company Maison Lesage, these two models represent camellias with tiny stitches in gold and silk thread, rose-cut diamonds, natural pearls and paillons in yellow and white gold. Because each dial—crafted upon a background of inky black fabric—is meticulously handmade, the embroiderer possesses a certain amount of liberty to express his or her own artistic vision within the confines of the dial. The use of needle and thread brings an ancient technique to horology, enriching it with elements from both the future and the past.

One model features leaves limned in strands of silk and golden thread, petals in fine circlets of yellow and white gold, and a natural pearl pistil; the other opts for a more highly stylized camellia, with a rose-cut diamond twinkling at the center like a drop of dew on a summer morning. These floral flights of fancy offer an intimate glimpse inside the world of Mademoiselle Chanel: her tastes, her inimitable aesthetic and her unwavering commitment to the highest quality.

Each timepiece is housed within an 18-karat yellow-gold case whose 37.5mm diameter is set with 60 brilliant-cut diamonds, totaling approximately one carat in weight. A high-precision quartz movement powers the hours and minute in a discreet display at five o'clock that complements the precious dial decorations. The chic black satin strap bears an 18-karat yellow-gold ardillon buckle set with 80 brilliant-cut diamonds, with a total weight of approximately 0.49 carat. The classic color combination of yellow gold, black fabric, white diamonds and natural white pearls, as well as the classic camellia form, would fit in seamlessly with any CHANEL couture collection in the Maison's long history. This collaboration with Maison Lesage only gives more perfect form to an aesthetic and a design philosophy that has given us innumerable stylistic classics over the years.

▲ **MADEMOISELLE PRIVÉ CAMELLIA EMBROIDERED**
Housed within a 37.5mm yellow-gold case, this model depicts several camellias with gold paillons and natural pearls.

◄ **MADEMOISELLE PRIVÉ CAMELLIA EMBROIDERED**
A product of CHANEL's undertaking with haute couture embroidery house Maison Lesage, this timepiece sparkles with brilliant-cut diamonds around the dial and one rose-cut diamond in the camellia's center.

MADEMOISELLE PRIVE COROMANDEL TWIN   REF. H3811

Movement: automatic-winding; 42-hour power reserve.
Functions: hours, minutes.
Case: 18K white gold; Ø 37.5mm; snow-set with 520 diamonds (approx. 4.45 carats); crown snow-set with 66 diamonds (approx. 0.15 carat).
Dial: miniature in Grand Feu enamel produced using Geneva technique.
Strap: black alligator leather; 18K white-gold folding buckle set with 80 brilliant-cut diamonds (approx. 0.49 carat).
Note: unique piece sold exclusively with H3812.

MADEMOISELLE PRIVE CAMELLIA   REF. H3567

Movement: automatic-winding; 42-hour power reserve.
Functions: hours, minutes.
Case: 18K yellow gold; Ø 37.5mm; set with 60 brilliant-cut diamonds (approx. 1 carat); water resistant to 3atm.
Dial: black lacquer decorated with yellow-gold camellias using Maki-e technique.
Strap: black satin; 18K yellow-gold ardillon buckle set with 80 brilliant-cut diamonds (approx. 0.49 carat).

MADEMOISELLE PRIVE CAMELLIA   REF. H3096

Movement: high-precision quartz.
Functions: hours, minutes.
Case: 18K white gold; Ø 37.5mm; set with 60 brilliant-cut diamonds (approx. 1 carat); onyx cabochon crown; water resistant to 3atm.
Dial: onyx decorated with camellia in mother-of-pearl marquetry; seven brilliant-cut diamond hour markers.
Strap: black satin; 18K white-gold ardillon buckle set with 80 brilliant-cut diamonds (0.49 carat).

MADEMOISELLE PRIVE COMET   REF. H2928

Movement: automatic-winding; 42-hour power reserve.
Functions: hours, minutes; comet revolves once every 60 seconds.
Case: 18K white gold; Ø 37.5mm; set with 60 brilliant-cut diamonds (approx. 1 carat); onyx cabochon crown; water resistant to 3atm.
Dial: black sapphire; whirling comet motif set with 31 brilliant-cut diamonds.
Strap: black satin; 18K white-gold ardillon buckle set with 80 brilliant-cut diamonds (approx. 0.49 carat).

J12 FLYING TOURBILLON HIGH JEWELRY REF. H3846

Movement: manual-winding; 40-hour power reserve.
Functions: hours, minutes; tourbillon with star at 6.
Case: 18K white gold; Ø 38mm; set with 82 baguette-cut diamonds (4 carats); crown set with 1 diamond; water resistant to 5atm.
Dial: set with 84 baguette-cut diamonds (4 carats) and 200 diamonds (approx. 0.86 carat); flange set with 74 diamonds (approx. 0.64 carat); tourbillon cabochon set with 19 diamonds (approx. 0.019 carat); tourbillon star set with 1 diamond (approx. 0.15 carat).
Bracelet: set with 502 baguette-cut diamonds (approx. 32.2 carats); 18K white-gold triple folding clasp.
Note: limited edition of five pieces.

J12 MOONPHASE CHROMATIC HIGH JEWELRY REF. H3460

Movement: automatic-winding; 42-hour power reserve.
Functions: hours, minutes; date; moonphase at 6.
Case: 18K white gold; Ø 38mm; set with 88 baguette-cut diamonds (approx. 5.73 carats); bezel set with 34 baguette-cut diamonds (approx. 3.3 carats); 18K white-gold crown set with one round faceted diamond (approx. 0.88 carat); 18K white-gold caseback; antireflective sapphire crystal; water resistant to 5atm.
Dial: gray; invisibly set with 32 baguette-cut diamonds (approx. 0.88 carat); aventurine moonphase.
Bracelet: set with 400 baguette-cut diamonds (approx. 20.28 carats).
Note: limited edition of 12 pieces.

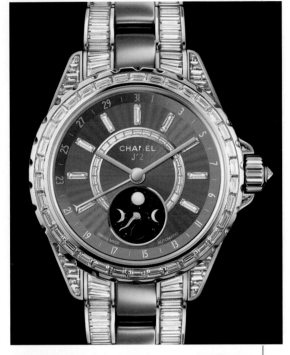

J12 FLYING TOURBILLON BEIGE GOLD REF. H4563

Movement: manual-winding; 40-hour power reserve.
Functions: hours, minutes; tourbillon with star at 6.
Case: white high-tech ceramic; Ø 38mm; 18K beige-gold bezel and crown, crown set with one diamond (approx. 0.15 carat); water resistant to 5atm.
Dial: mother-of-pearl set with 227 diamonds (approx. 0.78 carat); flange set with 74 diamonds (approx. 0.64 carat); tourbillon cabochon set with 19 diamonds (approx. 0.019 carat); tourbillon star set with 30 diamonds (approx. 0.037 carat); 18K beige-gold hands.
Bracelet: white high-tech ceramic; titanium folding buckle.

PREMIERE FLYING TOURBILLON REF. H3857

Movement: manual-winding, 40-hour power reserve.
Functions: hours, minutes; tourbillon at 6.
Case: 18K white gold; Ø 37mm; set with 47 baguette-cut pink sapphires (approx. 3.93 carats); crown set with 16 baguette-cut pink sapphires (approx. 0.034 carat) and 11 brilliant-cut diamonds (approx. 0.157 carat); water resistant to 3atm.
Dial: white high-tech ceramic set with 42 brilliant-cut diamonds (approx. 2.4 carats) and 52 brilliant-cut diamonds (approx. 1.48 carats); tourbillon cabochon set with 19 brilliant-cut diamonds (approx. 0.019 carat).
Strap: white alligator leather; 18K white-gold buckle set with 30 brilliant-cut diamonds (approx. 0.33 carat).

J12 365 BEIGE GOLD
REF. H3843

Movement: automatic-winding; 42-hour power reserve.
Functions: hours, minutes; small seconds at 6; date.
Case: white high-tech ceramic; Ø 36.5mm; 18K beige-gold bezel and crown; water resistant to 10atm.
Dial: opaline guilloché; flange set with 69 diamonds (approx. 0.6 carat); small seconds counter set with 68 diamonds (approx. 0.1 carat).
Bracelet: white high-tech ceramic; steel triple-folding buckle.

J12 COLLECTOR PASTEL BLUE
REF. H4341

Movement: automatic-winding; 42-hour power reserve.
Functions: hours, minutes, seconds; date.
Case: white high-tech ceramic and steel; Ø 38mm; unidirectional rotating pastel blue bezel; steel screw-down crown; water resistant to 20atm.
Dial: white.
Bracelet: white high-tech ceramic; steel triple-folding buckle.
Note: limited edition of 1,200 pieces.

J12-G10 CHROMATIC
REF. H4187

Movement: automatic-winding; 42-hour power reserve.
Functions: hours, minutes, seconds; date.
Case: titanium ceramic and steel; Ø 38mm; unidirectional rotating bezel; highly scratch-resistant; water resistant to 20atm.
Dial: vertical satin finish center with circular guilloché work on edge.
Strap: alligator leather; steel pin buckle and loops.

J12 SUPERLEGGERA
REF. H3409

Movement: automatic-winding; 42-hour power reserve; COSC-certified.
Functions: hours, minutes; small seconds at 3; date; chronograph: 30-minute counter, central seconds; tachometer.
Case: matte black high-tech ceramic and steel; Ø 41mm; screw-down pushbuttons and crown; steel caseback engraved with "J12 Superleggera"; water resistant to 20atm.
Dial: black.
Bracelet: matte black high-tech ceramic; steel triple folding buckle.

PREMIERE CHAIN LARGE SIZE FULL SET   REF. H3260

Movement: high-precision quartz.
Functions: hours, minutes.
Case: 18K white gold; 20x28mm, thickness: 6.6mm; set with 495 brilliant-cut diamonds (approx. 2.08 carats); water resistant to 3atm.
Dial: black lacquer.
Bracelet: 18K white gold; snow-set with 2,173 diamonds (approx. 9.16 carats).

PREMIERE ROCK PASTEL   REF. H4312

Movement: high-precision quartz.
Functions: hours, minutes.
Case: steel; 15.8x23.6mm, thickness: 6.2mm; steel cabochon crown.
Dial: white mother-of-pearl.
Strap: steel and nude leather ribbon interwoven; triple row.

PREMIERE ROCK METAL   REF. H4199

Movement: high-precision quartz.
Functions: hours, minutes.
Case: steel; 20x28mm, thickness: 6.6mm; water resistant to 3atm.
Dial: black lacquer.
Bracelet: steel; double row.

PREMIERE CHAIN LARGE SIZE BEIGE GOLD   REF. H4412

Movement: high-precision quartz.
Functions: hours, minutes.
Case: 18K beige gold; 20x28mm, thickness: 6.6mm; set with 56 brilliant-cut diamonds (approx. 0.43 carat); 18K beige-gold cabochon crown; water resistant to 3atm.
Dial: white mother-of-pearl.
Bracelet: 18K beige-gold chain and clasp.

CHAUMET
PARIS

SPRING BLOSSOMS

Celebrated since 1780 for its evocative timekeeping, **PARISIAN WATCHMAKER CHAUMET LIGHTS UP THE WRIST WITH A FLORAL-INSPIRED COLLECTION**.

The Hortensia High-Jewelry line of timepieces captures the sense of possibility inherent to a blossoming flower, combining natural and mechanical beauty in the process. Like gardens brightened by micro-mechanical intricacy, an 18-karat rhodium-plated white-gold interpretation begins with a shimmering setting of 123 brilliant-cut diamonds on the bezel and lugs. On the sides of the round 40mm structure, diamond-set, hand-engraved floral hydrangea patterns balance organic sensibility and luxurious tones. Powered by the hand-wound 24-jewel CP12V-IX caliber, which is shaped like a hydrangea, this luminous work of timekeeping art reveals a tourbillon within a meadow of hand-engraved corollas with Grand Feu enamel. Staged on a white Grand Feu base, the timepiece seamlessly integrates the tourbillon within an arrangement of lustrous flowers accentuated by their light pink tones and soft colors. Limited to 12 pieces, the splendidly ornamented timepiece continues the floral theme on the crown, where a brilliant-cut diamond sparkles atop an enameled engraving of a hydrangea.

◀ **HORTENSIA TOURBILLON**
This hand-wound timepiece's tourbillon is revealed within a bouquet of Grand-Feu enameled hydrangea flowers, proposing a serene harmony of nature and micro-mechanical sophistication.

Adorned with diamonds and other gems, these timepieces express their Hortensia personality with numerous techniques, all infused with floral beauty.

The Hortensia Secret Watch presents time as a secret reserved for the wearer, told on a white mother-of-pearl dial set with four diamond indexes. Housed within a generously adorned 18-karat pink-gold case set with a row of 46 brilliant-cut diamonds, the hours and minutes are concealed beneath a flowery décor resplendent with intricate adornments. The bouquet, composed of seven brilliant-cut diamonds, two large flowers paved with brilliant-cut diamonds and four marquise-cut pink tourmalines or one brilliant-cut pink sapphire, one large flower in angel skin opal set with a brilliant-cut diamond, and 11 small flowers sculpted in pink gold or pink opal, set with brilliant-cut diamonds, is lavishly finished with a prominent pear-cut pink tourmaline on the strap link at 6 o'clock. Chaumet's jewelry excellence transports the vigorous, colorful beauty of the floral universe to a world of precious gems, scintillating with each passing moment like a dewy flower under the sun's light.

A line of four Hortensia members of the collection finds delicate decadence within a refined white- or yellow-gold frame of 31mm. All adorned with diamond settings on the bezel, the four timepieces express their Hortensia personality with numerous techniques, all infused with the emotion of floral beauty. From a mixture of guilloché and kaleidoscope décor to a bouquet of lace-work hydrangea flowers, the radiant white mother-of-pearl dials let the flower take center stage with stunning detail, often surrounded by a shimmering corolla of diamonds. A pair of finely proportioned open-worked hands indicates the hours and minutes, further revealing the dials' artistry.

The Hortensia collection thus brings the house's jewelry expertise to bear upon nature's finest sculptures.

▲ **HORTENSIA SECRET WATCH**
A plethora of gem-set sculpted flowers adorns this magnificent display of finesse and high-jewelry virtuosity.

▼ **HORTENSIA METIERS D'ART**
These 31mm interpretations of the Hortensia spirit put Chaumet's technical skill to the test, adorning their mother-of-pearl dials with marvelous hydrangea-inspired motifs.

CHAUMET

LIENS   REF. W23610-01A

Movement: quartz.
Functions: hours, minutes, seconds.
Case: polished stainless steel; Ø 27mm (Ø 29mm with link); surrounding link crosses at 3 & 9, creating handles to hold bracelet; curved sapphire crystal; water resistant to 3atm.
Dial: white-silvered; center vertical-lined and two lateral arcs; applied curved stick hour markers and night blue Arabic numerals; pointed stick hands.
Bracelet: polished stainless steel; three rows with lateral border; double folding-clasp buckle with safety push-buttons.
Price: available upon request.
Also available: navy blue calfskin strap (ref. W23210-01A).

LIENS   REF. W23211-01A

Movement: quartz.
Functions: hours, minutes, seconds.
Case: polished stainless steel; Ø 27mm (Ø 29mm with link); bezel set with 56 diamonds (0.38 carat); surrounding link crosses at 3 & 9, creating handles to hold bracelet; curved sapphire crystal; water resistant to 3atm.
Dial: white-silvered; center vertical-lined and two lateral arcs; applied curved stick hour markers and night blue Arabic numerals; pointed stick hands.
Strap: charcoal-gray calfskin; stainess steel pin buckle with crossed link décor.
Price: available upon request.
Also available: stainless steel three-row bracelet (ref. W23611-01A).

LIENS   REF. W23010-02A

Movement: quartz.
Functions: hours, minutes, seconds.
Case: polished 18K 3N yellow gold; Ø 27mm (Ø 29mm with link); surrounding link crosses at 3 & 9, creating handles to hold bracelet; crown set with white mother-of-pearl cabochon; curved sapphire crystal; water resistant to 3atm.
Dial: white-silvered; center vertical-lined and two lateral arcs; applied curved stick hour markers and night blue Arabic numerals; pointed stick hands.
Strap: taupe-brown calfskin; 18K 3N yellow-gold pin buckle with crossed link décor.
Price: available upon request.

LIENS   REF. W23011-02A

Movement: quartz.
Functions: hours, minutes, seconds.
Case: polished 18K 3N yellow gold; Ø 27mm (Ø 29mm with link); bezel set with 56 diamonds (0.38 carat); surrounding link crosses at 3 & 9, creating handles to hold bracelet; crown set with white mother-of-pearl cabochon; curved sapphire crystal; water resistant to 3atm.
Dial: white-silvered; center vertical-lined and two lateral arcs; applied curved stick hour markers and night blue Arabic numerals; pointed stick hands.
Strap: black calfskin; 18K 3N yellow-gold pin buckle with crossed link décor.
Price: available upon request.

LIENS — REF. W23270-01A

Movement: automatic-winding; 42-hour power reserve; 25 jewels; 28,800 vph.
Functions: hours, minutes, seconds; date at 4:30.
Case: polished stainless steel; Ø 33mm (Ø 35mm with link); surrounding link crosses at 3 & 9, creating handles to hold bracelet; curved sapphire crystal; open caseback; water resistant to 3atm.
Dial: white-silvered; sunray fine-brushed center and two lacquered lateral arcs; applied curved stick hour markers and night blue Arabic numerals; pointed stick hands.
Strap: night blue alligator leather; stainless steel pin buckle with crossed link décor.
Price: available upon request.
Also available: stainless steel three-row bracelet (ref. W23670-01A).

LIENS — REF. W23671-01A

Movement: automatic-winding; 42-hour power reserve; 25 jewels; 28,800 vph.
Functions: hours, minutes, seconds; date at 4:30.
Case: polished stainless steel; Ø 33mm (Ø 35mm with link); bezel set with 64 diamonds (0.44 carat); surrounding link crosses at 3 & 9, creating handles to hold bracelet; curved sapphire crystal; open caseback; water resistant to 3atm.
Dial: white-silvered; sunray fine-brushed center and two lacquered lateral arcs; applied curved stick hour markers and night blue Arabic numerals; pointed stick hands.
Bracelet: polished stainless steel; three rows with a lateral border; double folding-clasp buckle with safety pushbuttons.
Price: available upon request.
Also available: brown alligator leather strap (ref. W23271-01A).

LIENS — REF. W23771-02A

Movement: automatic-winding; 42-hour power reserve; 25 jewels; 28,800 vph.
Functions: hours, minutes, seconds; date at 4:30.
Case: polished stainless steel; Ø 33mm (Ø 35mm with link); 18K 5N pink-gold bezel set with 64 diamonds (0.44 carat); surrounding link crosses at 3 & 9, creating handles to hold bracelet; 18K 5N pink-gold crown set with white mother-of-pearl cabochon; curved sapphire crystal; open caseback; water resistant to 3atm.
Dial: white-silvered; sunray fine-brushed center and two lacquered lateral arcs; applied curved stick hour markers and night blue Arabic numerals; pointed stick hands.
Bracelet: polished stainless steel and 18K 5N pink-gold; three rows with lateral border; double folding clasp buckle with safety pushbuttons.
Price: available upon request.

LIENS — REF. W23870-02A

Movement: automatic-winding; 42-hour power reserve; 25 jewels; 28,800 vph.
Functions: hours, minutes, seconds; date at 4:30.
Case: polished 18K 5N pink gold; Ø 33mm (Ø 35mm with link); surrounding link crosses at 3 & 9, creating handles to hold bracelet; crown set with white mother-of-pearl cabochon; curved sapphire crystal; open caseback; water resistant to 3atm.
Dial: white-silvered, sunray fine-brushed center and two lacquered lateral arcs; applied curved stick hour markers and night blue Arabic numerals; pointed stick hands.
Strap: white alligator leather; 18K 5N pink-gold pin buckle with crossed link décor.
Price: available upon request.
Also available: bezel set with 64 diamonds on taupe alligator leather strap (ref. W23871-02A).

HORTENSIA   REF. W20120-05D

Movement: quartz.
Functions: hours, minutes.
Case: polished 18K rhodium-plated white gold; Ø 31mm; bezel set with 55 diamonds (0.78 carat); curved sapphire crystal; water resistant to 3atm.
Dial: lavender blue seawater mother-of-pearl, engraved with floral pattern, inlaid in crown of 121 diamonds (0.24 carat) and adorned with white seawater mother-of-pearl lace, cut and applied to create the hydrangea décor; leaf-shaped skeletonized hands, with twist on minutes hand.

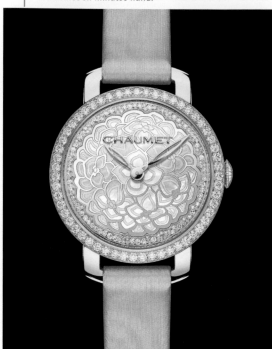

Strap: light blue brushed canvas satin; 18K rhodium-plated white-gold pin buckle set with 19 diamonds (0.16 carat).
Price: available upon request.

HORTENSIA   REF. W20021-04C

Movement: quartz.
Functions: hours, minutes.
Case: polished 18K 3N yellow gold; Ø 31mm; bezel set with 55 diamonds (0.78 carat); curved sapphire crystal; water resistant to 3atm.
Dial: white seawater mother-of-pearl marquetry, worked with 2 corollas around central flower to create the hydrangea décor, inlaid in crown of 121 diamonds (0.24 carat); leaf-shaped skeletonized hands, with twist on minutes hand.
Strap: brown brushed canvas satin; 18K 3N yellow-gold pin buckle set with 19 diamonds (0.16 carat).
Price: available upon request.

HORTENSIA   REF. W20020-04B

Movement: quartz.
Functions: hours, minutes.
Case: polished 18K 3N yellow gold; Ø 31mm; bezel set with 55 diamonds (0.78 carat); curved sapphire crystal; water resistant to 3atm.
Dial: white seawater mother-of-pearl, engraved with floral pattern, inlaid in crown of 121 diamonds (0.24 carat) and adorned with white seawater mother-of-pearl lace, cut and applied to create the hydrangea décor; leaf-shaped skeletonized hands, with twist on minutes hand.

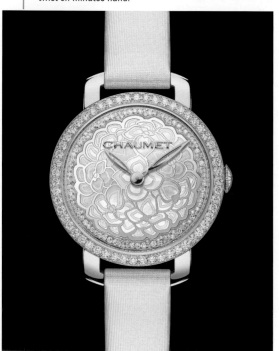

Strap: sand-colored satin; 18K 3N yellow-gold pin buckle set with 19 diamonds (0.16 carat).
Price: available upon request.

HORTENSIA   REF. W20121-05E

Movement: quartz.
Functions: hours, minutes.
Case: polished 18K rhodium-plated white gold; Ø 31mm; bezel set with 55 diamonds (0.78 carat); curved sapphire crystal; water resistant to 3atm.
Dial: mother-of-pearl marquetry, alternating squares of guilloché riverwater white mother-of-pearl and of seawater white & gold mother-of-pearl, cut and engraved then miniature-painted to create the hydrangea flower patterns; leaf-shaped skeletonized hands, with twist on minutes hand.

Strap: cream-beige satin; 18K rhodium-plated white-gold pin buckle set with 19 diamonds (0.16 carat).
Price: available upon request.

ATTRAPE-MOI... SI TU M'AIMES   REF. W16199-BC1

Movement: Chaumet exclusive automatic-winding caliber complication CP12V-XII; revisiting time reading thanks to mobile indexes moving on trajectories of distinct shapes.
Case: 18K rhodium-plated white gold with 5N pink gold cabochon markers; set with 204 diamonds (1.92 carat) on top, side and crown; engraved with web patterns; curved antireflective sapphire crystal; water resistant to 3atm.
Dial: three parts; rhodium-plated; hollowed-out cobweb pattern adorned with 43 curved polished mother-of-pearl waves; marqueted between decreasing metal filets set with 83 diamonds (0.30 carat).
Strap: pearly white alligator leather; 18K rhodium-plated white-gold jaw pin buckle with pink-gold polished spider; adorned with engraved web pattern and set with 7 diamonds (0.08 carat).
Price: available upon request.

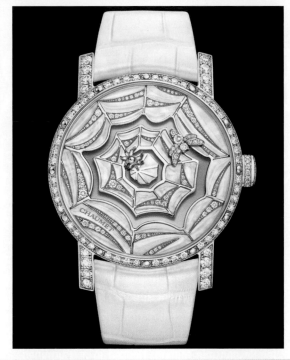

ATTRAPE-MOI... SI TU M'AIMES   REF. W16189-38D

Movement: automatic-winding; 42-hour power reserve; 20 jewels; 28,800 vph.
Functions: hours, minutes.
Case: 18K rhodium-plated white gold; Ø 35mm; polished and set on top with 58 diamonds on top (2.52 carats); one rose-cut diamond on crown (0.1 carat); curved sapphire crystal; open caseback; water resistant to 3atm.
Dial: butterflies' flight worked in applied agate and mother-of-pearl wings on sunray guilloché sky and diamond-made clouds (164 diamonds, 0.21 carat); leaf-shaped hands.
Strap: blue gros-grain satin; 18K rhodium-plated white-gold pin buckle set with 63 diamonds (0.21 carat).
Note: limited and numbered edition of 88 pieces; additional black alligator leather strap offered.
Price: available upon request.

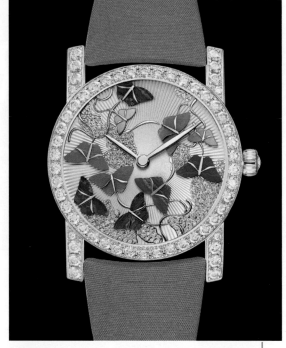

HORTENSIA   REF. W20190-01A

Movement: manual-winding CP12V-IX caliber; 120-hour power reserve; 24 jewels; 21,600 vph; tourbillon.
Functions: hours, minutes; tourbillon at 6.
Case: 18K rhodium-plated white gold; Ø39.9mm; set on top with 133 diamonds (4.06 carats); hydrangea flowers pattern engraved on sides; enameled crown; curved sapphire crystal; open caseback; water resistant to 3atm.
Dial: white gold; Grand Feu enamel; applied hydrangea flowers; sculpted, hand-engraved and Grand Feu enameled in blue and purple tones with silver foils in center; opening on tourbillon cage at 6; leaf-shaped hands.
Strap: night blue alligator leather; 18K rhodium-plated white-gold jaw pin buckle engraved with hydrangea flowers set in their center with 3 diamonds (0.09 carat).
Note: limited and numbered edition of 12 pieces; additional night blue alligator leather strap offered.
Price: available upon request.
Also available: Grand Feu enameled dial in white and pink tones on white alligator leather strap (ref. W20191-02A).

ATTRAPE-MOI... SI TU M'AIMES   REF. W16888-38H

Movement: automatic-winding caliber; 42-hour power reserve; 20 jewels; 28,800 vph.
Functions: hours, minutes.
Case: 18K 5N pink gold; Ø 35mm; polished and set on bezel with 152 diamonds (0.89 carat); one rose-cut diamond on crown (0.1 carat); curved sapphire crystal; open caseback; water resistant to 3atm.
Dial: butterflies worked in applied blackened gold, inlaid with red cornelian and white-colored wood marquetry, burr myrtle wood base, with three 18K pink-gold stalks set with 48 diamonds (0.09 carat); leaf-shaped hands.
Strap: taupe gros-grain satin; 18K 5N pink-gold pin buckle set with 63 diamonds (0.21 carat).
Note: limited and numbered edition of 88 pieces; additional white alligator leather strap offered.
Price: available upon request.

Chopard

TIME FOR A BETTER WORLD

From a statement of global citizenship and consciousness, to a timepiece that challenges the limits of mechanical performance or one that connects its wearer to the moon's eternal cycles, **CHOPARD AMAZES WITH AN ALL-INCLUSIVE EXHIBITION OF ITS ESTEEMED WATCHMAKING TALENTS**.

The L.U.C Tourbillon QF Fairmined is a striking demonstration that true elegance manifests itself below the surface. As its name implies, the hand-wound 43mm timepiece is crafted in gold mined responsibly in South America, with miners receiving fair payment and an overall premium. The first watch created from "Fairmined" gold, the L.U.C Tourbillon QF Fairmined brings attention to Chopard's proud partnership with the Alliance for Responsible Mining. Housed in a "Fairmined" 18-karat rose-gold case, the L.U.C 02.13-L caliber, certified by the Fleurier Quality Foundation and COSC, animates a refined dial-side display of the hours, minutes and a retrograde indication of the piece's impressive 216-hour power reserve, as well as a stunning tourbillon visible through an aperture in the sunburst satin-finished ruthenium face. The timepiece is available limited to 25 pieces and boasts an open caseback through which the wearer may enjoy Chopard's exquisite mastery of fine finishes and meticulous craftsmanship.

◄ **L.U.C TOURBILLON QF FAIRMINED**
This tourbillon timepiece is housed in a case composed of 18-karat rose gold mined according to the sustainable and ethical standards of Chopard's "The Journey" project and Alliance for Responsible Mining.

The L.U.C 8HF Power Control's combination of ultra-high frequency and certified precision makes for a statement of terrific evolution in the field of haute horology.

The commanding nature of the L.U.C 8HF Power Control's 42mm black ceramic case provides a high-tech aesthetic for a timepiece of spectacular mechanical excellence and extraordinary frequency. A COSC-certified 8Hz movement, the self-winding L.U.C 01.09-L caliber reveals, through an opening in the matte black ceramic caseback, its exceptional escapement beating at a rate of 57,600 vph—16 vibrations per second. This combination of ultra-high frequency and certified precision and reliability makes for a statement of terrific evolution in the field of haute horology. On the sunburst black dial, time passes against a decisively modern backdrop of tasteful asymmetry. Joining the central hours and minutes, a window between 5 and 6 o'clock indicates the date by way of a revolving disc and bright red arrow. At 7 o'clock, the timepiece showcases its caliber with tasteful subtlety, via a traditional small seconds subdial through which a vivid red hand smoothly travels, each pulse invisible to the human eye. A power reserve indicator, at 10 o'clock, highlights the watch's impressive single-barrel autonomy of 60 hours—a noteworthy feat given the sizeable energy demands of such a high-frequency escapement.

An inherent connection links humanity's relationship with time and the sky above us, which illuminates the day and shimmers in the night. Chopard's L.U.C Lunar Big Date encapsulates this bond with a design that honors the moon's continuous cycles and their significance within our conception of time. The timepiece's splendid moonphase display, at 7 o'clock, illustrates the journey of the moon, for both the Northern and Southern Hemispheres, throughout its synodic cycle of 29 days, 12 hours, 44 minutes and 2.8 seconds. This interval from one new moon to the next is precisely animated on a lively subdial complete with the Big Dipper and Southern Cross. Needing only a single-day adjustment every 122 years, the module is driven by a wheel comprising an impressive 135 teeth. A large display at 12 o'clock, playing off the dual-counter design of the silver-toned dial's lower half, indicates the date with optimal legibility thanks to a two-disc construction within the self-winding L.U.C 96.20-L caliber. The 42mm case, in 18-karat white gold, combines with the dial for the perfect monochrome effect to vibrantly showcase the artful colors of the lunar complication.

▲ L.U.C 8HF POWER CONTROL
Oscillating at a breathtaking frequency of 57,600 vph, this black ceramic wristwatch takes a cutting-edge approach to the concept of chronometric accuracy.

▼ L.U.C LUNAR BIG DATE
A visually stunning lunar complication takes the wearer on a brilliant journey through the moon's cyclical phases.

CHOPARD

GRAND PRIX DE MONACO HISTORIQUE AUTOMATIC   REF. 168568-3001

Movement: automatic-winding; Ø 37.20mm; 46-hour power reserve; 24 jewels; 28,800 vph; COSC-certified chronometer.
Functions: hours, minutes, seconds; date at 3.
Case: beadblasted titanium; Ø 44.5mm, thickness: 13.9mm; glareproof sapphire crystal; titanium crown; steel bezel with black aluminum insert, silver-toned transfer and yellow dots; caseback bearing the Automobile Club de Monaco logo; water resistant to 10atm.
Dial: snailed silver-toned dial; raised oversized Arabic numerals at 12 and 6; yellow inner bezel ring; metalized black hour and minute hands; yellow central sweep-seconds hand.

Strap: black Barenia calfskin strap with yellow stitching; optional black and yellow NATO strap; steel and titanium folding clasp.
Suggested price: $5,570

GRAND PRIX DE MONACO HISTORIQUE CHRONO   REF. 168570-3001

Movement: automatic-winding; Ø 37.20mm; 46-hour power reserve; 24 jewels; 28,800 vph; COSC-certified chronometer.
Functions: hours, minutes; small seconds at 9; date at 3; chronograph: 30-minute counter, 12-hour counter.
Case: beadblasted titanium; Ø 44.5mm, thickness: 13.9mm; glareproof sapphire crystal; titanium crown; steel bezel with black aluminum insert, silver-toned transfer and yellow dots; caseback bearing the Automobile Club de Monaco logo; water resistant to 10atm.
Dial: snailed silver-toned dial; hollowed silver-toned subdial at 9; metalized black hour and minute hands; yellow central sweep-seconds hand.

Strap: black Barenia calfskin strap with yellow stitching; optional black and yellow NATO strap; steel and titanium folding clasp.
Suggested price: $7,640

GRAND PRIX DE MONACO HISTORIQUE POWER CONTROL   REF. 168569-3001

Movement: automatic-winding; Ø 37.20mm; 46-hour power reserve; 24 jewels; 28,800 vph; COSC-certified chronometer.
Functions: hours, minutes, seconds; date at 3; power reserve indicator at 6.
Case: beadblasted titanium; Ø 44.5mm, thickness: 13.9mm; glareproof sapphire crystal; titanium crown; steel bezel with black aluminum insert, silver-toned transfer and yellow dots; caseback bearing the Automobile Club de Monaco logo; water resistant to 10atm.
Dial: snailed silver-toned dial; raised oversized Arabic numeral at 12; yellow inner bezel ring; metalized black hour and minute hands; yellow central sweep-seconds hand.

Strap: black Barenia calfskin strap with yellow stitching; optional black and yellow NATO strap; steel and titanium folding clasp.
Suggested price: $6,990

HAPPY SPORT MEDIUM AUTOMATIC TWO TONE   REF. 278559-6002

Movement: automatic-winding; Ø 26.20mm, thickness: 3.60mm; 42-hour power reserve; 25 jewels; 28,800 vph.
Functions: hours, minutes, seconds; date at 4:30.
Case: stainless steel and 18K rose gold; Ø 36mm, thickness: 12.08mm; 18K rose-gold crown set with a blue sapphire; polished 18K rose-gold bezel; 7 moving diamonds; glareproof sapphire crystal; exhibition caseback; water resistant to 3atm.
Dial: silver-toned dial; central guilloché motif; gold-toned hour, minute and seconds hands; gold-toned hour markers.

Bracelet: steel and 18K rose-gold.
Suggested price: $17,330

HAPPY SPORT TOURBILLON JOAILLERIE

REF. 274462-1001

Movement: manual-winding L.U.C 02.16-L caliber; Ø 29.70mm, thickness: 6.10mm; 216-hour (9-day) power reserve; 33 jewels; 28,800 vph; 4 barrels, Quattro® technology; Poinçon de Genève; COSC-certified chronometer.
Functions: hours, minutes; small seconds at 6; tourbillon.
Case: 18K white gold; Ø 42mm, thickness: 15.09mm; 18K white-gold crown; glareproof sapphire crystal; transparent caseback; water resistant to 3atm.
Dial: snow-set diamond pavé; diamond-set tourbillon bridge; 7 moving diamonds; blue dagger-type hour and minute hands; blue small seconds hand.
Strap: hand-sewn alligator leather; 18K white-gold pin buckle.
Price: available upon request.

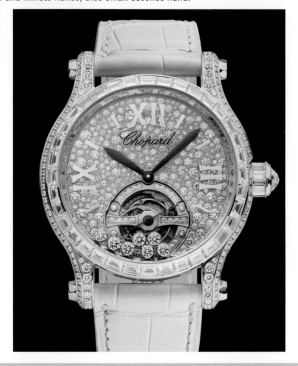

IMPERIALE

REF. 384242-5005

Movement: automatic-winding; Ø 26.20mm, thickness: 3.60mm; 42-hour power reserve; 25 jewels; 28,800 vph.
Functions: hours, minutes.
Case: 18K rose gold; Ø 36mm, thickness: 9.30mm; 18K rose-gold crown set with diamonds; 18K rose-gold bezel and horns set with diamonds; glareproof sapphire crystal; solid caseback; water resistant to 5atm.
Dial: white mother-of-pearl; brilliant-set indexes; Roman numerals.
Strap: white satin; 18K rose-gold pin buckle.
Suggested price: $45,690

L.U.C 1963

REF. 161963-5001

Movement: manual-winding L.U.C 63.01-L caliber; Ø 38mm, thickness: 5.50mm; 60-hour power reserve; 20 jewels; 21,600 vph; bridges adorned with Côtes de Genève motif; Poinçon de Genève; COSC-certified chronometer.
Functions: hours, minutes; small seconds at 9.
Case: 18K rose gold; Ø 44mm, thickness: 11.50mm; 18K rose-gold crown with L.U.C logo; glareproof sapphire crystal; exhibition caseback; water resistant to 5atm.
Dial: porcelain-style white dial; gilt hour, minute and small second hands.
Strap: hand-sewn alligator leather; 18K rose gold pin buckle.
Note: limited edition of 50 pieces.
Suggested price: $37,580
Also available: platinum (ref. 161963-9001) — limited edition of 50 pieces.

L.U.C 1963 CHRONOGRAPH

REF. 161964-5001

Movement: manual-winding L.U.C 03.07-L caliber; Ø 28.80mm, thickness: 5.62mm; 60-hour power reserve; 38 jewels; 28,800 vph; bridges adorned with Côtes de Genève motif; Poinçon de Genève; COSC-certified chronometer.
Functions: hours, minutes; small seconds at 6; chronograph: sweep seconds hand, 30-minute counter at 3; 12-hour counter at 9; date between 4 and 5.
Case: 18K rose gold, Ø 42mm, thickness: 11.50mm; 18K rose-gold crown with L.U.C logo; glareproof sapphire crystal; exhibition caseback; water resistant to 5atm.
Dial: sunburst satin-brushed silver-toned; matte silver-toned counters.
Strap: hand-sewn brown alligator leather; lined with cognac-toned alligator leather; 18K rose-gold pin buckle.
Note: limited edition of 50 pieces.
Suggested price: $44,440

CHOPARD

L.U.C XPS 35MM   REF. 121968-5001

Movement: automatic-winding L.U.C 96.12-L caliber; Ø 27.40mm, thickness: 3.30mm; 65-hour power reserve; 29 jewels; 28,800 vph; bridges adorned with Côtes de Genève motif; 2 barrels – Twin® technology; COSC-certified chronometer.
Functions: hours, minutes; small seconds at 6.
Case: 18K rose gold; Ø 35mm, thickness: 7.10mm; 18K rose-gold crown with L.U.C logo; polished bezel; glareproof sapphire crystal; exhibition caseback; water resistant to 5atm.
Dial: sunburst satin-brushed silver-toned dial; polished hour markers; gilded dauphine hour and minute hands; gilded triangular small seconds hand.
Strap: hand-sewn brown alligator leather with alligator lining; 18K rose-gold pin buckle.
Suggested price: $16,710

L.U.C XPS 35MM   REF. 131968-5001

Movement: automatic-winding L.U.C 96.12-L caliber; Ø 27.40mm, thickness: 3.30mm; 65-hour power reserve; 29 jewels; 28,800 vph; bridges adorned with Côtes de Genève motif; 2 barrels – Twin® technology; COSC-certified chronometer.
Functions: hours, minutes; small seconds at 6.
Case: 18K rose gold; Ø 35mm, thickness: 7.10mm; 18K rose-gold crown with L.U.C logo; diamond-set bezel; glareproof sapphire crystal; exhibition caseback; water resistant to 5atm.
Dial: shimmering white mother-of-pearl dial; diamond-set hour markers; gilded dauphine hour and minute hands; gilded triangular small seconds hand.
Strap: gray brushed canvas; 18K rose-gold pin buckle.
Suggested price: $27,080

L.U.C XPS POINÇON DE GENEVE   REF. 161932-9002

Movement: automatic-winding L.U.C 96.01-L caliber; Ø 27.40mm, thickness: 3.30mm; 65-hour power reserve; 29 jewels; 28,800 vph; bridges adorned with Côtes de Genève motif; 2 barrels – Twin® technology; Poinçon de Genève; COSC-certified chronometer.
Functions: hours, minutes; small seconds and 6; date at 3.
Case: platinum; Ø 39.50mm, thickness: 7.13mm; 18K white-gold crown with L.U.C logo; glareproof sapphire crystal; platinum exhibition caseback with "Poinçon de Genève" logo; water resistant to 3atm.
Dial: gray-blue sunburst satin-brushed dial with white "Poinçon de Genève" logo; rhodiumed hour markers; rhodiumed dauphine-type hours and minute hands; rhodiumed baton-type seconds hand.
Strap: hand-sewn matte blue alligator leather strap lined with marine blue-toned alligator leather; 18K white-gold pin buckle.
Suggested price: $25,650

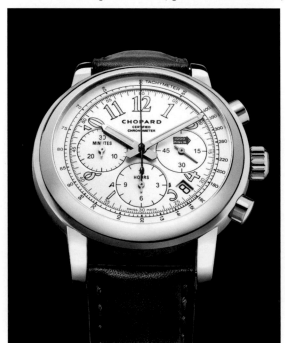

MILLE MIGLIA 2014   REF. 168511-3036

Movement: automatic-winding chronograph caliber; Ø 28.60mm; 42-hour power reserve; 37 jewels; 28,800 vph; COSC-certified chronometer.
Functions: hours, minutes, seconds; chronograph: hour, minute and seconds counters at 6, 9 and 3; date between 4 and 5.
Case: steel; Ø42mm, thickness: 12.31mm; glareproof sapphire crystal; steel crown and pushers; open caseback with special Mille Miglia logo around the rim; water resistant to 5atm.
Dial: matte beige dial with red, green and black transfers; metalized black baton-type hour and minute hands; red central sweep-seconds hand.
Strap: brown Barenia calfskin; steel pin buckle.
Note: limited edition of 2014 pieces.
Suggested price: $5,520
Also available: 18K rose gold, limited edition of 250 pieces (ref. 161274-5006).

MILLE MIGLIA ZAGATO CHRONOGRAPH REF. 168550-6001

Movement: automatic-winding chronograph caliber; Ø 30.40mm, thickness: 7.90mm; 46-hour power reserve; 25 jewels; 28,800 vph; COSC-certified chronometer.
Functions: hours, minutes; small seconds at 9; date at 3; central dual-time display; chronograph: 30-minute counter at 12, 12-hour counter at 6, central sweep seconds hand.
Case: DLC-coated steel; Ø 42.50mm, thickness: 14.85mm; crown in DLC-coated steel with "Z" logo; pushers in 18K rose gold; bezel in 18K rose gold with red aluminum insert; glareproof sapphire crystal; solid DLC-coated steel caseback with 1000 Miglia arrow logo and Zagato inscrip-

tion; water resistant to 5atm.
Dial: black dial with "Z" logo and snailed black counters at 12, 6 and 9; gold-toned hour and minute hands enhanced with Super-LumiNova; red-tipped center sweep-seconds hand; black GMT hand with SuperLumiNova-enhanced tip; white counter pointers.
Strap: integrated black Barenia leather strap with red or black stitching; folding clasp in DLC-coated steel.
Note: limited edition of 500 pieces.
Suggested price: $9,900
Also available: DLC-coated steel, limited edition of 500 pieces (ref. 168550-3004).

SUPERFAST AUTOMATIC REF. 168536-3001

Movement: automatic-winding Chopard 01.01-M caliber; Ø 28.8mm; 60-hour power reserve; 31 jewels; 28,800 vph; COSC-certified chronometer.
Functions: hours, minutes, seconds; date at 6.
Case: stainless steel; Ø 41mm, thickness: 11.3mm; black rubber-molded stainless steel crown with steering-wheel logo; glareproof sapphire crystal; open caseback; stainless steel bezel secured by 8 visible screws; water resistant to 10atm.
Dial: black dial with vertical anthracite stripes; SuperLumiNova-enhanced rhodiumed hour and minute hands and hour markers; red seconds hand.
Strap: black rubber strap (slick tire-tread motif); stainless steel folding clasp.
Suggested price: $9,230

SUPERFAST CHRONO REF. 168535-3001

Movement: automatic-winding Chopard 03.05-M caliber; Ø 28.8mm; 60-hour power reserve; 45 jewels; 28,800 vph; COSC-certified chronometer.
Functions: hours, minutes; small seconds at 6; date at 4:30; flyback chronograph: central sweep-seconds hand, 30-minute counter at 3, 12-hour counter at 9; tachometer.
Case: stainless steel; Ø 45mm, thickness: 15.18mm; black rubber-molded stainless steel crown with steering-wheel logo; black rubber-molded stainless steel pushers; glareproof sapphire crystal; open caseback; stainless steel bezel with tachometer secured by 8 visible screws; water resistant to 10atm.
Dial: black dial with vertical anthracite stripes; SuperLumiNova-enhanced rhodiumed hour and minute hands and hour markers; rhodiumed small seconds hand; red sweep-seconds hand with arrow tip; red hour and minute counters hands.
Strap: black rubber strap (slick tire-tread motif); stainless steel folding clasp.
Suggested price: $12,740

SUPERFAST POWER CONTROL REF. 168537-3001

Movement: automatic-winding Chopard 01.02-M caliber; Ø 28.8mm; 60-hour power reserve; 37 jewels; 28,800 vph; COSC-certified chronometer.
Functions: hours, minutes; small seconds at 6; date at 3; power reserve indicator at 9.
Case: stainless steel; Ø 45mm, thickness: 12.4mm; black rubber-molded stainless steel crown with steering-wheel logo; glareproof sapphire crystal; open caseback; stainless steel bezel secured by 8 visible screws; water resistant to 10atm.
Dial: black dial with vertical anthracite stripes; white power reserve indicator; Super-LumiNova-enhanced rhodiumed hour and minute hands and hour markers; rhodiumed small seconds hand; red power reserve indicator hand.
Strap: black rubber strap (slick tire-tread motif); stainless steel folding clasp.
Suggested price: $10,350

CHRISTOPHE CLARET

À LA FOLIE!

At its most transcendent, haute horology transports its admirers, accompanying them on a journey of wonderment and imagination, conquering the impossible and securing it to the wrist.

It was a simple visit to a watchmaker-restorer that ignited an inextinguishable passion for 14-year-old Christophe Claret. Devoting his undivided attention to timekeeping mechanics from there on, the French-born teenager would graduate, five years later, from the Geneva Watchmaking School before learning firsthand the intricacies of complex horology under the wing of watchmaking legend Roger Dubuis.

In 1989, at the age of 27, Christophe Claret would move on from the workshop he established in his Lyon family home, ready to take his talents to the incomparable watchmaking nucleus of La Chaux-de-Fonds, Switzerland. A master of minute repeaters and skeletonized architectures, among other feats, Claret would undertake a path of rare distinction, developing spectacular movements for the industry's most esteemed houses while remaining a relative unknown to haute horology's end consumers. All of this would change in 2009 when Christophe Claret launched his eponymous brand. Celebrating his manufacture's 20th anniversary, Claret's DualTow would propel the unveiled talent to the forefront of the watchmaking world. Now employing nearly a hundred of the finest minds in the field and boasting a number of state-of-the-art technological solutions, the Christophe Claret collection expresses the genius of its founder and namesake, producing highly sophisticated, unconventional timepieces. Freed from the boundaries of commissioned work, Christophe Claret creations continually reinvent the concept of watchmaking complications, upholding a standard of excellence in line with their creator's journey from a bright-eyed teenager to one of the most admired members of the haute horological elite.

▲ **CHRISTOPHE CLARET**

▶ **MARGOT**
Margot's romantic picking of a daisy's petals is driven by a highly sophisticated 95-jewel caliber ingeniously designed to maintain love's endless mystery.

The Margot's patented complication unpredictably picks the petals individually or as a pair to preserve the mystery of the game's resulting outcome.

GPHG
GRAND PRIX D'HORLOGERIE DE GENÈVE
2014
Prix de la Haute Mécanique
pour Dame

Christophe Claret makes its mark yet again on haute horology with an irresistibly feminine timepiece. The Swiss manufacture's Margot captures the delightful mystery of love and presents its wearer with an enchanting game of "He loves me… He loves me not."

With a simple push of the button at 2 o'clock, Margot picks a delicate petal, or two, from the daisy in the center of her dial. Simultaneously, through an opening in the watch's blue or pink mother-of-pearl outer dial, Margot reveals a new fortune. A visible hammer, observed at 8 o'clock on the timepiece's caseband and adorned with a prong-set ruby, strikes the mechanism's cathedral gong with each press of the button. Illuminating Margot's "sentiment display"—"il m'aime… un peu, beaucoup, passionnément,

à la folie or pas du tout" ("he loves me… a little, a lot, passionately, madly or not at all")—a snow or baguette setting of diamonds on the bezel scintillates upon the watch's red- or palladium-white-gold case. Victor Hugo's poem "Unité" adorns the dial's outer ring.

The self-winding EMT17 movement, boasting a staggering 731 components and 95 jewels, demonstrates the inventive genius of Christophe Claret. A press of the button at 4 o'clock returns all 12 satin-lacquered titanium petals to their place around the daisy's pistil and resets the window to an ellipsis. The caseback showcases the movement's intricate flower-shaped winding rotor, whose eight precious stones, take turns lining up with the red heart that surrounds them. Margot's four dazzling versions are each limited to 20 pieces.

223

MAESTOSO — REF. MTR.DTC07.030-050

Movement: manual-winding DTC07 caliber; 31x8.60mm; 80-hour power reserve; 301 components; 44 jewels; 14,400 vph; grade-5 titanium detent escapement; balance with gold screw; cylindrical balance spring; anti-over-banking security device; escapement mounted on shock absorbing bridge; balance stop system activated via crown; four parallel barrels; Charles X-style stepped bridges.
Functions: hours, minutes; constant force at 4.
Case: 5N red gold and anthracite PVD-treated grade-5 titanium; Ø 44mm, thickness: 13.59mm; 5N red-gold and anthracite PVD-treated grade-5 titanium crown; water resistant to 3atm.
Dial: skeletonized; black ceramic and anthracite PVD-treated hands with SuperLumiNova.
Strap: black hand-sewn alligator leather with black stitching.
Note: limited edition of 20 pieces.
Suggested price: $205,000
Also available: 5N red gold with black ceramic and anthracite PVD-treated hands with SuperLumiNova; white-gold and anthracite PVD-treated grade-5 titanium with ruby red and black PVD-treated hands with SuperLumiNova.

KANTHAROS — REF. MTR.MBA13.905

Movement: automatic-winding MBA13 caliber; 37.60x10.56mm; 48-hour power reserve; 558 components; 75 jewels; 21,600 vph; Swiss lever escapement; anthracite rhodium-plated mainplate and bridges; white-gold gears; sapphire bridge with gold chatons.
Functions: hours, minutes; monopusher chronograph; mechanical chime each time the function is changed (start, stop, reset); patented cathedral gong; constant force at 6.
Case: 5N red gold and anthracite PVD-treated grade-5 titanium; Ø 45mm, thickness: 15.80mm; 5N red-gold and anthracite PVD-treated grade-5 titanium crown; water resistant to 3atm.
Dial: 4N red gold; black ceramic and anthracite PVD-treated grade-5 titanium hands with SuperLumiNova.

Strap: black alligator leather with black stitching.
Note: numbered edition.
Suggested price: $134,000
Also available: titanium with rhodium-plated dial; black titanium with anthracite rhodium-plated dial; 5N red gold and anthracite PVD-treated grade-5 titanium with anthracite rhodium-plated dial; white gold and anthracite PVD-treated grade-5 titanium with anthracite rhodium-plated dial.

SOPRANO — REF. MTR.TRD98.020-028

Movement: manual-winding TRD98 caliber; 27.60x8.45mm; 72-hour power reserve; 450 components; 39 jewels; 21,600 vph; Swiss lever escapement; transparent sapphire crystal mainspring barrel; Charles X-style stepped bridges; parachute shock protection.
Functions: hours, minutes; four-note minute repeater playing Westminster chimes activated on left side of caseback; one-minute tourbillon at 6.
Case: white gold and anthracite PVD-treated grade-5 titanium; Ø 45mm, thickness: 15.32mm; white-gold and anthracite PVD-treated grade-5 titanium crown; water resistant to 3atm.
Dial: skeletonized, anthracite PVD and blue spinel hands.
Strap: black hand-sewn alligator leather with blue stitching.
Note: limited edition of eight pieces.
Suggested price: $547,000
Also available: white gold and anthracite PVD-treated grade-5 titanium with red ruby and anthracite PVD-treated hands; 5N red gold and anthracite PVD-treated grade-5 titanium with black spinel and anthracite PVD-treated hands.

ADAGIO — REF. MTR.SLB88.101-801

Movement: manual-winding SLB88 caliber; 34x8.10mm (without hands); 48-hour power reserve; 455 components; 46 jewels; 18,000 vph; Swiss lever escapement; anthracite rhodium-plated mainplate and bridges; rhodium gears; sapphire bridge with gold chatons.
Functions: hours, minutes, seconds at 9; large date at 6; GMT with day/night indicator at 2; minute repeater with cathedral gongs on demand.
Case: white gold; Ø 44mm, thickness: 13.91mm; white-gold crown; repeater mechanism activated by slide on left side; water resistant to 3atm.
Dial: lapis lazuli.
Strap: blue hand-sewn alligator leather with blue stitching.
Note: limited series of eight pieces.
Suggested price: $309,000.
Also available: platinum, grade-5 titanium, 5N red gold or black PVD-treated grade-5 titanium; different colored dials.

AVENTICUM   REF. MTR.AVE15.901

Movement: automatic-winding AVE15 caliber; 26.20x3.37mm (without hands); 72-hour power reserve; 186 components; 28 jewels; 28,800 vph; dual barrels; Swiss lever escapement; winding rotor incorporating high-definition metalized glass.
Functions: hours, minutes; mirascope with micro-engraved bust of Marcus Aurelius.
Case: 5N red gold and anthracite PVD-treated grade-5 titanium; Ø44mm, thickness: 18.49mm; 5N red-gold and anthracite PVD-treated grade-5 titanium crown with cabochon in black PVD-treated grade-5 titanium; water resistant to 3atm.
Dial: carbon fiber hands.
Strap: black hand-sewn alligator leather with black stitching.
Note: limited edition of 68 pieces.
Suggested price: available upon request.
Also available: white gold and anthracite PVD-treated grade-5 titanium.

POKER   REF. MTR.PCK05.001-020

Movement: automatic-winding PCK05 caliber; 38.60x9.92mm; 72-hour power reserve; 655 components; 72 jewels; 28,800 vph; dual barrels.
Functions: hours, minutes; two games: Poker Texas Hold'em with striking mechanism and roulette.
Case: white gold and black PVD-treated grade-5 titanium; Ø 45mm, thickness: 15.95mm; white-gold and black PVD-treated grade-5 titanium crown; water resistant to 3atm.
Dial: black PVD-treated skeletonized cards motif; white-gold blinds, ruby red and black PVD-treated hands with SuperLumiNova; front: five windows for community board which are activated on demand by utilizing pushbuttons at 8 and 10 with gongs; three sets of two windows which are adorned with blinds in order to conceal game; 3D roulette rotating in conjunction with movement.
Strap: black hand-sewn alligator leather with red stitching.
Note: limited edition of 20 pieces.
Suggested price: $198,000
Also available: black PVD-treated grade-5 titanium with ruby red or blue spinel and black PVD-treated hands with SuperLumiNova; 5N red-gold and black PVD-treated grade-5 titanium with orange ruby and black PVD-treated hands with SuperLumiNova.

X-TREM-1   REF. MTR.FLY11.090-098

Movement: manual-winding FLY11 caliber; 26.60x46.40mm, thickness: 11.94mm; 50-hour power reserve; 419 components; 64 jewels; 21,600 vph; dual barrels: one for movement gear train, one for time indications; Swiss lever escapement; flying tourbillon.
Functions: hours, minutes; small seconds on tourbillon carriage.
Case: 5N red gold/brown PVD-treated grade-5 titanium; 40.80x56.80mm, thickness: 15mm; fast time adjustment via integrated pushbutton on caseband at 12; water resistant to 3atm.
Dial: two Ø 4mm hollowed 4N pink-gold stainless steel spheres that move past sapphire scales marked with 5N red-gold metallized numerals and graduations beneath sapphire crystal; hours and minutes indication by spheres inside sapphire tubes diven by magnetic field.
Strap: brown hand-sewn alligator leather with rose stitching.
Note: limited edition of eight pieces.
Suggested price: $308,000
Also available: platinum or 5N red gold or white gold and PVD-treated grade-5 titanium case; white-gold case; red-gold case.

MARGOT   REF. MTR.EMT17.000.020

Movement: automatic-winding EMT17 caliber; 38.40x9.76mm; 72-hour power reserve; 731 components; 95 jewels; 28,800 vph; dual barrels; Swiss lever escapement.
Functions: hours, minutes; "he loves me…he loves me not;" 12 petals to pick off; sentiment displayed in window at 4; pushbutton at 2 picks off one or two petals while advancing the sentiment indicator by one sentiment; striking chime at pushbutton at 2; symbolic color-feeling on winding rotor.
Case: white gold with palladium alloy; Ø 42.5mm, thickness: 14.52mm; set with 68 diamonds (5.2 carats); white-gold crown; water resistant to 3atm.
Dial: blue mother-of-pearl; white-gold prong-set with pear-shaped diamonds; blued steel hands with 3N yellow-gold tips.
Strap: white alligator leather; white-gold clasp prong-set with pear-shaped diamond.
Note: limited edition of 20 pieces.
Suggested price: $320,000
Also available: white gold with palladium alloy and snow-set diamonds; 5N red gold with baguette or snow-set diamonds.

CORUM
LA CHAUX-DE-FONDS · SUISSE

FANTASTIC VOYAGE

As it prepares to celebrate its 60th anniversary, Swiss watchmaker Corum unveils **THE EVOLUTION OF THREE COLLECTIONS THAT EPITOMIZE THE BOLD CREATIVE SPIRIT OF THE BRAND**.

The La-Chaux-de-Fonds horologer has, since 1955, combined a profound respect for the traditions of watchmaking with a drive to innovate and imbue the art form with a sense of modernity. It is thus no surprise that Corum's iconic collections of timepieces have experienced remarkable longevity over the last six decades. Guided by the mantra that "to create is to live," the brand honors its founders and rich history by upholding standards of excellence and savoir-faire throughout the process of creating its movements.

The Admiral's Cup collection has been paying tribute to the legendary sailing race of the same name since 1960. Since its inception, the line of timepieces has become a global leader in the field of nautical timekeeping, accompanying renowned yachtsmen in racing challenges across the world. The sport-chic collection brilliantly marries the elegant authenticity of the sailing lifestyle with the rugged requirements of its competitive elements. The self-winding AC-One 45 Tides "provides its wearer with an in-depth illustration of some of sailing's most crucial information. Joining the hours, minutes, sweeping seconds and date, the CO 277 caliber animates, at 12 o'clock, indications of the moonphase as well as the strength of the tide. A subdial displaying the time of the next two tides operates in conjunction with a counter at 9 o'clock to determine the height of the tide as well as the strength of the current. Housed in a 45mm titanium case, the AC-One 45 Tides delivers the mysteries of the lunar cycle to the wrist of the courageous explorer of the open waters.

◄ AC-ONE 45 TIDES
This sophisticated nautical instrument elegantly provides an incredible depth of information on the ocean's tides and current.

The timeless nature of Corum's immense creativity lies in finding contemporary genius in the past and guiding today's enthusiasts on a voyage through bygone eras.

An icon of haute horology since 1980, Corum's Golden Bridge collection fascinates connoisseurs with its groundbreaking architecture and revealing transparency. Its legendary "baguette" movement construction exposes the internal organ's dynamic continuity while rejecting the conventional circular form. Mounted on a vertical axis in the center of the watch, the collection's signature Golden Bridge presents the time within a superb multi-dimensional display that highlights the movement's exquisite finishes. The Golden Bridge Automatic, housed in a tonneau-shaped case in 18-karat red gold, presents its golden linear mechanism in a two-part sapphire dial contrasted by a metallic striped motif on the rear sapphire crystal. The self-winding timepiece is finished with a platinum oscillating weight, which may be admired through a transparent caseback.

The Heritage collection honors the grand history of the watchmaking arts, bringing new life to some of the brand's most esteemed creations. Such rebirths of celebrated vintage timepieces exemplify the timeless nature of Corum's immense creativity; the brand finds contemporary genius in its own past and guides today's enthusiasts on a voyage to bygone eras and age-old refinements. The Feather Watch travels back in time to the 19th century, when plumasserie, or feather art, gained popularity for its visual poetry and magnificent hand-crafted finesse. The self-winding wristwatch's elegant two-hand display makes way for a backdrop boasting a regal peacock feather. The ornamental masterpiece, available with or without a dial-side setting of 120 diamonds, is presented in a 39mm 18-karat red-gold case and driven by the CO 082 caliber with an oscillating frequency of 28,800 vph.

▲ **GOLDEN BRIDGE AUTOMATIC**
Corum's legendary linear movement configuration is on full display thanks to a stunning visual transparency and multi-dimensional dial construction.

▶ **FEATHER WATCH**
A peacock feather adorns the luxurious dial of this self-winding timepiece, honoring the delicate refinement of an ancient ornamental technique.

ADMIRAL'S CUP AC-ONE 45 SQUELETTE REF. A082/02336

Movement: automatic-winding CO082 caliber; 13¼ lines; 42-hour power reserve; 27 jewels; 28,800 vph; rotor with Corum-dedicated decoration; gray colored rotor.
Functions: hours, minutes, seconds; date at 6.
Case: grade-5 titanium; Ø 45mm, thickness: 13.3mm; grade-5 titanium crown with engraved Corum key; grade-5 titanium crown protector with black PVD treatment; grade-5 titanium screw-down caseback cover; anti-reflective sapphire crystal; water resistant to 30atm.
Dial: no dial; rhodium-coated, faceted, skeletonized dauphine-variant hour and minute hands with white SuperLumiNova; rhodium-coated, bateau-shaped seconds hand with Corum key.

Strap: black crocodile leather; grade-5 titanium triple-folding clasp with engraved Corum key; opening and fastening system uses two pushbuttons.
Suggested price: $10,200

ADMIRAL'S CUP AC-ONE 45 REGATTA REF. A040/01991

Movement: automatic-winding CO040 caliber; 13¼ lines; 48-hour power reserve; 25 jewels; 28,800 vph; rotor with Corum-dedicated decoration.
Functions: hours, minutes; chronograph: 12-hour counter at 6, 30-minute counter at 12, central chronograph seconds hand; regatta countdown of 10 minutes.
Case: grade-5 titanium; Ø 45mm, thickness: 15.20mm; grade-5 titanium bezel and sides with black PVD treatment; grade-5 titanium crown with engraved Corum key; grade-5 titanium caseback; antireflective sapphire crystal; water resistant to 30atm.
Dial: black brass; nautical pennants transferred on flange; rhodium-coated hour markers with beige SuperLumiNova; applied rhodium-coated Corum logo; rhodium-coated, faceted, skeletonized dauphine-variant hour and minute hands with beige SuperLumiNova; red colored, baton-shaped chronograph hand with Corum key; red colored, dauphine-variant counter hands.

Bracelet: grade-5 titanium; grade-5 titanium triple-folding clasp with engraved Corum key; opening and fastening system uses two pushbuttons.
Suggested price: $12,100

ADMIRAL'S CUP AC-ONE 45 DOUBLE TOURBILLON REF. A108/02339

Movement: manual-winding CO108 caliber; 14 ¼ lines; 72-hour power reserve; 45 jewels; 21,600 vph.
Functions: hours, minutes; retrograde date; double tourbillon at 5 and 7 with small seconds; actual hour corrector.
Case: 5N 18K red gold; Ø 45mm, thickness: 14.4mm; 5N 18K red-gold crown with engraved Corum key on pushbutton; 5N 18K red-gold screw-down caseback cover; antireflective sapphire crystal; water resistant to 30atm.
Dial: black brass; nautical pennants transferred on flange, applied red-gold-coated hour markers, applied red-gold-coated Corum logo; red-gold-coated, faceted, skeleton dauphine-variant hour and minute hands with white SuperLumiNova; red colored, baton-shaped date hand with arrow head tip.

Strap: black crocodile leather; 5N 18K red-gold and stainless steel triple-folding clasp with engraved Corum key; opening and fastening system uses two pushbuttons.
Note: additional brown crocodile leather strap provided.
Suggested price: $96,500

ADMIRAL'S CUP AC-ONE 45 TIDES REF. A277/02401

Movement: automatic-winding CO277 caliber; 11½ lines, 42-hour power reserve; 21 jewels; 28,800 vph; rotor with Corum-dedicated decoration, skeletonized and circular shaped.
Functions: hours, minutes, seconds; date; moonphase and tides coefficient with timing of the next two high and low tides; current strength and tidal process indication.
Case: grade-5 titanium; Ø 45mm, thickness: 14.3mm; grade-5 titanium crown with engraved Corum key; blue composite resin crown protector; grade-5 titanium caseback cover; water resistant to 30atm.

Dial: blue brass; nautical pennants transferred on flange; applied rhodium-coated hour markers; applied rhodium-coated Corum logo; rhodium-coated, faceted, skeletonized dauphine-variant hour and minute hands with white SuperLumiNova; rhodium-coated, baton-shaped seconds hand with Corum key; rhodium-coated, faceted, dauphine-variant counter hands.
Strap: blue vulcanized rubber; grade-5 titanium triple-folding clasp with engraved Corum key; opening and fastening system uses two pushbuttons.
Suggested price: $9,350

ADMIRAL'S CUP AC-ONE 45 CHRONOGRAPH   REF. A132/01977

Movement: automatic-winding CO132 caliber; 12½ lines; 42-hour power reserve; 39 jewels; 28,800 vph; rotor with Corum-dedicated decoration, skeletonized and circular shaped.
Functions: hours, minutes; small seconds at 3; date at 4:30; chronograph: 12-hour counter at 6, 30-minute counter at 9, central chronograph seconds hand.
Case: grade-5 titanium with black PVD treatment; Ø 45mm, thickness 14.3mm; 5N 18K red-gold bezel, sides and pushbuttons; 5N 18K red-gold crown with engraved Corum key; grade-5 titanium crown cover with black PVD treatment; grade-5 titanium open caseback cover with black PVD treatment; antireflective sapphire crystal; water resistant to 30atm.

Dial: black brass; nautical pennants transferred on flange; applied red-gold-coated hour markers with white SuperLumiNova; applied red-gold-coated Corum logo; red-gold-coated, faceted, skeleton dauphine-variant hour and minute hands with white SuperLumiNova; red-gold-coated, baton-shaped chronograph hand with Corum key; red-gold-coated, dauphine-variant counter hands.

Strap: black crocodile leather; grade-5 titanium triple-folding clasp with black PVD treatment and engraved Corum key; opening and fastening system uses two pushbuttons.
Suggested price: $19,200

ADMIRAL'S CUP LEGEND 38 CHRONOGRAPH   REF. A132/01661

Movement: automatic-winding CO132 caliber; 12½ lines; 42-hour power reserve; 39 jewels; 28,800 vph; rotor with Corum-dedicated decoration.
Functions: hours, minutes; small seconds at 3; date at 4:30; chronograph: 12-hour counter at 6, 30-minute counter at 9, central chronograph seconds hand.
Case: stainless steel; Ø 38mm, thickness: 10.85mm, 5N 18K red-gold bezel set with 72 diamonds (0.59 carat); 5N 18K red-gold pushbuttons and crown engraved with Corum key; stainless steel open caseback cover; antireflective sapphire crystal; water resistant to 3atm.

Dial: white mother-of-pearl; nautical pennants transferred on flange; applied red-gold coated hour markers set with 11 diamonds (0.16 carat); applied red-gold-coated Corum logo; red-gold-coated, faceted, skeletonized dauphine-variant hour and minute hands with white SuperLumi-Nova, red-gold-coated, baton-shaped chronograph hand with Corum key; red-gold-coated, dauphine-variant counter hands.

Strap: white satin; stainless steel folding clasp with engraved Corum key; opening and fastening system uses two pushbuttons.
Suggested price: $14,500

ADMIRAL'S CUP LEGEND 42 CHRONOGRAPH   REF. A984/01245

Movement: automatic-winding CO984 caliber; 12 ½ lines; 42-hour power reserve; 37 jewels; 28,800 vph; rotor with Corum-dedicated decoration.
Functions: hours, minutes; small seconds; date; chronograph.
Case: stainless steel; Ø 42mm, thickness: 11.60mm; bezel and crown in stainless steel with engraved Corum key; screw-down open caseback cover in stainless steel; water resistant to 3atm.
Dial: black brass; applied rhodium-coated hour markers; nautical pennants transferred on the flange; rhodium-coated Corum logo applied on the dial; rhodium-coated, faceted, skeleton dauphine-variant hour and minute hands with white SuperLumiNo-va; rhodium-coated, baton-shaped chronograph hand with Corum key; rhodium-coated, dauphine-variant counter hands.

Bracelet: stainless steel; stainless steel triple-folding clasp with engraved Corum key; opening and fastening system uses two pushbuttons.
Suggested price: $5,125

ADMIRAL'S CUP LEGEND 38 MYSTERY MOON   REF. A384/01252

Movement: automatic-winding CO384 caliber; 13 lines; 42-hour power reserve; 30 jewels; 28,800 vph; rotor with Corum-dedicated decoration.
Functions: hours, minutes; date; moonphase; rotating dial.
Case: stainless steel; Ø 38mm, thickness: 12.2mm; stainless steel bezel set with 72 diamonds (0.58 carat); stainless steel crown with engraved Corum key; stainless steel screw-down open caseback; antireflective sapphire crystal; water resistant to 3atm.
Dial: black mother-of-pearl; Corum logo transferred under sapphire crystal; nautical pennants transferred on flange; rotating date and moonphase indicators complete one revolution in 31 days; moonphase indicator: inner disc changes every 23.5 hours, moonphase disc set with 6 diamonds (0.02 carat); rhodium-coated, faceted, skeleton dauphine-variant hour and minute hands with white SuperLumi-Nova.

Strap: gray satin; stainless steel folding clasp with engraved Corum key.
Suggested price: $15,000

GOLDEN BRIDGE
REF.B113/01043

Movement: manual-winding CO113 caliber; 14¾ x 5 lines; 40-hour power reserve; 19 jewels; 28,800 vph; 18K red-gold plate and bridges; bridge engraved with Corum logo.
Functions: hours, minutes.
Case: 5N 18K red gold; 34x51mm, thickness: 10.90mm; crown in 5N 18K red gold with engraved Corum key; open caseback cover in 5N 18K red gold with glareproof sapphire crystal; water resistant to 3atm.
Dial: no dial; red-gold-coated, skeleton, baton-shaped hour and minute hands.
Strap: crocodile leather; 5N 18K red-gold tongue buckle with engraved Corum key.
Suggested price: $31,300

MISS GOLDEN BRIDGE
REF. B113/00977

Movement: manual-winding CO113 caliber; 14¾ x 5 lines; 40-hour power reserve; 19 jewels; 28,800 vph; 18K red-gold plate and bridges; bridge engraved with Corum logo.
Functions: hours, minutes.
Case: 5N 18K red gold; 21x43mm, thickness: 11.24mm; set with 90 round diamonds (0.68 carat); screw-down 5N 18K red-gold crown with engraved Corum key; 5N 18K red-gold caseback cover; antireflective sapphire crystal; water resistant to 3atm.
Dial: no dial; black skeleton leaf-shaped hour and minute hands.
Bracelet: 5N 18K red gold; 5N 18K red-gold triple-folding clasp with engraved Corum key.
Suggested price: $41,200

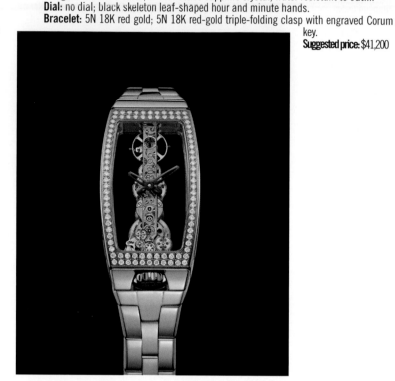

GOLDEN BRIDGE DRAGON
REF. B113/02349

Movement: manual-winding CO113 caliber; 14¾ x 5 lines, 40-hour power reserve; 19 jewels; 28,800 vph; 18K red-gold plate and bridges; bridge engraved with Corum logo.
Functions: hours, minutes.
Case: 5N 18K red gold, 34x51mm, thickness: 10.90mm; 5N 18K red-gold crown with engraved Corum key; 5N 18K red-gold screw-down caseback cover; antireflective sapphire crystal; water resistant to 3atm.
Dial: no dial; 5N 18K gold hand-engraved dragon with pearl set at tail; red-gold-coated, skeletonized baton-shaped hour and minute hands.

Strap: black crocodile leather; 5N 18K red-gold tongue buckle with engraved Corum key.
Suggested price: $81,000

GOLDEN BRIDGE AUTOMATIC
REF. B313/01612

Movement: automatic-winding CO313 caliber; 14¾ x 5 lines; 40-hour power reserve; 26 jewels; 28,800 vph; 18K red-gold plate and bridges; bridge engraved with Corum logo; platinum oscillating weight.
Functions: hours, minutes.
Case: 5N 18K red gold; 37.2x51.8mm, thickness 13.70mm; 5N 18K red-gold crown with engraved Corum key; 5N 18K red-gold caseback with antireflective sapphire crystal with metallized linear red-gold stripes; water resistant to 3atm.
Dial: sapphire crystal; minute circle transferred on flange; applied red-gold coated hour markers; red-gold-coated, skeletonized baton-shaped hour and minute hands.
Strap: crocodile leather; 5N 18K red-gold tongue buckle with engraved Corum key.
Suggested price: $44,800

HERITAGE FEATHER WATCH
REF. C082/02325

Movement: automatic-winding CO082 caliber; 11½ lines; 42-hour power reserve; 21 jewels; 28,800 vph; rotor with Corum-dedicated decoration.
Functions: hours, minutes.
Case: 5N 18K red gold; Ø 39mm, thickness: 10.30mm; 5N 18K red-gold crown with engraved Corum key; 5N 18K red-gold caseback cover; antireflective sapphire crystal; water resistant to 5atm.
Dial: peacock feather on brass, set with 120 diamonds (0.71 carat); applied 5N 18K red-gold Corum logo; red-gold-coated skeletonized dauphine hour and minute hands.
Strap: black crocodile leather; 5N 18K red-gold tongue buckle with engraved Corum key.
Note: limited edition of 100 pieces.
Suggested price: $37,000

HERITAGE COIN WATCH 50TH ANNIVERSARY
REF. C082/02495

Movement: automatic-winding CO082 caliber; 11½ lines; 42-hour power reserve; 21 jewels; 28,800 vph.
Functions: hours, minutes.
Case: 925 silver; Ø 43mm, thickness: 7.60mm; screw-down caseback cover: 925 silver 1US$ coin (minted in 2014); water resistant to 1atm.
Dial: 925 silver 1US$ coin (minted in 2014); black-colored baton-shaped hour and minute hands.
Strap: black crocodile leather; 925 silver tongue buckle with engraved Corum key.
Suggested price: $12,100

HERITAGE INGOT
REF. V082/02348

Movement: automatic-winding CO082 caliber; 11½ lines; 42-hour power reserve; 21 jewels; 28,800 vph; rotor with Corum-dedicated decoration.
Functions: hours, minutes.
Case: 3N 18K yellow gold; 30x40mm, thickness: 9.00mm; 3N 18K yellow-gold crown with engraved Corum key; 3N 18K yellow-gold caseback cover; water resistant to 3atm.
Dial: 24K gold ingot (15g) with engraved Corum logo; black colored baton-shaped hour and minute hands.
Strap: black crocodile leather, 3N 18K yellow-gold tongue buckle with engraved Corum key.
Suggested price: $26,300

HERITAGE COIN WATCH
REF. C293/00831

Movement: automatic-winding CO293 caliber; 11½ lines; 72-hour power reserve; 30 jewels; 28,800 vph; rotor with Corum-dedicated decoration.
Functions: hours, minutes.
Case: 3N 18K yellow gold; Ø 36mm, thickness: 6.40m; 3N 18K yellow-gold crown set with one diamond (0.17 carat); screw-down caseback cover: 22K yellow-gold "Double Eagle" coin; water resistant to 3atm.
Dial: 22K yellow gold "Double Eagle" coin, Corum logo transferred on coin; black colored baton-shaped hour and minute hands.
Strap: black crocodile leather, 3N 18K yellow-gold tongue buckle with engraved Corum key.
Suggested price: $20,800

DE BETHUNE

L'ART HORLOGER AU XXIᵉ SIÈCLE

MAXIMUM AXIS

De Bethune uses its **IMAGINATIVE, UNCONVENTIONAL GENIUS** as the foundation of three ground-breaking timepieces, pioneering a unique and intuitive demonstration of elapsed time.

The Swiss manufacture's DB28 Maxichrono represents an exciting evolution of the chronograph, from the original construction of its patented clutch system to the inventive modernity with which elapsed time is displayed. The hand-wound 45mm timepiece, unveiled in a rose-gold case with blackened zirconium floating lugs or in a monochromatic grade-5 titanium interpretation, juxtaposes timeless marine design accents with an imaginative caliber and reinvention of the chronograph readoff. Activated by a single retro crown at 12 o'clock, the timepiece's three-hand chronograph eschews traditional subdial-style architecture, opting instead for a multi-level dial expanding from the center. In the center of the silver-toned dial, a numbered ring is animated by a bright blued-steel hand that indicates the chronograph's unusual 24-hour capability. The elapsed minutes and seconds are intuitively read against a shared graduated scale on the periphery of the face, and are easily distinguished by the hands' contrasting hues—flame-blued steel for the seconds and rose gold for the minutes. This visual coexistence brilliantly echoes the DB28 Maxichrono's more conventional display of run-

ning time, as two skeletonized hands indicate the minutes against the chronograph's outer ring and the hours against a sequence of 12 Arabic numerals in a large modern typeface.

De Bethune extends this innovative vision to the watch's interior. The 384-component DB2030 caliber, whose rose-gold and hand-polished steel bridges may be admired through a sapphire caseback, boasts an astounding degree of sophistication, including the manufacture's patented "absolute clutch" system and chronograph's co-axial stacked wheels. Complementing the 36,000vph movement's self-regulating twin barrel, De Bethune's "absolute clutch" allows the three chronograph functions to act as semi-autonomous entities, governed by three column wheels. The system thus capitalizes on the benefits of both horizontal and vertical clutch modules to reduce friction and maximize the overall precision of the watch, regardless of the chronograph's activation.

The DB28 Maxichrono is worn on an extra-supple alligator leather strap that celebrates the watch's technical breakthroughs with a finishing touch of unquestionable elegance.

The fruit of seven years of research, the DB29 Maxichrono Tourbillon's 49-jewel DB2039 caliber complements De Bethune's mechanical innovations with a 63-part tourbillon in silicon and titanium.

The DB29 Maxichrono Tourbillon builds upon the triumphant exploits of the aforementioned DB28 Maxichrono with its incorporation of one of haute horology's most revered complications. The fruit of seven years of research, the timepiece's 49-jewel DB2039 caliber complements De Bethune's mechanical innovations—"absolute clutch" system, self-regulating twin barrel, silicon/white-gold balance wheel and silicon escape wheel—with a 63-part 30" tourbillon in silicon and titanium weighing only 0.18g. The 36,000vph tourbillon is showcased not on the silver-toned dial, but via a delightful quirk in the construction of the 46mm rose-gold case. A press of the discreet button at 4 o'clock, located just beneath the chronograph's all-inclusive crown, opens the caseback's cover to reveal the complication's superb construction, in addition to the three-column-wheel movement's bridges and creative architecture.

On the dial side, the hand-wound DB29 Maxichrono Tourbillon reflects the ingenious five-central-hand design of the DB28 Maxichrono, portraying the chronograph's minutes and seconds against a single peripheral numbered ring, the 24-hour counter against the face's innermost circle and the running hours and minutes with two open-tipped blued-steel hands.

GPHG
GRAND PRIX D'HORLOGERIE DE GENÈVE
———— 2014 ————
Chronograph Watch Prize

▲ DB29 MAXICHRONO TOURBILLON

Armed with an invisible hinge, the timepiece's caseback opens at the push of a button to reveal its movement's 36,000vph tourbillon and chronograph's innovative construction.

◄ DB28 MAXICHRONO

This limited-production wristwatch with a five-day power reserve rethinks the chronograph with an ingenious quintuple central-hand interpretation driven by the manufacture's groundbreaking "absolute clutch" system.

DE BETHUNE

DB29 MAXICHRONO TOURBILLON   REF. DB29RS1

Movement: manual-winding DB2039 caliber; Ø 30mm; 5-day power reserve; 410 components; 49 jewels; 36,000 vph; hand-crafted finishing and decoration; hand-polished steel; three column wheels; De Bethune absolute clutch; self-regulating twin barrel; silicon/white-gold balance wheel and balance spring with flat terminal curve; silicon escape wheel; De Bethune 30" silicon/titanium tourbillon.
Functions: hours, minutes; monopusher chronograph: 24-hour counter, 60-minute counter, 60-second counter; tourbillon.
Case: 5N rose gold; Ø 46mm, thickness: 11.7mm; crown at 3 with mono-pushbutton; push-

button for double back at 4; cone-shaped lugs; anti-reflective sapphire crystal; tourbillon visible through caseback; 5N rose-gold double back with invisible hinge.
Dial: silver toned; multi-level architecture; from center to periphery: central hours counter, hours inner ring, minutes ring and minutes counter, outer ring with chronograph seconds indication; five curved central hands: hand-polished and flame-blued steel for hours, minutes, hours chronograph and seconds chronograph hands, rose-gold minutes chronograph hands.
Strap: extra-supple alligator leather; pin buckle.
Note: limited annual production of 20 pieces.
Price: available upon request.

DB16 TOURBILLON REGULATOR PLATINUM   REF. DB16PS2

Movement: manual-winding DB2509 caliber; Ø 30mm; 4-day power reserve; 499 components; 48 jewels; 36,000 vph; hand-crafted finishing and decoration; Côtes de Bethune; self-regulating twin barrel; silicon and white-gold balance wheel and balance spring with flat terminal curve; silicon escape wheel.
Functions: hours, minutes; central jumping seconds; date by hand at 6; perpetual calendar: month at 3, day at 9, leap year indicator and spherical moonphase at 12, accurate to degree of one lunar day every 122 years; De Bethune tourbillon with 30-second indication; power indication; age of moon indication.

Case: platinum; Ø 43mm, thickness: 13.4mm; crown at 3 set in three positions; cone-shaped lugs; antireflective sapphire crystal; tourbillon, central jumping seconds mechanism, retrograde age of moon indicator and power indication all visible through caseback.
Dial: 5N rose gold; sunburst hand-guilloché motif; De Bethune star-studded sky in flame-blued steel set with gold stars, featuring platinum spherical moonphase indication and flame-blued steel leap year indication; hand-polished and flame-blued steel hands.
Strap: extra-supple alligator leather; pin buckle.
Note: limited annual production of five pieces.
Price: available upon request.

DB25 L PINK GOLD   REF. DB25LRS1V1

Movement: manual-winding DB 2105 V1 caliber; Ø 30mm; 6-day power reserve; 307 components; 29 jewels; 28,800 vph; hand-crafted finishing and decoration; Côtes De Bethune; chamfered and polished steel; self-regulating twin barrel; titanium and platinum balance-spring with flat terminal curve; triple pare-chute shock-absorbing system; silicon escape wheel.
Functions: hours, minutes; spherical moonphase at 12, accurate to degree of one lunar day every 122 years; power reserve indicator on caseback.
Case: pink gold; Ø 44mm; hollowed lugs; open caseback with linear power reserve

indicator.
Dial: silver-toned and hand-guilloché with 12 radiating sectors; flame-blued steel De Bethune star-studded sky inlaid with yellow-gold stars with platinum and flame-blued steel moonphase; curved hand-polished flame-blued steel hands.
Strap: extra-supple alligator leather; pin buckle.
Price: available upon request.
Also available: white gold.

DB25LT   REF. DB25LTP

Movement: manual-winding DB 2519 caliber; Ø 30mm; 5-day power reserve; 281 components; 31 jewels; 36,000 vph; self-regulating twin barrel; silicon and white-gold balance wheel, balance spring with flat terminal curve; silicon escape wheel.
Functions: hours, minutes; spherical moonphase at 12, accurate to degree of one lunar day every 1112 years; De Bethune tourbillon with 30-second indication on caseback at 9.
Case: platinum; Ø 44mm, thickness: 11.6mm; hollowed lugs; antireflective sapphire crystal; open caseback.
Dial: hand-guilloché 5N rose gold; De Bethune star-studded sky in mirror-polished

flame-blued steel inlaid with yellow-gold stars with spherical moonphase indicator in platinum and flame-blued steel at 12; hand-polished flame-blued curved steel hands.
Strap: extra-supple alligator leather; pin buckle.
Price: available upon request.

DB25 L STAR STUDDED SKY   REF. DB25LWS3V2

Movement: manual-winding DB 2105 V2 caliber; Ø 30mm; 6-day power reserve; 288 components; 27 jewels; 28,800 vph; hand-crafted finishing and decoration; chamfered and polished steel; self-regulating twin barrel; silicon and white-gold balance-spring with flat terminal curve; triple pare-chute shock-absorbing system; silicon escape wheel.
Functions: hours, minutes; spherical moonphase at 12, accurate to degree of one lunar day every 122 years; power reserve on caseback.
Case: white gold; Ø 44mm, thickness: 11.3mm; hollowed lugs; open caseback with linear power reserve indicator.
Dial: mirror-polished grade-5 titanium De Bethune star-studded sky inlaid with white-gold stars; platinum and flame-blued steel moonphase, can be personalized; curved hand-polished steel hands.
Strap: extra supple alligator leather; pin buckle.
Price: available upon request.

DB25 QP PINK GOLD   REF. DB25QPRS1

Movement: automatic-winding DB 2324QP caliber; Ø 30mm; 5-day power reserve; 420 components; 46 jewels; 28,800 vph; hand-crafted finishing and decoration; bridges and parts in blued grade-5 titanium; silicon escape wheel; self-regulating twin barrel; titanium and platinum wheel and balance spring with flat terminal curve; triple pare-chute shock-absorbing system; titanium and platinum oscillating weight.
Functions: hours, minutes; perpetual calendar: date at 6, month at 3, day at 9; spherical moonphase indication accurate to degree of one lunar day every 122 years and leap-year cycle at 12.
Case: rose gold; Ø 44mm, thickness: 11.2mm; hollowed lugs; open caseback.
Dial: silver-toned hand-guilloché in 12 radiating sectors with apertures for indications; flame-blued steel De Bethune star-studded sky inlaid with gold stars; platinum and flame-blued steel spherical moonphase indication; curved hand-polished flame-blued steel hands.
Strap: extra-supple alligator leather; pin buckle.
Price: available upon request.
Also available: white gold.

DB25SV RS1   REF. DB25

Movement: automatic-winding DB2024 caliber; Ø 30mm; 6-day power reserve; 287 components; 49 jewels; 28,800 vph; hand-decorated with chamfered and polished steel parts and natural fired-blue titanium bridge; self-regulating twin barrel; titanium/platinum balance wheel and balance spring with flat terminal curve; triple pare-chute shock-absorbing system; silicon escape wheel; titanium/platinum oscillating weight.
Functions: hours, minutes.
Case: rose gold; Ø 40mm, thickness: 8.5mm; crown at 3, setting in two positions; hollowed lugs; antireflective sapphire crystal; open caseback.
Dial: silver-toned; hand-guilloché with 12 radiating sectors; hand-polished flame-blued steel hands.
Strap: extra-supple alligator leather; pin buckle.
Price: available upon request.
Also available: white gold.

DB25QP BLACK GOLD   REF. DB25QPARS8R

Movement: automatic-winding DB2324QP caliber; Ø 30mm; 5-day power reserve; 420 components; 46 jewels; 28,800 vph; hand-crafted finishing and decoration; bridges and parts in blued grade-5 titanium; silicon escape wheel; self-regulating twin barrel; titanium/platinum balance wheel and balance spring with flat terminal curve; triple pare-chute shock absorbing system; titanium/platinum oscillating weight.
Functions: hours, minutes; perpetual calendar: date at 6, month at 3, day at 9; spherical moonphase and leap year indication at 12 (spherical moonphase indication accurate to degree of one lunar day every 122 years).
Case: rose gold; Ø 44mm, thickness: 11.2mm; hollowed lugs; open caseback.
Dial: black; hand-guilloché in 12 radiating sectors with apertures for indications; De Bethune star-studded sky in black mirror-polished steel set with yellow gold stars; spherical moonphase indication in blacked zirconium and palladium; rose-gold curved hands.
Strap: extra-supple alligator leather; pin buckle.
Price: available upon request.

DE BETHUNE

DB28 DIGITALE — REF. DB28D

Movement: manual-winding DB2144 caliber; Ø 30mm; 5-day power reserve; 329 components; 32 jewels; 28,800 vph; hand-crafted finishing and decoration; Côtes de Bethune; mirror-polished blued steel; self-regulating twin barrel; silicon/white-gold balance wheel and balance spring with flat terminal curve; triple pare-chute shock absorbing system; silicon escape wheel.

Functions: hours, minutes; jumping hour at 12; moonphase: spherical indicator at center, accurate to degree of one lunar day every 1,112 years.

Case: grade-5 titanium; Ø 43mm, Ø 45mm with titanium bezel, thickness: 11.6mm;

crown at 12; grade-5 titanium floating lugs; antireflective sapphire crystal; open caseback.

Dial: silver toned; hand-guilloché barleycorn motif; De Bethune star-studded sky in polished blued grade-5 titanium encrusted with white gold stars; analogue minutes indicator on silver-toned rotating disc; jumping hour aperture at 12.

Strap: extra-supple alligator leather; pin buckle.

Price: available upon request.

DB28 — REF. DB28TIS8

Movement: manual-winding DB 2115 caliber; Ø 30mm; 6-day power reserve; 299 components; 38 jewels; 28,800 vph; hand-crafted finishing and decoration; hand-polished and chamfered steel parts; Côtes De Bethune; self-regulating twin barrel; silicon and white-gold balance wheel and balance spring with flat terminal curve; triple pare-chute shock-absorbing system; silicon escape wheel.

Functions: hours, minutes; spherical moonphase indicator at 6, accurate to degree of one lunar day every 122 years; power reserve indicator on caseback; performance indicator between 2 and 3.

Case: grade-5 titanium; Ø 42.6mm, thickness: 9.2mm; distinctively shaped; grade-5 titanium short or long floating lugs; mirror-polished grade-5 titanium solid caseback.

Dial: black mirror-polished grade-5 titanium; silver-toned minute and hour ring; Côtes De Bethune performance-zone read-off between 2 and 3; platinum and blued-steel spherical moonphase; hand-polished steel hands.

Strap: extra supple alligator leather; pin buckle.

Price: available upon request.

DB27 TITAN HAWK ALL BLACK — REF. DB27ZS8

Movement: automatic-winding S233 caliber; Ø 30mm; 6-day power reserve; 271 components; 38 jewels; 28,800 vph; hand-crafted finishing and decoration; chamfered and polished steel parts; self-regulating twin barrel; silicon/white-gold balance wheel and balance spring with flat terminal curve; triple pare-chute shock absorbing system; titanium/platinum oscillating weight; silicon escape wheel.

Functions: hours, minutes; central date.

Case: sandblasted anthracite zirconium; Ø 43mm, thickness: 11mm; screw-down crown at 12 set in three positions; sandblasted anthracite zirconium short floating lugs; antireflective

sapphire crystal; solid sandblasted anthracite zirconium caseback with window revealing balance wheel.

Dial: black-toned microlight; chapter ring with Roman numerals; minutes circle with Arabic numerals placed around the rim; hand-polished steel hands.

Strap: extra-supple alligator leather; pin buckle.

Price: available upon request.

DB28 SKYBRIDGE — REF. DB28CE

Movement: manual-winding DB2105 caliber; Ø 30mm; 6-day power reserve; 240 components; 27 jewels; 28,800 vph; hand-crafted finishing and decoration; entirely mirror-polished blue steel; self-regulating twin barrel; silicon and palladium balance wheel, balance-spring with flat terminal curve; triple pare-chute shock-absorbing system; silicon escape wheel.

Functions: hours, minutes; spherical moonphase at 6, accurate to degree of one lunar day every 122 years.

Case: grade-5 titanium; Ø 43mm (Ø 45mm with titanium bezel); grade-5 titanium

floating lugs; open caseback.

Dial: De Bethune star-studded sky in blued mirror-polished grade-5 titanium encrusted with white gold and diamond stars; platinum and blued steel spherical moonphase; polished steel spherical hour markers; blued and mirror-polished steel hands.

Strap: extra-supple alligator leather; pin buckle.

Price: available upon request.

DB28 MAXICHRONO ROSE   REF. DB28MCRZN

Movement: manual-winding DB2030 caliber; Ø 30mm; 5-day power reserve; 384 components; 47 jewels; 36,000 vph; hand-crafted finishing and decoration; hand-polished steel; three column wheels; De Bethune absolute clutch; self-regulating twin barrel; silicon/white gold balance wheel and balance spring with flat terminal curve; silicon escape wheel.
Functions: hours, minutes; monopusher chronograph: 24-hour counter, 60-minute counter and 60-second counter.
Case: 5N rose gold; Ø 45mm, thickness: 11mm; crown with mono-pushbutton, set in two positions; mirror-polished black zirconium floating lugs; antireflective sapphire crystal; open caseback.
Dial: silver-toned; multi-level architecture; from center to periphery: hours counter, hours inner ring, minutes ring, minutes counter, outer ring with chronograph seconds indication; five curved central hands: hand-polished and blackened steel hours and minutes hands, flame-blued steel hours and seconds chronograph indicators, rose-gold minutes chronograph indicator.
Strap: extra-supple alligator leather; pin buckle.
Note: limited annual production of 20 pieces.
Price: available upon request.

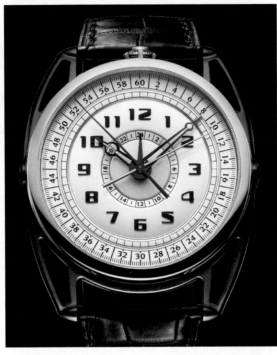

DB28 DARK SHADOWS   REF. DB28ZC8

Movement: manual-winding DB2115 caliber; Ø 30mm; 6-day power reserve; 299 components; 38 jewels; hand-crafted finishing and decoration; black mirror-polished steel parts; Côtes de Bethune; self-regulating twin barrel; silicon/white-gold balance wheel and balance spring with flat terminal curve; triple pare-chute shock absorbing system; silicon escape wheel.
Functions: hours, minutes; spherical moonphase at 6, accurate to degree of one lunar day every 122 years; power reserve indication; performance indication.
Case: sandblasted anthracite zirconium; Ø 42.6mm, thickness: 9.2mm; screw-down crown at 12 set in two positions; sandblasted anthracite zirconium floating lugs; antireflective sapphire crystal; open caseback with power reserve indication and rose-gold rack.
Dial: black; anthracite zirconium mirror-polished hours ring; black mirror-polished steel spherical hour markers; black steel parts; matte black ruthenium; Côtes De Bethune performance zone read-off between 2 and 3; palladium and anthracite moonphase; hand-polished steel hands.
Strap: extra-supple alligator leather; pin buckle.
Note: limited edition of 50 pieces.
Price: available upon request.

DB28 T   REF. DB28TTIS8

Movement: manual-winding DB 2019 caliber; Ø 30mm; 5-day power reserve; 298 components; 35 jewels; 36,000 vph; hand-crafted finishing and decoration; polished steel; self-regulating twin barrel; silicon and white-gold balance wheel and balance spring with flat terminal curve; silicon escape wheel.
Functions: hours, minutes; ultra-light De Bethune 30" silicon and titanium tourbillon at 6.
Case: grade-5 titanium; Ø 42.6mm; crown at 12, set in two positions; grade-5 titanium short or long floating lugs; solid mirror-polished grade-5 titanium caseback with linear power reserve indicator.
Dial: black mirror-polished steel; black minute and hour rings; hand-polished steel hands.
Strap: extra supple alligator leather; pin buckle.
Price: available upon request.

DB28ST BLACK   REF. DB28STTS5PN

Movement: manual-winding DB2119 caliber; Ø 30mm; 4-day power reserve; 333 components; 45 jewels; 36,000 vph; hand-crafted finishing and decoration; Côtes De Bethune; self-regulating twin barrel; silicon/white-gold balance wheel and balance spring with flat terminal curve; silicon escape wheel.
Functions: hours, minutes; central jumping seconds; De Bethune 30" silicon/titanium tourbillon at 6; power reserve indicator at 6.
Case: mirror-polished grade-5 titanium; Ø 45mm, thickness: 11.6mm; platinum bezel; crown at 12 set in two positions; grade-5 titanium floating lugs; antireflective sapphire crystal; solid mirror-polished grade-5 titanium caseback.
Dial: black; black mirror-polished steel parts; matte black ruthenium; Côtes De Bethune; grained and engraved silver chapter ring; Roman numerals and Arabic numerals; hand-polished steel hands.
Strap: extra-supple alligator leather; pin buckle.
Note: limited edition of 20 pieces.
Price: available upon request.

RESTLESS RADIANCE

DARING ALWAYS TO REACH FOR THE HEIGHTS OF HUMAN IMAGINATION, de GRISOGONO asserts its artistic virtuosity with three watch collections bejeweled to perfection in the luxurious tradition of the brand.

Born from the jubilant love of a father for his daughter, the Allegra collection is a resonant ode to joy, vivacity and boundless creativity. Fawaz Gruosi, the brand's founder and leader, has made exuberant passion his signature in horological design. An aesthete who spent his formative years in Florence, Gruosi imbues his creations with the daring imagination that took him from the Italian heart of the Renaissance to the epicenter of Swiss haute horology. Named after his daughter Allegra, the collection of timepieces adorns the perfect proportions of its double-square cases with a dazzling harmony of colors and precious stones. Varying in case materials from PVD steel to pink or white gold, diamond-set or sleek metal, and boasting bezels pulsating with the fiery exhilaration of white diamonds, emeralds, spinels, tsavorites, orange, yellow and pink sapphires, or amethysts, these vibrant wristwatches share a common joie de vivre emblematic of their designer.

The timepieces' spirited femininity shows up in their cases and inhabits their dials in lacquered black or white or pink, orange, red or black mother-of-pearl. The seemingly endless combinations mirror the uniqueness of life's most delightful moments. Reminiscent of the timepieces worn by Hollywood stars of the 1930s, Allegra watches are connected to their wearer by straps composed of 20 intertwining leather cords that speak a language of color, joyful suppleness and the youthful spirit. Each one unique, Allegra timepieces hold a common bond, a de GRISOGONO trademark: a black diamond on the crown, the brand's precious signature passed down from father to daughter.

ALLEGRA

This feminine timepiece completes the perfect symmetry of its gem-set double-square case with a bracelet composed of 20 supple leather cords.

de GRISOGONO

The Grappoli collection presents a set of scintillating wristwatches that harness the artistic power of chance. Set in a random style on cases in white or pink gold as to accentuate the pieces' textural effects, 585 white diamonds or 598 orange or blue sapphires, amethysts or emeralds burst with sparkling color. The Grappoli's dials enjoy a similarly opulent approach, as an additional 256 stones enliven the backdrop with a superb snow setting behind two white- or pink-gold dauphine hands. The effervescence of shimmering light enhances the sensuality of motion. Surrounding the sumptuous display of color, 70 briolette-cut white diamonds, emeralds, amethysts or blue or orange sapphires are attached to the case, moving freely with each motion of the wrist to reflect the light in an infinity of directions. The corolla thus enriches the timepiece with a delicate ballet, granting it an additional dimension of luxury. A galuchat strap, white or colored to match the timepiece, attaches the Grappoli to the wrist with character and tasteful distinction. The dance of each ray of light and the grace of each moving briolette remind us that beauty is in perpetual motion in the de GRISOGONO universe.

GRAPPOLI

Expertly sewn onto a gem-set case, 70 briolette-cut precious stones dance gracefully with the motions of the wrist of this watch's wearer.

de GRISOGONO
GENÈVE

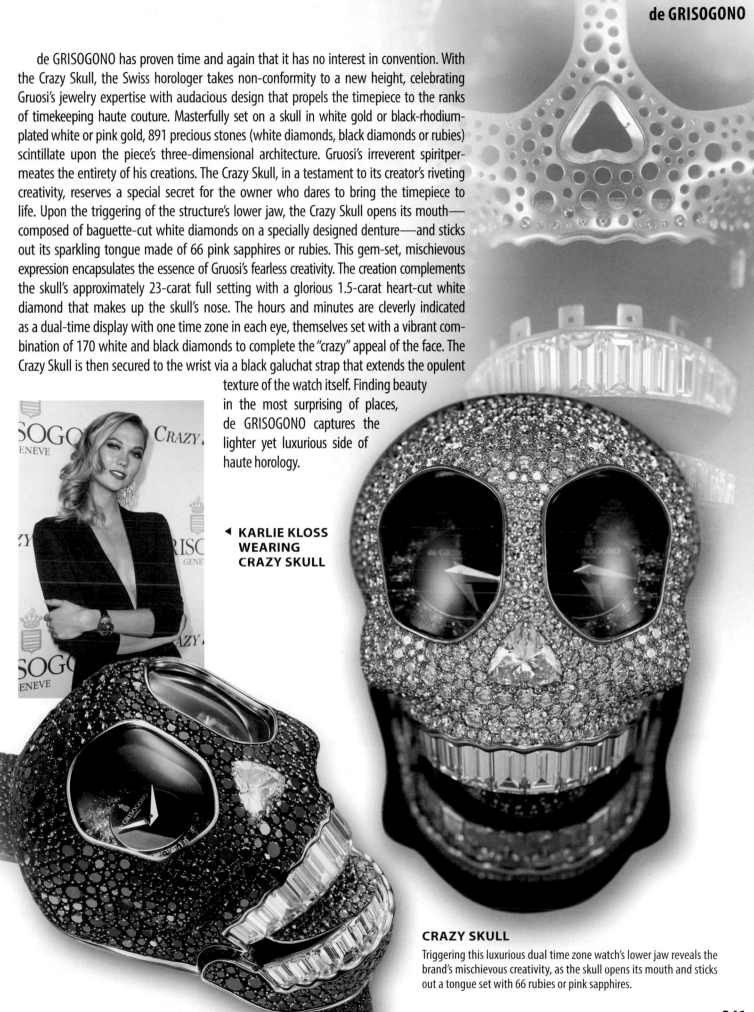

de GRISOGONO has proven time and again that it has no interest in convention. With the Crazy Skull, the Swiss horologer takes non-conformity to a new height, celebrating Gruosi's jewelry expertise with audacious design that propels the timepiece to the ranks of timekeeping haute couture. Masterfully set on a skull in white gold or black-rhodium-plated white or pink gold, 891 precious stones (white diamonds, black diamonds or rubies) scintillate upon the piece's three-dimensional architecture. Gruosi's irreverent spiritpermeates the entirety of his creations. The Crazy Skull, in a testament to its creator's riveting creativity, reserves a special secret for the owner who dares to bring the timepiece to life. Upon the triggering of the structure's lower jaw, the Crazy Skull opens its mouth—composed of baguette-cut white diamonds on a specially designed denture—and sticks out its sparkling tongue made of 66 pink sapphires or rubies. This gem-set, mischievous expression encapsulates the essence of Gruosi's fearless creativity. The creation complements the skull's approximately 23-carat full setting with a glorious 1.5-carat heart-cut white diamond that makes up the skull's nose. The hours and minutes are cleverly indicated as a dual-time display with one time zone in each eye, themselves set with a vibrant combination of 170 white and black diamonds to complete the "crazy" appeal of the face. The Crazy Skull is then secured to the wrist via a black galuchat strap that extends the opulent texture of the watch itself. Finding beauty in the most surprising of places, de GRISOGONO captures the lighter yet luxurious side of haute horology.

◄ **KARLIE KLOSS WEARING CRAZY SKULL**

CRAZY SKULL
Triggering this luxurious dual time zone watch's lower jaw reveals the brand's mischievous creativity, as the skull opens its mouth and sticks out a tongue set with 66 rubies or pink sapphires.

Dior
DIOR VIII MONTAIGNE

"Almost anything goes with gray, so it is a good color for accessories."

– Christian Dior

▲ **DIOR VIII MONTAIGNE**

Steel and sun-brushed colored dial, 32mm automatic - stainless steel, blue sun-brushed diamond-set dial (left); steel and pink gold 32mm quartz - stainless steel, pink gold, mother-of-pearl and diamonds (center); and steel and sun-brushed colored dial, 32mm automatic - stainless steel, pink sun-brushed diamond-set dial (right).

8: A MAGICAL NUMBER FOR CHRISTIAN DIOR, evoking in turn the 8th of October 1946, day of the opening of his Couture House; his address Avenue Montaigne, in the VIIIth arrondissement of Paris and "En Huit" (In Eight), the name of his first collection. So it was natural that the first ceramic timepiece imagined by Dior received, in addition to the name of the creator, those 4 simple and obvious characters: VIII.

And transposing all of the Dior codes onto the wrist was obvious too: the architectural line, the allusion to the "Bar" suit, the many precious and lightweight versions, celebrating at every moment of the day or night and the same approach to feminine elegance, fashioned with exquisiteness and refinement.

With Dior VIII Montaigne, Dior not only pays tribute to the House's historical address and to Parisian luxury but also pushes inspiration even further while faithfully returning to the basic color in the Christian Dior palette with its choice of steel. The emblematic colour of the French 18th century, gray was so highly prized by the couturier ("It is the most elegant neutral color," he wrote in his *Little Dictionary of Fashion* in 1954) that, in his hands, it was to become the legendary "Dior gray," draped on women's bodies and upholstered on the walls of his boutique.

For the Dior VIII Montaigne, steel gray is combined with pink, "the sweetest of all the colors," according to Christian Dior, recalling the color of his childhood home at Granville in Normandy and also the color of the flowers he loved so much. The pink of the gold placed on the second hand, the hour markers, the bezel, the bracelet or the caseback; the pink of the translucent lacquer delicately tinting the dial or the bolder pink on the galvanized steel dial of the Grand Bal "Plissé Soleil" model. Pale blue, "one of the prettiest colors" according to the couturier, is also present on this unprecedented model.

◄ **DIOR VIII MONTAIGNE**
Pink gold, 25mm quartz (left): Pink gold, mother-of-pearl and diamonds; pink gold, 25mm quartz (right): Pink gold, mother-of-pearl diamonds and black alligator.

The Dior VIII Montaigne is inhabited by this fashion culture from the caseback, groomed like the lining of a dress, to the refined details on the dial. Already a classic and eminently chic, the Dior VIII Montaigne possesses the soul of a genuine Parisienne, toying with colors, juggling with the codes and having fun with the diameters. Elegant and feminine, the Dior VIII Montaigne also knows how to vary its wardrobe, alternating the glow of the metal bracelets with the velvety light of the alligator strap. Timepiece by day, jewel by night, the Dior VIII Montaigne enchants every moment.

▲ DIOR VIII GRAND BAL "PLISSÉ SOLEIL"

Steel, mother-of-pearl and diamonds. 36mm automatic - Stainless steel, diamonds, mother-of-pearl and dark blue alligator / limited edition of 188 pieces.

◄ DIOR VIII GRAND BAL "PLISSÉ SOLEIL"

Pink gold and diamonds. 36mm automatic - Pink gold, diamonds and mother-of-pearl / Limited edition of 88 pieces.

More than ever, Dior VIII Montaigne unfurls the attractive features of femininity, but this time subtly revisited. The slenderized horns, the slimmed down case and bracelet and the pyramids with softened angles discreetly renew this timekeeper's couture spirit. Whether a "jewel" timepiece with a new 25mm diameter on a steel or pink gold bracelet or alligator strap; or a day timepiece in its 32mm or 36mm all steel version, embellished or not with a single hem of diamonds on the white mother-of-pearl dial, as well as in a two-tone version (steel bracelet and pink-gold bezel or mixed bracelet), Dior VIII Montaigne also knows how to play the perfect partner all night long, adorned, in its Grand Bal version, with a functional oscillating weight placed on top of the dial, in gold, mother-of-pearl and diamonds, recalling the hypnotic and swirling sun pleat pattern from the couture universe.

▲ **DIOR VIII GRAND BAL "PLISSÉ SOLEIL"**
Steel, mother-of-pearl and diamonds. 36mm automatic - Stainless steel, diamonds and mother-of-pearl / Limited edition of 188 pieces.

▲ **DIOR VIII GRAND BAL "PLISSÉ SOLEIL"**
Steel and mother-of-pearl. 36mm automatic - Stainless steel, diamonds and mother-of-pearl / Limited edition of 888 pieces.

DIOR HORLOGERIE

DIOR VIII – 33MM   REF. CD1231E4C001

Movement: quartz.
Functions: hours, minutes, seconds.
Case: white high-tech ceramic and stainless steel; Ø 33mm; bezel set with 70 diamonds (0.56 carat) and white mother-of-pearl ring; crown set with white ceramic insert; water resistant to 5atm.
Dial: white mother-of-pearl; set with 32 diamonds (0.1 carat).
Bracelet: white high-tech ceramic; stainless steel unfolding clasp.

DIOR VIII PINK METALLIC STRAP – 38MM   REF. CD1245EGA001

Movement: automatic-winding; 38-hour power reserve; sea-green lacquered oscillating weight.
Functions: hours, minutes, seconds.
Case: black high-tech ceramic and stainless steel; Ø 38mm; bezel set with black ceramic inserts; crown set with black ceramic insert; transparent sapphire crystal caseback; water resistant to 5atm.
Dial: black lacquer; set with 34 sapphires (0.18 carat).
Strap: pink metallic "mirror" calfskin; stainless steel ardillon buckle.

Note: limited edition of 188 pieces.
Also available: black high-tech ceramic bracelet with stainless steel unfolding clasp.

DIOR VIII MONTAIGNE – 25MM   REF. CD151110M001

Movement: quartz.
Functions: hours, minutes.
Case: stainless steel; Ø 25mm; bezel set with 53 diamonds (0.42 carat); water resistant to 5atm.
Dial: white mother-of-pearl; set with 28 diamonds (0.07 carat).
Bracelet: stainless steel; stainless steel unfolding clasp.

DIOR VIII MONTAIGNE – 32MM   REF. CD1525I0M001

Movement: automatic-winding; 40-hour power reserve; white lacquered oscillating weight.
Functions: hours, minutes, seconds.
Case: stainless steel; Ø 32mm; stainless steel bezel set with 18K pink-gold ring; 18K pink-gold crown; transparent sapphire crystal caseback; water resistant to 5atm.
Dial: white mother-of-pearl; set with 34 diamonds (0.11 carat).
Bracelet: 18K pink gold and stainless steel; stainless steel unfolding clasp.

DIOR VIII GRAND BAL "PLISSE SOLEIL" – 36MM   REF. CD153B10M001

Movement: automatic-winding "Dior Inversé 11 1/2" caliber; 42-hour power reserve; 22K white-gold oscillating weight set with 32 diamonds (0.08 carat) and white mother-of-pearl marquetry.
Functions: hours, minutes.
Case: stainless steel; Ø 36mm; bezel set with 71 diamonds (0.71 carat) and white mother-of-pearl ring; transparent sapphire crystal caseback; water resistant to 5atm.
Dial: sun-brushed with pink galvanic treatment.
Bracelet: stainless steel; stainless steel unfolding clasp.
Note: limited edition of 188 pieces.

DIOR VIII GRAND BAL "FIL DE SOIE" – 38MM   REF. CD124BH4A001

Movement: automatic-winding "Dior Inversé 11 1/2" caliber; 42-hour power reserve; 18K pink-gold oscillating weight set with 95 diamonds (0.24 carat) and pink silk thread.
Functions: hours, minutes.
Case: black high-tech ceramic and 18K pink gold; Ø 38mm; 18K pink-gold bezel set with 72 diamonds (0.72 carat) and black ceramic ring; 18K pink-gold crown set with black ceramic insert; black translucent sapphire crystal caseback; water resistant to 5atm.
Dial: black mother-of-pearl; set with 28 diamonds (0.04 carat).
Strap: black patent calfskin; 18K pink-gold ardillon; buckle set with diamonds (0.18 carat).
Note: limited edition of 88 pieces.
Also available: shiny black alligator leather strap.

DIOR VIII GRAND BAL PIECE UNIQUE N°8 – 36MM   REF. CD153B6ZA009

Movement: automatic-winding "Dior Inversé 11 1/2" caliber; 42-hour power reserve; 22K white-gold oscillating weight set with 68 diamonds (0.16 carat), 18 sapphires (0.03 carat), 5 lavender sapphires (0.01 carat), opal and mother-of-pearl.
Functions: hours, minutes.
Case: 18K white gold; Ø 36mm; bezel snow-set with 332 diamonds (2.08 carats); 18K white-gold crown set with rose-cut diamond (0.07 carat); opalescent sapphire crystal caseback; water resistant to 5atm.
Dial: 18K white gold; 534 snow-set sapphires (1.82 carats); 114 snow-set diamonds (0.37 carat).
Strap: blue metallic leather; 18K white-gold ardillon buckle set with 69 diamonds (0.26 carat).
Note: unique piece.
Also available: black satin strap.

DIOR GRAND SOIR N°29 ORIGAMI – 33MM   REF. CD13355ZA003

Movement: automatic-winding Elite 681 caliber by Zenith for Dior; 50-hour power reserve; peach lacquered oscillating weight.
Functions: hours, minutes.
Case: 18K yellow gold; Ø 33mm; 18K yellow-gold bezel set with 48 triangle-cut sapphires (4.8 carats); 18K pink-gold crown set with rose-cut diamond (0.05 carat); transparent sapphire crystal caseback; water resistant to 5atm.
Dial: white mother-of-pearl marquetry; set with 12 yellow sapphires (0.16 carat).
Strap: white satin and leather; 18K yellow-gold unfolding clasp set with 44 diamonds (0.28 carat).
Note: unique piece.
Also available: dark blue semi-matte alligator leather strap.

LA D DE DIOR "PRECIEUSE" – 21MM — REF. CD040166M001

Movement: quartz.
Functions: hours, minutes.
Case: 18K white gold; Ø 21mm; bezel set with 18 diamonds and 57 fancy pink diamonds (2.01 carats); 18K white-gold crown set with 24 fancy pink diamonds (0.08 carat); water resistant to 3atm.
Dial: 18K white gold; 167 snow-set fancy pink diamonds (0.55 carat).
Bracelet: 18K white gold; set with 46 diamonds and 632 fancy diamonds (6.77 carats); 18K white-gold jewelry unfolding clasp.

LA MINI D DE DIOR "MIRROR" – 19MM — REF. CD040110A015

Movement: quartz.
Functions: hours, minutes.
Case: stainless steel; Ø 19mm; bezel set with 40 diamonds (0.32 carat); crown set with 13 diamonds (0.03 carat); water resistant to 3atm.
Dial: black mother-of-pearl.
Strap: pink-gold "mirror" calfskin leather; stainless steel ardillon buckle set with 18 diamonds (0.11 carat).
Also available: black patent calfskin strap.

LA D DE DIOR – 25MM — REF. CD047111A003

Movement: quartz.
Functions: hours, minutes.
Case: stainless steel; Ø 25mm; bezel set with 50 diamonds (0.5 carat); crown set with 13 diamonds (0.3 carat); water resistant to 3atm.
Dial: white mother-of-pearl; set with 12 diamonds (0.06 carat).
Strap: black satin; stainless steel ardillon buckle set with 18 diamonds (0.18 carat).

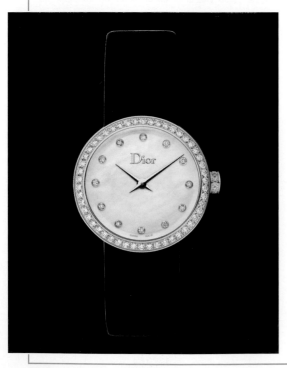

LA D DE DIOR – 38MM — REF. DC043171A003

Movement: quartz.
Functions: hours, minutes.
Case: 18K pink gold; Ø 38mm; 18K pink-gold bezel set with 72 diamonds (0.72 carat); 18K pink-gold crown set with 10 diamonds (0.06 carat); water resistant to 3atm.
Dial: jade; set with 12 diamonds (0.06 carat).
Strap: black satin; 18K pink-gold ardillon buckle set with 62 diamonds (0.45 carat).

DIOR CHRISTAL RED – 33MM   REF. CD143111M001

Movement: quartz.
Functions: hours, minutes, seconds.
Case: stainless steel; Ø 33mm; turning bezel set with red sapphire crystal inserts; crown set with red sapphire crystal insert; water resistant to 5atm.
Dial: red lacquer; set with 32 diamonds (0.1 carat).
Bracelet: stainless steel; set with three rows of red sapphire crystal inserts; stainless steel unfolding clasp.

DIOR CHRISTAL BLUE – 38MM   REF. CD144517M001

Movement: automatic-winding; 38-hour power reserve; blue lacquered oscillating weight.
Functions: hours, minutes, seconds.
Case: stainless steel; Ø 38mm; turning bezel set with blue sapphire crystal inserts; crown set with blue sapphire crystal insert; transparent sapphire crystal caseback; water resistant to 5atm.
Dial: blue mother-of-pearl; set with 34 diamonds (0.17 carat).
Bracelet: stainless steel; set with three rows of blue sapphire crystal inserts; stainless steel unfolding clasp.

CHIFFRE ROUGE A02 – 38MM   REF. CD084610M002

Movement: automatic-winding; 42-hour power reserve; COSC certified chronograph.
Functions: hours, minutes, seconds; date; chronograph.
Case: stainless steel; Ø 38mm; translucent black sapphire crystal caseback; water resistant to 5atm.
Dial: black galvanic.
Bracelet: stainless steel; stainless steel unfolding clasp.

CHIFFRE ROUGE C03 – 38MM   REF. CD084C11A003

Movement: automatic-winding Elite 691 caliber by Zenith for Dior; 50-hour power reserve; brushed oscillating weight engraved with "DIOR HOMME CALIBRE ZENITH 691."
Functions: hours, minutes; small seconds at 9; large date at 2; moonphase at 6.
Case: stainless steel; Ø 38mm; translucent black sapphire crystal caseback; water resistant to 5atm.
Dial: gray metallized mother-of-pearl.
Strap: black perforated calfskin; stainless steel ardillon buckle.
Note: limited edition of 100 pieces.

LAND, AIR, & SEA

Ernst Benz takes timekeeping on a journey through the world's roads, skies and deepest oceans. With its Great Circle series, the watchmaker, **INSPIRED BY THE WORLDS OF MOTORING, MILITARY AVIATION AND NAUTICAL VOYAGE**, offers a distinct trio of self-winding instruments, all with individually numbered dials and exhibition casebacks, suited for the world's most determined explorers.

The ChronoRacer opens the limited edition series with a tribute to the colors of some of history's finest racing automobiles. Housed in a 47mm or 44mm case in matte black DLC or brushed stainless steel, the timepiece displays a wealth of information on a blue dial that creates a vibrant contrast against the luminous orange or black Arabic numerals. The ChronoRacer, equipped with day and date apertures at 3 o'clock is available with a high-precision chronograph or as an understated three-hand variation for a more leisurely drive down a coastal highway.

As a chronograph or a three-hand variation, the ChronoCombat takes to the air with decisive character and clarity of design.

Unmistakable in its military inspiration, the ChronoCombat series honors the aviation legacy of the brand's namesake founder. Luminous orange numerals and hands join forces with the iconic combination of matte black and military green to endow the timepiece with a bold balance of legibility and rugged aesthetics. Each indicating the day and date via two openings on the right side of the dial, three models offer an array of stylistic flexibility. Whether as a 47mm chronograph with solid or black subdials, or as a 44mm three-hand variation, the ChronoCombat takes to the air with decisive character and clarity of design.

The third entry in the Great Circle series, the Nautical Star earns its name with the commanding exposition of the iconic seafaring emblem in the center of its dial. The 47mm timepiece, housed in a matte black DLC or brushed stainless steel case, complements its indication of the hours, minutes and seconds with two apertures displaying the day and date at 3 o'clock. Available in signature Ernst Benz red or in marine blue, the Nautical Star accompanies its wearer to the fascinating unknown of the farthest horizons.

◄ **CHRONORACER** *(far left)*

This motor-racing-inspired timepiece provides a highly legible cockpit for the world's most unforgettable drives.

◄ **CHRONOCOMBAT** *(center)*

The peripheral tachometer and militarized codes of design of the ChronoCombat express its spirited personality.

◄ **NAUTICAL STAR** *(left)*

This self-winding wristwatch adorns its displays of the day, date, hours, minutes and central running seconds with a bold nautical star emblematic of the sailing lifestyle.

CHRONOCOMBAT CHRONOSCOPE DLC   REF. GC10100-CC2-DLC

Movement: automatic-winding Valjoux 7750 caliber; Incabloc; Glucydur balance; Nivarox alloy hairspring.
Functions: hours, minutes; small seconds at 9; day and date at 3; chronograph: 12-hour counter at 6, 30-minute counter at 12, central chronograph seconds.
Case: black DLC-brushed stainless steel; Ø 47mm; knurled double O-ring sealed crown; antireflective sapphire crystal; water resistant to 5atm.
Dial: green; orange luminous numerals; black counters.
Strap: handmade aviator alligator leather; double stitching.

Suggested price: $6,500

CHRONORACER CHRONOSCOPE DLC   REF. GC10100-CR1-DLC

Movement: automatic-winding Valjoux 7750 caliber; Incabloc; Glucydur balance; Nivarox alloy hairspring.
Functions: hours, minutes; small seconds at 9; day and date at 3; chronograph: 12-hour counter at 6, 30-minute counter at 12, central chronograph seconds.
Case: black DLC-brushed stainless steel; Ø 47mm; knurled double O-ring sealed crown; antireflective sapphire crystal; water resistant to 5atm.
Dial: blue; black luminous numerals.
Strap: handmade aviator alligator leather.

Suggested price: $6,500

CHRONORACER CHRONOSCOPE   REF. GC10100-CR2

Movement: automatic-winding Valjoux 7750 caliber; Incabloc; Glucydur balance; Nivarox alloy hairspring.
Functions: hours, minutes; small seconds at 9; day and date at 3; chronograph: 12-hour counter at 6, 30-minute counter at 12, central chronograph seconds.
Case: brushed stainless steel; Ø 47mm; knurled double O-ring sealed crown; antireflective sapphire crystal; water resistant to 5atm.
Dial: blue; orange luminous numerals.
Strap: handmade matte aviator alligator leather.

Suggested price: $5,700

ERNST BENZ BY JOHN VARVATOS DLC CHRONOSCOPE   REF. GC10410-JV-5

Movement: automatic-winding Valjoux 7750 caliber; Incabloc; Glucydur balance; Nivarox alloy hairspring.
Functions: hours, minutes; small seconds at 9; day and date at 3; chronograph: 12-hour counter at 6, 30-minute counter at 12, central chronograph seconds.
Case: black DLC-brushed stainless steel; Ø 47mm; angled and polished bezel with square polished pushbuttons; knurled double O-ring sealed crown; antireflective sapphire crystal; water resistant to 5atm.
Dial: black matte; black luminous numerals.
Strap: handmade matte aviator alligator leather.
Suggested price: $7,800

CHRONOSCOPE DLC REF. GC10118-DLC

Movement: automatic-winding Valjoux 7750 caliber; Incabloc; Glucydur balance; Nivarox alloy hairspring.
Functions: hours, minutes; small seconds at 9; day and date at 3; chronograph: 12-hour counter at 6, 30-minute counter at 12, central chronograph seconds.
Case: black DLC-brushed stainless steel; Ø 47mm; angled and polished bezel with square polished pushbuttons; knurled double O-ring sealed crown; antireflective sapphire crystal; water resistant to 5atm.
Dial: yellow; black numerals.
Strap: handmade aviator alligator leather.
Suggested price: $6,225

CHRONOLUNAR OFFICER REF. GC10381

Movement: automatic-winding Valjoux 7750 caliber; Incabloc; Glucydur balance; Nivarox alloy hairspring.
Functions: hours, minutes; small seconds at 9; day and date at 3; chronograph: 12-hour counter at 6, 30-minute counter at 12, central chronograph seconds.
Case: polished stainless steel; Ø 47mm; knurled double O-ring sealed crown; antireflective sapphire crystal; water resistant to 5atm.
Dial: black; steel hands and numerals.
Strap: handmade alligator leather.
Suggested price: $7,625

NAUTICAL STARS REF. GC10200-NS2

Movement: automatic-winding ETA 2836-2 Incabloc; Glucydur balance; Nivarox alloy hairspring.
Functions: hours, minutes, seconds; day and date at 3.
Case: stainless steel; Ø 47mm; knurled O-ring sealed crown; antireflective sapphire crystal; water resistant to 5atm.
Dial: black; blue numerals.
Strap: aviator alligator leather.
Suggested price: $3,925

CHRONOSCOPE DLC REF. GC10119-DLC

Movement: automatic-winding Valjoux 7750 caliber; Incabloc; Glucydur balance; Nivarox alloy hairspring.
Functions: hours, minutes; small seconds at 9; day and date at 3; chronograph: 12-hour counter at 6, 30-minute counter at 12, central chronograph seconds.
Case: black DLC brushed stainless steel; Ø 47mm; knurled double O-ring sealed crown; antireflective sapphire crystal; water resistant to 5atm.
Dial: yellow; black numerals.
Strap: handmade aviator alligator leather.
Suggested price: $6,225

FREDERIQUE CONSTANT
GENEVE

TELLTALE HEART BEAT

THE MOST PRESTIGIOUS NAMES OF HAUTE HOROLOGY POSSESS MANUFACTURING FACILI-TIES WHERE THEY DESIGN AND CREATE THEIR OWN MOVEMENTS TO POWER THE WATCH WORLD'S MOST ICONIC PIECES. Since 2004, Frédérique Constant has been a member of this elite group, adding new models to its Heart Beat Manufacture line with each passing year.

To celebrate the collection's tenth anniversary in 2014, Frédérique Constant released the sleek Jubilee Edition 10 Years Heart Beat Manufacture Silicium, a limited edition of 18 pieces in platinum or 188 pieces in rose gold that is the culmination of the brand's horological advances over the last decade. Powered by the Heart Beat Manufacture FC-942 Silicium, this model takes advantage of the unique qualities of the element silicon to ensure the movement's reliability and longevity. Typical watches made with conventional materials require lubrication as a regular part of maintenance to reduce the friction between the movement's components. The more friction between the balance spring and the escapement, in particular, the less power is transferred to the balance wheel. The use of silicon, also known as silicium, obviates the need for lubrication, and its low friction means that the caliber requires less energy. Since silicon is so lightweight, it has decreased inertia, which increases the energy efficiency of the movement as a whole. The material is the basis for the movement's escapement wheel, anchor and plateau.

JUBILEE EDITION 10 YEARS HEART BEAT MANUFACTURE SILICIUM

Through a sapphire crystal caseback and Frédérique Constant's iconic Heart Beat aperture on the dial, this watch gives pride of place to the high-tech use of silicon as a material for watchmaking components.

Frédérique Constant's characteristic Heart Beat aperture swirls a tail behind it like an otherworldly comet in a pitch-black night sky.

This technical achievement from Frédérique Constant, as well as others, is on full display in the Jubilee Edition 10 Years Heart Beat Manufacture Silicium. The patented balance wheel bridge is displayed on the front of the caliber, and the silicon escapement wheel operates in full view through the Heart Beat dial cutout at six o'clock, playing peek-a-boo to striking effect. The sapphire crystal caseback provides an even more comprehensive view of the movement in action. Even the stationary components of the FC-942 are a pleasure to behold, finely finished with perlage and vertical Côtes de Genève decoration. With 25 jewels used in its construction, the movement oscillates at a frequency of 28,800 vph and has at its disposal a 42-hour power reserve.

Both the platinum and the 18-karat rose-gold models feature an individually numbered two-part case that is water resistant to 3atm. The curvilinear aesthetic of the chic black dial reflects the constant motion of the movement within. Frédérique Constant's characteristic Heart Beat aperture swirls a tail behind it like an otherworldly comet in a pitch-black night sky. Understated Arabic numerals at three and nine o'clock complement the hand-applied indexes and hand-polished hands. A pointer-style date display and moonphase indication share a subdial at twelve o'clock. The simple, stylish look of the dial and case complements the sophisticated use of nontraditional materials within—an expansion of haute horology's limits that opens our eyes to the potential that lies unnoticed all around us.

FREDERIQUE CONSTANT

HEART BEAT MANUFACTURE   REF. FC-945MC4H6

Movement: automatic-winding Manufacture FC-945 caliber; 42-hour power reserve; 26 jewels; silicium escapement wheel.
Functions: hours, minutes; date by hand and moonphase at 12; 24-hour indicator at 9; heartbeat at 6.
Case: stainless steel; Ø 42mm; convex sapphire crystal; water resistant to 5atm.
Dial: silver; guilloché with printed Roman numerals.
Strap: blue alligator leather.
Note: delivered in wooden gift box.

Suggested price: $6,500
Also available: 18K rose gold with brown alligator leather strap (ref. FC-945MC4H9).

SLIMLINE MANUFACTURE   REF. FC-710V4S4

Movement: automatic-winding Manufacture FC-710 caliber; 42-hour power reserve; 26 jewels; perlage and circular Côtes de Genève decoration.
Functions: hours, minutes, seconds; date by hand at 6.
Case: polished rose-gold-plated steel; Ø 42mm; convex sapphire crystal; transparent caseback; water resistant to 3atm.
Dial: silver; domed; hand-applied hour markers.
Strap: brown alligator leather.
Note: delivered in wooden gift box.

Suggested price: $3,095
Also available: polished stainless steel with black alligator leather strap (ref. FC-710S4S6).

SLIMLINE MOONPHASE MANUFACTURE   REF. FC-705S4S6B

Movement: automatic-winding Manufacture FC-705 caliber; 42-hour power reserve; 26 jewels; perlage and circular Côtes de Genève decoration.
Functions: hours, minutes; date by hand and moonphase at 6.
Case: polished stainless steel; Ø 42mm; convex sapphire crystal; transparent caseback; water resistant to 3atm.
Dial: silver domed; hand-applied nickel hour markers.
Bracelet: polished stainless steel; seven-link; butterfly buckle with pushbuttons.
Note: delivered in wooden gift box.

Suggested price: $3,795
Also available: polished stainless steel with domed navy dial and stainless steel bracelet (ref. FC-705N4S6B).

MANUFACTURE WORLDTIMER   REF. FC-718WM4H4

Movement: automatic-winding Manufacture FC-718 caliber; 42-hour power reserve; 26 jewels; perlage and circular Côtes de Genève.
Functions: hours, minutes, seconds; date by hand at 6; worldtime.
Case: polished rose-gold-plated stainless steel; Ø 42mm; convex sapphire crystal; transparent caseback; water resistant to 5atm.
Dial: silver with world map in center and rose-gold-plated luminescent hour markers; hand polished blue hands.
Strap: dark brown alligator leather; rose-gold pin buckle; water resistant inner lining.

Note: delivered in wooden gift box.
Suggested price: $4,395
Also available: polished stainless steel with silver dial and worldmap in center on stainless steel bracelet (ref. FC-718WM4H6B).

LADIES WORLD HEART FEDERATION AUTOMATIC   REF. FC-303WHF2PD2B3

Movement: automatic-winding FC-303 caliber; 38-hour power reserve; 26 jewels; rose-gold-plated rotor with "WHF logo" and "Heart of Children" engraving; sunray bridges.
Functions: hours, minutes, seconds; date at 6.
Case: rose-gold-plated stainless steel; Ø 34mm, thickness: 9.9mm; bezel set with 48 diamonds (0.74 carat); sapphire crystal; transparent caseback; water resistant to 6atm.
Dial: vanilla with WHF logo decoration in center; mother-of-pearl outer ring; hand-applied hour markers; ten diamonds (0.10 carat).
Bracelet: bi-color metal; butterfly folding buckle.
Note: delivered in special heart-shaped WHF box.
Suggested price: $4,695
Also available: vanilla dial with WHF logo decoration in center; mother-of-pearl outer ring with rose-gold-plated metal bracelet (ref. FC-303WHF2P-D4B3).

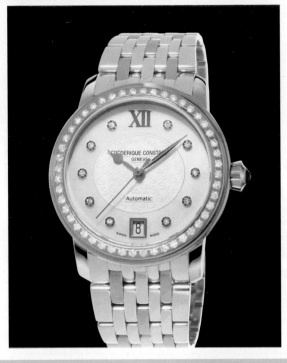

RUNABOUT CHRONOGRAPH   REF. FC-393RM5B6

Movement: automatic-winding FC-393 caliber; 46-hour power reserve; 25 jewels.
Functions: hours, minutes, seconds; date at 3; chronograph: 12-hour counter at 6, 30-minute counter at 12.
Case: stainless steel; Ø 42mm; convex sapphire crystal; transparent caseback; riva historical society flag on caseback glass; water resistant to 5atm.
Dial: silvered; guilloché decoration in center; applied pearl black Arabic numerals; luminescent minute hands.
Strap: blue crococalf strap; folding buckle.
Note: limited edition of 2,888 pieces, delivered in special gift box with runabout miniature.
Suggested price: $3,395
Also available: rose-gold-plated with brown crococalf strap (ref. FC-393RM5B4).

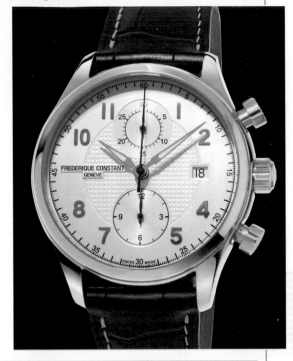

HEALEY GMT 24H   REF. FC-350CH5B4

Movement: automatic-winding FC-350 caliber; 38-hour power reserve; 26 jewels.
Functions: hours, minutes, seconds; date at 3; 24-hour GMT.
Case: rose-gold-plated; Ø 42mm; convex sapphire crystal; caseback with NOJ-393 car engraving and round opening revealing balance wheel; water resistant to 5atm.
Dial: chocolate brown; guilloché decoration; hand-applied rose-gold-plated hour markers; Healey logo at 6; white luminescent hour and minute hands; easy setup of local time via hour hand.
Strap: dark brown racing leather.
Note: limited edition of 2,888 pieces, delivered in special gift box with Healey NOJ 393 car miniature.
Suggested price: $2,795
Also available: stainless steel with black leather strap (ref. FC-350HS5B6).

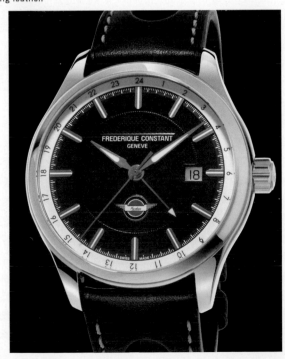

SLIMLINE LADIES MOONPHASE   REF. FC-206MPWD1SD6B

Movement: quartz; FC-206 caliber; 60-month battery life; 5 jewels.
Functions: hours, minutes; moonphase at 6.
Case: polished stainless steel; Ø 30mm; set with diamonds (0.56 carat); sapphire crystal; water resistant to 3atm.
Dial: mother-of-pearl; hand-applied diamond hour markers (0.2 carat); hand-polished hands; moonphase display at 6.
Bracelet: metal.
Suggested price: $2,895
Also available: stainless steel with black leather strap (ref. FC-206MPWD1SD6).

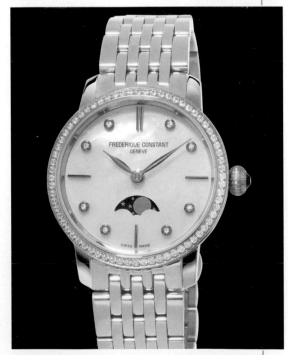

GP
GIRARD-PERREGAUX

HAUTE HOROLOGY'S
THIRD DIMENSION

Upholding a tradition of beauty inside and out, Girard-Perregaux's Tri-Axial Tourbillon embodies haute horology's **UNIQUE BLEND** of art and micro-mechanical engineering.

The 10-piece limited edition pink-gold masterpiece fulfills watchmaking's timeless quest for chronometric precision while exposing the fascinating dynamism of its high-precision three-dimensional regulator. Positioned at 9 o'clock under an elevated domed lens that ensures the module's freedom of mobility, the timepiece's 140-component tourbillon combats the Earth's gravitational pull on three separate axes. While the innermost tourbillon cage performs its complete rotation over the course of one minute, a secondary structure, within which it is integrated, undergoes a revolution of its own in the span of 30 seconds. This dual-axis mechanism is then incorporated within a final system that conducts its own two-minute rotation on a third independent axis, completing the marvelous tri-axial orbiting spectacle. The meticulously constructed tourbillon, weighing a total of 1.24g and containing a variable-inertia balance wheel with 16 pink-gold micro-screws, boasts support pillars in titanium or pink gold that act as ingenious counterweights in an exercise of perfect kinetic balance.

Girard-Perregaux demonstrates its faithful respect for Swiss watchmaking's purest traditions, hand-finishing the components of the manually wound GP09300 caliber with exquisite care and attention to detail—whether it be the perfect chamfering of the movement's numerous inward angles, the mirror polishing of its surfaces or the delicate circular graining of its precise gear train. Containing 34 jewels, 317 components and pink-gold two-arrow bridges, the spectacular movement also drives a display of the hours and minutes at 1 o'clock via two skeletonized pink-gold hands on a silver subdial decorated with Clous de Paris. At 4 o'clock, a gracefully curved gray empty space counters the vibrant complexity of the timepiece with a Zen-like air of visual simplicity, leading the eye to a subtle revelation of the movement's 52-hour power reserve indicator.

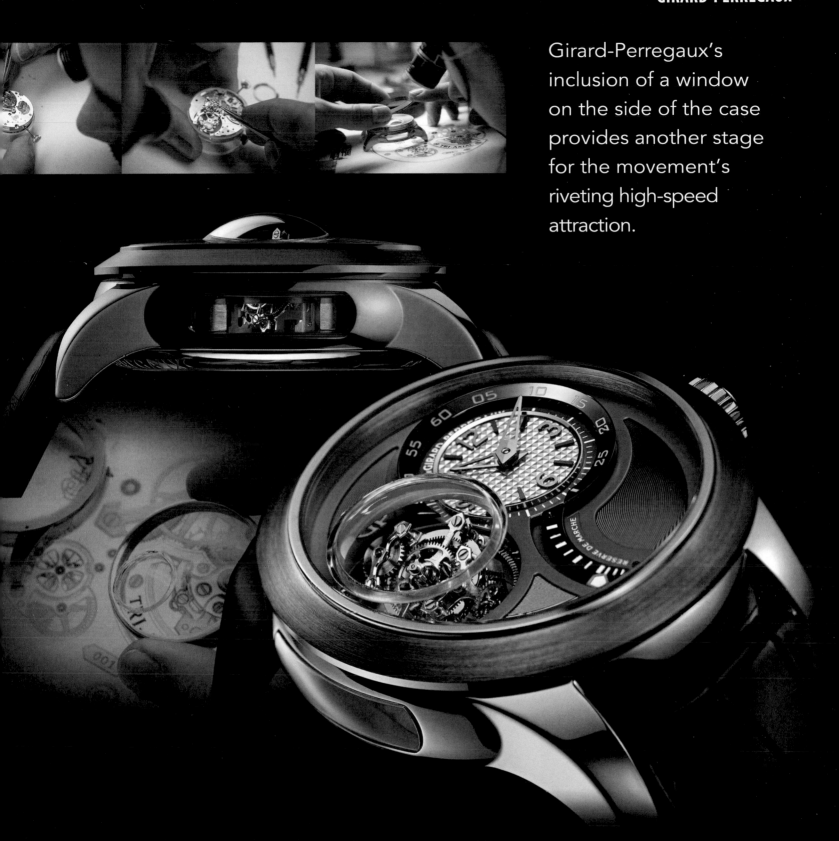

Girard-Perregaux's inclusion of a window on the side of the case provides another stage for the movement's riveting high-speed attraction.

The 21,600vph timepiece's transparent caseback provides a dazzling view of the caliber, including the tourbillon-differential's supporting circular bridge engraved with the words "Tri-Axial." However, as its name would suggest, two stages are not enough to truly honor the brilliance of the Tri-Axial Tourbillon. Girard-Perregaux's inclusion of a window, at 9 o'clock on the side of the case, grants the owner another exhibition stage for the movement's riveting high-speed attraction—a fitting third dimension to an already unforgettable performance.

TRI-AXIAL TOURBILLON
This limited edition masterpiece reveals, through a trio of windows, a highly sophisticated tourbillon that rotates on three separate axes.

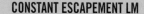

TRI-AXIAL TOURBILLON REF. 99815-52-251-BA6A

Movement: manual-winding GPE09300-0001 caliber; 16 lines; 52-hour power reserve; 34 jewels; 21,600 vph.
Functions: off-centered hours, minutes at 2; tri-axial tourbillon at 9; power reserve indicator.
Case: pink gold; Ø 48mm. thickness: 17.51mm (20.27mm with dome); sapphire crystal caseback secured by 6 screws; water resistant to 3atm.
Dial: constructed on several levels.
Strap: black alligator; pink-gold folding buckle.

Note: limited edition of 10 pieces.
Price: available upon request.

CONSTANT ESCAPEMENT LM REF. 93500-52-731-BA6D

Movement: manual-winding GP09100-0002 caliber; 17½ lines; 6-day power reserve; 271 components; 28 jewels; 21,600 vph.
Functions: off-centered hours, minutes at 12; central seconds; constant escapement; power reserve indicator at 9.
Case: pink gold; Ø 48mm, thickness: 14.63mm; sapphire crystal caseback secured by 6 screws; water resistant to 3atm.
Dial: white varnish on subdial for time indication.
Strap: black alligator leather; pink-gold folding buckle.

Price: available upon request.

NEO-TOURBILLON WITH THREE BRIDGES REF. 99270-52-000-BA6A

Movement: automatic-winding GP09400-0001 caliber; 16 lines; 70-hour power reserve; 245 components; 27 jewels; 21,600 vph.
Functions: hours, minutes; small seconds on tourbillon at 6.
Case: pink gold; Ø 45mm, thickness: 14.45mm; caseback secured by 6 screws; water resistant to 3atm.
Dial: skeletonized.
Strap: black alligator leather; pink-gold folding buckle.
Note: limited edition of 12 pieces.

Price: available upon request.

TOURBILLON WITH THREE GOLD BRIDGES REF. 99193-52-000-BA6A

Movement: automatic-winding GP09600C caliber; 13¾ lines; 48-hour power reserve; 262 components; 31 jewels; 21,600 vph.
Functions: hours, minutes; small seconds on tourbillon at 6.
Case: pink gold; Ø 41mm, thickness: 11mm; caseback secured by 6 screws; water resistant to 3atm.
Dial: skeletonized.
Strap: black alligator leather; pink-gold folding buckle.
Note: limited edition of 50 pieces.

Price: available upon request.

CONSTANT ESCAPEMENT LM
REF. 93500-53-131-BA6C

Movement: manual-winding GP09100-0002 caliber; 17½ lines; 6-day power reserve; 271 components; 28 jewels; 21,600 vph.
Functions: off-centered hours, minutes at 12; central seconds; constant escapement; power reserve indicator.
Case: white gold; Ø 48mm, thickness: 14.63mm; sapphire crystal caseback secured by 6 screws; water resistant to 3atm.
Dial: silvered with grained finish.
Strap: black alligator leather; titanium blade with white-gold cover folding buckle.
Price: available upon request.

BI-AXIAL TOURBILLON
REF. 99810-81-000-BA6A

Movement: manual-winding GPE07-0002 caliber; 15 lines; 70-hour power reserve; 28 jewels; 21,600 vph.
Functions: hours, minutes; bi-axial tourbillon at 6.
Case: tantalum and sapphire bridges; Ø 45mm, thickness: 19.25mm; sapphire crystal caseback secured by 6 screws; water resistant to 3atm.
Dial: guilloché motif with galvanic gray finishing.
Strap: black alligator leather; sandblasted steel folding buckle.
Note: limited edition of 12 pieces.
Price: available upon request.

TOURBILLON WITH THREE GOLD BRIDGES
REF. 99193B52H001-BA6A

Movement: automatic-winding GP09600-0022 caliber; 13¾ lines; 48-hour power reserve; 256 components; 31 jewels; 21,600 vph.
Functions: hours, minutes; small seconds on tourbillon at 6.
Case: pink gold; Ø 41mm, thickness: 11.1mm; set with 88 baguette-cut diamonds (11.70 carats); sapphire crystal caseback secured by 6 screws; water resistant to 3atm.
Dial: skeletonized.
Strap: black alligator leather; pink-gold folding buckle set with 18 brilliant-cut diamonds (0.2 carat).
Note: limited edition of 18 pieces.
Price: available upon request.

TOURBILLON WITH THREE GOLD BRIDGES LADY
REF. 99240D52A701-CK7A

Movement: automatic-winding GP09600-0025 caliber; 13 lines; 48-hour power reserve; 233 components; 31 jewels; 21,600 vph.
Functions: hours, minute; small seconds on tourbillon at 6.
Case: pink gold; Ø 38mm, thickness: 11.16mm; set with 48 brilliant-cut diamonds (1.45 carats); caseback secured by 6 screws; water resistant to 3atm.
Dial: white natural mother-of-pearl; interior flange set with 70 brilliant-cut diamonds (0.35 carat).
Strap: navy blue alligator; pink-gold folding buckle set with 18 brilliant-cut diamonds (0.2 carat).
Price: available upon request.

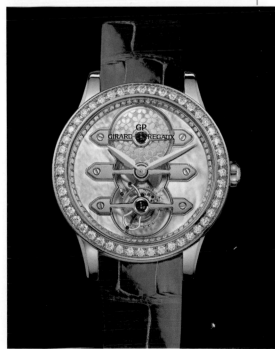

GIRARD-PERREGAUX

VINTAGE 1945 XXL LARGE DATE & MOON-PHASES REF. 25882-52-222-BB6B

Movement: automatic-winding GP03300-0105 caliber; 11½ lines; 46-hour power reserve; 32 jewels; 28,800 vph.
Functions: hours, minutes; small seconds on moonphase at 6; large date at 12.
Case: pink gold; 36.1x35.25mm, thickness: 11.74mm; sapphire crystal caseback secured by 4 screws; water resistant to 3atm.
Dial: skeletonized; 3 applied Arabic numerals; 9 applied hour markers.
Strap: black alligator leather; pink-gold folding buckle.
Price: available upon request.

Also available: steel.

VINTAGE 1945 XXL LARGE DATE & MOON-PHASES REF. 25882-52-121-BB6B

Movement: automatic-winding GP03300-0062 caliber; 11½ lines; 46-hour power reserve; 32 jewels; 28,800 vph.
Functions: hours, minutes; small seconds on moonphase at 6; large date at 12.
Case: pink gold; 36.1x35.25mm, thickness: 11.74mm; sapphire crystal caseback secured by 4 screws; water resistant to 3atm.
Dial: opaline; 11 applied Arabic numerals; railroad minute track.
Strap: black alligator leather; pink-gold folding buckle.
Price: available upon request.

Also available: steel.

VINTAGE 1945 XXL SMALL SECOND REF. 25880-11-421-BB4A

Movement: automatic-winding GP03300-0051 caliber; 11½ lines; 46-hour power reserve; 32 jewels; 28,800 vph.
Functions: hours, minutes; small seconds at 6.
Case: steel; 36.20x35.25mm, thickness: 10.83mm; sapphire crystal caseback secured by 4 screws; water resistant to 3 atm.
Dial: blue; 11 applied Arabic numerals; railroad minute track.
Strap: blue alligator leather; steel folding buckle.
Price: available upon request.

VINTAGE 1945 LADY REF. 25860D11A1A1-11A

Movement: automatic-winding GP02700-0003 caliber; 8¾ lines; 36-hour power reserve; 26 jewels; 28,800 vph.
Functions: hours, minutes; date at 6.
Case: steel; 28.2x27.86mm, thickness: 10.21mm; set with 30 brilliant-cut diamonds (0.55 carat); sapphire crystal caseback secured by 4 screws; water resistant to 3atm.
Dial: opaline; railroad track set with 42 brilliant-cut diamonds (0.105 carat); 3 applied Arabic numerals.
Bracelet: steel; triple-safety steel folding buckle.

Price: available upon request.

TRAVELLER JOHN HARRISON   REF. 49655-52-133-BBBA

Movement: automatic-winding GP03300-0093 caliber; 13½ lines; 46-hour power reserve; 35 jewels; 28,800 vph.
Functions: hours, minutes; small seconds on moonphase at 7:30; large date at 12; GMT: second time zone, day/night indicator at 4:30; power reserve indicator.
Case: pink gold; Ø 44mm, thickness: 12.1mm; sapphire crystal caseback secured by 6 screws; water resistant to 10 atm.
Dial: opaline; 6 applied luminescent-tipped hour markers.
Strap: brown alligator leather; titanium blade with pink-gold cover folding buckle.
Note: limited edition of 50 pieces.
Price: available upon request.

TRAVELLER WW.TC   REF. 49700-52-134-BB6B

Movement: automatic-winding GP03300-0084 caliber; 13 lines; 46-hour power reserve; 476 components; 63 jewels; 28,800 vph.
Functions: hours, minutes; small seconds at 3; date at 1:30; chronograph: 12-hour counter at 6, 30-minute counter at 9, central chronograph seconds hand; worldtime with day/night indicator.
Case: pink gold; Ø 44mm, thickness: 13.65mm; sapphire crystal caseback secured by 6 screws; water resistant to 10 atm.
Dial: opaline; 9 applied hour markers with luminescent material.
Strap: rubber covered in brown alligator leather; pink-gold folding buckle.
Price: available upon request.
Also available: steel.

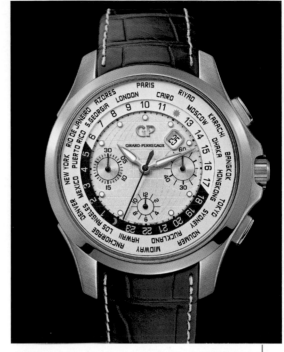

CHRONO HAWK   REF. 49970-34-633-BB6B

Movement: automatic-winding GP03300-0076 caliber; 13 lines; 46-hour power reserve; 61 jewels; 28,800 vph.
Functions: hours, minutes; small seconds at 3; date at 6; chronograph: 30-minute counter at 9, central chronograph seconds hand.
Case: pink gold; Ø 44mm, thickness: 15.85mm; sapphire crystal caseback secured by 6 screws; water resistant to 10 atm.
Dial: black; emblematic Girard-Perregaux bridge motif; 12 applied hour markers with luminescent material.
Strap: rubber covered with black alligator leather; PVD titanium with ceramic cover folding buckle.
Price: available upon request.

SEA HAWK   REF. 49960-32-632-FK6A

Movement: automatic-winding GP03300-0074 caliber; 11½ lines; 46-hour power reserve; 27 jewels; 28,800 vph.
Functions: hours, minutes; small seconds at 10; date at 1:30; power reserve indicator at 6.
Case: ceramic; Ø 44mm, thickness: 17.8mm; caseback secured by 6 screws; water resistant to 30atm.
Dial: black; emblematic Girard-Perregaux bridge motif; 12 applied hour markers with luminescent material.
Strap: black rubber; PVD titanium with ceramic cover folding buckle.
Price: available upon request.

GIRARD-PERREGAUX

GIRARD-PERREGAUX 1966 DUAL TIME   REF. 49544-52-231-BB60

Movement: automatic-winding GP03300-0094 caliber; 11½ lines; 46-hour power reserve; 27 jewels; 28,800 vph.
Functions: hours, minutes, seconds; date by hand at 6; GMT with 24-hour indicator.
Case: pink gold; Ø 40mm, thickness: 11.7 mm; sapphire crystal caseback; water resistant to 3 atm.
Dial: anthracite; 12 applied hour markers; railroad minute circle.
Strap: black alligator leather, pink-gold pin buckle.
Price: available upon request.

GIRARD-PERREGAUX 1966 COLUMN-WHEEL CHRONOGRAPH   REF. 49529-52-231-BA6A

Movement: manual-winding GP03800-0001 caliber; 11½ lines; 56-hour power reserve; 31 jewels; 28,800 vph.
Functions: hours, minutes; small seconds at 9; date at 6; column-wheel integrated chronograph: 30-minute counter at 3, central chronograph seconds hand.
Case: pink gold; Ø 40mm, thickness: 11.25mm; sapphire crystal caseback; water resistant to 3atm.
Dial: anthracite; 12 applied hour markers; railroad minute circle.
Strap: black hand-sewn alligator; pink-gold folding buckle.

Price: available upon request.

GIRARD-PERREGAUX 1966 38 MM   REF. 49525-52-432-BB4A

Movement: automatic-winding GP03300-0030 caliber; 11½ lines; 46-hour power reserve; 27 jewels; 28,800 vph.
Functions: hours, minutes, seconds; date at 3.
Case: pink gold; Ø 38mm, thickness: 8.62 mm; sapphire crystal caseback; water resistant to 3atm.
Dial: blue; 4 applied hour markers.
Strap: blue alligator leather; pink-gold pin buckle.
Price: available upon request.

GIRARD-PERREGAUX 1966 LADY 38 MM   REF. 49525D52ABD2-BK8A

Movement: automatic-winding GP03300-0066 caliber; 11½ lines; 46-hour power reserve; 26 jewels; 28,800 vph.
Functions: hours, minutes.
Case: pink gold; Ø 38mm, thickness: 8.62mm; set with 72 brilliant-cut diamonds (0.85 carat); sapphire crystal caseback; water resistant to 3atm.
Dial: mother-of-pearl marquetry; pathway set with 47 brilliant-cut diamonds (0.1 carat); 2 applied Roman numerals.
Strap: white alligator leather; pink-gold pin buckle.

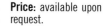

Price: available upon request.

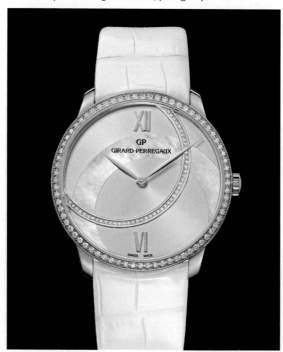

CAT'S EYE HIGH JEWELRY REF. 91702B53P7B1-KK6A

Movement: automatic-winding GP03300-0072 caliber; 11½ lines; 46-hour power reserve; 27 jewels; 28,800 vph.
Functions: hours, minutes; small seconds at 9.
Case: white gold; 38.63x33.63mm, thickness: 12.9 mm; set with 150 emerald-cut diamonds (14.52 carats); crown set with one rose-cut diamond (0.14 carat); sapphire crystal caseback secured by 4 screws; water resistant to 3atm.
Dial: set with 102 emerald-cut diamonds (6.6 carats); "Clous de Paris" hobnail motif.
Strap: technological satin; white-gold pin buckle set with 13 baguette-cut diamonds (0.67 carat).
Price: available upon request.

CAT'S EYE DAY AND NIGHT REF. 80488D52A251-CK2A

Movement: automatic-winding GP03300-0090 caliber; 11½ lines; 46-hour power reserve; 32 jewels; 28,800 vph.
Functions: hours, minutes; small seconds; day/night indicator at 6.
Case: pink gold; 35.44x30.44mm, thickness: 11.29mm; set with 62 brilliant-cut diamonds (0.8 carat); sapphire crystal caseback secured by 4 screws; water resistant to 3atm.
Dial: gray mother-of-pearl with guilloché motif; 18 applied brilliant-cut diamonds (0.6 carat); applied Arabic numeral.
Strap: gray alligator leather; pink-gold folding buckle.
Price: available upon request.

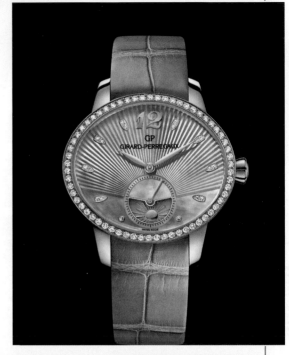

CAT'S EYE ANNIVERSARY REF. 80476D11A701-CK7A

Movement: automatic-winding GP03300-0097 caliber; 11½ lines; 46-hour power reserve; 27 jewels; 28,800 vph.
Functions: hours, minutes.
Case: steel; 37.84x32.84mm, thickness: 11.22mm; set with 64 brilliant-cut diamonds (0.95 carat); sapphire crystal caseback secured by four screws; water resistant to 3atm.
Dial: white natural mother-of-pearl with lace motif.
Strap: gray alligator; steel folding buckle.
Price: available upon request.

CAT'S EYE ANNIVERSARY REF. 80489D53A601-CK6A

Movement: automatic-winding GP03300-0101 caliber; 11½ lines; 46-hour power reserve; 27 jewels; 28,800 vph.
Functions: hours, minutes.
Case: white gold; 35.44x30.44mm, thickness: 11.29mm; set with 62 brilliant-cut diamonds (0.8 carat); sapphire crystal caseback secured by four screws; water resistant to 3 atm.
Dial: onyx; 73 applied brilliant-cut diamonds (0.36 carat).
Strap: black alligator leather; white-gold folding buckle.
Price: available upon request.

ORIGINAL

PANORAMIC PROSPECTS

German watchmaker Glashütte Original presents two flyback chronographs that **EPITOMIZE THE MANUFACTURE'S UNIQUE BLEND OF SIMPLICITY AND SOPHISTICATION.**

SEVENTIES CHRONOGRAPH PANORAMA DATE

This self-winding column-wheel flyback chronograph combines a vintage code of design with the 37-02 caliber's refined complexity.

The Senator Chronograph Panorama Date's juxtaposition of Roman and Arabic numerals exemplifies the timepiece's subtle fusion of past and present.

The German watchmaker honors the 1970s, an era of exciting design developments, with a timepiece as appealing for its vintage allure as for its modern, sophisticated movement. The Seventies Chronograph Panorama Date enlivens its rounded square stainless steel case with architectural symmetry and legibility. Driven by a self-winding column-wheel caliber whose simplified construction—with an accompanying reduction of components —has led to an increase in precision and durability, the wristwatch boasts a flyback chronograph permitting an instantaneous restart of the complication with the press of a single button. A trio of dial options (in blue, galvanized ruthenium or galvanized silver) displays the movement's multiple indications within a distinct and ingenious configuration. While the chronograph's slender central hand is joined at 3 o'clock by a traditional 30-minute subdial, Glashütte Original's exposure of the stopwatch's 12-hour counter, through a window at 12 o'clock, echoes the disposition of the large date aperture at 6 o'clock in a play on the shape of the 40x40mm case. Glashütte Original further demonstrates its commitment to clarity with the integration of a dual-function subdial at 9 o'clock that integrates both the running seconds and 70-hour power reserve while preserving the elegant symmetry of the watch. Designed with a penchant for refined simplicity and vintage understatement, the Seventies Chronograph Panorama Date sports four gold screws on the balance rim instead of a module on the spring for the regulatory mechanism.

The Senator Chronograph Panorama Date strikes a superb equilibrium of classicism and horological modernity. The self-winding satin-brushed platinum timepiece measures time on a dial whose rich luster represents an achievement in itself. A process of "silver plating by friction," in which a fine silver powder is meticulously hand-applied to the gold backdrop, results in a vibrant finish that offers a bright contrast by the wristwatch's numerous blued steel hands. The juxtaposition of Roman numerals in the chapter ring and Arabic numerals on the laser-engraved tachometric scale exemplifies the timepiece's subtle fusion of past and present and frames a highly legible visualization of the column-wheel caliber's several coexisting functions. Three hands, central for the seconds and at 12 and 3 o'clock for the 12-hour and 30-minute counters, display a precise measure of elapsed time driven by the movement's flyback chronograph mechanism. A large panoramic date aperture in the center of the dial's lower half breaks from the hand-driven configuration, while the integration of the power reserve indicator within the seconds subdial at 9 o'clock maintains an understated aura. On the caseback, a sapphire crystal window reveals the 37-01 caliber's chronograph bridges, 21-karat gold skeletonized rotor and four gold regulating screws. Finished with a blue sapphire cabochon on the crown, the platinum Senator Chronograph Panorama Date is worn on a blue Louisiana alligator leather strap. An additional red-gold version with grained lacquered silver dial plays the case's luxurious warmth against the cool allure of its six blued-steel hands.

▲ **SENATOR CHRONOGRAPH PANORAMA DATE**
This 42mm timepiece in platinum or red gold combines the excellence of a column-wheel flyback chronograph with a classical aesthetic.

SENATOR TOURBILLON
REF. 1-94-03-04-04-04

Movement: automatic-winding 94-03 caliber; Ø 32.2mm, thickness: 7.65mm; 48-hour power reserve; 50 jewels; two diamond endstones; 21,600 vph; screw balance with 18 weighted screws; beveled and polished edges; polished steel parts; blued screws; plate with Glashütte stripe finish; skeletonized rotor with 21K gold oscillating weight.
Functions: hours, minutes; small seconds on the flying tourbillon at 6; Panorama date at 12.
Case: 18K white gold; Ø 42mm; water resistant to 5atm.

Dial: varnish gray-grainé with engraved Roman numerals and railroad chapter.
Strap: gray Louisiana Nubuck alligator leather.
Suggested price: $118,600

PANOLUNAR TOURBILLON
REF. 1-93-02-05-05-05

Movement: automatic-winding 93-02 caliber; Ø 32.2mm, thickness: 7.65mm; 48-hour power reserve; 48 jewels; two diamond endstones; 21,600 vph; screw balance with ten weighted screws and eight regulation screws; beveled and polished edges; polished steel parts; blued screws; plate with Glashütte stripe finish; skeletonized rotor with 21K gold oscillating weight; fine adjustment by regulating screws.
Functions: off-centered hours, minutes; flying tourbillon with small seconds; Panorama date; moonphase.
Case: 18K red gold; Ø 40mm; water resistant to 5atm.

Dial: galvanized silver with gold appliqués.
Strap: brown nubuck Louisiana alligator leather.
Suggested price: $117,400
Also available: black Louisiana alligator leather strap.

SENATOR CHRONOGRAPH PANORAMA DATE
REF. 1-37-01-02-03-30

Movement: automatic-winding 37-01 caliber; Ø 31.6mm, thickness: 8mm; 70-hour power reserve; 65 jewels; 28,800 vph; screw balance with four 14K gold adjustment screws; Anachron balance spring; Incabloc shock protection; exquisitely finished with beveled and polished edges, polished steel parts, polished blued screws; plate with Glashütte stripe finish; skeletonized rotor with 21K gold oscillating weight; fine adjustment by adjustment screws.
Functions: hours, minutes; small seconds at 9; second stop; Panorama date at 6; flyback chronograph: 12-hour counter at 12, 30-minute counter at 3, central seconds hand, stop seconds; power reserve indicator.
Case: platinum; Ø 42mm, thickness: 14mm; antireflective sapphire crystal; water resistant to 5atm.
Dial: solid gold; hand silver plating by friction with Roman and Arabic numerals; tachometer scale: numerals and scale engraved, inlaid by hand; blued stainless steel hands.
Strap: blue Louisiana alligator leather.
Suggested price: $55,600
Also available: 18K red-gold case; silver varnish grainé with black Roman and Arabic numerals; black Louisiana alligator leather strap.

SENATOR PERPETUAL CALENDAR
REF. 100-02-25-05-05

Movement: automatic-winding 100-02 caliber; Ø 31.15mm, thickness: 7.1mm; 55-hour power reserve; 59 jewels; 28,800 vph; screw balance with 18 weighted screws; beveled edges; polished and brushed steel parts; swan-neck fine adjustment; divided three-quarter plate with Glashütte ribbed finish; skeletonized rotor with 21K gold oscillating weight.
Functions: hours, minutes, seconds; reset function; Panorama date; perpetual calendar with day, month, leap year and moonphase.
Case: 18K red gold; Ø 42mm; water resistant to 5atm.

Dial: black varnish grainé; white Roman numerals and railroad chapter.
Strap: black Louisiana alligator leather.
Suggested price: $37,100
Also available: steel case; silver varnish grainé; rubber strap; steel bracelet.

PANOGRAPH
REF. 1-61-03-25-15-05

Movement: manual-winding 61-03 caliber; Ø 32.2mm; thickness: 7.2mm; 42-hour power reserve; 41 jewels; 28,800 vph; screw balance with 18 weighted screws; beveled edges; polished and brushed steel parts; screwed gold chatons; blued screws; swan-neck fine adjustment; hand-engraved balance cock.
Functions: off-centered hours, minutes; small seconds; Panorama date; flyback chronograph: 30-minute counter; stop seconds.
Case: 18K red gold; Ø 40mm, thickness: 13.7mm; antireflective sapphire crystal; water resistant to 5atm.
Dial: galvanized silver; gold appliqués.
Strap: nubuck brown Louisiana alligator leather.
Suggested price: $34,600
Also available: black Louisiana alligator leather strap.

PANOMATIC LUNAR
REF. 1-90-02-42-32-05

Movement: automatic-winding 90-02 caliber; Ø 32.6mm, thickness: 7mm; 42-hour power reserve; 47 jewels; 28,800 vph; screw balance with 18 weighted screws; beveled edges; polished and brushed steel parts; blued screws; duplex swan-neck fine adjustment; hand-engraved balance bridge; Glashütte three-quarter plate with ribbed finish; off-center skeletonized rotor with 21K gold oscillating weight.
Functions: off-centered hours, minutes; small seconds; stop seconds; Panorama date; moonphase.
Case: stainless steel; Ø 40mm, thickness: 12.7mm; antireflective sapphire crystal; water resistant to 5atm.
Dial: galvanized silver.
Strap: black Louisana alligator leather.
Suggested price: $11,500
Also available: galvanized ruthenium dial; 18K red-gold case; steel bracelet; brown Nubuck strap.

PANOMATIC INVERSE
REF. 1-91-02-02-02-30

Movement: automatic-winding 91-02 caliber; Ø 38.2mm, thickness: 7.1mm; 42-hour power reserve; 49 jewels; 28,800 vph; screw balance with 18 weighted screws; Anachron balance spring; Incabloc shock protection; balance and fine adjustment on the dial side; exquisitely finished; beveled edges; polished steel parts; polished and blued screws; skeletonized rotor with 21K gold oscillating weight; plate with Glashütte stripe finish; duplex swan-neck fine adjustment.
Functions: off-centered hours, minutes; off-centered small seconds; Panorama date.
Case: stainless steel; Ø 42mm; antireflective sapphire crystal; water resistant to 5atm.
Dial: galvanized rhodium; blue appliqués; stainless steel hands with SuperLumiNova.
Strap: blue alligator leather.
Suggested price: $14,900
Also available: 18K red-gold case; brown Louisiana nubuck leather strap.

SENATOR MANUAL WINDING SKELETONIZED EDITION
REF. 1-49-18-01-05-30

Movement: manual-winding 49-18 caliber; Ø 35mm, thickness: 4.2m; 40-hour power reserve; 19 jewels, including five screwed gold chatons; 28,800 vph; Anachron balance spring; Incabloc protection; exquisitely finished; skeletonized; hand engraved; beveled and polished edges; polished steel parts; blued screws; swan-neck fine adjustment.
Functions: hours, minutes.
Case: 18K red gold; Ø 42mm, thickness: 9.5mm; antireflective sapphire crystal; water resistant to 5atm.
Dial: skeletonized; galvanized silver with black Roman numerals. blued stainless steel hands.
Strap: black Louisiana alligator leather; red-gold standard fold fastener.
Suggested price: $37,100

SENATOR CHRONOMETER REGULATOR   REF. 1-58-04-04-04-04

Movement: manual-winding 58-04 caliber; Ø 35mm, thickness: 6.47mm; 45-hour power reserve; 58 jewels; 28,800 vph; screw balance with 18 weighted screws; beveled and polished edges; polished steel parts; blued screws; Glashütte three-quarter plate with stripe finish; swan-neck fine adjustment; engraved balance cock; German chronometer certificate.
Functions: hours at 12, central minutes; seconds reset with couple minute ratched; Panorama date at 3; power reserve indicator; day/night indicator.
Case: 18K white gold; Ø 42mm; water resistant to 5atm.

Dial: varnish silver graniné with black Roman and Arabic numerals.
Strap: black Louisiana alligator leather.
Suggested price: $33,400
Also available: 18K red-gold case.

SENATOR OBSERVER   REF. 100-14-05-02-05

Movement: automatic-winding 100-14 caliber; Ø 31.15mm, thickness: 6.5mm; 55-hour power reserve; 28,800 vph; screw balance with 16 weighted screws; beveled edges; polished and brushed steel parts; swan-neck fine adjustment; divided three-quarter plate with Glashütte ribbed finish, skeletonized rotor with 21K gold oscillating weight.
Functions: hours, minutes; small seconds at 9; stop seconds; Panorama date at 6; power reserve indicator at 3.
Case: steel; Ø 44mm, thickness: 12mm; water resistant to 5atm.

Dial: varnish silver-graniné; railroad chapter.
Strap: brown calfskin leather.
Suggested price: $11,800
Also available: gray varnish graniné dial; steel bracelet; black Louisiana alligator leather.

SENATOR PANORAMA DATE   REF. 100-03-32-45-04

Movement: automatic-winding 100-03 caliber; Ø 31.15mm, thickness: 5.8mm; 55-hour power reserve; 51 jewels; 28,800 vph; screw balance with 18 weighted screws; Anachron balance spring; exquisitely finished; beveled edges; polished steel parts; divided Glashütte three-quarter plate with stripe finish; skeletonized rotor with 21K gold oscillating weight; swan-neck fine adjustment.
Functions: hours, minutes, seconds; Panorama date at 4.
Case: 18K red gold; Ø 40mm, thickness: 11.52mm; antireflective sapphire crystal; water resistant to 5atm.

Dial: varnish silver graniné; black Roman numerals; blued stainless steel hands.
Strap: black Louisiana alligator leather.
Suggested price: $22,700
Also available: steel case; steel bracelet.

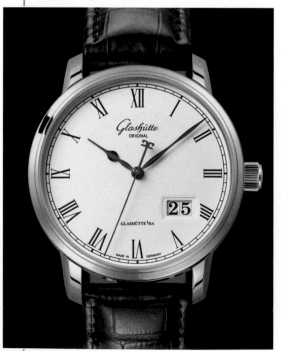

SENATOR DATE DISPLAY   REF. 1-39-58-02-02-04

Movement: automatic-winding 39-58 caliber; Ø 26.2mm, thickness: 4.3mm; 40-hour power reserve; 28,800 vph; beveled edges; polished and brushed steel parts; swan-neck fine adjustment; skeletonized rotor with 21K gold oscillating weight; Glashütte three quarter plate with stripe finish.
Functions: hours, minutes; small seconds at 9; date by hand at 3.
Case: polished stainless steel; Ø 40mm, thickness: 11.2mm; crown with double-G logo; antireflective sapphire crystal; water resistant to 5atm.
Dial: galvanized silver; surface fine matte; rhodium-plated applied hour markers; printed scales; rhodium-plated hands partially inlaid with luminous substance.
Strap: black Louisiana alligator leather.
Suggested price: $6,400
Also available: steel bracelet.

SIXTIES PANORAMA DATE   REF. 2-39-47-06-02-04

Movement: automatic-winding 39-47 caliber; Ø 30.95mm, thickness: 5.9mm; 40-hour power reserve; 39 jewels; 28,800 vph; smooth balance rim; beveled edges; polished steel parts; Glashütte three-quarter plate with stripe finish; skeletonized rotor with 21K gold oscillating weight; swan-neck fine adjustment.
Functions: hours, minutes, seconds; Panorama date at 6.
Case: steel; Ø 42mm; water resistant to 3 atm.
Dial: galvanized blue with sunburst decoration; white numerals; milled hour markers with luminous spots.
Strap: flank blue Louisiana alligator leather.
Suggested price: $9,300
Also available: 18K red-gold case; galvanized black or silver dial; black Louisiana alligator leather strap.

SEVENTIES CHRONOGRAPH PANORAMA DATE   REF. 1-37-02-03-02-30

Movement: automatic-winding 37-02 caliber; Ø 31.6mm, thickness: 8mm; 70-hour power reserve; exquisitely finished; beveled and polished edges; polished steel parts; polished and blued screws; plate with Glashütte stripe finish; skeletonized rotor with 21K gold oscillating weight; fine adjustment by adjustment screws.
Functions: hours, minutes; small seconds at 9; second stop; Panorama date at 6; flyback chronograph: 12-hour display at 12; 30-minute counter at 3, central seconds hand; power reserve indicator.
Case: stainless steel; 40x40mm, thickness: 13.5mm; antireflective sapphire crystal; water resistant to 10atm.
Dial: galvanized blue with sunburst decoration; white-gold appliqués, SuperLumiNova; white-gold Pfinodal hands with SuperLumiNova.
Strap: blue Louisiana alligator leather; stainless steel standard-fold fastener.
Suggested price: $14,900
Also available: steel bracelet; rubber black strap; galvanized silver; galvanized ruthenium.

PANOMATIC LUNA   REF. 1-90-12-01-12-04

Movement: automatic-winding 90-12 caliber; Ø 32.6mm, thickness: 7mm; 42 hour power reserve; 47 jewels; 28,800 vph; screw balance with 18 weighted gold screws; Nivarox flat balance spring; Incabloc shock protection; Glashütte three-quarter plate with stripe finish; polished steel parts; beveled edges; blued screws; hand-engraved balance bridge; off-centered, skeletonized rotor with Glashütte stripe finish and 21K gold oscillating weight; duplex swan-neck fine adjustment.
Functions: off-centered hours, minutes; small seconds; Panorama date; moonphase.
Case: stainless steel; Ø 39.4mm, thickness: 12mm; set with diamonds; antireflective sapphire crystal; water resistant to 3atm.
Dial: mother of pearl; set with diamonds.
Strap: white rubber.
Suggested price: $20,400
Also available: dark colored mother-of-pearl dial; Louisiana alligator leather strap; black rubber.

PAVONINA   REF. 1-03-01-28-05-02

Movement: quartz 03-01 caliber; Ø 18.6mm, thickness: 2.4mm; 48-month power reserve with battery at full capacity; 8 jewels; 32,768 Hz; silver-oxide cell 1.55V battery; exquisitely finished, Glashütte stripe finish; electronic fine adjustment; anti-magnetic protective cage.
Functions: hours, minutes; date at 6.
Case: 18K red gold; 31x31mm, thickness: 7.5mm; crown with one diamond (approx. 0.03 carat); domed antireflective sapphire crystal on both sides; red-gold caseback; 18K red-gold links set with 42 diamonds (0.14 carat); water resistant to 5atm.
Dial: galvanized black with guilloché; 12 diamond hour markers (approx. 0.06 carat); red-gold plated hands.
Strap: black Louisiana alligator leather; red-gold buckle.
Suggested price: $14,900
Also available: red-gold bracelet; brown patent leather strap; Roma-satin strap (purple, gray, petrol); steel and red-gold bracelet; steel bracelet; mother-of-pearl dial with guilloché; galvanized ruthenium or silver dial; brown or white-gold enamel; steel case.

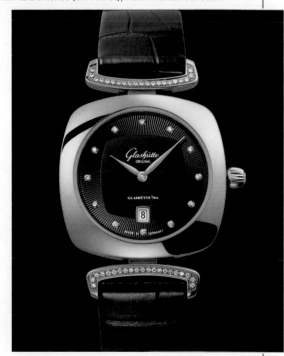

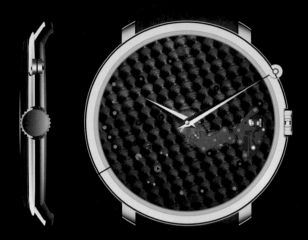

LESS IS SO MUCH MORE

Guy Ellia revisits its superb masculine classic, the Time Space, **WITH AN AVANT-GARDE CREATION THAT UNITES CASE AND CALIBER IN AN ULTRA-SLENDER EXHIBITION OF THE BRAND'S ARCHITECTURAL INGENUITY**.

Housed in a 41mm 18-karat white-gold case, the Time Space II reveals the raw purity of its movement, replacing the dial with a spectacle of mechanical finesse and minimalist elegance. A double anti-reflective sapphire crystal permits the wearer to extend his admiration of the instrument's intricacies through the timepiece's transparent caseback.

As with the Time Space, this novel interpretation is constructed around Blancpain's PGE 15 caliber, a 1.9mm-thin hand-wound movement oscillating at a frequency of 21,600 vph.

Guy Ellia, through a revolutionary assembly system, achieves a virtually level configuration of the bezel and exquisite dial-side mainplate, as the sleek edges of the glass are integrated between the movement and the frame to accentuate the refined dimensions of the 3.5mm-thin timepiece.

Stripped of its encompassing matter to the strict minimum by the innovative construction, the caliber, nearly palpable, is free to be showcased in all of its stunning nobility.

All that is left is for the time to be told with fitting precision and delicacy by two solid-gold dauphine hands that confirm the graceful elegance of a genuine horological work of art.

▶ **TIME SPACE II**
A revolutionary construction merges case and caliber in this 3.5mm-thin demonstration of courageous innovation and watchmaking savoir-faire.

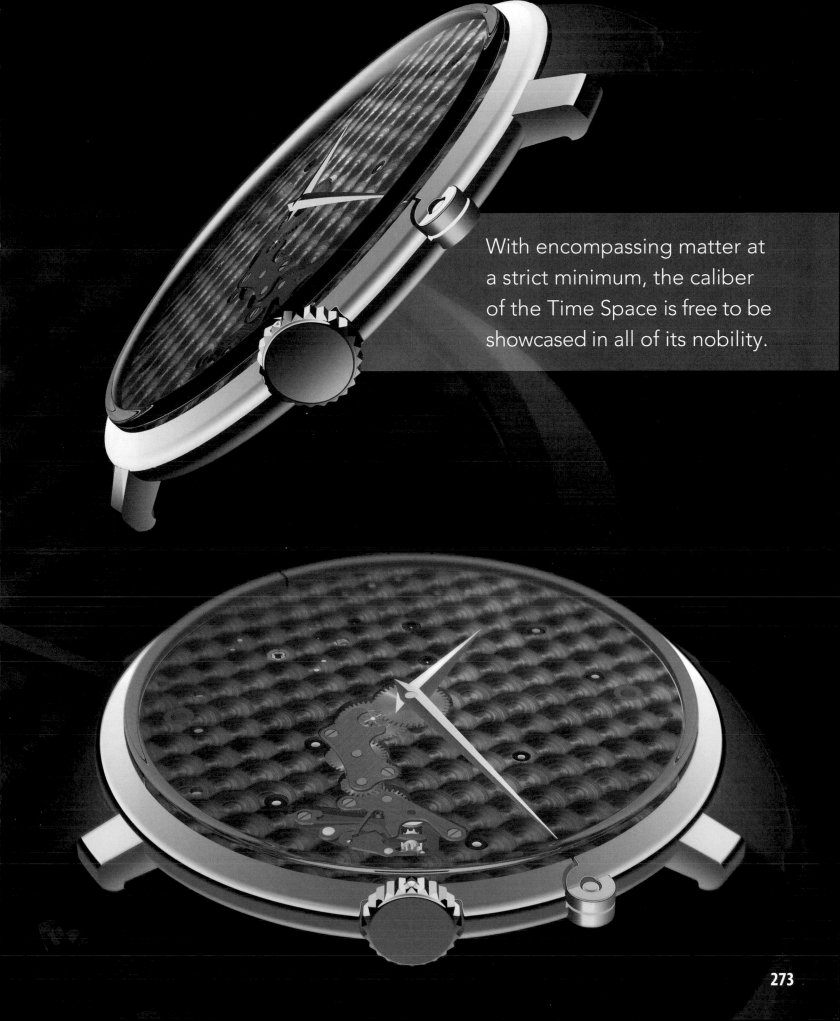

With encompassing matter at a strict minimum, the caliber of the Time Space is free to be showcased in all of its nobility.

GUY ELLIA

CIRCLE "LA PETITE"

Movement: quartz; Frédéric Piguet caliber PGE 820; Ø 18.8mm, thickness: 1.95mm.
Functions: hours, minutes.
Case: polished 18K white gold (43.7g); Ø 45mm, thickness: 6mm; bezel set with 105 diamonds (0.71 carat); crown set with one diamond (Ø 2.8mm); sapphire glass with thermal counter-shock marking; caseback set with one diamond on the "I" of ELLIA (Ø 0.95mm); water resistant to 3atm.
Dial: mirror white; hour markers set with 192 brilliant-cut diamonds (0.58 carat); 18K white-gold dauphine-shaped hands.

Bracelet: solid 18K white gold (113.3g).
Also available: case: pink gold, yellow gold; dial: shiny black, opal or navy, mirror or matte gold white, pink and yellow; markers: mirror-polished gold, diamonds set; strap: alligator leather with 18K solid gold pin buckle set with one diamond (Ø 0.9mm).

CIRCLE "LA PETITE"

Movement: quartz; Frédéric Piguet caliber PGE 820; Ø 18.8mm, thickness: 1.95mm.
Functions: hours, minutes.
Case: polished 18K pink gold (41g); Ø 45mm, thickness: 6mm; bezel set with 105 diamonds (0.71 carat); crown set with one diamond (Ø 2.8mm); sapphire glass with thermal counter-shock marking; caseback set with one diamond on the "I" of ELLIA (Ø 0.95mm); water resistant to 3atm.
Dial: black; pink-gold mirror-polished hour markers; 18K pink-gold dauphine-shaped hands.

Bracelet: solid 18K pink gold (106.6g).
Also available: case: pink gold, yellow gold; white gold, dial: opal, navy, matte gold, full set; markers: mirror-polished gold, diamonds set; strap: alligator leather with 18K solid gold pin buckle set with one diamond (Ø 0.9mm).

CIRCLE

Movement: quartz; Frédéric Piguet caliber PGE 820; Ø 18.8mm, thickness: 1.95mm.
Functions: hours, minutes.
Case: polished 18K pink gold (80.13g); Ø 52mm, thickness: 7mm; bezel set with 124 diamonds (Ø 1.15mm); crown set with one diamond (Ø 2.8mm); sapphire glass with thermal counter-shock marking; mirror-polished caseback set with one diamond on the "I" of ELLIA (Ø 0.95mm); water resistant to 3atm.
Dial: opal; pink-gold hour markers; 18K pink-gold dauphine-shaped hands.
Strap: alligator leather; solid 18K pink-gold pin buckle set with 86 diamonds (0.38 carat); pin set with one diamond (Ø 0.9mm).

Also available: case: black gold, yellow gold, white gold; dial: opal, mirror or matte gold, white, pink, yellow, full set; markers: diamond set, full set.

CIRCLE

Movement: quartz; Frédéric Piguet caliber PGE 820; Ø 18.8mm, thickness: 1.95mm.
Functions: hours, minutes.
Case: matte 18K black gold (83.86g); Ø 52mm, thickness: 7mm; bezel set with 124 diamonds (Ø 1.15mm); crown set with one diamond (Ø 2.8mm); sapphire glass with thermal counter-shock marking; caseback set with one diamond on the "I" of ELLIA (Ø 0.95mm); water resistant to 3atm.
Dial: matte black; hour markers set with 168 brilliant-cut diamonds (1 carat); 18K white-gold dauphine-shaped hands.

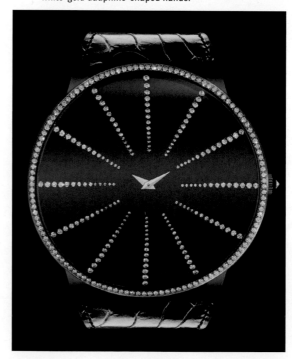

Strap: alligator leather; solid 18K black-gold pin buckle set with 86 diamonds (0.38 carat); pin set with one diamond (Ø 0.9mm).
Also available: case: pink gold, yellow gold, white gold; dial: opal, mirror or matte gold, black, white, pink, yellow, full set; markers: gold, full set.

ELYPSE

Movement: quartz; Frédéric Piguet caliber PGE 820; Ø 18.8mm, thickness: 1.95mm.
Functions: hours, minutes.
Case: 18K white gold (53.38g); 52x35mm, thickness: 5.6mm; set with 80 diamonds; crown set with one diamond (Ø 2.3mm); sapphire glass with thermal counter-shock marking; mirror-polished caseback set with one diamond on the "I" of ELLIA (Ø 0.95mm) and deep mechanical engraving; water resistant to 3atm.
Dial: 18K solid gold black painted; matte-gold Roman numerals; 18K white-gold dauphine-shaped hands.
Strap: black alligator leather; 18K white-gold pin buckle set with nine diamonds (Ø 1.5mm); pin set with one diamond (Ø 0.9mm).
Also available: case: pink and yellow gold; dial: Roman numeral versions: matte black, matte chocolate, brilliant gold, matte khaki, brilliant Burgundy, matte Burgundy, brilliant blue, matte orange; matte lilac, pink salmon, matte beige; dial: mirror or polished gold (white, pink and yellow), brilliant black, black matte, pearly white, light brown matte, navy pearly;, light blue matte, opale (only for yellow gold cases).

ELYPSE

Movement: quartz; Frédéric Piguet caliber PGE 820; Ø 18.8mm, thickness: 1.95mm.
Functions: hours, minutes.
Case: 18K white gold (53.38g); 52x35mm, thickness: 5.6mm; bezel set with 80 diamonds; crown set with one diamond (Ø 2.3mm); sapphire glass with thermal counter-shock marking; mirror-polished caseback set with one diamond on the "I" of ELLIA (Ø 0.9mm) and deep mechanical engraving; water resistant to 3atm.
Dial: 18K pearly navy white gold; brilliant blue painted Roman numerals; 18K white-gold dauphine-shaped hands.
Strap: blue alligator leather; 18K white-gold buckle set with nine diamonds (Ø 1.5mm); pin set with one diamond (Ø 0.9mm).
Also available: case: pink and yellow gold; dial: Roman numeral versions: matte black, matte chocolate, brilliant gold, matte khaki, brilliant Burgundy, matte Burgundy, matte orange, matte lilac, pink salmon, matte beige, dial: mirror or polished gold (white, pink and yellow); brilliant black, black matte, light brown matte, navy pearly, light blue matte; opale (only for yellow gold cases).

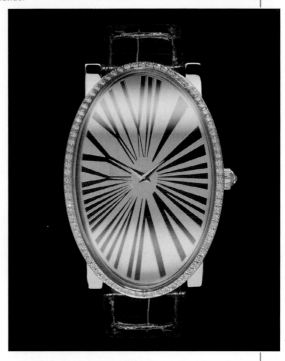

QUEEN

Movement: quartz; Frédéric Piguet caliber PGE 820; Ø 18.8mm, thickness: 1.95mm.
Functions: hours, minutes.
Case: 18K white gold (64.7g); 52x38.5mm, thickness: 7.2mm; bezel set with 96 diamonds (0.89 carat); crown set with one diamond (Ø 2.3mm); sapphire glass with thermal counter-shock marking; mirror-polished caseback set with one diamond on the "I" of ELLIA (Ø 0.95mm) and deep mechanical engraving; water resistant to 3atm.
Dial: navy mother-of-pearl; white-gold Roman numerals.
Strap: alligator leather; solid 18K white-gold pin buckle (3.98g) set with 86 diamonds (0.38 carat).
Also available: case: pink gold, yellow gold; dial: mirror or matte gold (white, pink and yellow), mother-of-pearl: white, ivory, brown or black; full set; markers: gold Roman numerals or diamonds set.

QUEEN

Movement: quartz; Frédéric Piguet caliber PGE 820; Ø 18.8mm, thickness: 1.95mm.
Functions: hours, minutes.
Case: 18K pink gold (62.12g); 52x38.5mm, thickness: 7.2mm; fully set with 409 diamonds (3.05 carats); crown set with one diamond (Ø 2.3mm); sapphire glass with thermal counter-shock marking; mirror-polished caseback set with one diamond on the "I" of ELLIA (Ø 0.95mm) and deep mechanical engraving; water resistant to 3atm.
Dial: fully set with 450 diamonds (2.19 carats); pink-gold Roman numerals.
Strap: alligator leather; solid 18K pink-gold buckle and pin (3.67g) set with 86 diamonds (0.38 carat).
Also available: case: white gold, yellow gold; dial: mirror or matte gold (white, pink, yellow), mother-of-pearl: white, ivory, navy, brown, black; markers: gold Roman numerals or diamonds set.

DOUZE

Movement: quartz; Frédéric Piguet caliber PGE 820; Ø 18.8mm, thickness: 1.95mm.
Functions: hours, minutes.
Case: 18K pink gold (74.44g); 52.5x35.5mm, thickness: 5.8mm; bezel set with 82 diamonds (Ø 2.5mm); crown set with one diamond (Ø 2.3mm); sapphire glass with thermal counter-shock marking; mirror-polished caseback set with one diamond on the "I" of ELLIA (Ø 0.95mm) and deep mechanical engraving; water resistant to 3atm.
Strap: navy alligator leather; 18K pink-gold pin buckle set with 40 diamonds (Ø 1.5mm); pin set with one diamond (Ø 0.9mm).

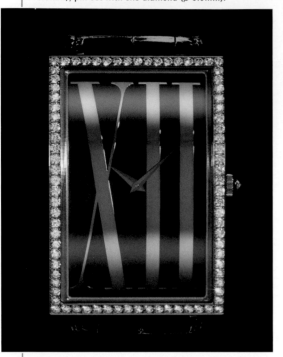

Also available: case and pin buckle: yellow gold, white gold; dial: opal, gray, black, chocolate, burgundy; markers: mirror-polished gold (yellow, white).

DOUZE

Movement: quartz; Frédéric Piguet caliber PGE 820; Ø 18.8mm, thickness: 1.95mm.
Functions: hours, minutes.
Case: 18K pink gold (74.44g); 52.5x35.5mm, thickness: 5.8mm; bezel set with 82 diamonds (Ø 2.5mm); crown set with one diamond (Ø 2.3mm); sapphire glass with thermal counter-shock marking; mirror-polished caseback set with one diamond on the "I" of ELLIA (Ø 0.95mm) and deep mechanical engraving; water resistant to 3atm.
Strap: light brown alligator leather; 18K pink-gold pin buckle set with 40 diamonds (Ø 1.5mm); pin set with one diamond (Ø 0.9mm).

Also available: case and pin buckle: yellow gold, white gold; dial: navy, gray, black, chocolate, burgundy; markers: mirror-polished gold (yellow, white).

CONVEX

Movement: quartz; Frédéric Piguet caliber PGE 820; Ø 18.8mm, thickness: 1.95mm.
Functions: hours, minutes.
Case: 18K white gold (59.17g); 41x41mm, thickness: 7.1mm; bezel set with 100 diamonds (Ø 1.5mm); crown set with one diamond (Ø 2.3mm); sapphire glass with thermal counter-shock marking; mirror-polished caseback set with one diamond on the "I" of ELLIA (Ø 0.95mm) and deep mechanical engraving; water resistant to 3atm.
Dial: solid 18K white gold (25.65g); fully set with 578 diamonds (2.28 carats); four gold Arabic numerals; 18K white-gold dauphine-shaped hands.

Strap: black alligator leather; 18K white-gold pin buckle set with 40 diamonds (Ø 1.5mm); pin set with one diamond (Ø 0.9mm).
Also available: case: yellow gold, pink gold; dial: solid 18K gold (white, yellow, pink), mother-of-pearl: navy, jeans, pink beige); markers: diamond set with 204 diamonds (0.79 carat), gold: (white, yellow, pink), outlined.

CONVEX

Movement: quartz; Frédéric Piguet caliber PGE 820; Ø 18.8mm, thickness: 1.95mm.
Functions: hours, minutes.
Case: 18K pink gold (56.61g); 41x41mm, thickness: 7.1mm; bezel set with 100 diamonds (Ø 1.5mm); crown set with one diamond (Ø 2.3mm); sapphire glass with thermal counter-shock marking; mirror-polished caseback set with one diamond on the "I" of ELLIA (Ø 0.95mm) and deep mechanical engraving; water resistant to 3atm.
Dial: navy mother-of-pearl with four Arabic numerals; 18K gold dauphine-shaped hands.

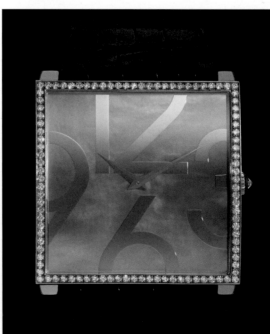

Strap: dark blue alligator leather; 18K pink-gold pin buckle set with 40 diamonds (Ø 1.5mm); pin set with one diamond (Ø 0.9mm).
Also available: case: yellow gold, white gold; dial: fully set 18K gold (white, yellow, pink), mother-of-pearl: navy, jeans, pink beige; markers: diamond set with 204 diamonds (0.79 carat), gold: (white, yellow, pink), outlined.

TIME SPACE

Movement: manual-winding Frédéric Piguet caliber PGE 15; Ø 35.64mm, thickness: 1.9mm; 43-hour power reserve; 20 jewels; 21,600 vph; five position adjustment; Côtes de Genève finished bridges with black PVD treatment; "GE" engraved on stippled plate with black PVD treatment.
Functions: hours, minutes.
Case: 18K full-set black gold (30.64g); Ø 46.8mm, thickness: 4.9mm; bezel set with 234 diamonds (1.83 carats); crown set with one diamond (Ø 1.3mm); bottom plate set with 366 diamonds (1.03 carats); sapphire glass with antireflective coating; water resistant to 3atm.
Strap: black alligator leather; 18K black-gold pin buckle (3.70g) set with 31 diamonds (0.41 carats).
Also available: white gold; set-bezel white gold; full-set white gold; pink gold; set-bezel pink gold; full-set pink gold; black gold; set-bezel black gold.

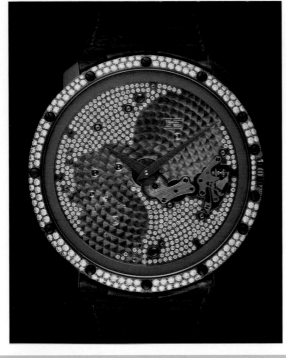

TIME SPACE

Movement: manual-winding Frédéric Piguet caliber PGE 15; Ø 35.64mm, thickness: 1.9mm; 43-hour power reserve; 20 jewels; 21,600 vph; five position adjustment; Côtes de Genève finished bridges with black PVD treatment; "GE" engraved on stippled plate with black PVD treatment.
Functions: hours, minutes.
Case: 18K pink gold (31.42g); Ø 46.8mm, thickness: 4.9mm; crown set with one diamond (Ø 1.3mm); sapphire glass with antireflective coating; water resistant to 3atm.
Strap: 18K brown alligator leather; 18K pink-gold pin buckle (4.28g).
Also available: white gold; set-bezel white gold; full-set white gold; set-bezel pink gold; full-set pink gold; black gold; set-bezel black gold; full-set black gold.

TIME SPACE QUANTIEME PERPETUEL

Movement: manual-winding Frédéric Piguet PGE 5615 D caliber; Ø 35.64mm, thickness: 4.7mm; 43-hour power reserve; 20 jewels; 21,600 vph; five-position adjustment; Côtes de Genève-finished bridges with black PVD treatment; GUY ELLIA logo engraved on stippled plate with black PVD treatment; watch box with an integrated specific automatic winder.
Functions: hours, minutes; perpetual calendar: day, date, month, leap-year cycle; moonphase.
Case: 18K black gold (32.61g); Ø 46.8mm, thickness: 7.75mm; crown set with one diamond (Ø 1.3mm); sapphire middle ring; sapphire glass with antireflective coating; water resistant to 3atm.
Strap: black alligator leather; 18K black-gold pin buckle (4.82g).
Also available: black-gold bezel set, full-set black gold; white gold, white-gold bezel set, full-set white gold; pink gold, pink-gold bezel set, full-set pink gold.

TIME SPACE QUANTIEME PERPETUEL

Movement: manual-winding Frédéric Piguet caliber PGE 15; Ø 35.64mm, thickness: 4.7mm; 43-hour power reserve; 20 jewels; 21,600 vph; five position adjustment; Côtes de Genève finished bridges with black PVD treatment; "GE" engraved on stippled plate with black PVD treatment; watch box with an integrated specific automatic winder.
Functions: hours, minutes; perpetual calendar: day, date, month, leap-year cycle; moonphase.
Case: 18K white gold (32.61g); Ø 46.8mm, thickness: 4.7mm; crown set with one diamond (Ø 1.3mm); sapphire middle ring; sapphire glass with antireflective coating; water resistant to 3atm.
Strap: black alligator leather; 18K white-gold pin buckle (4.82g).
Also available: set-bezel white gold; full-set white gold; pink gold; set-bezel pink gold; full-set pink gold; black gold; set-bezel black gold; full-set black gold.

JUMBO CHRONO

Movement: automatic-winding Frédéric Piguet caliber PGE 1185; Ø 26.2mm, thickness: 5.5mm; 45-hour power reserve; chronograph with column wheel; Côtes de Genève finished bridges with rhodium plating; "GUY ELLIA" engraved on rotor with rhodium plating.
Functions: hours, minutes at 12; small seconds at 6; date at 2; column-wheel chronograph: 12-hour counter at 8, 30-minute counter at 4, central sweep seconds hand.
Case: 18K pink gold (85.75g); Ø 50mm, thickness: 11.5mm; sapphire glass with thermal antireflective coating; water resistant to 3atm.

Strap: brown alligator leather; 18K pink-gold folding buckle (11.90g).
Also available: black gold; set black-gold bezel; full-set black gold; white gold; set white-gold bezel; full-set white gold; set pink-gold bezel; full-set pink gold.

JUMBO CHRONO

Movement: automatic-winding Frédéric Piguet caliber PGE 1185; Ø 26.2mm, thickness: 5.5mm; 45-hour power reserve; chronograph with column wheel; Côtes de Genève finished bridges with rhodium plating; "GUY ELLIA" engraved on rotor with rhodium plating.
Functions: hours, minutes at 12; small seconds at 6; date at 2; column-wheel chronograph: 12-hour counter at 8, 30-minute counter at 4, central sweep seconds hand.
Case: 18K solid matte white gold (90.14g); Ø 50mm, thickness: 11.5mm, bezel full set with 323 diamonds (7.93 carats); sapphire glass with antireflective coating; water resistant to 3atm.

Strap: gray alligator leather; 18K white-gold folding buckle (12.53g); set with 35 diamonds (0.35 carat).
Also available: black gold; set black-gold bezel; full-set black gold; white gold; set white-gold bezel; pink gold; set pink-gold bezel; full-set pink gold.

JUMBO HEURE UNIVERSELLE

Movement: automatic-winding caliber PGE 1150; Ø 36.2mm, thickness: 6.24mm; 72-hour power reserve; 37 jewels; five position adjustment; blue sapphire disc; Côtes de Genève-finished bridges with rhodium plating; "GUY ELLIA" engraved on rotor with rhodium plating.
Functions: hours, minutes; 24-hour time zone indicator; large date; day/night indicator.
Case: 18K gray gold (82.9g); Ø 50mm, thickness: 11mm; sapphire glass with antireflective coating; openwork caseback with sapphire crystal; water resistant to 3atm.
Dial:

Strap: gray alligator leather; 18K gray-gold folding buckle (12.53g).
Also available: white gold; black gold.

JUMBO HEURE UNIVERSELLE

Movement: automatic-winding Frédéric Piguet caliber PGE 1150; Ø 36.2mm, thickness: 6.24mm; 72-hour power reserve; 37 jewels; five position adjustment; blue sapphire disc; Côtes de Genève-finished bridges with rhodium plating; "GUY ELLIA" engraved on rotor with rhodium plating.
Functions: hours, minutes; 24-hour time zone indicator; large date; day/night indicator.
Case: 18K black gold (82.9g); Ø 50mm, thickness: 11mm; sapphire glass with antireflective coating; openwork caseback with sapphire glass; water resistant to 3atm.
Strap: black alligator leather; 18K black-gold folding buckle (12.53g).

Also available: white gold; pink gold.

TOURBILLON ZEPHYR

Movement: manual-winding Christophe Claret caliber GES 97; 37x37mm, thickness: 6.21mm; 110-hour power reserve; 233 components; 17 jewels; 21,600 vph; winding ring set with 36 baguette-cut diamonds (1.04 carats) or engine turning; mysterious winding tourbillon; entirely hand-chamfered cage; bottom plate and bridges in blue sapphire; five-position adjustment.
Functions: hours, minutes; tourbillon.
Case: white sapphire case with platinum sides (54.9g); 54x45.3mm, thickness: 15.4mm; crown set with one diamond (Ø 1mm); water resistant to 3atm.
Strap: alligator leather; solid 18K white-gold folding buckle (15.64g).
Note: limited edition of 12 number pieces.
Also available: pink gpld case; bottom plate and bridges sapphire: white, smokey.

REPETITION MINUTE ZEPHYR

Movement: manual-winding Christophe Claret GEC 88 caliber; 41.2x38.2mm, thickness: 9.41mm; 48-hour power reserve; 720 components; 72 jewels; 18,000 vph; flat balance-spring; gear wheels with different platings; five-position adjustment.
Functions: hours, minutes; power reserve indicator; minute repeater; five time zones with day/night indicators.
Case: sapphire crystal block and titanium; 53.6x43.7mm, thickness: 14.8mm; sapphire and titanium crown set with a diamond (Ø 2.2mm); water resistant to 3atm.
Strap: black rubber with titanium and white gold folding buckle (17.27g).
Note: limited edition of 20 numbered pieces.
Also available: pink gold and white gold; alligator leather strap.

TOURBILLON MAGISTERE

Movement: manual-winding Christophe Claret caliber PGE 97; 37.4x29.9mm, thickness: 5.4mm; 110-hour power reserve; 20 jewels; 21,600 vph; flat balance-spring; mysterious winding; skeletonized barrel and ratchet wheel; entirely hand-chamfered cage; white-gold bottom plate and bridges.
Functions: hours, minutes; tourbillon.
Case: pink gold (73.09g); 43.5x36mm, thickness: 10.9mm; sapphire glass with anti-reflective coating; water resistant to 3atm.
Strap: brown alligator leather; solid 18K pink-gold folding buckle (15g).
Also available: white gold; platinum; bezel set with 52 baguette diamonds (2.15 carats); full set with 172 baguette diamonds (19.56 carats); full set with 535 brilliants (8.25 carats).

TOURBILLON MAGISTERE II

Movement: manual-winding Christophe Claret caliber MGE 97; 38.4x30.9mm, thickness: 5.71mm; 90-hour power reserve; 266 components; 33 jewels; 21,600 vph; flat balance-spring; mysterious winding; skeletonized ratchet and wheels with curved arms and wolf-teeth; entirely hand-chamfered cage; 18K white-gold tourbillon and barrel bridges.
Functions: hours, minutes; tourbillon.
Case: white gold (125g); 44x36.7mm, thickness: 15mm; antireflective sapphire glass; transparent caseback; water resistant to 3atm.
Strap: black alligator leather; solid 18K white-gold folding buckle (18.77g).
Note: limited edition of 12 numbered pieces.
Also available: 5N red gold.

HARRY WINSTON

DAZZLING LEGACY

Honoring its founder's devotion to the world's most magnificent diamonds, Harry Winston dazzles watchmaking enthusiasts with **INVENTIVE CONCEPTS, SHIMMERING STONES AND EXQUISITE CRAFTSMANSHIP**.

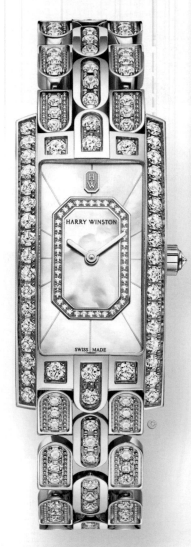

The very name "Harry Winston" is synonymous with imposing gemstones and innovative jewelry craftsmanship. How fitting, then, that the house has created a discreet timepiece tucked away within an attention-getting diamond-set jewel. With a small moveable panel that conceals or reveal the watch face at will, the cunning design lends itself to admiration as a sautoir necklace, brooch or ribbon-mounted wristwatch. Alluding to Mr. Winston's favorite shape, the Emerald Signature places an emerald-cut diamond at the very center of its piece, limned by expanding, concentric rows of brilliant-cut diamonds—343 in all, with a total carat weight of approximately 1.96 carats. A white mother-of-pearl dial provides a softly shimmering backdrop for the time indication.

The classic emerald shape also guides the aesthetic of the Avenue C Emerald, with an eight-angled chapter ring set with 44 diamonds. Within the border, a mother-of-pearl backdrop lends a soft luster to the diamonds, fulfilling the jeweler's objective to maximize the brilliance of each gemstone. Around the chapter ring is another mother-of-pearl backdrop, with engraved indexes to subtly demarcate the hours and reflect the 43 diamonds set into the 19x39.5mm white-gold case. Expressing Mr. Winston's belief that there was "no limit to beauty," the gems spill over to adorn each individual link of the white-gold bracelet for a total of 225 brilliant-cut diamonds on this exquisite High Jewelry timepiece.

▲ EMERALD SIGNATURE
Mixing eye-catching gems with a secret time indication, the Emerald Signature interprets the eponymous cut with brilliants radiating out from a 0.65-carat central diamond.

◄ AVENUE C EMERALD
Harry Winston's preferred diamond shape, the emerald cut, creates a chapter ring on the Avenue C Emerald that divides a lustrous mother-of-pearl dial.

The cascading arrangement of diamonds enlivens the Midnight Diamond Drops' dark blue hue with an air of weightless motion.

A more colorful but equally sophisticated model, Midnight Diamond Drops 39mm, exhibits the watchmaker's finesse and creativity with near-invisible diamond settings that ensure an undistracted admiration of the precious stones, arranged in a snow setting. The cascading arrangement of 214 brilliant-cut gems enlivens the dial's satin-finished dark blue hue with an air of weightless motion. A moonphase indication near the center of the dial sets a nighttime scene to match the elegant dial and alligator strap. The 91 brilliant-cut diamonds that adorn the white-gold case delineate where mundane reality ends and delicious fantasy begins.

The newest member of the house's Project Z series, the revolutionary Project Z8 combines avant-garde architecture with the pioneering use of Zalium™ in the 44mm case. The zirconium-based alloy, lighter and harder than titanium, enhances the Project Z8's powerful demeanor with a matte gunmetal hue. Equally imaginative, the dial's three-dimensional architecture serves as a captivating stage for the self-winding HW2502 caliber. The 281-component mechanical movement complements its off-centered, transparent home-time subdial at 1 o'clock with a retrograde hours indicator on the left of the expressive dial, representing the second time zone. The retrograde module is ingeniously fitted with an additional clutch system that permits adjustment in both directions. A shuriken, the signature of the collection, confirms the movement's running operation just below the main time display. A sapphire crystal caseback grants the wearer an exhibition of the caliber's exquisite workmanship and Côtes de Genève decoration available in a limited edition of 300 pieces..

▲ MIDNIGHT DIAMOND DROPS 39MM

This vibrant 18-karat white-gold wristwatch displays a lustrous moonphase upon a starry-sky dial set with 214 brilliant-cut diamonds.

▶ PROJECT Z8

This timepiece's innovative use of Zalium™, an alloy lighter and harder than titanium, initiates a narrative of ultra-modern masculinity epitomized by a three-dimensional dial that throws convention to the wind.

HARRY WINSTON

HARRY WINSTON MIDNIGHT MOON PHASE AUTOMATIC 42MM REF. MIDAMP42RR002

Movement: automatic-winding; 65-hour power reserve; 28 jewels; 28,800 vph.
Functions: hours, minutes; moonphase; retrograde date.
Case: 18K rose gold; Ø 42mm; sapphire crystal caseback; water resistant to 3atm.
Dial: black; broad snailed-finish base; sunray satin-brushed and fine snailed-finish chapter rings; slate texture on the moon phase disc, one brilliant-cut diamond at 6.
Strap: black hand-sewn alligator leather; 18K rose-gold ardillon buckle.

HARRY WINSTON MIDNIGHT RETROGRADE SECOND AUTOMATIC 42MM REF. MIDARS42WW001

Movement: automatic-winding; 72-hour power reserve; 34 jewels; 28,800 vph.
Functions: hours, minutes; retrograde seconds at 6.
Case: 18K white gold; Ø 42mm; sapphire crystal caseback; water resistant to 3atm.
Dial: silver toned; sunray satin-brushed finish.
Strap: black hand-sewn alligator leather; 18K white-gold ardillon buckle.

HARRY WINSTON MIDNIGHT MONOCHROME AUTOMATIC REF. MIDAHD42WW003

Movement: automatic-winding; 45-hour power reserve; 27 jewels; 28,800 vph.
Functions: hours, minutes; date at 6.
Case: 18K white gold; Ø 42mm; sapphire crystal caseback; water resistant to 3atm.
Dial: metallic; slate impression.
Strap: black hand-sewn alligator leather; 18K white-gold ardillon buckle.

HARRY WINSTON MIDNIGHT SKELETON REF. MIDAHM42RR001

Movement: automatic-winding; 42-hour power reserve; 29 jewels; 21,600 vph.
Functions: hours, minutes.
Case: 18K rose gold; Ø 42mm; sapphire crystal caseback; water resistant to 3atm.
Dial: skeletonized; circular satin-brushed from center of rotor; engravings; rhodium-plated.
Strap: brown hand-sewn alligator leather; 18K rose-gold ardillon buckle.

HARRY WINSTON MIDNIGHT MOON PHASE 39MM   REF. MIDQHM39RR002

Movement: quartz.
Functions: hours, minutes; date; moonphase.
Case: 18K rose gold; Ø 39mm; set with 91 brilliant-cut diamonds (0.98 carat); water resistant to 3atm.
Dial: champagne rose tone; stamped wave pattern; applied moonphase and date aperture; set with 70 brilliant-cut diamonds including hour markers at 3 and 9 set with four brilliant-cut diamonds and hour markers at 6 set with three brilliant-cut diamonds.
Strap: taupe hand-sewn alligator leather; 18K rose-gold ardillon buckle.

HARRY WINSTON MIDNIGHT DIAMOND SECOND 39MM   REF. MIDASS39RR001

Movement: automatic winding; 68-hour power reserve; 30 jewels; 28,800 vph.
Functions: hours, minutes; small seconds at 6.
Case: 18K rose gold; Ø 39mm; set with 91 brilliant-cut diamonds (0.98 carats); sapphire crystal caseback; water resistant to 3atm.
Dial: champagne rose tone; sunray satin-brushed finish; flower-motif seconds indicator; hour markers set with nine brilliant-cut diamonds; seconds set with three brilliant-cut diamonds.
Strap: taupe hand-sewn alligator leather; 18K rose-gold ardillon buckle.

HARRY WINSTON MIDNIGHT DIAMOND DROPS 39MM   REF. MIDQMP39WW004

Movement: quartz.
Functions: hours, minutes; moonphase; date at 6.
Case: 18K white gold; Ø 39mm; set with 91 brilliant-cut diamonds (0.98 carats); water resistant to 3atm.
Dial: blue; sunray satin-brushed finish; snow-set with 211 brilliant-cut diamonds (0.54 carat); applied hour marker at 9 set with three brilliant-cut diamonds.
Strap: navy blue hand-sewn alligator leather; 18K white-gold ardillon buckle.

HARRY WINSTON MIDNIGHT MONOCHROME 32MM   REF. MIDQHM32RR004

Movement: quartz.
Functions: hours, minutes.
Case: 18K rose gold; Ø 32mm; set with 76 brilliant-cut diamonds (0.73 carat); water resistant to 3atm.
Dial: silver toned white metallic; slate impression; hour markers at 12, 3, 6 and 9 set with three brilliant-cut diamonds each.
Strap: satin; 18K rose-gold ardillon buckle.

HARRY WINSTON

PREMIER CHRONOGRAPH 40MM   REF. PRNQCH40RR002

Movement: quartz.
Functions: hours, minutes; small seconds and date at 6; chronograph: 12-hour counter at 2, 30-minute counter at 10, central chronograph seconds hand.
Case: 18K rose gold; Ø 40mm; set with 59 brilliant-cut diamonds (2.93 carats) including one diamond on crown and four diamonds on the strap integration parts; water resistant to 3atm.
Dial: Tahitian mother-of-pearl; applied set counter detours; numeral hour markers; date aperture; set with total of 135 brilliant-cut diamonds.

Strap: taupe alligator leather; 18K rose-gold set ardillon buckle.

PREMIER PRECIOUS MARQUETRY 36MM   REF. PRNQHM36WW015

Movement: quartz.
Functions: hours, minutes.
Case: 18K white gold; Ø 36mm; set with 67 brilliant-cut diamonds (1.4 carats), including one diamond on crown and four diamonds on strap integration parts, water resistant to 3atm.
Dial: white gold with white matte mother-of-pearl base; set with 54 diamonds (0.28 carat) and eleven blue pear-shaped sapphires cabochons (0.95 carat); eight white mother-of-pearl cabochons; blue gradation of enamel dusted with gold flecks; freshwater mother-of-pearl engraved; white mother-of-pearl engraved; pearled mother-of-pearl; pink mother-of-pearl engraved.
Strap: black hand-sewn alligator leather; 18K white-gold set ardillon buckle.

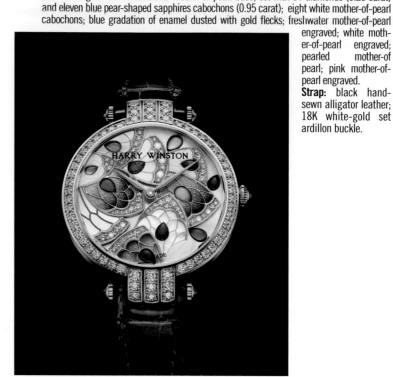

PREMIER CHRONOGRAPH 40MM   REF. PRNQCH40WW001

Movement: quartz.
Functions: hours, minutes; small seconds and date at 6; chronograph: 12-hour counter at 2, 30-minute counter at 10, central chronograph seconds hand.
Case: 18K white gold; Ø 40mm; set with 59 brilliant cut-diamonds (2.93 carats) including one diamond on crown and four diamonds on strap integration parts; water resistant to 3atm.
Dial: white pearled mother-of-pearl with blue varnish; applied set counter detours; numeral hour markers; date aperture; set with total of 135 brilliant-cut diamonds.

Strap: alligator leather; 18K white-gold set ardillon buckle.

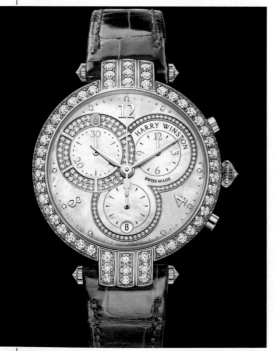

PREMIER LADIES 36MM AUTOMATIC   REF. PRNAHM36WW002

Movement: automatic-winding; 42-hour power reserve; 29 jewels; 21,600 vph.
Functions: hours, minutes.
Case: 18K white gold; Ø 36mm; set with 67 brilliant-cut diamonds (1.4 carats), including one diamond on the crown and four diamonds on strap integration parts; water resistant to 3atm.
Dial: beaded white mother-of-pearl, mosaic matte and shiny décor; hour markers set with 12 brilliant-cut diamonds.
Strap: 18K white gold with folding clasp.

SUBLIME TIMEPIECE — REF. HJTQHM25WW001

Movement: quartz.
Functions: hours, minutes.
Case: 18K white gold; 20.2x36.5mm; set with 178 brilliant cut diamonds (1.75 carats), 2 baguette-cut diamonds and 2 marquise-cut diamonds; water resistant to 3atm.
Dial: gray mother-of-pearl.
Strap: satin; 18K white gold; ardillon buckle set.

EMERALD SIGNATURE — REF. HJTQHM24WW005

Movement: quartz.
Functions: hours, minutes.
Case: 18K white gold; 24x27mm; secret watch; set with 1 emerald-cut diamond (0.65 carat) and 302 brilliant-cut diamonds (1.71 carats); water resistant to 3atm.
Dial: white mother-of-pearl.
Strap: satin; 18K white gold; ardillon buckle set.
Chain: 18K white gold; 650 mm length.
Note: Emerald Signature can be worn as a pendant, a wristwatch or a brooch.

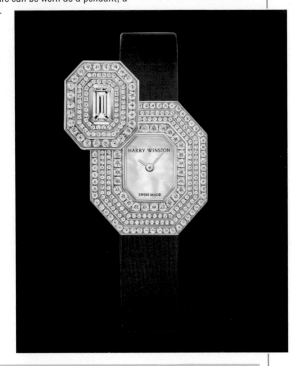

PREMIER LADIES WITH BAGUETTE-CUT DIAMONDS — REF. PRNQHM39WW006

Movement: quartz.
Functions: hours, minutes.
Case: 18K white gold; Ø 39mm; set with 130 baguette-cut diamonds (5.89 carats); water resistant to 3atm.
Dial: fully set with 156 baguette-cut diamonds (9.52 carats).
Bracelet: 18K white gold; set with 254 baguette-cut diamonds (16.1 carats).

PREMIER LADIES WITH BRILLIANT-CUT DIAMONDS — REF. PRNQHM39WW004

Movement: quartz.
Functions: hours, minutes.
Case: 18K white gold; Ø 39mm; set with 187 brilliant-cut diamonds (5.57 carats); water resistant to 3atm.
Dial: fully set with 280 brilliant-cut diamonds (5.6 carats).
Bracelet: 18K white gold; set with 376 brilliant-cut diamonds (5.65 carats).

HISTOIRE DE TOURBILLON 4 — REF. HCOMTT47WZ001

Movement: manual-winding; 50-hour power reserve; 59 jewels; 345 components; 21,600 vph.
Functions: hours, minutes; 300 seconds indication on the tourbillon; tri-axial tourbillon; power reserve indicator.
Case: 18K white gold; Ø 47mm; Zalium™ with DLC-treated caseband, arches, lugs and tourbillon bezel; sapphire crystal caseback; water resistant to 3atm.
Dial: three dimensional; black gold finish with apertures on movement; black galvanic flange and appliqués; curved sapphire crystal on the tourbillon.
Strap: black hand-sewn alligator leather; 18K white-gold double-ardillon buckle.
Note: limited edition of 20 pieces.

OCEAN TOURBILLON JUMPING HOUR — REF. OCEMTJ45WW001

Movement: manual-winding; 110-hour power reserve; 41 jewels; 28,800 vph.
Functions: jumping hour; minutes; power indicator (shuriken) on the tourbillon; power reserve indicator on caseback.
Case: 18K white gold; Ø 45.6mm; sapphire crystal caseback; water resistant to 5atm.
Dial: black sapphire delimited by the metallization of the engraved dial train and markers; rhodium-plated hour aperture; sandblasted emerald-shaped HW logo.
Strap: black hand-sewn alligator leather; 18K white-gold ardillon buckle.
Note: limited edition of 75 pieces.

OCEAN BIRETROGRADE 36MM — REF. OCEABI36WW049

Movement: automatic-winding; 65-hour power reserve; 35 jewels; 28,800 vph.
Functions: hours, minutes; retrograde seconds and days; date.
Case: 18K white gold; Ø 36mm; set with 57 brilliant-cut diamonds (2.9 carats); water resistant to 10atm.
Dial: white pearled mother-of-pearl; blue varnish; rectangular hour marker appliqués; date aperture; set with 23 diamonds.
Strap: dark blue hand-sewn alligator leather; 18K white-gold set ardillon buckle.

OCEAN MOON PHASE 36MM — REF. OCEQMP36RR029

Movement: quartz.
Functions: hours, minutes; moonphase; date at 6.
Case: 18K rose gold; Ø 36mm; set with 57 brilliant-cut diamonds (2.9 carats); water resistant to 10atm.
Dial: bluish white mother-of-pearl set with 58 brilliant-cut diamonds; central moonphase covered with openworked grid; date aperture.
Strap: taupe hand-sewn alligator leather; 18K rose-gold set ardillon buckle.

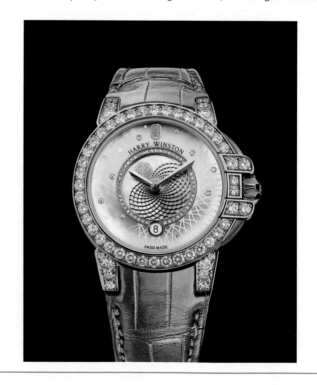

HARRY WINSTON AVENUE CLASSIC   REF. AVEQHM21RR123

Movement: quartz.
Functions: hours, minutes; small seconds at 6.
Case: 18K rose gold; 21x36mm; set with 29 brilliant-cut diamonds (2.27 carats); water resistant to 3atm.
Dial: silver-toned; snow-set with 42 brilliant-cut diamonds.
Bracelet: 18K rose gold with folding clasp.

HARRY WINSTON AVENUE DIAMOND DROPS   REF. AVEQHM21WW280

Movement: quartz.
Functions: hours, minutes.
Case: 18K white gold; 21x36mm; set with 29 brilliant-cut diamonds (2.27 carats); water resistant to 3atm.
Dial: black; snow-set with 129 brilliant-cut diamonds.
Strap: black hand-sewn alligator leather; 18K white-gold folding clasp.

HARRY WINSTON AVENUE C™ EMERALD   REF. AVCQHM19WW138

Movement: quartz.
Functions: hours, minutes.
Case: 18K white gold; 19x39.5mm; set with 43 brilliant-cut diamonds (1.55 carats); water resistant to 3atm.
Dial: mix of smoky pink varnished white mother of pearl and light lilac varnished pearled mother-of-pearl at the center; set with 44 brilliant-cut diamonds.
Bracelet: 18K white gold set with 138 brilliant-cut diamonds; 18K white-gold folding clasp.

HARRY WINSTON AVENUE C™ MINI LILY CLUSTER   REF. AVCQHM16RR042

Movement: quartz.
Functions: hours, minutes.
Case: 18K rose gold; 15.6x32.3mm; set with 47 brilliant-cut diamonds (0.72 carat); water resistant to 3atm.
Dial: white mother of pearl; Lily cluster pattern set with 34 brilliant-cut diamonds.
Bracelet: 18K rose gold with folding clasp.

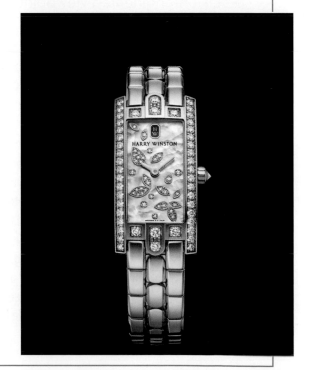

SILK, STONE, CRYSTAL AND TIME

DRAWING INSPIRATION FROM SOURCES AS FAR-FLUNG IN SPACE AND TIME AS IMPERIAL JAPAN AND 19TH-CENTURY FRANCE, Hermès introduces two collections that reinterpret diverse artistic pursuits using the precision-engineered viewpoint of haute horology.

Cross-pollination is one of the most powerful influences in culture. Using Japanese elements in a Western art form, the Arceau Temari from Hermès effects several transformations. The exquisitely soft silken scraps left over from sewing kimonos in the Japanese Imperial court became elaborately knotted balls known as "temari" and inspired a design for an Hermès silk carré, leading in turn to the Arceau Temari's abstracted geometrical motif. This constant give-and-take between influences and materials engenders a creative tension that makes for a charming, unexpected miniature work of art.

The dial's marquetry, crafted in 20 delicate slices of white mother-of-pearl, onyx, lapis lazuli or opal, must be precisely cut and inlaid to create the seamless effect of knotted silken threads. However, the diamond bands that weave in and out among the slivers of stone are crafted using a technique called snow-setting, in which artisans select each small diamond individually, place it in a custom-made claw and proceed according to the visual interplay between the gems, as opposed to a rigid preset plan. Each dial in the Arceau Temari collection is thus unique, with an inimitable sparkle from 176 diamonds.

▶ **ARCEAU TEMARI**
Using meticulously designed marquetry in onyx, opal, mother-of-pearl and other fine stones, Hermès introduces an element of uniqueness to each dial with 176 diamonds mounted with the snow-setting technique.

The marquetry of the Arceau Temari dial is precisely cut and inlaid to create the seamless effect of knotted silken threads.

After the diamond-setting is complete, the colored stones take their places within the white-gold framework, completing a tableau much greater than the sum of its parts. The case that frames this work of art is equally expert in its construction, which also entails snow-set diamonds. It takes 700 diamonds and almost three weeks for an expert gem-setter to create a case of such sophistication. Even the crown scintillates, set with 27 diamonds, with a rose-cut diamond at its end.

Powered by the automatic-winding Hermès H1912 caliber, the Arceau Temari lavishes the same attention on its interior as on its exterior. The mainplate sports a circular grain and snailing, and the bridges bear their own insignia: a satin-brushed finish with a design of seemingly randomly placed "H"s. The rhodium-plated oscillating weight, in addition to the "H" motif, is also engraved with "Hermès Paris." The standard-setting luxury brand thus continues to make its mark in the world of precious jewelry watches. This artistic watch writes a new chapter in the evolution of the temari—from a leftover scrap of silk, to a knotted ball, to a decorative element in its own right, to a silk scarf, to a precious timepiece.

Another intricate design, and another age-old art, take center stage in the Arceau Millefiori collection. "Millefiori" means "one thousand flowers" in Italian, and the 19th-century Millefiori paperweights from the Cristalleries royales de Saint-Louis inspire this exuberant collection, whose dials and covers are meticulously crafted by expert glassblowers. The process of creating these intricate designs is a complex one, and begins with a furnace in which bubble several pots of molten crystal, each one home to a distinct color. As the artisans work with this fragile material, the color builds in intensity with each layer of crystal. The glassblowers pull the glass into threads that measure several meters long and just a few millimeters across, placing different colors of glass side by side to create a cheerful design element that will truly be realized only in cross-section. Once this step of the process is complete, the artisans slice the multi-colored rods they have created into small slivers just 10mm long. Using tweezers to place each minute cylindrical rod with exquisite care, the glassworkers create a stunning bouquet in a cast-iron bowl, bloom by bloom.

The tiny buds then receive a covering of molten crystal, a protective coating for the fragile elements. Encased in glass, the bouquet returns to the furnace, where the glassblowers mold and shape the circular tableau with a wooden pallet or even paper, removing extraneous glass until they achieve the desired final form. The crystal covering adds a contradictory dimension to the glass flowers: they now seem both more solid and more delicate, fleeting yet permanent. When the face is completed, the true beauty of the "thousand flowers" is finally apparent: an edge-to-edge motif of intricate circular designs sweeps across the dial. The hand of the artisan glassblower is necessarily apparent in each piece, as the organic form of each rod and the artistic judgment of the assembler ensure the uniqueness of each dial. The transparent glass coating adds richness and depth to the free-spirited art below, fixing it in place even as it bends the light in unexpected ways.

Available in 34mm and 41mm sizes, the white-gold case of the Arceau Millefiori houses movements from the Hermès Manufacture (H1912 and H1837, respectively) that sport the special Hermès decoration of small "H"'s. A sapphire crystal caseback ensures that the reverse of the watch holds as much visual interest as the face.

▲ **ARCEAU MILLEFIORI**

The Arceau Millefiori 34mm frames a crystal dial crafted using the same technique as 19th-century paperweights from the Cristalleries royales de Saint-Louis.

▲ **ARCEAU MILLEFIORI**

Mounted on a smooth raspberry alligator leather strap, the white-gold case of the Arceau Millefiori bears 60 diamonds, with a total weight of 0.76 carat, as well as a 0.07-carat diamond set in the crown.

▶ **ARCEAU MILLEFIORI**

Each element of the Arceau Millefiori 41mm is crafted using minute rods of colored crystal placed side by side and exposed in cross-section.

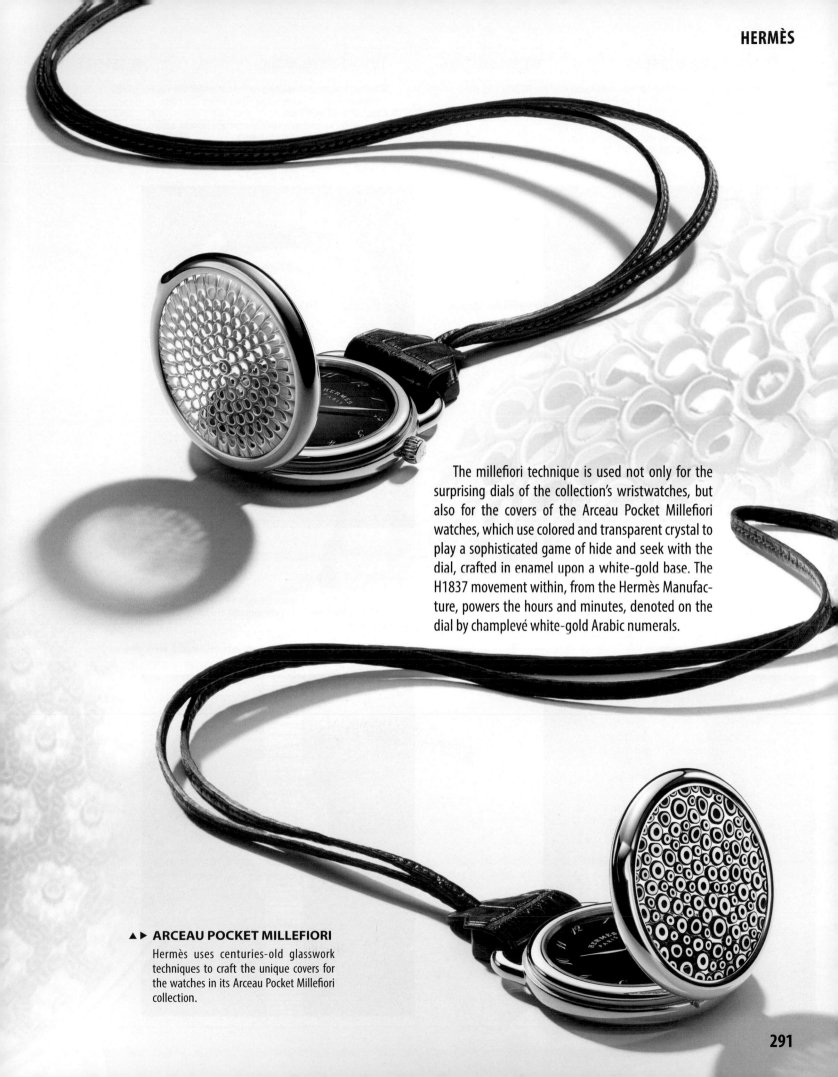

The millefiori technique is used not only for the surprising dials of the collection's wristwatches, but also for the covers of the Arceau Pocket Millefiori watches, which use colored and transparent crystal to play a sophisticated game of hide and seek with the dial, crafted in enamel upon a white-gold base. The H1837 movement within, from the Hermès Manufacture, powers the hours and minutes, denoted on the dial by champlevé white-gold Arabic numerals.

▲▶ **ARCEAU POCKET MILLEFIORI**
Hermès uses centuries-old glasswork techniques to craft the unique covers for the watches in its Arceau Pocket Millefiori collection.

HERMÈS

DRESSAGE L'HEURE MASQUEE — REF. DR5.870.221/MHA

Movement: automatic-winding Hermès manufacture caliber H1925.
Functions: hours, minutes; GMT; "Time Veiled" function.
Case: rose gold; 40.5x38.4mm.
Dial: opaline silvered with vertical central guilloché motif.
Strap: matte Havane alligator leather.
Price: available upon request.
Also available: steel.

DRESSAGE L'HEURE MASQUEE — REF. DR5.810.220/MHA

Movement: automatic-winding Hermès manufacture caliber H1925.
Functions: hours, minutes; GMT; "Time Veiled" function.
Case: steel; 40.5x38.4mm.
Dial: opaline silvered with vertical central guilloché motif.
Strap: matte Havane alligator leather.
Price: available upon request.
Also available: rose gold.

MEDOR PM FULL SET WITH DIAMONDS — REF. ME3.230.282/ZNO

Movement: quartz.
Functions: hours, minutes.
Case: steel; 23x23mm; dial fully set with 499 diamonds (1.31 carats).
Dial: silvered.
Strap: black alligator leather; two steel pyramids fully set with 352 diamonds each (0.93 carat each).
Price: available upon request.
Also available: rose gold; non set; partially set; other strap colors.

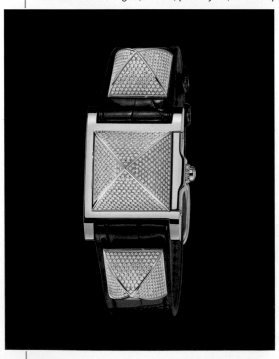

FAUBOURG — REF. FG1.171.111/3801

Movement: Swiss quartz.
Functions: hours, minutes.
Case: rose gold; Ø 15.5mm; set with 44 diamonds (0.1 carat).
Dial: lacquered white dial; set with one diamond.
Bracelet: rose gold.
Price: available upon request.
Also available: strap; without diamonds; yellow gold; white gold.

NANTUCKET
REF. NA2.250.220/WW9T1

Movement: Swiss quartz.
Functions: hours; minutes.
Case: silver; 20x27mm.
Dial: opaline silver with central stamped motif.
Strap: interchangeable double tour smooth Capucine calfskin.
Price: available upon request.
Also available: with diamonds; other strap colors.

NANTUCKET SET WITH DIAMONDS
REF. NA2.251.220/ZZ8C

Movement: Swiss quartz.
Functions: hours, minutes.
Case: silver; 20x27mm; set with 56 diamonds (1.12 carats).
Dial: opaline silver with central stamped motif.
Strap: interchangeable smooth elephant alligator leather.
Price: available upon request.
Also available: without diamonds; other strap colors.

CAPE COD TONNEAU
REF. CT1.750.220/VBA1

Movement: Swiss quartz.
Functions: hours, minutes; date.
Case: silver; 33.6x30mm.
Dial: opaline silver with central stamped motif.
Strap: interchangeable Barenia calfskin.
Price: available upon request.
Also available: with diamonds; other strap colors; smaller size.

CAPE COD TONNEAU SET WITH DIAMONDS
REF. CT.251.220/ZZ5L

Movement: Swiss quartz.
Functions: hours, minutes.
Case: silver; 26.8x24mm; set with 52 full-cut diamonds (1.3 carats).
Dial: opaline silver with central stamped motif.
Strap: interchangeable ultraviolet alligator leather.
Price: available upon request.
Also available: without diamonds; other strap colors; larger size.

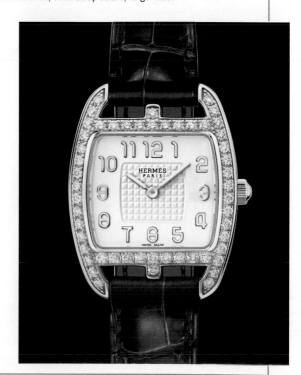

HUBLOT

GRACE, POWER, SPORT

The official timekeeper of the FIFA World Cup Brazil introduces three stunning timepieces whose vibrant colors highlight their mechanical sophistication. With its newest creations, **HUBLOT BRINGS AN INTERNATIONAL COMPETITIVE SPIRIT TO THE HEART OF TIMEKEEPING**, from the ingenuity of a bi-retrograde chronograph to a sporty, elegant watch befitting its athletic namesake.

Hublot's Big Bang Ferrari Ceramic dazzles with a poised synergy of power and refined precision, a fitting tribute to the legendary Italian sports cars. The bezel and 45.5mm case, in black carbon fiber and polished white ceramic respectively, combine strength and elegance, as the open dial reveals the movement's meticulous craftsmanship. A rugged yet striking open architecture brings this mechanical expertise to the forefront: juxtaposed gears, sharp lines and precise mechanical artistry evoke the unparalleled racing engines with which the Big Bang Ferrari shares its name.

Oscillating at the heart of the watch, the HUB 1241 Unico automatic caliber boasts a balance of robustness and reliability made possible by Hublot's unflagging devotion to mechanical progress. A flyback chronograph, operated via the activators on the right side of the case, allows the owner to restart the stopwatch with the single push of a button. A key resource when functioning at Ferrari-like speeds, the flyback function lets the wearer bypass the task of manually stopping and resetting the complication. From the silicon construction of its pallet fork and escapement wheel, to the barrel's direct drive of the hour counter, the 28,800vph, 330-component movement powers the timepiece to the highest chronometric standards. Two motoring-inspired pushbuttons at 2 and 4 o'clock lend the finishing touches to the racing theme expressed by accents on the chronograph counter, the dial's date window, the wheel-rim shape of the oscillating weight and Ferrari's famed stallion at 9 o'clock. Beneath the finely tuned motion of the watch's three luminescent hands and 60-minute counter, six commanding Arabic numerals ensure a superb degree of legibility—a synchronicity of design, purpose and masculine personality. The Big Bang Ferrari Ceramic, with its 72-hour power reserve, is worn on a strap in white leather and black rubber that echoes the notes of its two-toned case and demonstrative dial.

▲ Hublot with Team AF Corse wins the 2014 24 Heures du Mans race in the GTE PRO category.

Two motoring-inspired pushbuttons lend the finishing touches to the racing theme expressed by the dial's date window, the wheel-rim shape of the oscillating weight and Ferrari's famed stallion.

◄ **BIG BANG FERRARI CERAMIC**
Equipped with a flyback chronograph, this white ceramic timepiece brings a high-speed racing attitude to its innate horological elegance.

▲ Soccer legend Pelé and Hublot CEO Ricardo Guadalupe.

▲ Jean-Claude Biver, Chairman of Hublot and President of the Watches Division LVMH Group.

How did the official timekeeper of the 2014 World Cup celebrate the planet's most-watched sporting event? It created a watch that defies convention by using "the beautiful game" as inspiration inside and out. Framed by a carbon-fiber bezel and 45mm case in 18-karat King Gold, the dial's ingenious architecture turns the self-winding timepiece into a soccer fanatic's indispensable companion. A circular arc between 10 and 2 o'clock, along with two centrally driven hands in the colors of Brazil's national flag, allows the wearer to accurately measure the elapsed time of each gripping match. While the module's intuitive two-button mechanism operates with seamless simplicity, the engine beneath represents an impressive first for the Swiss watchmaker. Never before seen in an Hublot timepiece, the chronograph's bi-retrograde display allows both hands to move from left to right before returning instantaneously to their starting point, after each minute for the green seconds hand and at the end of each of the game's halves for the yellow minutes stem. An aperture at 12 o'clock **even clari-**fies which stage of the match is currently being played. Naturally the time of day, along with the running seconds, can be observed continuously via two subdials at 6 and 9 o'clock respectively. The Big Bang Unico Bi-Retrograde Chrono Official Watch of the 2014 FIFA World Cup Brazil, nicknamed Soccer Bang, boasts a self-winding manufacture movement optimized to withstand the difficult requirements of its inventive complication. With 385 components constructed from materials carefully chosen to maximize energy efficiency and minimize friction, the HUB 1260 Unico caliber the fruit of 18 months of intensive research, honors the captivating tournament with uncompromising mechanical sophistication. This daring and imaginative timepiece is secured to the wrist by a ribbed black rubber strap, is limited to 100 numbered pieces, and boasts a power reserve of 72 hours. A second variation, with a case in black ceramic, is limited to 200 numbered pieces.

Hublot steps off the soccer field—but just barely—with its presentation of the King Power "Special One." The 48mm titanium wristwatch pays tribute to brand ambassador and legendary soccer coach José Mourinho, nicknamed "The Special One." In line with the manager's signature color, the timepiece's carbon-fiber bezel boasts a rich dark blue that demonstrates Hublot's technical prowess. Using a brand-new process, the color was directly integrated into the mold's fibers before pressurization, saturating the material with the hue from the inside out. The dial, which mirrors the two-tone aesthetics of the watch's outer structure, also reveals the flyback chronograph's column wheel and horizontal double clutch via an openworked architecture. Two counters—at 3 o'clock for the stopwatch's elapsed minutes and 9 o'clock for the running seconds—are complemented by an aperture at 4 o'clock, whose black background clearly highlights the day's date from a wheel of revealed Arabic numerals. Driven from the center of the dial, two sword-shaped rhodium-plated hands indicate the hours and minutes with optimal clarity thanks to their blue luminescent material and are joined by the chronograph's seconds hand, sharply distinguished by its open red arrow tip. The caseback bears José Mourinho's autograph and exhibits the self-winding 28,800vph HUB 1240 caliber's oscillations through the sapphire crystal. A strap of blue alligator leather and black rubber, and blue accents on the titanium crown and pushbuttons, provide the sporty finishing touches to this limited edition watch.

◀ **SOCCER BANG**

Hublot's first-ever bi-retrograde display turns this watch's chronograph into the ideal soccer companion.

▶ **KING POWER "SPECIAL ONE"**

This 250-piece limited edition wristwatch boasts a carbon-fiber bezel whose deep blue tone saturates the material from the very beginning of the production process.

▶ **JOSÉ MOURINHO**

BIG BANG DEPECHE MODE   REF. 311.SX.8010.VR.DPM14

Movement: automatic-winding HUB4214 caliber; 42-hour power reserve; 257 components; 27 jewels; 28,800 vph; HUBLOT-designed black-coated tungsten openwork rotor, Swiss lever escapement.
Functions: hours, minutes; small seconds at 9; date at 4:30; chronograph: 12 hour counter at 6, 30-minute counter at 3, central chronograph seconds hand.
Case: satin-finished stainless steel; Ø 44mm; microblasted and satin-finished stainless steel bezel with "Clous Pyramide" decoration and six H-shaped black PVD-titanium screws; satin-finished stainless steel crown with black rubber insert pushbuttons;

black composite resin lug and lateral inserts; titanium screws; satin-finished stainless steel caseback with printed "Depeche Mode" and "Charity: Water" logos; antireflective sapphire crystal with HUBLOT logo on inner side; water resistant to 10atm.
Dial: metallic gray; skeletonized; microblasted rhodium-plated "Clous Pyramide" appliqués; satin-finished, rhodium-plated, black luminescent hands.
Strap: black rubber and gray calfskin with "Clous Pyramide" decoration; stainless steel deployant buckle clasp.
Note: limited edition of 250 pieces.
Suggested price: $19,400

BIG BANG DARK JEANS CERAMIC   REF. 301.CI.2770.NR.JEANS14

Movement: automatic-winding HUB4100 caliber; 42-hour power reserve; 252 components; 27 jewels; 28,800 vph; HUBLOT-designed black-coated tungsten openwork rotor; Swiss lever escapement.
Functions: hours, minutes; small seconds at 9; date at 4:30; chronograph: 12-hour counter at 6, 30-minute counter at 3, central chronograph seconds hand.
Case: microblasted black ceramic; Ø 44mm; microblasted black ceramic bezel with 6 H-shaped black PVD titanium screws; black PVD stainless steel crown and pushbuttons with black rubber insert; black composite resin bezel lug and lateral inserts;

microblasted black ceramic caseback; antireflective sapphire crystal with HUBLOT logo on inner side; water resistant to 10atm.
Dial: genuine dark jeans and black matte; satin-finished, rhodium-plated, black luminescent appliqués and hands.
Strap: black rubber and genuine dark jeans strap with orange stitching; microblasted black PVD stainless steel deployant buckle clasp.
Note: limited edition of 250 pieces.
Suggested price: $17,100

BIG BANG POP ART STEEL BLUE   REF. 341.SL.5199.LR.1907.POP14

Movement: automatic-winding HUB4300 caliber; 42-hour power reserve; 278 components; 37 jewels; 28,800 vph; HUBLOT-designed oscillating weight; black PVD tungsten openwork rotor; Swiss lever escapement.
Functions: hours, minutes; small seconds at 3; date at 4:30; chronograph: 12-hour counter at 6, 30-minute counter at 9, central chronograph seconds hand.
Case: polished and satin-finished stainless steel; Ø 41mm; polished 18K white-gold bezel set with 48 baguette-cut blue topazes; polished and satin-finished stainless steel crown and pushbuttons with blue rubber inserts; blue composite resin bezel

lug and lateral inserts; titanium screws; satin-finished stainless steel caseback; antireflective sapphire crystal; water resistant to 10atm.
Dial: matte dark blue; rhodium-plated printed purple and blue appliqués; rhodium-plated hands.
Strap: purple and blue alligator leather; stainless steel deployant buckle clasp.
Note: limited edition of 200 pieces.
Suggested price: $25,200
Also available: steel purple; yellow-gold rose; yellow-gold apple.

BIG BANG UNICO 2014 FIFA WORLD CUP BRAZIL   REF. 412.OQ.1128.RX

Movement: automatic-winding HUB1260 UNICO caliber; 72-hour power reserve; 385 components; 44 jewels.
Functions: off-centered hours, minutes; date at 12; central chronograph; retrograde minutes and seconds.
Case: 18K King Gold; Ø 45mm; carbon fiber bezel with six H-shaped titanium screws, countersunk, polished and locked; black composite resin bezel lugs; 18K King Gold black overmolded rubber crown with Hublot logo; satin-finished 18K King Gold caseback; antireflective sapphire crystal; water resistant to 10atm.

Dial: black, matte and satin-finished; yellow retrograde display and minute hand; green retrograde display and minute hand.
Strap: structured and ribbed natural black rubber; black PVD titanium deployant buckle with 18K King Gold insert.
Note: limited edition of 100 numbered pieces.
Suggested price: $42,400
Also available: ceramic, limited edition of 200 numbered pieces (ref. 412.CQ.1127.RX).

BIG BANG UNICO ALL BLACK   REF. 411.CI.1110.RX

Movement: automatic-winding HUB 1242 Unico caliber; 72-hour power reserve; black PVD-coated oscillating weight.
Functions: hours, minutes; date at 4:30; automatic flyback chronograph.
Case: black ceramic; Ø 45.5mm; black micro-blasted ceramic bezel set with six H-shaped matte titanium screws, countersunk, polished and locked; black PVD titanium crown; black composite resin bezel lugs and black anodized aluminum bezel rings; black composite resin lateral inserts; black PVD titanium pushbuttons; black micro-blasted PVD titanium caseback; antireflective sapphire crystal with Hublot logo; water resistant to 10atm.
Dial: matte black varnished and skeletonized; black-plated counter ring; black-plated hands with black SuperLumiNova.
Strap: structured ribbed black rubber strap; black PVD titanium clasp with black ceramic inserts.
Note: limited edition of 1,000 numbered pieces.
Suggested price: $21,700
Also available: Big Bang Unico Carbon (ref. 411.QX.1170.RX).

CLASSIC FUSION 2014 FIFA WORLD CUP BRAZIL   REF. 515.OX.0210.LR.FIF14

Movement: manual-winding HUB1301.4 caliber; thickness: 2.9mm; 90-hour power reserve; 123 components; 21 jewels; 21,600 vph.
Functions: hours, minutes; small seconds at 7.
Case: polished and satin-finished 18K King Gold; Ø 45mm; polished and satin-finished 18K King Gold bezel with six H-shaped titanium screws; polished 18K King Gold crown with engraved HUBLOT logo; black composite resin bezel lug; satin-finished 18K King Gold caseback; antireflective sapphire crystal with HUBLOT logo on inner side; water resistant to 5atm.
Dial: satin-finished 18K King Gold; 18K King Gold 2014 FIFA World Cup Brazil™ logo appliqué; 18K King Gold polished appliqués; polished gold-plated hands.
Strap: black rubber and alligator leather; 18K red gold and black PVD stainless steel deployant buckle clasp.
Note: limited edition of 100 pieces.
Suggested price: $33,200

CLASSIC FUSION AEROFUSION CHRONOGRAPH PELE   REF. 525.VX.0179.VR.PEL14

Movement: automatic-winding HUB1155 caliber; 42-hour power reserve; 207 components; 60 jewels; 28,800 vph; HUBLOT-designed oscillating weight; tungsten openwork rotor.
Functions: hours, minutes; small seconds at 3; date at 6; skeletonized chronograph: 30-minute counter at 9, central chronograph seconds hand.
Case: polished and satin-finished 18K 3N gold; vertical satin-finished and polished 18K 3N gold bezel with six H-shaped titanium screws; polished black ceramic crown and pushbuttons with HUBLOT logo on crown; black composite resin bezel lug; polished satin-finished 18K 3N gold caseback with printed PELE logo and signature; antireflective sapphire crystal; water resistant to 5atm.
Dial: sapphire; polished gold-plated appliqués and hands.
Strap: black rubber and black calfskin with football décor; 18K 3N gold and black PVD stainless steel deployant buckle clasp.
Note: limited edition of 500 pieces.
Suggested price: $39,400

CLASSIC FUSION BLACK MAGIC   REF. 581.CM.1770.RX

Movement: quartz HUB2912 caliber; 3-5-year power reserve; 38 components; three jewels.
Functions: hours, minutes, seconds; date at 3.
Case: polished and satin-finished black ceramic; Ø 33mm; vertical satin-finished black ceramic bezel with six H-shaped titanium screws; polished black PVD titanium crown engraved with HUBLOT logo; black composite resin bezel lug; polished and microblasted black ceramic caseback engraved with HUBLOT logo; antireflective sapphire crystal.
Dial: carbon fiber; satin-finished rhodium-plated appliqués; polished rhodium-plated hands.
Strap: black lined rubber; black PVD stainless steel deployant buckle clasp.
Suggested price: $7,200
Also available: with black magic diamonds (ref. 581.CM.1170.LR.1104).

CLASSIC FUSION CHRONOGRAPH TOUR AUTO 2014   REF. 521.NX.1472.VR.TRA14

Movement: automatic-winding HUB1143 caliber; 42-hour power reserve; 280 components; 59 jewels; 28,800 vph; HUBLOT-designed oscillating weight; black-coated tungsten openwork rotor; Swiss lever escapement.
Functions: hours, minutes; small seconds at 3; date at 7; chronograph: 30-minute counter at 9, central chronograph seconds hand.
Case: polished and satin-finished titanium; Ø 45mm; vertical satin-finished titanium bezel with six H-shaped titanium screws; polished titanium crown and pushbuttons, crown engraved with TOUR AUTO logo; black composite resin bezel lug; full polished and satin-finished titanium caseback engraved with TOUR AUTO logo; antireflective sapphire crystal; water resistant to 5atm.
Dial: black sunray satin-finish; silver counters; printed French flag colors; satin-finished rhodium-plated appliqués; polished rhodium-plated hands.
Strap: black rubber and black perforated calfskin with printed French flag colors; stainless steel deployant clasp.
Note: limited edition of 100 pieces.
Suggested price: $13,700

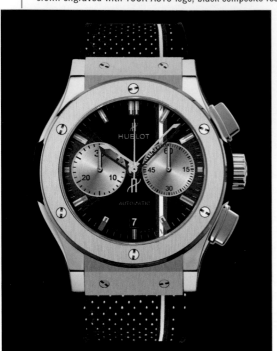

CLASSIC FUSION POWER RESERVE 8 DAYS   REF. 516.OX.1480.LR

Movement: manual-winding HUB1601 caliber; 8-day power reserve; 209 components; 33 jewels; 21,600 vph; Swiss lever escapement.
Functions: hours, minutes, small seconds at 6; date at 3; power reserve indicator at 10.
Case: polished and satin-finished 18K King Gold; vertical satin-finished 18K King Gold bezel with six H-shaped titanium screws; polished 18K King Gold crown engraved with HUBLOT logo; black composite resin bezel lug; satin-finished 18K King Gold caseback; antireflective sapphire crystal; water resistant to 5atm.
Dial: black sunray with satin finish; polished gold-plated appliqués and hands.
Strap: 18K red gold and black PVD stainless steel deployant buckle clasp.
Suggested price: $32,500
Also available: titanium (ref. 516.NX.1470.LR).

CLASSIC FUSION TOURBILLON NIGHT OUT   REF. 505.CS.1270.VR

Movement: manual-winding HUB6012 caliber; 120-hour power reserve; 155 components; 19 jewels; 21,600 vph.
Functions: hours, minutes; tourbillon at 6.
Case: polished black ceramic; Ø 45mm; polished black ceramic bezel with six H-shaped titanium screws; polished black ceramic crown with black rubber insert; black composite resin bezel lug.
Dial: black lacquer; rhodium-plated appliqués; set with ten baguette-cut diamonds (0.36 carat); polished rhodium-plated hands.
Strap: black rubber and black shiny calfskin; black PVD stainless steel deployant buckle clasp.
Note: limited edition of 30 pieces.
Suggested price: $92,000

KING POWER PARIS SAINT-GERMAIN   REF. 716.CI.0123.RX.PSG14

Movement: automatic-winding HUB4245 caliber; 42-hour power reserve; 249 components; 28 jewels; 28,800 vph; HUBLOT-designed oscillating weight; black-coated tungsten openwork rotor; Swiss lever escapement.
Functions: hours, minutes; date at 4; chronograph.
Case: microblasted black ceramic; Ø 48mm; microblasted black ceramic and black rubber bezel with six H-shaped black PVD titanium screws; black PVD titanium crown with black rubber insert; black composite resin bezel lug and lateral inserts; black PVD titanium pushbuttons at 2 and 4 with rubber inserts (blue at 2, white at 4); microblasted black ceramic caseback; antireflective sapphire crystal; water resistant to 10atm.
Dial: sapphire with printed Paris Saint-Germain logo; satin-finished black plated blue luminescent appliqués and hands.
Strap: black rubber with blue décor; microblasted black ceramic and black PVD titanium King Power deployant buckle clasp.
Note: limited edition of 200 pieces.
Suggested price: $25,200

KING POWER SPECIAL ONE   REF. 701.NQ.0137.GR.SPO14

Movement: automatic-winding HUB1240 UNICO caliber; 72-hour power reserve; 330 components; 38 jewels; 28,800 vph; tungsten oscillating weight with microblasted surface treated in black ruthenium; Swiss lever escapement.
Functions: hours; minutes; date at 4:30; chronograph; calendar.
Case: satin-finished titanium; Ø 48mm; blue carbon fiber and dark blue rubber with six H-shaped black PVD titanium screws; satin-finished titanium crown and pushers with dark blue rubber insert; black composite resin bezel lug and lateral inserts; satin-finished titanium caseback printed with José Mourinho signature; antireflective sapphire crystal; water resistant to 10atm.
Dial: sapphire; satin-finished, rhodium-plated, dark blue luminescent appliqués and hands.
Strap: black rubber and dark blue gummy alligator leather with black stitching; titanium blue carbon King Power deployant buckle clasp.
Note: limited edition of 250 pieces.
Suggested price: $24,500
Also available: King Gold Blue Carbon (ref. 701.OQ.0138. GR.SPO14).

MP-06 TOURBILLON KING GOLD   REF. 906.OX.0138.LR

Movement: manual-winding HUB9006.H1.8 caliber; 120-hour power reserve; 155 components; 19 jewels; 21,600 vph; polished gold-plated balance.
Functions: hours, minutes; tourbillon at 6.
Case: satin-finished 18K King Gold; satin-finished and microblasted 18K King Gold bezel set with six H-shaped titanium screws; satin-finished 18K King Gold crown with black rubber insert; satin-finished 18K King Gold caseback; antireflective sapphire crystal; water resistant to 3atm.
Dial: satin-finished, gold-plated, white luminescent appliqués and hands.
Strap: black rubber and brown alligator leather; satin-finished microblasted 18K King Gold black PVD titanium deployant buckle clasp.
Suggested price: $161,000
Also available: titanium (ref. 906.NX.0137. LR).

SPIRIT OF BIG BANG   REF. 601.NX.0173.LR

Movement: automatic-winding HUB4700 caliber; 50-hour power reserve; 278 components; 31 jewels; 36,000 vph; HUBLOT-designed tungsten openwork rotor; Swiss lever escapement.
Functions: hours, minutes, seconds; chronograph; perpetual calendar.
Case: satin-finished titanium; satin-finished, polished and microblasted titanium bezel; satin-finished titanium crown and pushbuttons with black rubber insert; satin-finished titanium caseback; antireflective sapphire crystal; water resistant to 10atm.
Dial: sapphire; satin-finished, rhodium-plated, white luminescent appliqués and hands.
Strap: black rubber and alligator leather; titanium deployant buckle clasp.
Suggested price: $24,000
Also available: King Gold (ref. 601.OX.0183.LR).

BIG BANG FERRARI TITANIUM CARBON   REF. 401.NQ.0123.VR

Movement: automatic-winding HUB 1241 UNICO caliber; 72-hour power reserve;
Functions: hours, minutes; small seconds and date at 3; flyback chronograph.
Case: titanium; Ø 45.5mm; carbon fiber bezel; black composite resin bezel lugs and lateral insert with carbon insert at 9; satin-finished titanium crown, black rubber insert with Hublot logo and red lacquered Ferrari logo on stop; circular micro-basted and satin finished titanium caseback; red antireflective sapphire crystal; water resistant to 10atm.
Dial: sapphire with white Hublot logo transfer; satin-finished rhodium-plated hands; minute counter hand and chronograph with Ferrari red coating; yellow date window.
Strap: black rubber; titanium deployant buckle.
Note: limited edition of 1,000 pieces.
Suggested price: $28,600
Also available: King Gold, limited edition of 500 pieces (ref. 401. OX.0123.VR); Ceramic Carbon, limited edition of 1,000 pieces (ref. 401.CW.0129.VR).

THE EVOLVING ART OF WATCHMAKING

With three diver's timepieces of distinct elegance, Swiss watchmaking icon **IWC PAYS A VIBRANT HOMAGE TO CHARLES DARWIN AND THE GALAPAGOS ISLANDS SO INEXTRICABLY LINKED WITH HIS RESEARCH**.

IWC's Aquatimer Chronograph Edition "Expedition Charles Darwin" honors one of history's finest minds with a devotion to time-keeping that befits the great naturalist's own dedication. A statement resounds in the very material of the piece's 44mm case. Crafted in bronze, the self-winding wristwatch evokes the accents of the HMS Beagle, the ship that carried Darwin to the Galapagos Islands for some of his most groundbreaking discoveries. The metal's propensity to develop a rich patina ensures an "evolution" of its own throughout the life of the diving instrument. Outfitted with luminescent elements for optimal underwater legibility, the timepiece boasts a mechanical external/internal rotating bezel that ensures the safety of its submerged owner. Its unidirectional range of motion guarantees that the dive-time may only be shortened, never accidentally extended. A date display and small hacking seconds complete a high-contrast dial architecture that reflects the deep, warm hues of the watch's dominant material. Turned over, the Aquatimer Chronograph Edition "Expedition Charles Darwin" reveals a detailed engraving of Darwin's portrait.

The Aquatimer Chronograph Edition "50 Years Science For Galapagos" honors the archipelago's ecosystem with precision and rugged elegance.

The limited series Aquatimer Chronograph Edition "50 Years Science For Galapagos" pays a refined, robust tribute to the half-century of countless contributions of the archipelago's Charles Darwin Research Station. Powered by the self-winding 89365 caliber, the rubber-coated stainless steel wristwatch presents a high-precision chronograph display optimally suited for the diving needs of its wearer. Highly luminescent and designed for excellent clarity, the 44mm timepiece is equipped with a mechanical external/internal rotating bezel, complete with the security of the SafeDive system. Joining the chronograph's central seconds hand and 60-minute counter, a date aperture and small hacking seconds complete the comprehensive yet unassuming design of the watch's deep black dial. An extension of IWC's partnership with the Charles Darwin Foundation, the Aquatimer Chronograph Edition "50 Years Science For Galapagos" honors the earthly paradise of the archipelago's magnificent ecosystem with precision and rugged elegance.

A balance of sophisticated engineering and aesthetic refinement, the Aquatimer Perpetual Calendar Digital Date-Month incorporates a perpetual calendar within a diver's code of design, graced by subtle notes of visual transparency. An 18-karat red-gold and rubber-coated titanium case sets the stage for the timepiece's functional luxury. On a dial framed by an external/internal rotating bezel fitted with the SafeDive system, the 49mm wristwatch demonstrates IWC's architectural expertise with a number of inventive design choices and luminescent elements. At 12 o'clock, a totalizer combines the chronograph's minutes and hours counters into a single easy-to-read display. The perpetual calendar's date and month indications appear at 3 and 9 o'clock respectively, ensuring excellent readability amid the wealth of information. Finally, a subdial at 6 o'clock combines the running seconds and leap-year indication within the confines of a golden circlet. Driven by the self-winding 89801 caliber equipped with flyback function, the Aquatimer Perpetual Calendar Digital Date-Month presents highly sophisticated watchmaking with style and visual simplicity.

◄ **AQUATIMER CHRONOGRAPH EDITION "EXPEDITION CHARLES DARWIN"**

Equipped with a flyback chronograph, this white ceramic timepiece brings a high-speed racing attitude to its innate horological elegance.

▲ **AQUATIMER CHRONOGRAPH EDITION "50 YEARS SCIENCE FOR GALAPAGOS"**

This diver's timepiece presents a brilliant balance of architectural clarity and robust mechanical construction. A portion of the proceeds is directed to the Charles Darwin Foundation.

▲ **AQUATIMER PERPETUAL CALENDAR DIGITAL DATE-MONTH**

This sophisticated diver's chronograph is equipped with a comprehensive and ingeniously constructed perpetual calendar.

IWC

AQUATIMER AUTOMATIC   REF. IW329001

Movement: automatic-winding 30120 caliber; 42-hour power reserve; 21 jewels; 28,800 vph.
Functions: hours, minutes, hacking seconds; date at 3.
Case: stainless steel; Ø 42mm, thickness: 14mm; rotating inner bezel with SafeDive system; screw-down crown; antireflective sapphire crystal; water resistant to 3atm.
Dial: black; hands and markers with luminescent material.
Strap: black rubber; stainless steel ardillon buckle.
Suggested price: $5,750

Also available: with stainless steel bracelet, $6,750 (ref. IW329002).

AQUATIMER AUTOMATIC   REF. IW329003

Movement: automatic-winding 30120 caliber; 42-hour power reserve; 21 jewels; 28,800 vph.
Functions: hours, minutes; stop seconds; date at 3.
Case: stainless steel; Ø 42mm, thickness: 14mm; rotating inner bezel; screw-down crown; antireflective sapphire crystal; water resistant to 3atm.
Dial: silver; hands and markers with luminescent material.
Strap: black rubber; stainless steel ardillon buckle.
Suggested price: $5,750

Also available: with stainless steel bracelet, $6,750 (ref. IW329004).

AQUATIMER DEEP THREE   REF. IW355701

Movement: automatic-winding 30120 caliber; 42-hour power reserve; 21 jewels; 28,800 vph.
Functions: hours, minutes; stop seconds.
Case: titanium; Ø 46mm, thickness: 16.5mm; rotated inner bezel with SafeDive system; antireflective sapphire crystal; water resistant to 10atm.
Dial: black; hands and markers with luminescent material.
Strap: black rubber.
Suggested price: $19,100

AQUATIMER CHRONOGRAPH   REF. IW376801

Movement: automatic-winding 79320 caliber; 44-hour power reserve; 25 jewels; 28,800 vph.
Functions: hours, minutes; small seconds at 9; day and date at 3; chronograph: 12-hour counter at 6, 30-minute counter at 12, central chronograph seconds hand.
Case: finished steel; Ø 44mm, thickness: 17mm; rotating inner bezel with SafeDive system; antireflective sapphire crystal; water resistant to 3atm.
Dial: silver; hands and markers with luminescent material.
Strap: black rubber.

Suggested price: $7,000
Also available: finished steel bracelet, $8,000 (ref. IW376802).

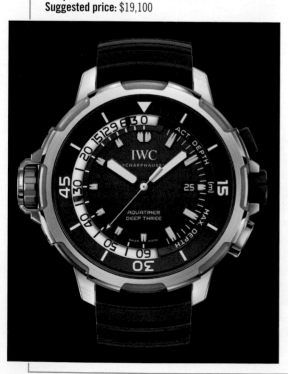

AQUATIMER CHRONOGRAPH   REF. IW376803

Movement: automatic-winding 79320 caliber; 44-hour power reserve; 25 jewels; 28,800 vph.
Functions: hours, minutes; small seconds at 9; day and date at 3; chronograph: 12-hour counter at 6, 30-minute counter at 12, central chronograph seconds hand.
Case: finished steel; Ø 44mm, thickness: 17mm; rotating inner bezel with SafeDive system; antireflective sapphire crystal; water resistant to 3atm.
Dial: black; hands and markers with luminescent material.
Strap: black rubber.
Suggested price: $7,000
Also available: finished steel bracelet, $8,000 (ref. IW376804).

AQUATIMER QP DATE-MONTH   REF. IW379401

Movement: automatic-winding 89801 caliber; 68-hour power reserve; 51 jewels; 28,800 vph.
Functions: hours, minutes, seconds; flyback chronograph: hours, minutes, small seconds counter at 12; perpetual calendar: large two-digit date and month display at 10 and 2.
Case: titanium ring coated with rubber; Ø 49mm, thickness: 19mm; 18K red-gold rotating bezel with SafeDive system; 18K red-gold caseback; antireflective sapphire crystal.
Dial: black; hands with luminescent material.
Strap: black rubber inlaid with black alligator leather; red-gold buckle.
Note: limited edition of 50 pieces.
Suggested price: $56,300

AQUATIMER GALAPAGOS   REF. IW379502

Movement: automatic-winding 89365 caliber; 68-hour power reserve; 35 jewels; 28,800 vph.
Functions: hours, minutes; small hacking seconds; date at 3; chronograph; stopwatch function.
Case: rubber-coated stainless steel; Ø 44mm, thickness: 17mm; bezel with SafeDive system; screw-down crown; antireflective sapphire crystal; water resistant to 3atm.
Dial: black; hands with luminescent material.
Strap: black rubber.
Suggested price: $11,100

AQUATIMER CHARLES DARWIN   REF. IW379503

Movement: automatic-winding 89365 caliber; 68-hour power reserve; 35 jewels; 28,800 vph.
Functions: hours, minutes; small hacking seconds; date at 3; chronograph; stopwatch function.
Case: bronze; Ø 44mm, thickness: 17mm; bezel with SafeDive system; screw-down crown; antireflective sapphire crystal; water resistant to 3atm.
Dial: black; hands with luminescent material.
Strap: black rubber; bronze ardillon buckle.
Suggested price: $11,100

AQUATIMER JACQUES YVES COUSTEAU REF. IW376805

Movement: automatic-winding 79320 caliber; 44-hour power reserve; 25 jewels; 28,700 vph.
Functions: hours, minutes; small hacking seconds at 9; day and date at 3; chronograph: 12-hour counter at 6, 30-minute counter at 12, central chronograph seconds hand.
Case: stainless steel; Ø44mm, thickness: 17mm; bezel with SafeDive system; screw-down crown; antireflective sapphire crystal; water resistant to 3atm.
Dial: blue; hands with luminescent material.
Strap: black rubber; steel ardillon buckle.

Suggested price: $7,200

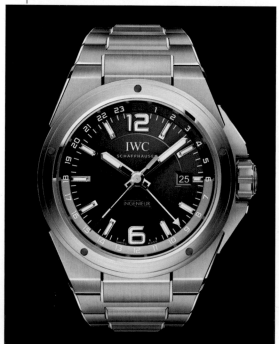

INGENIEUR AUTOMATIC CARBON PERFORMANCE CERAMIC REF. IW322404

Movement: automatic-winding 80110 caliber; 44-hour power reserve; 28 jewels; 28,800 vph.
Functions: hours, minutes, hacking seconds; date at 3.
Case: carbon fiber; Ø 46mm, thickness: 14.5mm; ceramic bezel and crown protection; titanium screws and caseback ring; caseback engraved with "ONE OUT OF 1,000"; water resistant to 12atm.
Dial: carbon fiber; green numerals on minute track.
Strap: black rubber with embossed calfskin inlay and green stitching;

Note: limited edition of 1,000 pieces.
Suggested price: $24,600

INGENIEUR DUAL TIME REF. IW324402

Movement: automatic-winding 35720 caliber; 42-hour power reserve; 27 jewels; 28,800 vph.
Functions: hours, minutes, hacking seconds; date at 3; 24-hour display (second local time); Time Zone Corrector.
Case: stainless steel; Ø 43mm, thickness: 13.5mm; screw-down crown; antireflective sapphire crystal; water resistant to 10atm.
Dial: black.
Bracelet: stainless steel.

Suggested price: $9,700

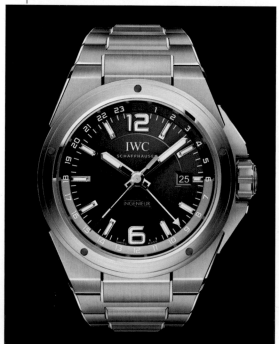

INGENIEUR DUAL TIME REF. IW324404

Movement: automatic-winding 35720 caliber; 42-hour power reserve; 27 jewels; 28,800 vph.
Functions: hours, minutes, hacking seconds; date at 3; 24-hour display (second local time); Time Zone Corrector.
Case: stainless steel; Ø 43mm, thickness: 13.5mm; screw-down crown; antireflective sapphire crystal; water resistant to 10atm.
Dial: silver-plated.
Bracelet: stainless steel.

Suggested price: $9,700

PORTUGUESE GRANDE COMPLICATION   REF. IW377401

Movement: automatic-winding 79091 caliber; 21K gold rotor.
Functions: hours, minutes, small seconds; chronograph; stopwatch function; perpetual calendar: four-digit year, month, day and date displays; minute repeater; moonphase.
Case: platinum; Ø 45mm; arched edge; antireflective sapphire crystal on both sides.
Dial: white.
Strap: black alligator leather with platinum stitching.
Price: available upon request.

PORTUGUESE TOURBILLON MYSTERE RETROGRADE   REF. IW504401

Movement: Pellaton automatic-winding 51900 caliber; Glucydur beryllium alloy balance with high-precision adjustment cam on balance arms; Breguet spring; rotor with 18K gold medallion.
Functions: hours, minutes; flying minute tourbillon; retrograde date; power reserve indicator.
Case: platinum; Ø 44.2mm; antireflective sapphire crystal on both sides.
Dial: gray.
Strap: black alligator leather; platinum folding clasp and pin buckle.
Price: available upon request.

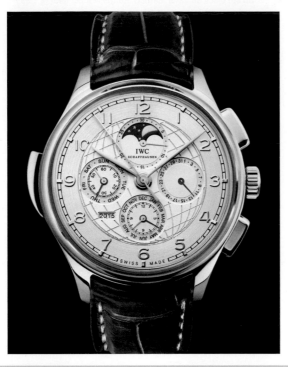

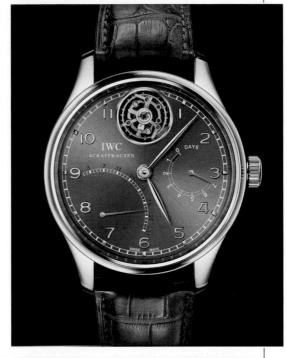

PORTUGUESE PERPETUAL CALENDAR   REF. IW503202

Movement: automatic-winding Pellaton caliber; Glucydur beryllium allow balance with high-precision adjustment cam on balance arms; Breguet spring; rotor with 18K gold precision.
Functions: hours, minutes; small seconds; perpetual calendar: four-digit year, month, day and date displays; moonphase: double moonphases for northern and southern hemispheres, countdown display showing phases until next full moon; power reserve indicator.
Case: 18K red gold; Ø 44.2mm; convex antireflective sapphire crystal on both sides.
Dial: black.
Strap: brown alligator leather; 18K red-gold folding clasp and pin buckle.
Price: available upon request.

PORTUGUESE PERPETUAL CALENDAR   REF. IW502307

Movement: Pellaton automatic winding 51613 caliber; Glucydur beryllium alloy balance with high-precision adjustment cam on balance arms; Breguet spring; rotor with 18K gold medallion.
Functions: hours, minutes; small seconds; perpetual calendar: four-digit year, month, day and date displays; power reserve indicator; moonphase.
Case: 18K white gold; Ø 44.2mm; antireflective sapphire crystal on both sides.
Dial: gray.
Strap: brown alligator leather; 18K white-gold folding clasp and pin buckle.
Price: available upon request.

PILOT'S WATCH CHRONOGRAPH EDITION "LE PETIT PRINCE"   REF. IW377706

Movement: automatic-winding 79320 caliber; 44-hour power reserve; 25 jewels; 28,800 vph.
Functions: hours, minutes, small hacking seconds at 9; day and date at 3; chronograph: 12-hour counter at 6, 30-minute counter at 12, central chronograph seconds hand, stopwatch function.
Case: stainless steel; Ø 43mm, thickness: 15mm; screw-in crown; antireflective sapphire crystal; caseback engraved with Little Prince; water resistant to 6atm.
Dial: midnight blue; hands and hour markers coated with SuperLumiNova.

Strap: brown calfskin with quilted stitching; stainless steel pin buckle.
Note: boutique edition.
Suggested price: $6,250

PILOT'S WATCH CHRONOGRAPH EDITION "JU-AIR"   REF. IW387809

Movement: automatic-winding 89365 caliber; 68-hour power reserve; 35 jewels; 28,800 vph.
Functions: hours, minutes; small hacking seconds at 6; flyback chronograph: 60-minute counter at 12, central chronograph seconds hand, flyback function.
Case: stainless steel; Ø 43mm, thickness: 15.5mm; screw-down crown, JU-52 aircraft engraved on caseback; antireflective sapphire crystal; water resistant to 6atm.
Dial: rhodium-plated; hands an appliqués coated with SuperLumiNova.
Strap: black alligator leather; stainless steel folding clasp.

Note: limited edition of 500 pieces.
Suggested price: $11,600

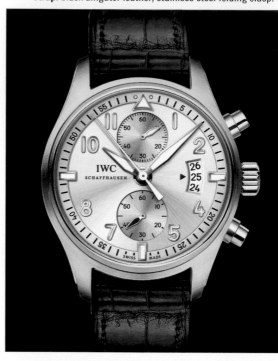

PORTUGUESE CHRONOGRAPH CLASSIC EDITION "LAUREUS SPORT FOR GOOD FOUNDATION"   REF. IW390406

Movement: automatic-winding 89361 caliber; 68-hour power reserve; 38 jewels; 28,800 vph.
Functions: hours, minutes, small hacking seconds at 6; date at 3 flyback chronograph: 12-hour and 60-minute counter combined in totalizer at 12, central chronograph seconds hand, stopwatch function.
Case: stainless steel; Ø 42mm, thickness: 14.5mm; sealed caseback with special engraving depicting the winning picture in "Time to play" drawing competition; arched antireflective sapphire crystal; water resistant to 3atm.

Dial: blue; rhodium-plated hands.
Strap: black Santoni alligator leather; stainless steel folding clasp.
Suggested price: $13,200

PORTUGUESE GRAND COMPLICATION   REF. IW377402

Movement: automatic-winding 79091 caliber; 44-hour power reserve; 75 jewels; 28,800 vph; 21K gold rotor.
Functions: hours, minutes seconds; small hacking seconds; perpetual calendar: date, day, month, four-digit year display; moonphase; minute repeater; stopwatch function.
Case: 18K red gold; Ø 45mm, thickness: 16.5mm; engraved caseback; antireflective sapphire crystal; water resistant to 3atm.
Dial: silver plated; 18K red-gold plated numerals.
Strap: brown alligator leather.

Note: limited edition of 100 pieces per year.
Suggested price: $233,000

PORTUGUESE GRAND COMPLICATION
REF. IW377401

Movement: automatic-winding 79091 caliber; 44-hour power reserve; 75 jewels; 28,800 vph; 21K gold rotor.
Functions: hours, minutes seconds; small hacking seconds; perpetual calendar: date, day, month, four-digit year display; moonphase; minute repeater; stopwatch function.
Case: platinum; Ø 45mm, thickness: 16.5mm; engraved caseback; antireflective sapphire crystal; water resistant to 3atm.
Dial: silver plated; rhodium plated numerals.
Strap: black alligator leather.
Note: limited edition of 100 pieces per year.
Suggested price: $260,000

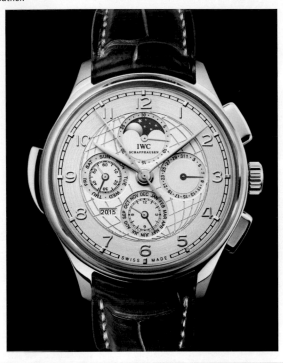

PORTUGUESE TOURBILLON HAND-WOUND
REF. IW546301

Movement: manual-winding 98900 caliber; 54-hour power reserve; 21 jewels; 28,800 vph; tourbillon: consists of 64 components, 0.801g; nickel silver plate and three-quarter bridge.
Functions: hours, minutes; small seconds at 6; flying one-minute tourbillon at 9.
Case: 18K white gold; Ø 43mm, thickness: 11mm; sapphire crystal; water resistant to 3atm.
Dial: slate colored.
Strap: dark brown Santoni alligator leather; 18K white-gold folding clasp.
Suggested price: $66,200

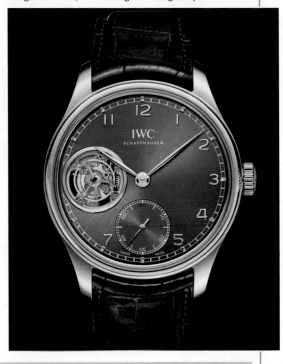

PILOT'S WATCH CHRONOGRAPH EDITION "THE LAST FLIGHT"
REF. IW388004

Movement: automatic-winding 89361 caliber; 68-hour power reserve; 38 jewels; 28,800 vph.
Functions: hours, minutes, small hacking seconds at 6 and date at 6; flyback chronograph: 12-hour and 60-minute counter combined in totalizer at 12, central chronograph seconds hand, stopwatch function.
Case: brown silicon nitride ceramic; Ø 46mm, thickness: 16.5mm; titanium crown, push-buttons and caseback; antireflective sapphire crystal; caseback with special engraving in memory of Antoine de Saint-Exupéry's last flight; water resistant to 6atm.
Dial: brown; black counters; rhodium-plated hands and appliqués with SuperLumi-Nova.
Strap: brown calfskin with quilted stitching; pin buckle
Note: limited edition of 1,700 pieces.
Suggested price: $14,800
Also available: with red gold, limited edition of 170 pieces (ref. IW388006); with platinum, limited edition of 17 pieces (ref. IW388008).

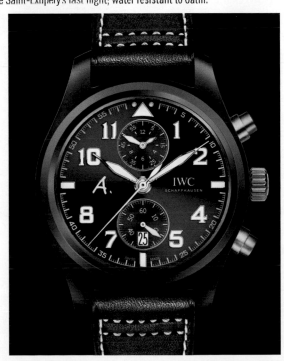

PORTUGUESE TOURBILLON HAND-WOUND
REF. IW546302

Movement: manual-winding 98900 caliber; 54-hour power reserve; 21 jewels; 28,800 vph; tourbillon: consists of 64 components, 0.801g; nickel silver plate and three-quarter bridge.
Functions: hours, minutes; small seconds at 6; flying one-minute tourbillon at 9.
Case: 18K red gold; Ø 43mm, thickness: 11mm; sapphire crystal; water resistant to 3atm.
Dial: silver colored.
Strap: dark brown Santoni alligator leather; 18K red-gold folding clasp.
Suggested price: $62,100

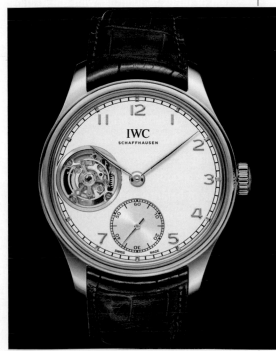

JACOB & CO
GENÈVE

WORLD ON THE WRIST

Whether depicting the grandeur of our celestial surroundings, inebriating every millimeter of a wristwatch with heady precious stones, or taking horology on a nostalgic trip around the world, Jacob & Co. expresses in its creations a **SPECTACULAR AND UNIQUE VISION OF THE TELLING OF TIME**.

The watchmaker's Astronomia Tourbillon transports its wearer on a journey into the heart of haute horology through its hypnotic exhibition of time in motion. In a poetic demonstration of time's relationship with the cosmos, the 18-piece limited edition timepiece depicts an aventurine midnight sky invigorated by the celebrated watchmaker's ingenuity. The multi-dimensional architecture is brought to life by the constant motion of a centrally driven four-arm carrier that completes a full revolution of the dial every twenty minutes. The hand-wound JCEM01 caliber's tourbillon, attached to one of the arms, adds to the twenty-minute orbit two more axes of rotation—around the arm's axis every five minutes and around its own every 60 seconds—for a spellbinding zero-gravity effect. An openworked hours-and-minutes subdial, on the opposite end of the central carrier, bestows upon the timepiece a sense of balance and continuity, thanks to a sophisticated differential-system mount that counters the overall rotation of the module and ensures the constant uppermost position of the "XII" marker. A 56-facet diamond Moon, whose own 60-second rotation presents a spectacle of light, and white-gold Earth with translucent blue enamel complete the fascinating arrangement, housed inside a 47mm case in 18-karat rose gold. Finished to the finest detail, the Astronomia Tourbillon is a dramatic exploration of space and motion.

▲ ASTRONOMIA TOURBILLON

This three-dimensional masterpiece boasts four orbiting modules, each endowed with additional axes of rotation for a harmonious exhibition of perpetual motion.

Framed by 205 icy-blue sapphires and 48 white diamonds, the Brilliant Skeleton Tourbillon Art Deco's hand-wound movement reveals its complexity via a skeletonized construction.

Jacob & Co. adorns the Brilliant Skeleton Tourbillon Art Deco with touches of gem-setting virtuosity that blur the line between the arts of haute joaillerie and haute horology. Framed by an 18-karat white-gold case invisibly set with 205 baguette icy-blue sapphires and 48 baguette white diamonds, as well as 15 additional sapphires on the crown, the watch's hand-wound JCAM05 movement reveals its complexity via a skeletonized construction that permits the wearer a riveting view of even its most delicate components. The 172-component exhibition caliber is further elevated by the integration of sapphire plates into the architecture, and illuminated by 178 diamonds meticulously set onto the bridges themselves. This one-of-a-kind chef d'oeuvre is worn on an alligator strap whose 18-karat white-gold buckle sports an additional 20 baguette-cut icy-blue sapphires.

The 18-karat rose-gold Epic SF24 takes on the digital display of worldtime zone concept with ingenuity and nostalgic artistry. Reminiscent of information boards In the world's most prominent travel terminals, the self-winding wristwatch indicates the time in a secondary location via a dual split-flap system. With a simple press of the button on the left of the mechanism, the wearer may choose from one of 24 global cities and admire as the right-side indication instantaneously transforms into the appropriate hour in said location. The creative display is contrasted, on the dial, by a contemporary architecture that reveals a number of the caliber's components. Combining modern aesthetics with Old-World sensibilities, the Epic SF24 not only accompanies its owner around the world on unforgettable journeys, but creates beautiful memories of its own.

▲ BRILLIANT SKELETON TOURBILLON ART DECO

Sapphire plates, bejeweled bridges and an invisible setting of precious stones lends this 47mm skeletonized tourbillon timepiece a balance of endless opulence and extraordinary technical craftsmanship.

▶ EPIC SF24

This timepiece indicates a secondary time zone via the first-ever digital display of worldtime zone, incorporated in a wristwatch.

JACOB & CO.

ASTRONOMIA TOURBILLON   REF. 750.100.94.AB.SD.1NS

Movement: manual-winding exclusive Jacob&Co. JCEM01 caliber; Ø 40mm, thickness: 15.9mm; 72-hour power reserve; 42 jewels; motor barrel construction; gravitational orbital tourbillon; finished plate and bridges: hand-angled and polished, circular graining, polished sink, hand-polished screws; barrel: circular graining; pinions: wood grinding-wheel polished; spring: Philips curve; PE 3000.
Functions: hours, minutes, seconds rotating every 20 minutes in 20 minutes on central axis; differential gears system; briolette diamond rotating in 60 seconds on two axes (56 faceted round diamonds, 1 carat); 18K white-gold hand-engraved enamel globe rotating in 60 seconds on 2 axes; gravitational orbital tourbillon cage rotating in on three axes: 1st axis: tourbillon cage rotating in 60 seconds, 2nd axis: in 5 minutes, 3rd axis: central axe in 20 minutes.
Case: 18K rose gold and diamond microparticule policarbonate fiber; Ø 47mm; caseback: 18K rose gold, bows: winding and time setting via 18K rose-gold lift out rotating bows at caseback; skylayer front case: aventurine Goldfluss and 18K rose gold; domed antireflective sapphire crystal; water resistant to 3atm.
Dial: skeletonized.
Strap: alligator leather; 18K rose-gold folding buckle.
Note: limited edition of eighteen pieces.
Price: available upon request.

EPIC SF24 TITANIUM   REF. 500.100.20.NS.PY.1NS

Movement: automatic-winding exclusive Jacob&Co. JCAA02 caliber; 48-hour power reserve.
Functions: hours, minutes, seconds; 24-hour world time indication.
Case: grade-5 titanium; Ø 45mm; satin-finished, micro-blasted and polished.
Dial: open-worked with micro-blasted gray center; red skeletonized hands with white LumiNova accent.
Strap: alligator leather; deployment buckle.
Suggested price: $85,000

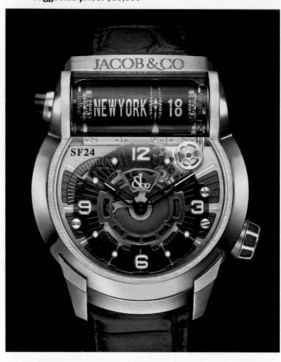

Also available: 18K white gold; 18K rose gold; black DLC titanium.

QUENTTIN   REF. 700.100.20.NS.AA.4NS

Movement: manual-winding exclusive Jacob&Co. JCBM04 caliber; 31-day power reserve; 21,600 vph; seven spring barrels.
Functions: hours, minutes; world premiere one-minute vertical tourbillon; power reserve indicator.
Case: grade-5 titanium; 56x47x21.55mm, curved; carbon fiber applications; tourbillon visible through side window; caseback with sapphire crystal.
Dial: indications on slowly revolving cylindrical drums; SuperLumiNova Arabic numerals.
Strap: black rubber; grade-5 titanium deployment buckle.

Note: limited edition of 18 pieces.
Suggested price: $350,000

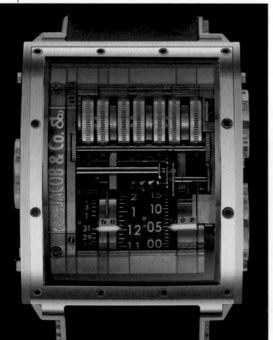

EPIC X RACING BLACK WITH WHITE INSERTS   REF. 550.100.21.WR.PY.4NS

Movement: manual-winding exclusive Jacob&Co. JCAM02 caliber; Ø 14.25mm; 48-hour power reserve; 21 jewels; 28,800 vph; barrel and balance vertically aligned; visible time setting mechanism on caseback; finishing:
Functions: hours, minutes; time setting spring with three functions ("octopus spring"): ratchet, lever and setting lever.
Case: black DLC grade-5 titanium; Ø 44mm, thickness: 12.3mm; white neoralithe inserts; finishing: microblasted and satin-finished; Jacob & Co. logo in inner ring; antireflective sapphire crystal; water resistant to 5atm.

Dial: skeletonized; open-worked hands.
Strap: alligator leather and rubber; black DLC buckle.
Suggested price: $19,800

PALATIAL TOURBILLON HOURS & MINUTES   REF. 150.250.40.NS.QR.1NS

Movement: manual-winding Jacob&Co. JCBM01 caliber; 100-hour power reserve; 29 jewels; 194 components; titanium balance with gold timing screw; satin-finished, hand-polished angles and draw-finished flanks finishes.
Functions: hours, minutes; one-minute flying tourbillon; power reserve indicator.
Case: 18K rose gold, circular satin-finished and polished; Ø 43mm; 18K rose-gold polished crown and outer lugs; sapphire glass on caseback; water resistant to 3atm.
Dial: red mineral crystal; 18K rose-gold applied polished Jacob & Co. logo and Roman numeral hour markers.
Strap: alligator leather; 18K rose-gold tang buckle.
Note: limited edition of 36 pieces.
Suggested price: $115,000

PALATIAL TOURBILLON JUMPING HOUR   REF. 150.510.24.NS.PB.1NS

Movement: manual-winding Jacob&Co. JCMB02 caliber; 100-hour power reserve; 251 components; 21,600 vph; titanium balance with gold timing screw; Côtes de Genève; satin-finished, hand-polished angles and draw-finished flanks.
Functions: jumping hours, retrograde minutes; one-minute flying tourbillon.
Case: 18K rose gold; Ø 43mm; circular satin-finished and polished; 18K rose-gold polished crown and outer lugs; sapphire crystal caseback; water resistant to 3atm.
Dial: blue mineral crystal; 18K rose-gold applied polished Jacob & Co. logo; jumping hour at 10 with instantaneous-jump disc.
Strap: alligator leather; 18K rose-gold tang buckle.
Note: limited edition of 36 pieces.
Suggested price: $125,000

PALATIAL MINUTE REPEATER   REF. 150.500.40.NS.OR.1NS

Movement: manual-winding Jacob&Co. JCMB03 caliber; 90-hour power reserve; 308 components; 21,600 vph; titanium balance with gold timing screw; Côtes de Genève; hand-polished angles and finely drawn-finished edges.
Functions: hours, minutes, minute repeater; one-minute flying tourbillon.
Case: 18K rose gold, satin-finished and polished; Ø 43mm; polished 18K rose-gold crown and minute repeater lever; sapphire crystal on caseback; water resistant to 3atm.
Dial: green mineral crystal; 18K rose-gold applied polished Jacob & Co. logo and brushed G clef.
Strap: alligator leather; 18K rose-gold tang buckle.
Note: limited edition of 36 pieces.
Suggested price: $265,000

PALATIAL CLASSIC MANUAL BIG DATE   REF. 110.400.40.NS.NA.1NS

Movement: manual-winding Jacob&Co. JCCM01 caliber; Ø 30.4mm, thickness: 5.8mm; 50-hour power reserve; 18 jewels; 28,800 vph; anti-shock; Glucydur balance; finishing: Côtes de Genève, circular graining and vertical satin-finish.
Functions: hours, minutes; big date at 12; power reserve indicator at 6.
Case: 18K rose gold; Ø 42mm, thickness: 13.5mm; water resistant to 5atm.
Dial: anthracite with guilloché pattern; polished applied Jacob & Co. logo; polished hands; applied polished faceted hour markers.
Strap: alligator leather; 18K rose-gold square polished tang buckle.
Suggested price: $22,500

JACOB & CO.

CALIGULA ROSE GOLD   REF. 400.100.40.NS.AA.1NS

Movement: automatic-winding exclusive Jacob&Co. JCAA01 caliber; Ø 35mm, thickness: 8.7mm; 25 jewels; 236 components; 46-hour power reserve; 28,800 vph; anti-shock; Glucydur balance; circular-grained; Côtes de Genève, sand-blasted.
Functions: hours, minutes, manually-wound automaton scene.
Case: 18K rose gold, polished; Ø 45mm; case side with fishnet engraving; antireflective sapphire crystal; water resistant to 3atm.
Dial: fishnet guilloché; rotalive; inner ring with hour markers which covers aperture that opens to reveal concealed erotic scene, hand-painted by miniature artist André Martinez; blue PVD 18K gold hands.
Strap: alligator leather; 18K rose-gold tang buckle.
Note: limited edition of 69 pieces.
Suggested price: $69,000

GHOST CARBON   REF. 300.100.11.NS.PC.4NS

Movement: Exclusive Jacob&Co. Swiss made digital caliber JCDQ01; quartz (32,768Hz; 20 ppm); battery lithium-polymere 3.7V, 80 mAh; LCD FFSTN negative.
Functions: LCD screen; digital multiple time zone display; 20 pre-set cities displayed on first four screen shows local time in chosen city, as well as date and battery power; automatic daylight savings time change and leap year, custom LCD display system, manual time setting possible; rechargeable battery via special USB cable (port on caseback).
Case: black PVD stainless steel; Ø 47mm, thickness: 16.2mm; rubberized carbon fiber bezel; red anodized aluminum pushbuttons; microblasted caseback with polished screws and engraved Jacob&Co. logo; water resistant to 3atm.
Dial: display colors: red, orange, yellow, green, blue, purple, white.
Strap: vulcanized rubber; black PVD stainless steel deployant buckle.
Note: warranty of two years.
Suggested price: $5,300.

PALATIAL FIVE TIME ZONE PIRATE DIAMOND BEZEL   REF. 100.500.10.NS.NP.1NS

Movement: Swiss quartz; one ETA caliber 976.001 and four ETA calibers 280.002.
Functions: hours, minutes; five time zones.
Case: stainless steel with black PVD coating; Ø 45mm; black PVD bezel set with 60 round diamonds (1.94 carats); water resistant to 5atm.
Dial: black PVD with pirate design set with 112 round diamonds (approx. 0.36 carat); polished Jacob & Co. logo; four time zone dials displaying New York, Los, Angeles, Tokyo and Paris; polished faceted rhodium-plated steel hands.
Strap: alligator leather; polished square tang stainless steel buckle.
Note: interchangeable bezels: plain or diamond set.
Suggested price: $12,500

EPIC X   REF. 550.100.20.NS.OX.4NS

Movement: manual-winding Jacob&Co. JCAM02 caliber; Ø 14.24mm, thickness: 5.9mm; 48-hour power reserve; 158 components; 21 jewels; 28,800 vph; barrel with sliding clamp system; balance screws visible through front side; time setting spring with three functions (octopus spring); ratchet, lever and setting level; anti-shock; finishing: Jacob&Co. upper bridge, sand blasted, angled and drawn-finished bridges; anthracite and red-lacquered Epic X engraving on right ride bridge; mirror-polished finishing screws; circular grained bridges on caseback.
Functions: hours, minutes.
Case: grade-5 titanium; Ø 44mm, thickness: 12.3mm; finishing: micro-blasted and satin-finished; Jacob&Co. logo in inner ring; sapphire crystal; water resistant to 5atm.
Dial: skeletonized hands.
Strap: openworked Honeycomb rubber; adjustable deployant clasp.
Note: warranty of two years.
Suggested price: $18,000.

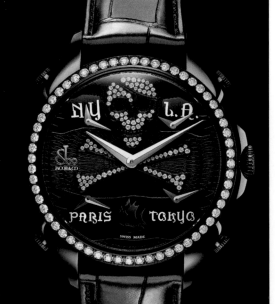

PALATIAL OPERA
REF. 150.820.40.BD.BD.1BD

Movement: manual-winding Jacob&Co. caliber JCBM01; 100-hour power reserve; 194 components; 29 jewels; 21,600 vph; titanium balance with gold timing screw; satin-finished, hand-polished angles and drawn-finished flanks.
Functions: hours, minutes; one minute flying tourbillon.
Case: 18K rose gold; Ø 47m; invisibly set with 142 baguette diamonds (approx. 11.7 carats); bezel set with 50 baguette diamonds (approx. 8.1 carats); 18K rose-gold polished crown set with nine baguette diamonds and one rose cut diamond (approx. 0.55 carat); circular satin-finished and polished; 18K rose-gold outer lugs; sapphire crystal caseback; water resistant to 3atm.
Dial: 18K rose gold; invisibly set with 174 baguette diamonds (approx. 10.9 carats).
Strap: alligator leather; 18K rose-gold deployment buckle set with 23 baguette diamonds (approx. 1.5 carats).
Note: limited edition of 18 pieces.
Suggested price: $720,000

CAVIAR TOURBILLON
REF. 600.201.30.BK.BK.1BK

Movement: manual-winding exclusive Jacob&Co. JCBM05 caliber; 100-hour power reserve; 169 components; 21,600 vph; titanium balance with gold timing screw.
Functions: hours, minutes; one minute flying tourbillon at 6.
Case: 18K white gold; Ø 47mm; invisibly set with 232 baguette black diamonds (approx. 26.2 carats); crown set with 16 baguette and one rose-cut black diamond (approx. 0.82 carat); power reserve indication on caseback; antireflective sapphire crystal.
Dial: invisibly set with 140 baguette black diamonds (approx. 10.6 carats).
Strap: alligator leather; 18K white-gold tang buckle set with 36 baguette black diamonds (approx. 1.52 carats).
Note: limited edition of three pieces.
Suggested price: $900,000

EPIC X TOURBILLON BAGUETTE
REF. 550.500.30.BD.BD.1BD

Movement: manual-winding exclusive Jacob&Co. JCAM03 caliber; Ø 34mm; 48-hour power reserve; 21,600 vph; barrel and tourbillon balance wheel vertically aligned; visible time setting mechanism on caseback; finishing: Jacob & Co. upper bridge, sandblasted, angled and drawn finished bridges, anthracite and red lacquered "Epic X" engraving on right side bridge, mirror-polished finishing screws, circular-grained bridges on caseback.
Functions: hours, minutes; seconds on tourbillon cage at 6; time setting spring with three functions ("octopus spring"): ratchet, lever and setting lever.
Case: 18K white gold; Ø 44mm, thickness: 12.3mm; 86 baguette diamonds; finishing: microblasted and satin-finished; "Jacob & Co." logo in inner ring; antireflective sapphire crystal; water resistant to 5atm.
Dial: skeletonized; skeletonized hands.
Strap: alligator leather; adjustable deployment clasp set with 11 baguette diamonds (approx. 1.13 carats).
Suggested price: $600,000

GHOST, ROSE-GOLD SET BEZEL
REF. 300.100.14.RP.MR.4NS

Movement: exclusive Swiss made Jacob&Co. JCDQ01 caliber; quartz (32,768Hz; 20ppm); battery Lithium-Polymere 3.7V 80mAh; LCD FFSTN negative.
Functions: LCD screen; digital multiple time zone display; 20 pre-set cities displayed on first four screens; fifth screen shows local time in chosen city, as well as day, date, month and battery power.
Case: black PVD stainless steel; Ø 47mm; pentagon-shaped; 18K rose-gold bezel set with 105 white round diamonds (approx. 3.48 carats); 18K rose gold pushbuttons.
Dial: 20 pre-set cities on first four screens; fifth screen shows local time in chosen city as well as day, date, month and battery power; display colors: red, orange, yellow, green, blue, purple, white.
Strap: vulcanized rubber; black PVD stainless steel deployment buckle.
Suggested price: $24,800
Also available: interchangeable bezels: carbon fiber, black PVD set with diamonds; rose gold set with diamonds.

JACOB & CO.

BRILLIANT RAINBOW — REF. 210.536.40.GR.KW.3RD

Movement: automatic-winding exclusive Jacob&Co. JCFA01 caliber; Ø 25.6mm, thickness: 3.6mm; 42-hour power reserve; 25 jewels; finishing: openworked, hand-engraved.
Functions: hours, minutes.
Case: 18K rose gold; Ø 44mm, thickness: 25mm; set with 48 rainbow baguette-cut sapphires (approx. 5.28 carats); crown set with 31 white round diamonds (approx. 0.38 carat); skeletonized caseback with inner ring set with 48 white round-cut diamonds (approx. 0.76 carat); antireflective sapphire crystal; water resistant to 3atm.

Dial: white mother-of-pearl set with 11 rainbow sapphire hour markers (approx. 0.88 carat); center pavé set with 50 white round-cut diamonds (approx. 0.96 carat); leaf-shaped hands.
Strap: alligator leather; buckle set with 42 white round-cut diamonds (approx. 0.76 carat).
Note: total carat weight: 129 white round diamonds (approx. 2.86 carats), 48 white round-cut diamonds (approx. 5.28 carats), eleven sapphires (approx. 0.88 carat), total sapphires (approx. 6.16 carats).
Suggested price: $65,000

BRILLIANT SKELETON JEWELRY — REF. 210.531.40.RD.CB.3RD

Movement: manual-winding exclusive Jacob&Co. JCAM01 caliber; Ø 32mm, thickness: 5.8mm; 46-hour power reserve; 21 jewels; finishing: angled bridges with sandblasted finishing, angled steel elements with drawn-finishing, open-worked anthracite with rose-gold bridges, gears and logo.
Functions: hours, minutes.
Case: 18K rose gold; Ø 44mm; polished and pavé-set with 294 round diamonds (approx. 8.88 carats); crown set with 31 white round diamonds (approx. 0.39 carat).
Dial: skeletonized.

Strap: satin; 18K rose-gold tang buckle set with 42 white round diamonds (approx. 0.72 carat).
Note: limited edition of 101 pieces.
Suggested price: $79,000

BRILLIANT MYSTERY PAVE ROSE-GOLD — REF. 210.526.40.RD.RD.3RD

Movement: Swiss quartz ETA caliber E01.701.
Functions: hours, minutes.
Case: 18K rose gold; Ø 38mm; invisible setting with 298 round white diamonds (approx. 6.5 carats); bezel set with 89 round white diamonds (approx. 0.55 carat); antireflective sapphire crystal.
Dial: center set with 56 round white diamonds (approx. 0.9 carat); two floating black triangle hands.
Strap: satin; 18K rose-gold tang buckle set with 33 round white diamonds (approx. 0.48 carat).
Note: limited edition of 18 pieces.
Suggested price: $75,000

BRILLIANT TWO ROWS — REF. 210.030.10.RT.KR.3NS

Movement: Swiss quartz ETA caliber 955.432; ETA caliber 901.001; Ø 24mm.
Functions: hours, minutes.
Case: polished stainless steel; Ø 44mm, thickness: 11.6mm; set with 177 round diamonds (approx. 2.36 carats); crown set with round diamonds; circular satin-finished caseback with engraving; antireflective crystal; water resistant to 3atm.
Dial: white mother-of-pearl; set with 11 multi-colored sapphire hour markers (approx. 0.88 carat); center pavé set with 50 round diamonds (approx. 0.96 carat); leaf-shaped hands.
Strap: satin; stainless steel polished tang buckle.
Note: warranty of two years.
Suggested price: $21,000

BRILLIANT SKELETON BAGUETTE   REF. 210.530.30.BR.AA.3BR

Movement: manual-winding exclusive JCAM01 caliber; Ø 32mm, thickness: 5.8mm; 46-hour power reserve; 21 jewels; finishing: angled bridges with sandblasted finishing, angled steel elements with drawn finishing, open-worked anthracite movement with rose-gold bridges, gears and logo.
Functions: hours, minutes.
Case: 18K rose gold; Ø 44mm; polished and set with 239 baguette diamonds (10.4 carats).
Dial: skeletonized.
Strap: alligator leather; 18K rose-gold tang buckle set with 21 baguette diamonds (approx. 1.17 carats).
Note: limited edition of 101 pieces.
Suggested price: $260,000

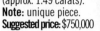

BRILLIANT SKELETON TOURBILLON ART DECO ICY BLUE   REF. 210.545.30.BC.RB.1BC

Movement: manual-winding exclusive JCAM05 caliber; Ø 32mm, thickness: 6.65mm; 72-hour power reserve; 19 jewels; finishing: open-worked with sapphire plates and bridges finely set with 178 round diamonds (0.56 carat); hand-polished angles.
Functions: hours, minutes.
Case: 18K white gold; Ø 47mm; polished and invisibly set with 205 icy blue baguette sapphires (approx. 20.98 carats); inside upper bezel with 48 white baguette diamonds (approx. 1.98 carats); crown set with 14 icy blue baguette sapphires (approx. 0.8 carat); one rose-cut icy blue sapphire (0.49 carat).
Dial: skeletonized.
Strap: alligator leather; 18K white-gold tang buckle set with 20 icy blue baguette sapphires (approx. 1.49 carats).
Note: unique piece.
Suggested price: $750,000

BRILLIANT MYSTERY DIAL BAGUETTE DIAMOND/RUBY   REF. 210.526.30.BD.BR.3BD

Movement: Swiss quartz ETA E01.701 caliber.
Functions: hours, minutes.
Case: 18K white gold; Ø 38mm; invisible setting with baguette-cut diamonds and baguette-cut rubies, total of 371 stones (approx. 27.5 carats); antireflective sapphire crystal.
Dial: hours, minutes; two floating black triangle hands.
Strap: satin; 18K white-gold tang buckle set with 28 baguette-cut diamonds (approx. 0.9 carat).
Suggested price: $290,000

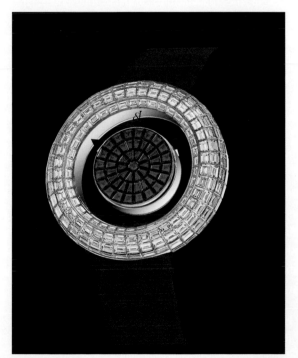

BRILLIANT FLYING TOURBILLON ARLEQUINO   REF. 210.543.40.HX.HX.1HX

Movement: manual-winding Jacob & Co. caliber JCBM01; 100-hour power reserve; 206 components; 21,600 vph; titanium balance with gold timing screw; satin-finished, hand-polished angles and drawn-finished flanks.
Functions: hours, minutes; one-minute flying tourbillon at 6.
Case: 18K rose gold; Ø 47mm; invisibly set with 68 baguette multicolor sapphires (approx. 6.01 carats) and 137 baguette white diamonds (approx. 11.3 carats); crown set with nine baguette multicolor sapphires (approx. 0.6 carat), five baguette diamonds (approx. 0.21 carat) and one rose-cut yellow sapphire (approx. 0.32 carat); power reserve indicator on caseback; antireflective sapphire crystal.
Dial: invisibly set with 90 baguette multicolor sapphires (approx. 9.1 carats), 66 baguette white diamonds (approx. 3.68 carats).
Strap: alligator leather; 18K rose-gold tang buckle set with 13 baguette multicolor sapphires (approx. 0.97 carat) and seven baguette white diamonds (approx. 0.41 carat).
Note: limited edition.
Suggested price: $770,000

JAEGER-LECOULTRE

HYBRIS VIGOR

New entries in Jaeger-LeCoultre's Hybris Mechanica and Hybris Artistica collections **EMBODY HAUTE HOROLOGY'S SYNERGY OF INGENUITY AND PERFORMANCE**.

Rejecting conventional mechanical construction, the Hybris Mechanica 11 boasts not only a flying tourbillon, but one endowed with a flying balance wheel. The audacious architecture permits an unprecedented view of the timepiece's heartbeat, while reducing the thickness of the movement and enabling the watch's record-breaking thinness of 7.9mm: an astounding feat for such a complex minute repeater. Suggested by a musical clef at 8 o'clock, the Hybris Mechanica 11's sonorous complication boasts another of the manufacture's inspired innovations. Traditional minute repeaters leave an audible pause in the chiming sequence when a quarter-hour strike is unnecessary—at 1:04 for example. The Jaeger LeCoultre Calibre 362 recognizes this gap and seamlessly erases the time lapse, creating a smooth transition between the sound of the hours and minutes. Even the choice of material for the 41mm case was made with functionality in mind. The 18-karat extra-white-gold case provides the hand-decorated 471-component movement with an optimal acoustic chamber. In a further demonstration of Jaeger-LeCoultre's dedication to innovative excellence, the self-winding caliber's platinum oscillating weight—visible through narrow openings on the outer section of the face—is installed as a peripheral module, thus optimizing use of space while presenting an additional dynamic spectacle. Finished with a retractable minute-repeater pushbutton that preserves the silhouette's geometric elegance, the limited edition Hybris Mechanica 11, the beneficiary of eight individual patents, is a testament to Jaeger-LeCoultre's horological genius.

◄ **HYBRIS MECHANICA 11**
This flying tourbillon minute repeater measures a mere 7.9mm in thickness—a triumph of ceaseless ingenuity and eight separate patents.

Fitted with a transparent sapphire bridge, the Duomètre Sphérotourbillon Pocket Watch appears to weightlessly suspend the complication in midair.

The manufacture's Duomètre Sphérotourbillon Pocket Watch, part of the brand's newest Hybris Artistica collection, wows with a flying tourbillon of its own, the world's first Sphérotourbillon presented in a pocket watch. Fitted with a transparent sapphire bridge, the tourbillon appears to be weightlessly suspended in midair. The 48mm case, in white gold with pronounced accents in blue enamel, brings to the creation a vivid personality in tune with the dial's tones and dynamic gyroscopic regulator. Three Grand Feu enamel subdials, at 12, 3 and 9 o'clock, indicate the hours and minutes, flyback seconds, and world time respectively. Power reserve indicators to the left and right of the principal subdial confirm the watch's elegant symmetry and accentuate the rich texture of the hand-engraved white-gold dial.

Another entry in the multi-faceted Hybris Artistica collection, the Master Gyrotourbillon 1 complements mechanical excellence with a dial of remarkable artistry. Pierced by an aperture at 6 o'clock exposing the Jaeger-LeCoultre 177 caliber's spherical tourbillon, the hand-wound timepiece's face is composed of a skeletonized aventurine plate that gives the watch its unique stained glass character. On the upper half of the dial, the hour and minute hands are joined by a third stem whose solar tip indicates a running equation-of-time functionality. This rare complication depicts variable discrepancies between civil time and "true solar time"—an astronomical concept that takes into account variations in the day's length caused by the earth's elliptical orbit. Presenting this divergence on the same axis as the conventional hours and minutes is particularly impressive, given the need for a single caliber to drive two separate measures of time. The Master Gyrotourbillon 1 also boasts a perpetual calendar with retrograde indications, including a retrograde leap-year indicator on the watch's caseback. Made of 18-karat white gold, the 43mm case emphasizes the intense hues and exceptional craftsmanship of the timepiece's dial.

▲ **DUOMETRE SPHEROTOURBILLON POCKET WATCH**
The tourbillon's transparent sapphire bridge results in an optimal view of the complication while furthering its visual effect of weightless suspension.

▶ **MASTER GYROTOURBILLON 1**
The exquisite craftsmanship of this hand-wound timepiece's skeletonized aventurine dial befits the stunning sophistication of its internal heartbeat.

JAEGER-LeCOULTRE

HYBRIS MECHANICA 11 — REF. 131 35 20

Movement: automatic-winding Jaeger-LeCoultre caliber 362; thickness: 4.8mm; 45-hour power reserve; 471 components; 68 jewels; 21,600 vph; two barrels.
Functions: hours, minutes; minute repeater; tourbillon.
Case: white gold; Ø 41mm, thickness: 7.9mm; water resistant to 3atm.
Dial: silver grained; dauphine hands.
Strap: alligator leather; pin buckle.
Note: limited edition of 75 pieces.
Suggested price: $143,472

MASTER GRANDE TRADITION A QUANTIEME PERPETUEL 8 JOURS SQ — REF. 506 35 SQ

Movement: manual-winding Jaeger-LeCoultre caliber 876SQ; thickness: 6.6mm; 8-day power reserve; 262 components; 37 jewels; 28,800 vph; two barrels.
Functions: hours, minutes; perpetual calendar: date, day, month, year, day/night indicator; moonphase; red security zone; 8-day power reserve.
Case: white gold; Ø 42mm, thickness: 11.6mm; water resistant to 5atm.
Dial: front, skeletonized enamel; back, skeletonized; feuille hands.
Strap: alligator leather; pin buckle.
Note: limited edition of 200 pieces.
Suggested price: $121,000

MASTER GRANDE TRADITION TOURBILLON CYLINDRIQUE A QUANTIEME PERPETUEL — REF. 504 25 20

Movement: automatic-winding Jaeger-LeCoultre caliber 985; thickness: 8.15mm; 48-hour power reserve; 431 components; 49 jewels; 28,800 vph; one barrel.
Functions: hours, minutes, seconds; perpetual calendar: date, day, month, year; moonphase; cylindrical tourbillon.
Case: pink gold; Ø 42mm, thickness: 13.1mm; water resistant to 5atm.
Dial: silver grained; dauphine hands.
Strap: alligator leather; pin buckle.
Suggested price: $143,000

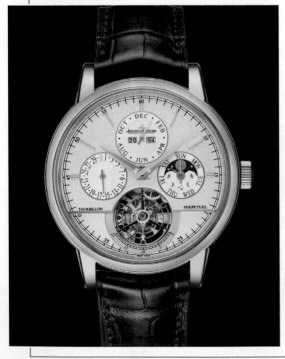

DUOMETRE UNIQUE TRAVEL TIME — REF. 606 25 20

Movement: Jaeger-LeCoultre caliber 383; thickness: 7.25mm; 50-hour power reserve; 498 components; 54 jewels; 28,800 vph; two barrels.
Functions: hours, minutes, seconds; jumping hour; GMT: second time zone, world map, day/night indicator, world time.
Case: pink gold; Ø 42mm, thickness: 13.7mm; water resistant to 5atm.
Dial: silvered; feuille hands.
Strap: alligator leather; pin buckle.
Suggested price: $46,300

MASTER ULTRA THIN 1907   REF. 129 25 20

Movement: manual-winding Jaeger-LeCoultre caliber 849; thickness: 1.85mm; 35-hour power reserve; 123 components; 19 jewels; 21,600 vph; one barrel.
Functions: hours, minutes.
Case: pink gold; Ø 39mm, thickness: 4.1mm; water resistant to 3atm.
Dial: white grained; dauphine hands.
Strap: alligator leather; pin buckle.
Suggested price: $18,600

MASTER ULTRA THIN GRAND FEU   REF. 129 35 E1

Movement: manual-winding Jaeger-LeCoultre caliber 849; thickness: 1.85mm; 35-hour power reserve; 123 components; 19 jewels; 21,600 vph; one barrel.
Functions: hours, minutes.
Case: 18K white gold; Ø 39mm, thickness: 5.04mm; polished finish; water resistant to 3atm.
Dial: white Grand Feu enamel; rhodium leaf-type hands.
Strap: alligator leather; pin buckle.
Note: boutique edition.
Suggested price: $32,200

MASTER ULTRA THIN DATE   REF. 128 25 10

Movement: automatic-winding Jaeger-LeCoultre caliber 899; thickness: 3.3mm; 43-hour power reserve; 219 components; 32 jewels; 28,800 vph; one barrel.
Functions: hours, minutes, seconds; date at 6.
Case: pink gold; Ø 40mm, thickness: 7.5mm; water resistant to 5atm.
Dial: eggshell beige; dauphine hands.
Strap: alligator leather; pin buckle.
Suggested price: $16,700

GEOPHYSIC 1958   REF. 800 85 20

Movement: automatic-winding Jaeger-LeCoultre caliber 898; thickness: 4.05mm; 43-hour power reserve; 202 components; 29 jewels; 28,800 vph.
Functions: hours, minutes, seconds.
Case: stainless steel; Ø 38.5mm, thickness: 12.4mm.
Dial: white; baton hands.
Strap: black alligator leather; pin buckle.
Note: limited edition of 800 pieces.
Suggested price: $9,800
Also available: pink gold: limited edition of 300 pieces, $20,800; platinum: limited edition of 58 pieces, $32,000.

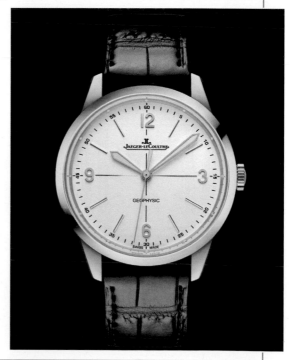

GRANDE REVERSO NIGHT & DAY — REF. 380 25 20

Movement: automatic-winding Jaeger-LeCoultre caliber 967B; thickness: 4.05mm; 42-hour power reserve; 200 components; 28 jewels; one barrel.
Functions: hours, minutes; 24-hour display.
Case: pink gold; 46.8x27.4mm, thickness: 9.1mm.
Dial: silvered satin-brushed and Clous de Paris; black transferred numerals; baton hands.
Strap: alligator leather; pin buckle.
Suggested price: $19,200

Also available: stainless steel: $9,750.

GRANDE REVERSO ULTRA THIN 1931 — REF. 278 25 60

Movement: manual-winding Jaeger-LeCoultre caliber 822/2; thickness: 2.94mm; 45-hour power reserve; 108 components; 19 jewels; 21,600 vph; one barrel.
Functions: hours, minutes, seconds.
Case: pink gold; 46.8x27.4mm, thickness: 7.3mm; water resistant to 3atm.
Dial: brilliant chocolate; gilt hour markers; baton hands.
Strap: cordovan alligator leather; pin buckle.
Suggested price: $18,800

GRANDE REVERSO ULTRA THIN 1948 — REF. 278 85 2J

Movement: manual-winding Jaeger-LeCoultre caliber 822/2; thickness: 2.94mm; 45-hour power reserve; 108 components; 19 jewels; 21,600 vph; one barrel.
Functions: hours, minutes, seconds.
Case: stainless steel; 46.8x27.4mm, thickness: 7.3mm; water resistant to 3atm.
Dial: silver grained; struck hour markers; baton hands.
Strap: alligator leather; pin buckle.
Note: boutique edition.
Suggested price: $9,450

REVERSO DUETTO CLASSIQUE — REF. 256 24 07

Movement: manual-winding Jaeger-LeCoultre caliber 865; thickness: 3.45mm; 48-hour power reserve; 130 components; 19 jewels; 21,600 vph; one barrel.
Functions: hours, minutes (on front and back).
Case: pink gold; 38.5x23.1mm, thickness: 9.5mm; water resistant to 3atm.
Dial: front: gem-set with 437 diamonds (approx. 1.8 carats), baton hands; back: black sunray brushed, gilt floral numerals, dauphine hands.
Strap: satin; double folding buckle.
Suggested price: $52,000

RENDEZ-VOUS DATE — REF. 351 25 20

Movement: automatic-winding Jaeger-LeCoultre caliber 966; thickness: 4.2mm; 214 components; 28 jewels; 28,800 vph; one barrel.
Functions: hours, minutes, seconds; date at 6.
Case: pink gold; Ø 27.5mm, thickness: 8.2mm; set with 60 diamonds (approx. 0.42 carat); water resistant to 3atm.
Dial: silvered guilloché; florale hands.
Strap: alligator leather; pin buckle.
Suggested price: $20,400

RENDEZ-VOUS NIGHT & DAY — REF. 346 84 90

Movement: automatic-winding Jaeger-LeCoultre caliber 967A; thickness: 4.05mm; 42-hour power reserve; 203 components; 28 jewels; one barrel.
Functions: hours, minutes, seconds; day/night indicator.
Case: stainless steel; Ø 29mm, thickness: 8.7mm; water resistant to 3atm.
Dial: mother-of-pearl; set with 11 diamonds (0.02 carat); florale hands.
Strap: alligator leather; double folding buckle.
Suggested price: $10,300
Also available: pink gold: $18,100; stainless steel with bracelet: $11,200.

MASTER COMPRESSOR CHRONOGRAPH CERAMIC — REF. 205 C5 70

Movement: automatic-winding Jaeger-LeCoultre caliber 757; thickness: 6.26mm; 65-hour power reserve; 300 components; 45 jewels; 28,800 vph; two barrels.
Functions: hours, minutes; small seconds at 6; date at 4:30; chronograph: 12-hour counter at 9, 30-minute counter at 3; second time zone; day/night indicator; movement operating indicator.
Case: ceramic; Ø 46mm, thickness: 14.3mm; water resistant to 10atm.
Dial: black; luminescent trapezoid hour markers; trapezium shaped skeletonized hands.
Strap: high-tech material; pin buckle.
Suggested price: $15,600

AMVOX2 TRANSPONDER — REF. 192 T4 8A

Movement: automatic-winding Jaeger-LeCoultre caliber 751E; thickness: 5.65mm; 280 components; 41 jewels; 65-hour power reserve; 28,800 vph; two barrels.
Functions: hours, minutes; date at 4:30; vertical trigger chronograph: 30-minute counter, 60-second counter; movement operating indicator; transponder.
Case: titanium; Ø 44mm, thickness: 15.4mm; water resistant to 5atm.
Dial: black satin; luminescent numerals and hour markers; faceted baton hands.
Strap: calfskin; double folding buckle.
Suggested price: $29,500

JD

JAQUET DROZ

PIECES OF EIGHT

UNRESTRICTED BY CONVENTIONAL CODES OF DESIGN, Jaquet Droz imbues each of its timepieces with the fruits of its boundless imagination, and for three new presentations, the sinuous elegance of the "figure eight."

The Swiss watchmaker's Grande Seconde Quantième Ivory Enamel encapsulates the pure elegance of timekeeping. Its self-winding 2660Q2.P caliber reflects the aesthetic refinement of the timepiece with a number of major technical evolutions, showcasing the brand's characteristic quest for excellence.

Incorporating silicon in the construction of its balance spring, the 43mm red-gold timepiece boasts a remarkable resistance to magnetism, shock and variations in temperature and pressure. Upon a dial in Grand Feu enamel, the wristwatch presents its display of time in the form of the watchmaker's emblematic figure eight.

Hours and minutes are told against a ring of Roman numerals within the upper subsection, while a larger subdial intersects the latter and gives subtle depth to the architecture. Articulating both the seconds (on the periphery) and the date (via a hand in the recessed portion of the counter), Jaquet Droz ingeniously maximizes its use of space and transforms a comprehensive timekeeping display into a picture of uncluttered elegance.

The Grande Seconde Quantième Ivory Enamel also grants its owner a magnificent view of its double-barrel movement, embellished with an array of exquisite finishes and decorated with Côtes de Genève, through an exhibition caseback.

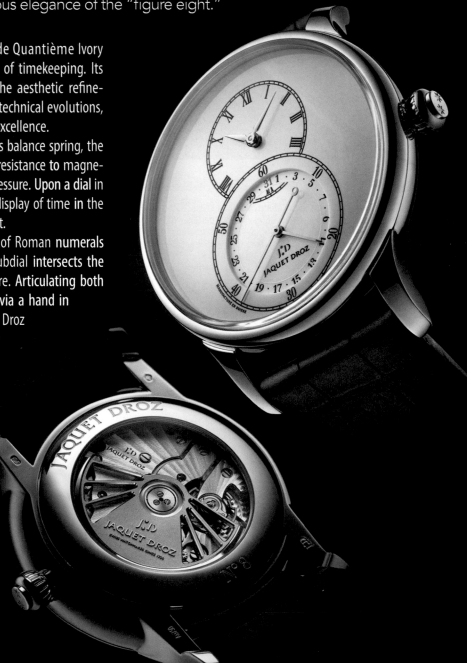

▶ **GRANDE SECONDE QUANTIEME IVORY ENAMEL**

The ingenious integration of the date in a recessed section of its large seconds display allows this self-winding timepiece's Grand Feu enamel dial to maintain its sober elegance.

The Grande Seconde SW Steel asserts its captivating personality with a robust steel case and a dial that blends bold geometric lines with Côtes de Genève décor.

A sporty interpretation of the brand's iconic Grande Seconde concept, the Grande Seconde SW Steel finds elegance in a dynamic balance of masculinity and finesse.

The 45mm timepiece asserts its captivating personality from the onset, with a robust steel case and a dial that blends bold geometric lines with background Côtes de Genève décor. Two subdials, one depicting the hours and minutes via two skeletonized hands, and the other the seconds within a generous frame on the watch's lower half, are seamlessly united into a symbolic figure eight, thanks to a tasteful transition from Roman to Arabic numerals in the center of the dial. Driven by the self-winding 2663A-S caliber with double-barrel construction, and boasting a 68-hour power reserve, the Grande Seconde SW Steel is a brilliant statement of contemporary elegance: a synergy of luxurious refinement and decisive masculinity.

The Lady 8 Mother-of-Pearl takes on horological architecture with opulent style. The self-winding 35mm wristwatch embodies feminine beauty with a magnificent interplay of lights, texture and sinuous architecture. Invigorated by 128 shimmering diamonds, the timepiece's 18-karat red-gold case extends beyond the circumference of the dial, gently wrapping itself around a large white pearl that lends the luxurious design a vibrant three-dimensional aesthetic. The lavish design is brightly echoed by a dial in white mother-of-pearl, upon which two lender 18-karat red-gold hands echo the warm tones of the case and hand-made brown alligator leather strap. Finished with a mother-of-pearl cabochon in the crown at 3 o'clock and endowed with a 68-hour power reserve and oscillation frequency of 28,800 vph, the Lady 8 Mother-of-Pearl takes timekeeping on a journey of radiant femininity.

▲ GRANDE SECONDE SW STEEL

This sporty take on the brand's "figure eight" juxtaposes its robust identity with the finesse of a dial decorated with Côtes de Genève.

▶ LADY 8 MOTHER-OF-PEARL

Illuminated at every turn by a combination of diamonds, white mother-of-pearl and a large pearl at 12 o'clock, this feminine wristwatch interprets the "figure eight" with incomparable radiance.

JAQUET DROZ

PETITE HEURE MINUTE 35 SHINY   REF. J005003220

Movement: automatic-winding; 68-hour power reserve.
Functions: off-centered hours, minutes at 12.
Case: 18K red gold; Ø 35mm; set with 685 diamonds (2.76 carats).
Dial: 18K red gold; set with 565 diamonds (1.31 carats).
Strap: 18K red-gold ardillon buckle set with 22 diamonds (0.072 carat).
Note: limited edition of 28 pieces.
Suggested price: $62,000

PETITE HEURE MINUTE 35 PIETERSIT   REF. J005004270

Movement: automatic-winding; 68-hour power reserve.
Functions: off-centered hours, minutes at 12.
Case: 18K white gold; Ø 35mm.
Dial: pietersite.
Strap: navy blue.
Note: limited edition of 28 pieces.
Suggested price: $21,700

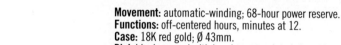

PETITE HEURE MINUTE HORSE   REF. J005013204

Movement: automatic-winding; 68-hour power reserve.
Functions: off-centered hours, minutes at 12.
Case: 18K red gold; Ø 39mm.
Dial: ivory Grand Feu enamel.
Strap: brown.
Note: limited edition of 88 pieces.
Suggested price: $30,500

PETITE HEURE MINUTE LOW RELIEF HORSE   REF. J005033201

Movement: automatic-winding; 68-hour power reserve.
Functions: off-centered hours, minutes at 12.
Case: 18K red gold; Ø 43mm.
Dial: black enamel with hand-engraved and champlevé-enameled 22K red-gold horse appliqué.
Strap: brown.
Note: limited edition of 88 pieces.
Suggested price: $57,800

GRANDE SECONDE OFF CENTERED IVORY ENAMEL — REF. J006033200

Movement: automatic-winding; 68-hour power reserve.
Functions: off-centered hours, minutes at 1; seconds at 7.
Case: 18K red gold; Ø 43mm.
Dial: ivory Grand Feu enamel.
Strap: black.
Suggested price: $20,000

GRAND SECONDE QUANTIEME COTES DE GENEVE — REF. J007010241

Movement: automatic-winding; 68-hour power reserve.
Functions: hours, minutes at 12; seconds and date by hand at 6.
Case: stainless steel; Ø 39mm.
Dial: Côtes de Genève; silver opaline ring.
Strap: black.
Suggested price: $9,300

GRANDE SECONDE QUANTIEME IVORY ENAMEL — REF. J007013200

Movement: automatic-winding; 68-hour power reserve.
Functions: hours, minutes at 12; seconds, date by hand at 6.
Case: 18K red gold; Ø 39mm.
Dial: ivory Grand Feu enamel; double level.
Strap: black.
Suggested price: $19,400

GRANDE SECONDE QUANTIEME IVORY ENAMEL — REF. J007034200

Movement: automatic-winding; 68-hour power reserve.
Functions: hours, minutes at 12; seconds, date by hand at 6.
Case: 18K white gold; Ø 43mm.
Dial: ivory Grand Feu enamel; double level.
Strap: black.
Suggested price: $20,000

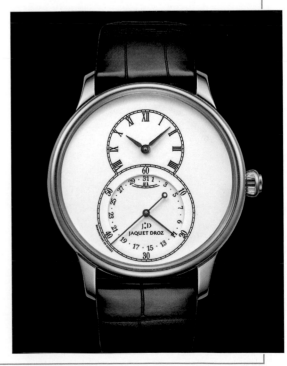

JAQUET DROZ

THE TWELVE CITIES AVENTURINE   REF. J010110270

Movement: automatic-winding 5153 caliber; 68-hour power reserve; 28 jewels; 28,800 vph; double barrel; heavy metal oscillating weight.
Functions: minutes; jumping hours through aperture at 12; 12 time zones indicated by city name at 6.
Case: stainless steel; Ø 39mm, thickness: 12.27mm; pushbutton at 2 for city selection; caseback engraved with individual serial number; water resistant to 3atm.
Dial: aventurine; white inlaid mother-of-pearl center; rhodium-treated hands.
Strap: blue rolled-edge handmade alligator leather; stainless steel ardillon buckle.

Suggested price: $17,300

THE ECLIPSE MOTHER OF PEARL   REF. J012614570

Movement: automatic-winding Jaquet Droz 6553L2 caliber; 68-hour power reserve; 28 jewels; 28,800 vph; double barrel; 22K white-gold oscillating weight.
Functions: hours, minutes; date by hand; month and day at 12; retrograde moonphase at 6.
Case: 18K white gold; Ø 39mm, thickness: 12.7mm; set with 248 diamonds (1.62 carats); caseback engraved with individual serial number; water resistant to 3atm.
Dial: white mother-of-pearl; white-gold moon and stars appliqués with rhodium treatment; 18K white-gold hands; white mother-of-pearl moonphase.
Strap: gray rolled-edge handmade satin; 18K white-gold ardillon buckle set with 24 diamonds (0.15 carat).
Suggested price: $36,500

THE ECLIPSE ONYX   REF. J012630270

Movement: automatic-winding Jaquet Droz 6553L2 caliber; 68-hour power reserve; 28 jewels; 28,800 vph; double barrel; heavy metal oscillating weight.
Functions: hours, minutes; date by hand; month and day at 12; retrograde moonphase at 6.
Case: stainless steel; Ø 43mm, thickness: 12.44mm; caseback engraved with individual serial number; water resistant to 3atm.
Dial: black onyx; rhodium-treated hands, star and moon appliqués; black onyx moonphase.
Strap: black rolled-edge handmade alligator leather; stainless steel ardillon buckle.
Suggested price: $17,900

GRANDE SECONDE TOURBILLON AVENTURINE   REF. J013014270

Movement: automatic-winding; 7-day power reserve.
Functions: hours, minutes at 6; tourbillon at 12.
Case: 18K white gold; Ø 39mm; set with 260 diamonds (1.47 carats).
Dial: aventurine with white mother-of-pearl; 18K white-gold ring set with 90 diamonds (0.14 carat).
Strap: navy blue.
Note: limited edition of 28 pieces.
Suggested price: $115,400

LADY 8 BLACK CERAMIC
REF. J014500240

Movement: automatic-winding; 68-hour power reserve.
Functions: hours, minutes.
Case: stainless steel; Ø 35mm; set with 48 diamonds (approx. 0.53 carat); black ceramic ball bearing at 12 and black ceramic crown cabochon.
Dial: dome-shaped black ceramic.
Strap: black.
Suggested price: $14,600

GRANDE HEURE GMT
REF. J015233200

Movement: automatic-winding Jaquet Droz 5N50.4 caliber; 68-hour power reserve; 28 jewels; 28,800 vph; double barrel; 22K white-gold oscillating weight.
Functions: central hours for the first and second time zones.
Case: 18K red gold; Ø 43mm, thickness: 11.85mm; caseback engraved with individual serial number; water resistant to 3atm.
Dial: ivory Grand Feu enamel; 18K red-gold and blued steel hands.
Strap: black rolled-edge handmade alligator leather; 18K red-gold ardillon buckle.
Suggested price: $26,400

GRANDE SECONDE SW STEEL
REF. J029030243

Movement: automatic-winding; 68-hour power reserve.
Functions: hours, minutes at 12; seconds at 6.
Case: stainless steel; crown with rubber cast.
Dial: blue; Côtes de Genève.
Strap: blue.
Suggested price: $14,700

PERPETUAL CALENDAR ECLIPSE IVORY ENAMEL
REF. J030533201

Movement: automatic-winding 5853LR.4 caliber; 68-hour power reserve; 34 jewels; 28,800 vph; double barrel; 22K white-gold oscillating weight.
Functions: hours, minutes; perpetual calendar: retrograde day and date, pointer-type month display at 12, leap year indicator at 12, moonphase at 6.
Case: 18K red gold; Ø 43mm, thickness: 13.2mm; caseback engraved with individual serial number; water resistant to 3atm.
Dial: ivory Grand Feu enamel; 18K red-gold hands; ivory Grand Feu enamel moonphase.
Strap: black rolled-edge handmade alligator leather, 18K red gold folding clasp.
Suggested price: $54,600

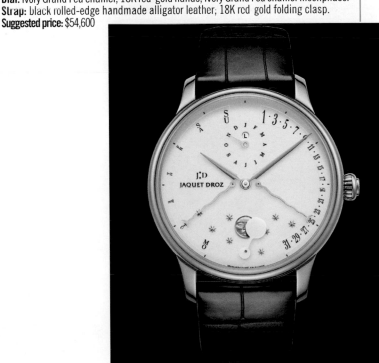

JR

JEANRICHARD
1681

ELEGANCE ON AND OFF THE PITCH

PARTNERING WITH LEGENDARY LONDON FOOTBALL CLUB ARSENAL FC, JEANRICHARD unites two worlds that share much more than meets the eye.

Honoring the legacy of 17th-century pioneer Daniel Jeanrichard, the Swiss watchmaker upholds a tradition of furthering the next generation's pursuit of excellence in the field of horology. This dedication to passing down not just its extraordinary expertise, but also its profound philosophy, which encompasses authenticity, passion to loyalty and team synergy, accounts for the culture of apprenticeship that drives the industry to this day. The Gunners of Arsenal, under the guidance of their manager Arsène Wenger, have long demonstrated a commitment to the recruitment of young players and their development into some of the sport's brightest stars, a rare philosophy among football clubs of such global success. The result is two organizations driven by youth and team spirit that proudly display a sincere respect for their rich heritages.

▲ **ARSENAL AEROSCOPE LIMITED EDITION**
Displaying the running seconds via a hand molded in the shape of Arsenal's emblematic canon, this titanium chronograph boasts a 43-jewel self-winding caliber with 42-hour power reserve.

◄ **ARSENAL TERRASCOPE SPECIAL EDITION**
This stainless steel timepiece displays Arsenal's famous logo within a design of understated elegance.

▲ Arsenal Manager Arsène Wenger and JEANRICHARD CEO Bruno Grande

▲ JEANRICHARD CEO Bruno Grande and Arsenal team players

▲ Arsenal stars Theo Walcott, Mathieu Flamini and Per Mertesacker showcase their specially designed timepieces alongside JEANRICHARD CEO Bruno Grande.

At 6 o'clock, an engraved Gunners logo joins the numerous luminescent red notes of the design and leaves no doubt as to the identity of the time-piece—Arsenal through and through.

The "off-field" philosophy of these two giants resembles their approach to their "in-game" performance. Arsenal's distinct and widely appealing attention to timing, elegance and style makes it a perfect partner for JEANRICHARD, a watchmaker founded on savoring each moment and the commitment to extraordinary designs and high-performance mechanisms. Now a global partner and "Official Watch" of Arsenal, JEANRICHARD unveils a duo of timepieces to adorn the wrists of the English club's talented players as stunning parts of their match-day outfits.

The Arsenal Terrascope Special Edition exudes the team's spirit of stylish elegance within a sporty design that echoes the club's own aesthetic. Housed in a 44mm stainless steel case, the self-winding timepiece displays the hours, minutes and seconds via centrally driven hands as well as the date through an elegant opening at 3 o'clock. At 6 o'clock, an engraved Gunners logo joins

the numerous luminescent red notes of the design and expresses its identity—Arsenal through and through. The wristwatch is powered by the JR60 caliber oscillating at a frequency of 28,800 vph.

With the Arsenal Aeroscope Limited Edition, JEANRICHARD asserts Arsenal's personality in a timepiece full of youthful dynamism and timekeeping sophistication. The watch's case in sandblasted black DLC-coated titanium sets a bright and imposing contrast against a red dial with honeycomb motif, where the JR66 caliber's chronograph presents the measure of elapsed time by way of a central seconds hand as well as 12-hour and 30-minute counters at 6 and 9 o'clock. Positioned just above the date aperture, the small seconds provide a resounding nod to the football club, as the traditional hand is replaced with an indicator in the shape of the Gunners' iconic canon.

TERRASCOPE — REF. 60500-11-601-FK6A

Movement: automatic-winding JR60 caliber; 11½ lines; 38-hour power reserve; 26 jewels; 28,800 vph.
Functions: hours, minutes, seconds; date.
Case: polished and vertically satin-finished steel; Ø 44 mm, thickness: 12.6mm; engraved screw-down caseback; water resistant to 10atm.
Dial: black; vertically satin-finished.
Strap: black rubber; steel folding buckle.
Price: available upon request.

TERRASCOPE — REF. 60500-56-603-BB60

Movement: automatic-winding JR60 caliber; 11½ lines; 38-hour power reserve; 26 jewels; 28,800 vph.
Functions: hours, minutes, seconds; date.
Case: sandblasted and vertically satin-finished black DLC-coated steel; Ø 44mm, thickness: 12.6mm; pink-gold bezel; engraved screw-down black caseback; water resistant to 10atm.
Dial: black; matte.
Strap: black alligator leather; black PVD-coated steel folding buckle.
Price: available upon request.

TERRASCOPE ARSENAL FC — REF. 60500-11-20E-FK6A

Movement: automatic-winding JR60 caliber; 11½ lines; 38-hour power reserve; 26 jewels; 28,800 vph.
Functions: hours, minutes, seconds; date.
Case: polished and vertically satin-finished steel; Ø 44mm, thickness: 12.6mm; engraved screw-down caseback; water resistant to 10 atm.
Dial: gray; engraved Gunners logo.
Strap: blue rubber; steel folding buckle.
Price: available upon request.

TERRASCOPE — REF. 60500-10-702-FK4B

Movement: automatic-winding JR60 caliber; 11½ lines; 38-hour power reserve; 26 jewels; 28,800 vph.
Functions: hours, minutes, seconds; date.
Case: polished and vertically satin-finished blue, red, and green aluminum; Ø 44mm, thickness: 12.6mm; engraved screw-down black caseback; water resistant to 10atm.
Dial: white; matte.
Strap: blue rubber; steel folding buckle.
Price: available upon request.

AQUASCOPE REF. 60400-11E701-FK7A

Movement: automatic-winding JR60 caliber; 11½ lines; 38-hour power reserve; 26 jewels; 28,800 vph.
Functions: hours, minutes, seconds; date.
Case: polished and vertically satin-finished steel; Ø 44mm, thickness: 13.05mm; circular satin-finished steel bezel; engraved screw-down caseback; water resistant to 30atm.
Dial: white; matte.
Strap: white rubber; steel folding buckle.
Price: available upon request.

AQUASCOPE REF. 60400-11D705-FB4A

Movement: automatic-winding JR60 caliber; 11½ lines; 38-hour power reserve; 26 jewels; 28,800 vph.
Functions: hours, minutes, seconds; date.
Case: polished and vertically satin-finished steel; Ø 44mm, thickness: 13.05mm; circular blue eloxed aluminum bezel; engraved screw-down caseback; water resistant to 30atm.
Dial: white; matte.
Strap: blue rubbergator; steel folding buckle.
Price: available upon request.

AQUASCOPE REF. 60400-11B402-FK4A

Movement: automatic-winding JR60 caliber; 11½ lines; 38-hour power reserve; 26 jewels; 28,800 vph.
Functions: hours, minutes, seconds; date.
Case: polished and vertically satin-finished blue PVD-coated steel; Ø 44mm, thickness: 13.05mm; circular satin-finished steel bezel; engraved screw-down caseback; water resistant to 30atm.
Dial: blue; engraved "Hokusai" style.
Strap: blue rubber; steel folding buckle.
Price: available upon request.

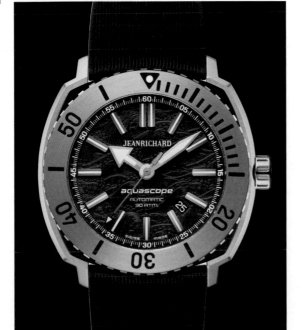

AQUASCOPE REF. 60400-11G606-FK6A

Movement: automatic-winding JR60 caliber; 11½ lines; 38-hour power reserve; 26 jewels; 28,800 vph.
Functions: hours, minutes, seconds; date.
Case: sandblasted and vertically satin-finished black PVD-coated steel; Ø 44mm, thickness: 13.05mm; circular satin-finished black eloxed aluminum bezel; engraved screw-down caseback; water resistant to 30atm.
Dial: black; engraved "Hokusai" style.
Strap: black rubber; black PVD-coated steel folding buckle.
Price: available upon request.

JEANRICHARD

AEROSCOPE ARSENAL FC   REF. 60650-21PH51-FK6A

Movement: automatic-winding JR66 caliber; 12½ lines; 42-hour power reserve; 43 jewels; 28,800 vph.
Functions: hours, minutes; small seconds; date; chronograph.
Case: sandblasted black DLC-coated titanium; Ø 44mm, thickness: 12.8mm; engraved screw-down titanium caseback; water resistant to 10atm.
Dial: red; stamped honeycomb pattern.
Strap: black rubber; black DLC-coated titanium folding buckle.
Note: numbered and limited edition of 250 pieces.

Price: available upon request.

NEROSCOPE   REF. 60650-21K614-FK6A

Movement: automatic-winding JR66 caliber; 12½ lines; 42-hour power reserve; 43 jewels; 28,800 vph.
Functions: hours, minutes; small seconds; date; chronograph.
Case: sandblasted and vertically satin-finished black DLC-coated titanium; Ø 44mm, thickness: 12.8mm; engraved screw-down titanium caseback; water resistant to 10atm.
Dial: black; vertically satin-finished.
Strap: black rubber; black PVD-coated steel folding buckle.
Note: numbered and limited edition of 500 pieces.
Price: available upon request.

AEROSCOPE   REF. 60650-21L252-FK6A

Movement: automatic-winding JR66 caliber; 12½ lines; 42-hour power reserve; 43 jewels; 28,800 vph.
Functions: hours, minutes; small seconds; date; chronograph.
Case: sandblasted titanium; Ø 44mm, thickness: 12.8mm; engraved screw-down titanium caseback; water resistant to 10atm.
Dial: gray; stamped honeycomb pattern.
Strap: black rubber; titanium folding buckle.
Price: available upon request.

AEROSCOPE   REF. 60650-21M652-FK6A

Movement: automatic-winding JR66 caliber; 12½ lines; 42-hour power reserve; 43 jewels; 28,800 vph.
Functions: hours, minutes; small seconds; date; chronograph.
Case: sandblasted and black DLC-coated titanium; Ø 44mm, thickness: 12.8mm; engraved screw-down titanium caseback; water resistant to 10atm.
Dial: black; stamped honeycomb pattern.
Strap: black rubber; black DLC-coated titanium folding buckle.
Price: available upon request.

AEROSCOPE
REF. 60660-21G651-FK6A

Movement: automatic-winding JR60 caliber; 11½ lines; 38-hour power reserve; 26 jewels; 28,800 vph.
Functions: hours, minutes, seconds; date.
Case: sandblasted titanium; Ø 44mm, thickness: 12.6mm; engraved screw-down titanium caseback; water resistant to 10atm.
Dial: black; grained.
Strap: black rubber; titanium folding buckle.
Price: available upon request.

1681
REF. 60320-11-652-HB6A

Movement: automatic-winding JR1000 caliber; 11½ lines; 48-hour power reserve; 27 jewels; 28,800 vph.
Functions: hours, minutes, seconds; date.
Case: sandblasted black DLC-coated steel; Ø 44mm, thickness: 11.27mm; screw down sapphire crystal caseback; water resistant to 10atm.
Dial: black; matte.
Strap: black Barenia® calfskin; black PVD-coated steel folding buckle.
Price: available upon request.

TERRASCOPE 39MM
REF. 60510-11-401-11A

Movement: automatic-winding JR60 caliber; 11½ lines; 38-hour power reserve; 26 jewels; 28,800 vph.
Functions: hours, minutes, seconds; date.
Case: polished and vertically satin-finished steel; Ø 39mm, thickness: 10.3mm; engraved screwed-down sapphire crystal caseback; water resistant to 10atm.
Dial: blue; textured.
Strap: steel; butterfly buckle.
Price: available upon request.

TERRASCOPE 39MM
REF. 60510-11-901-BBDA

Movement: automatic-winding JR60 caliber; 11½ lines; 38-hour power reserve; 26 jewels; 28,800 vph.
Functions: hours, minutes, seconds; date.
Case: polished and vertically satin-finished steel; Ø 39mm, thickness: 10.3mm; engraved screwed-down sapphire crystal caseback; water resistant to 10atm.
Dial: pale pink; mother-of-pearl.
Strap: pink alligator leather; steel folding buckle.
Price: available upon request.

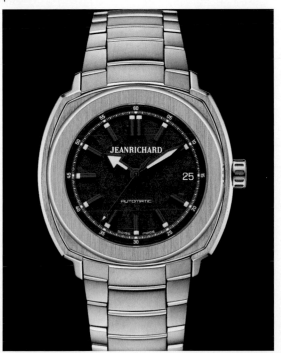

CONQUEST CLASSIC MOONPHASE

LONGINES CELEBRATES THE REFINED ELEGANCE OF EQUESTRIAN SPORTS

The "Conquest" brand was patented through the WIPO on 25 May 1954. Since then this name has been used for many successful models produced by Longines across the years. With its rich equestrian heritage dating back to 1878, it was natural for Longines to dedicate an entire collection to equestrian sports enthusiasts, for whom these disciplines are a source of excitement, passion and devotion. Hence it presented the Conquest Classic line. Building on the success of the Conquest Classic line, the Swiss watch brand was keen to further celebrate the equestrian sports and one of their essential dimensions, elegance. This is why Longines has come out with a new chronograph with a moonphase display: the Conquest Classic Moonphase. The sophistication of this model, including a moonphase display, makes it an eminently refined timepiece and echoes the excellence and elegance of the stars of the equestrian universe.

With a diameter of 42mm, this chronograph houses the self-winding mechanical chronograph movement L678. The case is available in steel, in steel and rose-gold cap or in 18-karat rose gold. The black or silvered dial is set with 9 applied indices coated with SuperLumiNova® and makes an elegantly contrasting background to the moonphase display. It features the 12-hour counter at 6 o'clock, the 24-hour indicator and the subdial for the seconds at 9 o'clock, as well as the 30-minute counter and the day-and-month display at 12 o'clock. The date is indicated by a half-moon central hand. Water resistant to 5 bar, these models display a transparent caseback through which its scintillating movement can be observed. These chronographs are fitted on a black alligator strap or a steel or steel and rose-gold cap bracelet, all having a triple-folding safety clasp.

LONGINES

LONGINES EQUESTRIAN LÉPINE

A TRIBUTE TO A LONG-LASTING PASSION

To mark the year of the horse in 2014, the Swiss watch brand launched its Longines Equestrian Lépine, a pocket watch in rose gold. Echoing the brand's passion for equestrian sport, the back cover of this exceptional creation is decorated with a horse flying over a jump. The model that served as an inspiration for this new product is a metal Lépine pocket watch dating from 1927, which is now on display at the Longines Museum in Saint-Imier.

Longines has been passionate about equestrian sports for many years. Today, it is involved in endurance competitions, show jumping and flat racing. In each discipline the brand is a partner of the most exciting and prestigious events all around the world, as well as of a number of major institutions in the field. Many racecourses and showgrounds boast the Longines colors today.

In 2014, Longines celebrated the year of the horse with an exceptional creation, a rose-gold pocket watch whose back cover is decorated with a horse flying over a jump. This model is a reissue of a metal pocket watch dating from 1927, which is currently on display in the Longines Museum. Given the name of Longines Equestrian Lépine, this new product is a tribute to a noble animal that has fascinated man from time immemorial. Imposing and proud, the horse embodies prestige as well as elegance and performance—two of the core values of the Swiss watch brand known by its winged hourglass logo.

With a diameter of 49.50mm, this new model is fitted with a manually wound L506 caliber, shows the hours and minutes and has a small seconds at 6 o'clock. Its white dial features a railway track minute-ring, large painted black Arabic numerals and a second minute-ring with red numerals. Pink Breguet hands complete the harmony of the dial while the sides and the bow are finely worked in imitation of the original model. The back cover is decorated with a stamped out horse motif and opens to reveal a solid caseback.

ELEGANCE IS AN ATTITUDE

The world of flat racing and Longines both share
common values, the most iconic of those being Elegance.
Longines celebrates the refined elegance of equestrian sports.

LONGINES

LONGINES PRIMALUNA — REF. L8.110.5.79.6

Movement: quartz caliber L250.2.
Functions: hours, minutes, seconds; date at 3.
Case: stainless steel and rose gold; Ø 26.5mm; set with 44 Top Wesselton VVS diamonds (0.299 carat); anti-reflective sapphire crystal; water resistant to 3atm.
Dial: silvered with "flinqué" decoration; 11 blue Roman numerals; blued steel hands.
Bracelet: stainless steel and rose gold; folding safety clasp and pushpieces.

LA GRANDE CLASSIQUE DE LONGINES "TONNEAU" — REF. L4.205.4.11.6

Movement: quartz caliber L209.
Functions: hours, minutes.
Case: stainless steel; ultra-thin; 22.2x24.5mm; sapphire crystal; water resistant to 3atm.
Dial: white; black Roman numerals; blackened steel hands.
Bracelet: stainless steel; triple-folding safety clasp and pushpieces.

LA GRANDE CLASSIQUE DE LONGINES 100 DIAMONDS — REF. L4.308.0.97.6

Movement: quartz caliber L209.
Functions: hours, minutes.
Case: stainless steel; Ø 29mm; set with 100 Top Wesselton VVS diamonds (0.760 carat); scratch-resistant sapphire crystal; water resistant to 3atm.
Dial: sunray blue; 12 diamond hour markers; silvered polished hands.
Bracelet: stainless steel; triple-folding safety clasp and pushpieces.

THE ELEGANT COLLECTION — REF. L4.309.5.88.7

Movement: automatic-winding caliber L595; 8¾ lines; 40-hour power reserve; 20 jewels; 28,800 vph.
Functions: hours, minutes, seconds, date at 3.
Case: stainless steel and rose gold; Ø 25.5mm; set with 52 Top Wesselton VVS diamonds (0.353 carat); scratch-resistant sapphire crystal; transparent caseback with sapphire crystal; water resistant to 3atm.
Dial: white mother-of-pearl; 12 diamond hour markers; black hands.
Bracelet: stainless steel and rose gold; triple-folding safety clasp and pushpieces.

CONQUEST CLASSIC   REF. L2.786.4.56.6

Movement: automatic-winding caliber L688.2; column-wheel chronograph; 13¼ lines; 54-hour power reserve; 27 jewels; 28,800 vph.
Functions: hours, minutes; small seconds at 9; date at 4:30; chronograph: 12-hour counter at 6, 30-minute counter at 3, central sweep seconds.
Case: stainless steel; Ø 41mm; scratch-resistant sapphire crystal with several layers of anti-reflective coating on the underside; transparent caseback with sapphire crystal; water resistant to 5atm.
Dial: black; 1 Arabic numeral and 11 applied hour markers with SuperLumiNova; rhodium-plated hands with SuperLumiNova.
Bracelet: stainless steel; triple-folding safety clasp and pushpieces.

CONQUEST CLASSIC   REF. L2.285.5.88.7

Movement: automatic-winding caliber L595.2; 8¾ lines; 40-hour power reserve; 20 jewels; 28,800 vph.
Functions: hours, minutes, seconds; date at 3.
Case: stainless steel and rose gold; Ø 29.5mm; set with 30 Top Wesselton VVS diamonds (0.501 carat); scratch-resistant sapphire crystal with several layers of anti-reflective coating; screw-down caseback with sapphire crystal; water resistant to 5 atm.
Dial: white mother-of-pearl; 12 diamond hour markers; rose-gold polished hands with SuperLumiNova.
Bracelet: stainless steel and rose gold; triple-folding safety clasp and pushpieces.

THE LONGINES MASTER COLLECTION   REF. L2.673.4.78.3

Movement: automatic-winding caliber L678; 13¼ lines; 48-hour power reserve; 25 jewels; 28,800 vph.
Functions: hours, minutes; small seconds and 24-hour indicator at 9; date; day and month at 12; moonphase at 6; chronograph: 12-hour counter at 6, 30-minute counter at 12, central seconds hand.
Case: stainless steel; Ø 40mm; anti-reflective sapphire crystal; sapphire crystal caseback; water resistant to 3atm.
Dial: silver-finished stamped "barleycorn"; nine Arabic numerals; blued steel hands; black-painted minute track, 31-day calendar.
Strap: dark brown alligator leather; triple-folding safety clasp.

LONGINES EVIDENZA   REF. L2.643.4.73.4

Movement: automatic-winding caliber L650; 12½ lines; 42-hour power reserve; 37 jewels; 28,800 vph.
Functions: hours, minutes; small seconds at 3; date at 6; chronograph: 12-hour counter at 6, 30-minute counter at 9, central seconds hand.
Case: stainless steel; 34.9x40mm; anti-reflective sapphire crystal; water resistant to 3atm.
Dial: silvered "flinqué"; 10 blue-painted Arabic numerals; blued steel hands.
Strap: dark brown alligator leather; triple-folding safety clasp.

LONGINES

CONQUEST   REF. L3.687.4.99.6

Movement: automatic-winding caliber L704.2; 16½ lines; 48-hour power reserve; 24 jewels; 28,800 vph.
Functions: hours, minutes, seconds; date at 3; second time zone.
Case: stainless steel; Ø 41mm; scratch-resistant sapphire crystal with several layers of anti-reflective coating on the underside; screw-in caseback and screw-in crown with protective shoulder; water resistant to 5atm.
Dial: blue dial; 2 applied Arabic numerals and 9 applied hour markers with Super-LumiNova; 24-hour scale; rhodium-plated hands with SuperLumiNova; red 24-hour hand with SuperLumi-Nova.
Bracelet: stainless steel; triple-folding safety clasp and pushpieces.

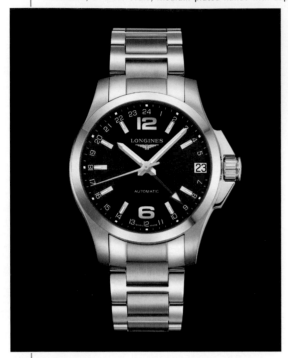

HYDROCONQUEST   REF. L3.696.4.53.6

Movement: automatic-winding caliber with a column-wheel chronograph mechanism L688.2; 13¼ lines; 54-hour power reserve; 27 jewels; 28,800 vph.
Functions: hours, minutes; small seconds at 9; date at 4; chronograph: dragging 30-minute counter at 3, dragging 12-hour counter at 6.
Case: stainless steel, Ø 41mm; scratch-resistant sapphire crystal with a single layer of anti-reflective coating; unidirectional turning bezel; screw-in crown with crown protection; screw-down caseback; water resistant to 30atm.
Dial: black; 8 Arabic numerals with SuperLumiNova; black bezel; rhodium-plated hands with SuperLumiNova.
Bracelet: integrated stainless steel bracelet; double-folding safety clasp; integrated diving extension.

CONQUEST 1/100TH HORSE RACING   REF. L3.700.4.76.6

Movement: quartz chronograph caliber L440.
Functions: hours, minutes; small seconds at 6; date at 4; chronograph: 30-minute counter at 2, 12-hour counter at 10, central 1/100th of second.
Case: stainless steel; Ø 41mm; scratch-resistant sapphire crystal with several layers of anti-reflective coating on the underside; screw-in caseback and screw-in crown with protective shoulder; water resistant to 3atm.
Dial: silvered; 1 applied Arabic numeral and 11 applied hour markers with SuperLumiNova; rhodium-plated hands; red 1/100th of second hand.
Bracelet: stainless steel; triple-folding safety clasp and pushpieces.

FLAGSHIP HERITAGE   REF. L4.795.4.78.2

Movement: automatic-winding caliber L615.2; 11½ lines; 42-hour power reserve; 27 jewels; 28,800 vph.
Functions: hours, minutes; small seconds and date at 6.
Case: stainless steel; Ø 38.5mm; anti-reflective sapphire crystal; water resistant to 3atm.
Dial: stainless steel; 11 golden hour markers; golden dauphine-style hands with SuperLumiNova.
Strap: brown alligator leather with buckle.

HERITAGE DIVER
REF. L2.796.4.52.9

Movement: automatic-winding chronograph caliber L651.3; 12½ lines; 42-hour power reserve; 37 jewels; 28,800 vph.
Functions: hours, minutes, seconds; date at 6; chronograph: 60-second counter at 3, 30-minute counter at 9.
Case: stainless steel; Ø 43mm; scratch-resistant sapphire crystal with several layers of anti-reflective coating on the underside; screw-in bezel, caseback and crown; water resistant to 3atm.
Dial: black satin-finish dial; 9 applied hour markers with SuperLumiNova; bidirectional rotating inner flange, graduated from 60 to 0 with minute zones indicated in red; rhodium-plated hands with Super-LumiNova; red second hand.
Strap: black rubber; diving folding clasp.

AVIGATION
REF. L2.831.4.53.2

Movement: automatic-winding caliber L704.2; 16½ lines; 48-hour power reserve; 24 jewels; 28,800 vph.
Functions: hours, minutes, seconds; date at 3; second time zone.
Case: stainless steel; Ø 44mm; scratch-resistant sapphire crystal with several layers of anti-reflective coating on the underside; screw-down caseback; water resistant to 3atm.
Dial: black lacquered and polished dial; 11 applied Arabic numerals with SuperLumi-Nova; red 24-hour scale; rhodium-plated skeleton baton hands with SuperLumiNova; red 24-hour diamond-shaped skeleton hand with SuperLumiNova.
Strap: black alligator with buckle.

THE LONGINES HERITAGE 1935
REF. L2.794.4.53.0

Movement: automatic-winding caliber L615; 11½ lines; 42-hour power reserve; 27 jewels; 28,800 vph.
Functions: hours, minutes; small seconds and date at 6.
Case: stainless steel; Ø 42mm; scratch-resistant sapphire crystal with several layers of anti-reflective coating on the underside; water resistant to 3atm.
Dial: matte black dial; 11 painted Arabic numerals with SuperLumiNova; rhodium-plated pear skeleton hands with SuperLumiNova.
Strap: black alligator with buckle.

LONGINES TWENTY-FOUR HOURS SINGLE PUSH-PIECE CHRONOGRAPH
REF. L2.797.4.73.0

Movement: automatic-winding caliber with a single pushpiece and column-wheel chronograph mechanism L789.2; 13¼ lines; 54-hour power reserve; 27 jewels; 28,800 vph.
Functions: hours (24-hour scale), minutes; small seconds; chronograph; date at 12; small seconds at 18.
Case: stainless steel; Ø 47.50mm; scratch-resistant sapphire crystal with several layers of anti-reflective coating on the underside; single pushpiece integrated into the crown; water resistant to 3atm.
Dial: silvered dial with black outer minute ring and 24-hour scale with SuperLumiNova; blued steel hands.
Strap: brown alligator; buckle with aviator's extension.

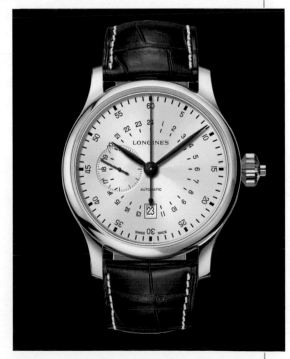

LOUIS MOINET
1806

BEAUTY FROM THE INSIDE OUT

UNVEILING THE MOST INTRICATE DETAILS OF ITS MOVEMENTS, Louis Moinet dazzles with three timepieces that combine sophisticated calibers with a riveting degree of horological artistry.

Through an uninhibited architecture that brings the movement's mechanical subtleties to the forefront, the 20-Second Tempograph represents an exploration of watchmaking's endless possibilities. The 43.5mm pink-gold timepiece expresses its distinct aesthetic with a Clous de Paris finish on the bezel of the robust case. The dial reveals the delicate technical and decorative skill of the Swiss watchmaker throughout the exposed components of its three-dimensional construction. While the hours and minutes are told in traditional form on a subdial at 4 o'clock, using two blue-tinted hands with signature dewdrop tips, the seconds are the principal attraction. A central stem performs a continuous 20-second sweep across an arc in the upper-right quadrant, completing its journey three times per minute. At 9 o'clock, a subtle openworked disc pinpoints the steps of the seconds indication. Directly beneath it, Louis Moinet uses the in-house caliber's unique configuration to expose the minimalist spiral shape of the mechanism's retrograde cam—an understated declaration of the horologer's immense expertise.

◄ **20-SECOND TEMPOGRAPH**

A continuous retrograde seconds hand at the center of the dial provides a twist on conventional timekeeping by executing a 20-second sweep before instantly reinitiating its journey.

A first in haute horology, the Vertalor's tourbillon revolves beneath a three-armed bridge made of solid gold.

The Vertalor demonstrates Louis Moinet's mastery of the multi-dimensional concept, suspension and mechanical sophistication. Upon a dial decorated with Côtes du Jura, the hand-wound timepiece boasts a pair of precious bridges that exhibit the caliber's superb construction. A first in haute horology, the Vertalor's tourbillon, at 6 o'clock, executes its 60-second revolution beneath a three-armed bridge made of solid gold. A luminous star-shaped seconds hand with axis at the center of the bridge honors the design of Louis Moinet's legendary 1825 Julius Caesar clock. The 18-karat rose-gold timepiece, housed in a 47mm case composed of 59 parts, features a second openworked revelation at 12 o'clock: the watch's barrel is gracefully contained within a circular frame that echoes the tourbillon carriage. Between these two spectacles, the movement's winding cog connects the crown to the barrel. At the center of the dewdrop-tipped hour and minute hands, a fragment of moon meteorite celebrates the audacious creativity of the Neuchâtel watchmaker.

Louis Moinet pays tribute to the city that never sleeps with a remarkable hand-engraved timepiece. The stunning dial of the limited edition grade-5 titanium Mecanograph NY combines the fascinating details of its movement, the magnificent craftsmanship of Louis Moinet's expert engravers and a fragment of the "New York meteorite," set at 1 o'clock within the landscape's night sky. The satin-finished engraving, which owes its rich metallic aesthetic to a delicate balance of matte and shiny accents, features some of the city's most renowned landmarks, from America's tallest skyscraper, One World Trade Center, to the Chrysler Building and Empire State Building, both the world's tallest at the time of their construction, and the world-famous Brooklyn Bridge. To the left of the mesmerizing tableau, the 43.5mm timepiece shows the self-winding LM31 caliber's intricately finished mechanism, topped with an openworked small-seconds subdial at 9 o'clock above the dynamic aperture.

▲ **VERTALOR**

Revealing its movement's barrel and winding cog on a rich multi-dimensional dial, this hand-wound timepiece boasts the first tourbillon cage hung from a solid-gold three-armed bridge.

▲ **MECANOGRAPH NY**

This tribute to New York boasts a spectacular hand-engraved depiction of the city's skyline adorned with an exclusive fragment of the famous "New York meteorite."

LOUIS MOINET

20-SECOND TEMPOGRAPH   REF. LM-39.50.80

Movement: automatic-winding caliber LM39, developed and manufacture-made by Louis Moinet and Concepto; 48-hour power reserve; 36 jewels; 28,800 vph.
Functions: hours, minutes; 20-second retrograde mechanism.
Case: 5N 18K rose gold; Ø 43.5mm, thickness: 15.6mm; caseback equipped with seven screws, engraved with individual number and Louis Moinet symbols; antireflective sapphire crystal; water resistant to 5atm.
Dial: skeletonized; blued steel dewdrop hands.
Strap: Louisiana hand-sewn alligator leather with alligator leather lining; 316L stainless steel folding clasp; 18K rose-gold pin buckle.
Note: limited edition of 60 pieces.
Suggested price: $49,500
Also available: grade-5 titanium (ref. LM-39.20.80); 18K white gold (ref. LM-39.70.80).

VERTALOR   REF. LM-35.50.55

Movement: manual-winding; 14½ lines; 72-hour power reserve; 21,600 vph; 19 jewels; side lever escapement; Côtes du Jura engraving, blued steel screws; tourbillon rotates once every 60 seconds.
Functions: hours, minutes; tourbillon with small seconds at 6.
Case: 18K rose gold; Ø 47mm; caseback secured with six screws, engraved with individual number and Louis Moinet markings; antireflective sapphire crystal; water resistant to 3atm.
Dial: Côtes du Jura decoration; 18K gold three-armed bridge; diamond-cut hour markers; fragment of meteorite in center; dewdrop hour and minute hands; luminous star-shaped seconds hand inspired by Julius Caesar clock made by Louis Moinet in 1825.
Strap: hand-sewn Louisiana alligator leather; 18K rose-gold folding clasp with Louis Moinet symbol.
Note: limited edition of 28 pieces.
Suggested price: $199,500
Also available: 18K white gold (LM-35.70.50).

MECANOGRAPH NEW YORK   REF. LM-31.20.NY

Movement: automatic-winding caliber LM31, developed and manufacture-made by Louis Moinet and Concepto; 13¼ lines; 48-hour power reserve; 182 components; 26 jewels; 28,800 vph; Glucydur balance; rotor mounted on high-tech ceramic ball bearings featuring Côtes du Jura design.
Functions: hours, minutes; running seconds at 9.
Case: grade-5 titanium with polished and matte finishing; Ø 43.5mm, thickness: 15.6mm; six-screw bezel; caseback equipped with seven screws, engraved with individual number and Louis Moinet symbols; antireflective sapphire crystal; water resistant to 5atm.
Dial: New York hand engravings; New York meteorite carefully set into glossy, blue, star-studded New York City skyline; visible mechanism; rhodium-plated dewdrop hands.
Strap: Louisiana hand-sewn alligator leather with alligator leather lining; stainless steel folding clasp.
Note: limited edition of 60 pieces.
Suggested price: $29,900
Also available: 5N 18K rose gold (ref. LM-31.50.NY).

MECANOGRAPH   REF. LM-31.50.65

Movement: automatic-winding caliber LM31, developed and manufacture-made by Louis Moinet and Concepto; 13¼ lines; 48-hour power reserve; 182 components; 26 jewels; 28,800 vph; Glucydur balance; rotor mounted on high-tech ceramic ball bearings featuring Côtes du Jura design.
Functions: hours, minutes.
Case: 5N 18K rose gold, polished finishing; Ø 43.5mm, thickness: 15.6mm; six-screw bezel; caseback equipped with seven screws and engraved with individual number and Louis Moinet symbols; antireflective sapphire crystal; water resistant to 5atm.
Dial: Côtes du Jura design; visible mechanism.
Strap: Louisiana hand-sewn alligator leather with alligator leather lining; 18K rose-gold pin buckle.
Suggested price: $45,500
Also available: grade-5 titanium with silver dial (ref. LM-31.20.60); grade-5 titanium with black dial (ref. LM-31.20.50); grade-5 titanium and 18K rose gold with silver dial (ref. LM-31.40.65); grade-5 titanium and 18K rose gold with black dial (ref. LM-31.40.55).

STARDANCE
REF. LM-32.20DD.80

Movement: automatic-winding caliber, developed and manufacture-made by Louis Moinet and Concepto; 11½ lines; 42-hour power reserve; 28 jewels; 28,800 vph; rotor designed with Louis Moinet theme of sun and moon; Glucydur balance.
Functions: hours, minutes; small seconds at 6; moonphase at 12 .
Case: 18K white gold; Ø 35.6mm, thickness: 12.1mm; bezel set with six cabochons and 297 diamonds; caseback equipped with seven screws, engraved with individual number, Louis Moinet symbols and star-studded sky and shooting star.
Dial: genuine mother-of-pearl, Côtes du Jura design; aventurine moonphase surround and sky backdrop; rhodium-plated dewdrop hands; sun-motif small seconds counter.
Strap: Louisiana hand-sewn alligator leather with alligator leather lining; grade-5 titanium folding clasp and 316L stainless steel buckle.
Note: limited edition of 60 pieces.
Suggested price: $35,500
Also available: grade -5 titanium and ceramic with diamonds (ref. LM-32.20DIA.80); grade-5 titanium with ceramic, 54 diamonds and six sapphires (ref. LM-32.20DS.80); titanium and 18K white gold with 291 diamonds and six sapphires (ref. LM-32.20DDS.80)

DERRICK TOURBILLON
REF. LM-14.70.03DB

Movement: manual-winding exclusive tourbillon escapement with representation of oil derrick; 14½ lines; 72-hour power reserve; 21,600 vph; 19 jewels; side lever escapement; Côtes du Jura engraving, blued steel screws.
Functions: hours, minutes; tourbillon; working representation of oil well pumpjack.
Case: 18K white gold; Ø 47mm; caseback secured with six screws, engraved with individual number and Louis Moinet markings; antireflective sapphire crystal; water resistant to 3atm.
Dial: petrol blue; Côtes du Jura decoration.
Strap: Louisiana hand-sewn alligator leather; 18K white-gold and black titanium folding clasp with Louis Moinet symbol.
Note: limited edition of 12 pieces.
Suggested price: $310,000

GEOGRAPH
REF. LM-24.10.62

Movement: automatic-winding; 13¼ lines; 48-hour power reserve; 25 jewels; 28,800 vph; Glucydur balance; Louis Moinet designed rotor.
Functions: hours, minutes; small seconds and date at 9; chronograph. 12-hour counter at 6, 30-minute counter at 12, central chronograph seconds hand; dual time via central hand.
Case: 316L stainless steel, polished and matte finishing; Ø 45.5mm, thickness: 17.0/mm; six-screw bezel; chronograph pushbuttons with champagne cork design and atlas engraving; caseback equipped with seven screws, engraved with individual number and Louis Moinet symbols, engraving inspired by Montgolfier brothers who made first human flight in 1783 and by James Cook, famous explorer and cartographer; antireflective sapphire crystal; water resistant to 5atm.
Dial: Côtes du Jura design; 24-hour display featuring two applied zones; faceted hour markers; counters featuring genuine watch jewels made using Verneuil process; blued steel dewdrop hands; small seconds counter with sun motif.
Strap: Louisiana hand-sewn alligator leathert with alligator leather lining; 316L stainless steel folding clasp.
Suggested price: $13,950
Also available: steel with black dial (ref. LM-24.10.52); steel with midnight blue dial (ref. LM-24.10.25); steel with Havana dial (ref. LM-24.10.95); steel and 18K rose gold with silver-toned dial (ref. LM-24.30.65); steel and 18K rose gold with black dial (ref. LM-24.30.55); steel and 18K rose gold with midnight blue dial (ref. LM-24.30.25); steel and 18K rose gold with Havana dial (ref. LM-24.30.95).

DRAGON TOURBILLON
REF. LM-14.44.14B

Movement: manual-winding exclusive tourbillon escapement; 14½ lines; 72-hour power reserve; 19 jewels; 21,600 vph; one tourbillon rotation every 60 seconds; side lever escapement; Côtes du Jura engraving, blued steel screws.
Functions: hours, minutes; tourbillon.
Case: 18K rose gold; Ø 47mm; caseback secured with six screws, engraved with individual number and Louis Moinet markings; antireflective sapphire crystal; water resistant to 3atm.
Dial: 18K white-gold hand-engraved dragon; black jade.
Strap: ostrich hand-sewn leather; 18K rose-gold folding clasp with Louis Moinet symbol.
Note: limited edition of twelve pieces.
Suggested price: $240,000

PARMIGIANI
FLEURIER

A SIDEWAYS LOOK AT HAUTE HOROLOGY

With its two newest presentations, the acclaimed manufacture showcases its comprehensive mastery of the horological arts—**FROM AVANT-GARDE, MOTORING-INSPIRED WATCHMAKING TO UNDERSTATED CLASSICISM.**

The Bugatti Mythe does more than celebrate a decade of prestigious partnership between Parmigiani and legendary car manufacturer Bugatti: it celebrates the inventive spirit of the Swiss watchmaker.

The futuristic timepiece turns convention on its side from the very first glance. Housed in an 18-karat rose-gold case that evokes the aerodynamic excellence of a finely tuned sportscar, the hand-wound wristwatch proposes a unique and highly demonstrative configuration. Occupying the top of the architecture, where the time would traditionally be read, the horizontally-mounted PF370 caliber takes center stage like a racecar's engine revealed through a transparent window. The 314-component, 37-jewel movement is showcased with marvelous clarity, its gears in perfect synchrony. Powered by two series-coupled barrels, the timepiece reveals the remainder of its impressive 10-day autonomy via a clever integration of engraved Arabic numerals on a rotating drum in the heart of the construction. The time indication also evokes the high-performance motoring lifestyle, as the hours and minutes are showcased vertically on the side of the watch, transposed on a dial that echoes the striking aesthetics of the iconic Bugatti Type 57 grille. This Art Deco sensibility works with the "industrial" accents of the mechanical exposition in fusing the automotive and horological arts, and symbolizing the two brands' ten years of fruitful collaboration. Enhancing the ergonomic qualities of the watch while injecting it with an added touch of sophisticated modernity, the Bugatti Mythe's rich two-toned case eschews a crown. The winding of the barrels is instead accomplished via an ingenious dynamometric starter. This celebration of a decade-long collaboration that began with the creation of the groundbreaking Bugatti 370 is worn on an Hermès ebony calf strap.

▲ **BUGATTI MYTHE**

This Bugatti-inspired timepiece is worn like a racing engine on the wrist thanks to the assembling of its sophisticated movement on a horizontal axis.

The Tonda Qualité Fleurier's Calibre 4000 is a statement of modern mechanical excellence that boasts superb finishings and certification under the rigorous demands of the COSC.

At the other end of the haute horology spectrum, the Tonda Qualité Fleurier conceals its mechanical sophistication to express a timeless elegance founded on vintage simplicity.

The 18-karat red-gold timepiece indicates the hours, minutes, sweeping seconds and date on a bright white lacquered dial that exudes refined classicism. The Arabic numerals, like the markers between them, are painted in the spirit of the finest watchmaking tradition. A red-gold frame at 6 o'clock echoes the luxurious material of the luminous hands and moon-crescent-tipped seconds stem, enhancing the legibility of the date indication contained within. However, things are not always as they seem. Concealed beneath the unassuming face, the Tonda Qualité Fleurier's Calibre 4000 is a statement of modern mechanical excellence. The superbly finished movement, whose Côtes de Genève decoration and gold oscillating weight can be admired through the watch's transparent caseback, boasts certification under the rigorous demands of the COSC. Parmigiani does not stop there in its quest for timekeeping perfection. The caliber's sophisticated mounting of its double barrel in series ensures an exceptional level of stability as the constant level of energy transmission ensures equal precision regardless of the movement's remaining tension. The Tonda Qualité Fleurier meets the restrained sobriety of its aesthetics with an extraordinary standard of chronometric excellence.

▲ **TONDA QUALITE FLEURIER**
This 55-hour power reserve timepiece conceals a caliber of exceptional distinction and sophistication beneath the refined classicism of its design.

PARMIGIANI

TONDA METROGRAPHE STEEL GRAINED WHITE   REF. PFC274-0002400

Movement: automatic-winding PF315 caliber; Ø 28mm, thickness: 6mm; 42-hour power reserve; 46 jewels; 351 components; 28,800 vph; two series-coupled barrels; Côtes de Genève; beveled bridges.
Functions: hours, minutes; small seconds at 3; date at 6; ¼-second chronograph: 12-hour counter at 6, 30-minute counter at 9, central seconds hand.
Case: polished steel; Ø 40mm, thickness: 12.2mm; crown: Ø 7mm; antireflective sapphire crystal; caseback engraved with individual number; water resistant to 3atm.
Dial: grained white brass; grained finition, azur counters; rose-gold-plated appliqués;

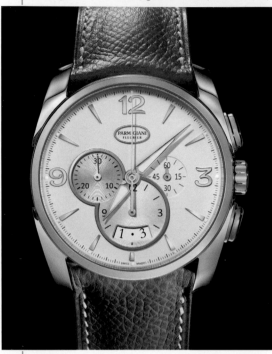

delta-shaped hands with luminescent coating.
Strap: gold Hermès calfskin; steel folding buckle.
Suggested price: $12,200

TONDA METROGRAPHE STEEL BLACK SUPERLUMINOVA REF. PFC274-0001401-833002

Movement: automatic-winding PF315 caliber; Ø 28mm, thickness: 6mm; 42-hour power reserve; 46 jewels; 351 components; 28,800 vph; two series-coupled barrels; Côtes de Genève; beveled bridges.
Functions: hours, minutes; small seconds at 3; date at 6; ¼-second chronograph: 12-hour counter at 6, 30-minute counter at 9, central seconds hand.
Case: polished steel; Ø 40mm, thickness: 12.2mm; crown: Ø 7mm; antireflective sapphire crystal; caseback engraved with individual number; water resistant to 3atm.
Dial: black; snailed exterior; opaline interior; luminescent couters; rhodium-plated appliqués with luminescent coating; delta-shaped hands with luminescent coating.
Strap: black Hermès calfskin; steel folding buckle.
Suggested price: $12,200.

TONDA METROGRAPHE CREME DE MENTHE   REF. PFC274-0005600

Movement: automatic-winding PF315 caliber; Ø 28mm, thickness: 6mm; 42-hour power reserve; 46 jewels; 351 components; 28,800 vph; two series-coupled barrels; Côtes de Genève; beveled bridges.
Functions: hours, minutes; small seconds at 3; date at 6; ¼-second chronograph: 12-hour counter at 6, 30-minute counter at 9, central seconds hand.
Case: polished steel; Ø 40mm, thickness: 12.2mm; crown: Ø 7mm; antireflective sapphire crystal; caseback engraved with individual number and "EDITION SPECIALE"; water resistant to 3atm.

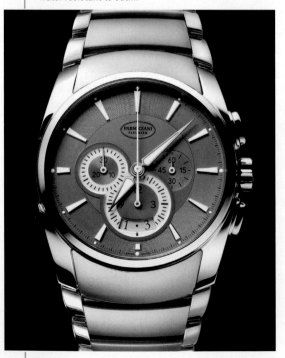
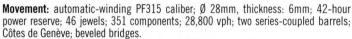

Dial: pale green brass; rhodium-plated appliqués with luminescent coating; delta-shaped hands with luminescent coating.
Bracelet: satin-finished and polished titanium and steel; folding buckle.
Suggested price: $12,900

TONDA 1950 ROSE GOLD GRAINED WHITE   REF. PFC267-1002400

Movement: automatic-winding PF701 caliber; Ø 30mm, thickness: 2.6mm; 42-hour power reserve; 29 jewels; 21,600 vph; one barrel; Côtes de Genève; beveled bridges; oscillating micro-weight.
Functions: hours, minutes; small seconds at 6.
Case: polished 18K rose gold; Ø 39mm, thickness: 7.8mm; crown: Ø 7mm; antireflective sapphire crystal; caseback engraved with individual number; water resistant to 3atm.
Dial: grained white; opaline background; diamond-polished appliqués; delta-shaped hands with luminescent coating.
Strap: alligator leather; polished rose-gold ardillon buckle.
Suggested price: $17,900

TONDA 1950 WHITE GOLD GRAPHITE   REF. PFC267-1200300

Movement: automatic-winding PF701 caliber; Ø 30mm, thickness: 2.6mm; 42-hour power reserve; 29 jewels; 21,600 vph; one barrel; Côtes de Genève; beveled bridges; oscillating micro-weight.
Functions: hours, minutes; small seconds at 6.
Case: polished 18K white gold; Ø 39mm, thickness: 7.8mm; crown: Ø 7mm; antireflective sapphire crystal; caseback engraved with individual number; water resistant to 3atm.
Dial: graphite; diamond-polished appliqués; delta-shaped hands with luminescent coating.
Strap: alligator leather; polished white-gold ardillon buckle.
Suggested price: $17,900

TONDA HEMISPHERES RED GOLD WHITE   REF. PFC231-1002400

Movement: automatic-winding PF337 caliber; Ø 35.6mm, thickness: 5.1mm; 50-hour power reserve; 216 components; 38 jewels; 28,800 vph; two series coupled barrels; Côtes de Genève; beveled bridges.
Functions: hours, minutes; small seconds and day/night indicator at 6; date at 9; second time zone at 12.
Case: polished 18K rose gold; Ø 42mm, thickness: 11.15mm; crowns: Ø 5.5mm, Ø 7mm; antireflective sapphire crystal; caseback engraved with individual number; water resistant to 3atm.
Dial: grained white: grained "velvet" center, azur counters; rose-gold-plated appliqués; delta-shaped hands with luminescent coating.
Strap: Havana Hermès alligator leather; ardillon buckle.
Suggested price: $17,900

TONDA QUATOR RED GOLD SABLE   REF. PFC272-1002400

Movement: automatic-winding PF339 caliber; Ø 27.1mm, thickness: 5.5mm; 50-hour power reserve; 380 components; 32 jewels; 28,800 vph; two series-coupled barrels; Côtes de Genève; beveled bridges.
Functions: hours, minutes, seconds; retrograde annual calendar: month at 3, day at 9, date by hand; precision moonphase at 6.
Case: polished 18K rose gold; Ø 40mm, thickness: 11.2mm; crown: Ø 6mm; antireflective sapphire crystal; caseback engraved with individual number; water resistant to 3atm.
Dial: black brass; opaline outer ring, grain-barley center; rose-gold plated appliqués; delta-shaped hands with luminescent coating.
Strap: black Hermès alligator leather; ardillon buckle.
Suggested price: $35,500

KALPAGRAPHE WHITE GOLD SAND   REF. PFC128-1202600

Movement: automatic-winding PF334 caliber; Ø 30.3mm, thickness: 6.81mm; 50-hour power reserve; 68 jewels; 303 components; 28,800 vph; two series-coupled barrels; Côtes de Genève; beveled bridges.
Functions: hours, minutes; small seconds at 3; date at 12; ¼ second chronograph: 12-hour counter at 6, 30-minute counter at 9, central seconds hand.
Case: polished 18K white gold; 44.5x39.2mm, thickness: 12.8mm; crown: Ø 7mm; antireflective sapphire crystal; caseback engraved with individual number; water resistant to 3atm.
Dial: sable colored; Côtes de Genève, "velvet" center; azur counters; black appliqués; delta-shaped hands with luminescent coating.
Strap: Havana Hermès alligator leather; ardillon buckle.
Suggested price: $32,200

BUGATTI AEROLITHE ABYSS   REF. PFC329-3400-600

Movement: automatic-winding PF335 caliber; Ø 30.3mm, thickness: 6.81mm; 50-hour power reserve; 68 jewels; 311 components; 28,800 vph; two series-coupled barrels; Côtes de Genève; beveled bridges.
Functions: hours, minutes; small seconds at 9; date at 6; ¼-second flyback chronograph: 30-minute counter at 3, central seconds hand.
Case: titanium; Ø 41mm, thickness: 12.55mm; 18K white-gold bezel; white-gold crown: Ø 7mm; white-gold pushbuttons at 8 and 10; antireflective sapphire crystal; caseback engraved with consecutive number; water resistant to 3atm.

Dial: abyss blue; satin-finished flange; opaline center; snailed counters; rhodium-plated appliqués with luminescent coating; delta-shaped hands with luminescent coating.
Strap: Hermès Epsom calfskin with adjustable titanium folding safety clasp.
Suggested price: $27,000

BUGATTI AEROLITHE CREME DE MENTHE   REF. PFC329-3405-600

Movement: automatic-winding PF335 caliber; Ø 30.3mm, thickness: 6.81mm; 50-hour power reserve; 68 jewels; 311 components; 28,800 vph; two series-coupled barrels; Côtes de Genève; beveled bridges.
Functions: hours, minutes; small seconds at 9; date at 6; ¼-second flyback chronograph: 30-minute counter at 3, central seconds hand.
Case: titanium; Ø 41mm, thickness: 12.55mm; 18K white-gold bezel; white-gold crown: Ø 7mm; white-gold pushbuttons at 8 and 10; antireflective sapphire crystal; caseback engraved with individual number; water resistant to 3atm.

Dial: pale mint green; satin exterior, opaline center, snailed counters; rhodium-plated appliqués; delta-shaped hands with luminescent coating.
Strap: gold Hermès calfskin; folding buckle.
Suggested price: $27,000

TONDA METROPOLITAINE BLACK SET – LEATHER STRAP   REF. PFC273-0061400

Movement: automatic-winding PF310 caliber; Ø 23.3mm, thickness: 3.9mm; 50-hour power reserve; 32 jewels; 193 components; 28,800 vph; two series-coupled barrels; Côtes de Genève; beveled bridges.
Functions: hours, minutes; small seconds and date at 6.
Case: polished steel; Ø 34mm, thickness: 8.65mm; set with 72 diamonds (0.51 carat); crown: Ø 5.5mm; antireflective sapphire crystal; caseback engraved with individual number; water resistant to 3atm.
Dial: black brass; décor frappé, azur counters; delta-shaped hands with luminescent coating.

Strap: Hermès Epson black calfskin; steel folding ardillon buckle.
Suggested price: $11,100

TONDA METROPOLITAINE MOTHER OF PEARL SET LEATHER STRAP   REF. PFC273-0003300

Movement: automatic-winding PF310 caliber; Ø 23.3mm, thickness: 3.9mm; 50-hour power reserve; 32 jewels; 193 components; 28,800 vph; two series-ccoupled barrels; Côtes de Genève; beveled bridges.
Functions: hours, minutes; small seconds and date at 6.
Case: polished steel; Ø 34mm, thickness: 8.65mm; set with 72 diamonds (0.51 carat); crown: Ø 5.5mm; antireflective sapphire crystal; caseback engraved with individual number; water resistant to 3atm.
Dial: white mother-of-pearl brass; delta-shaped hands with luminescent coating.

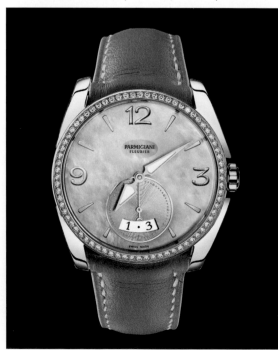

Strap: Hermès Oakum calfskin; steel folding ardillon buckle.
Suggested price: $11,500

TONDA METROPOLITAINE CREME DE MENTHE   REF. PFC272-0065600

Movement: automatic-winding PF310 caliber; Ø 23.3mm, thickness: 3.9mm; 50-hour power reserve; 32 jewels; 193 components; 28,800 vph; two series-coupled barrels; Côtes de Genève; beveled bridges.
Functions: hours, minutes; small seconds and date at 6.
Case: polished steel; Ø 34mm, thickness: 8.65mm; set with 72 diamonds (0.51 carat); crown: Ø 5.5mm; antireflective sapphire crystal; caseback engraved with individual number; water resistant to 3atm.
Dial: pale mint green; stamped decoration, snailed counter; rhodium-plated appliqués; delta-shaped hands with luminescent coating.
Bracelet: polished steel; folding buckle.
Suggested price: $11,500

TONDA 1950 RED GOLD SET TAHITI MOTHER OF PEARL   REF. PFC267-1063-800

Movement: automatic-winding PF701 caliber; Ø 30mm, thickness: 2.6mm; 42-hour power reserve; 145 components; 29 jewels; 21,600 vph; Côtes de Genève; 950 platinum oscillating micro-weight.
Functions: hours, minutes; small seconds at 6.
Case: 18K rose gold; Ø 39mm, thickness: 7.8mm; bezel set with 84 brilliant-cut Top Wesselton VVS diamonds (approx. 0.65 carat); crown: Ø 5mm; antireflective sapphire crystal; caseback engraved with individual number.
Dial: Tahitian mother-of-pearl; diamond-polished appliqués; delta-shaped hands with luminescent coating.
Strap: elephant gray Hermès alligator leather; 18K rose-gold ardillon buckle, polished finish.
Suggested price: $24,900

TONDA 1950 WHITE GOLD SET WHITE MOTHER OF PEARL REF. PFC267-1263300

Movement: automatic-winding PF701 caliber; Ø 30mm, thickness: 2.6mm; 42-hour power reserve; 21,600 vph; 29 jewels; 145 components; one barrel; Côtes de Genève beveled bridges.
Functions: hours, minutes; small seconds at 6.
Case: polished 18K white gold; Ø 39mm, thickness: 7.8mm; set with 84 diamonds (0.646 carat) crown: Ø 5mm; antireflective sapphire crystal; caseback engraved with individual number; water resistant to 3atm.
Dial: white mother-of-pearl; rhodium-plated hour marker appliqués; delta-shaped hands with luminescent coating.
Strap: Hermès red alligator leather; red ardillon buckle.
Suggested price: $24,900

KALPARISMA AGENDA RED GOLD IVORY   REF. PFC123-1000-700

Movement: automatic-winding PF331.02 caliber; 55-hour power reserve; 32 jewels; 28,800 vph; double barrel; Côtes de Genève.
Functions: hours, minutes; date at 6.
Case: 18K rose gold; 37.5x31.2mm, thickness: 8.4mm; crown: Ø 5.5mm; antireflective sapphire crystal; caseback engraved with consecutive number.
Dial: sunray guilloché; hour marker appliqués; delta-shaped hands with luminescent coating.
Bracelet: rose gold; Kalpa type metal; deployant clasp.
Suggested price: $37,300

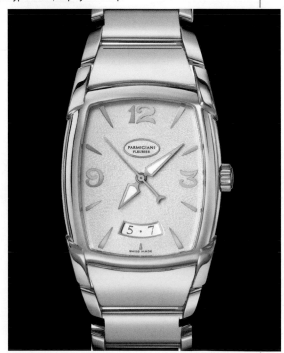

PATEK PHILIPPE
GENEVE

SIMPLY COMPLICATED

Patek Philippe endows each creation with the full breadth of more than 160 years of perpetual innovation, attention to detail and respect for watchmaking tradition. The manufacture's newest multi-complication timepieces epitomize its mastery of true sophistication: **A SUPREME EQUILIBRIUM OF COMPLEX-ITY, ELEGANCE AND FLAWLESS FUNCTIONALITY**.

The Nautilus Travel Time Chronograph is a picture of true design virtuosity, showcasing decisive sophistication within a clean aesthetic of high legibility and seeming simplicity.

Naturally rugged thanks to the bold masculinity of the iconic Nautilus case in stainless steel, the self-winding timepiece reflects its wearer's dynamic, globetrotting lifestyle with a duo of complications perfectly suited for the 21st century. A pair of local/home-time day/night apertures at 3 and 9 o'clock upon the black brass dial provides a clear indication of the watch's role as an essential travel companion. The seamless dual time zone personality is completed with fitting subtlety by a skeletonized 18-karat white-gold secondary hour hand driven from the central axis, beneath the luminescent local hour and minute hands in the same precious metal. A fourth central indicator animates the movement's sophisticated column-wheel flyback chronograph with a simple press of the pushers at 2 and 4 o'clock on the timepiece's elegantly geometric case. Counters at 12 and 6 o'clock, displaying the analog date and chronograph's 60-minute counter respectively, accentuate the symmetry of the dial and play off the linear motif of the horizontal embossed pattern and crisp lines of the stainless steel bracelet. Naturally, the Nautilus Travel Time Chronograph is driven by a caliber of supreme distinction. The 370-component CH 28-520 C FUS movement, with a frequency of 28,800 vph, boasts the ingenious integration of the patented Patek Philippe Spiromax hairspring, permitting oscillation on a single plane and thus reducing the overall size of the mechanism without the slightest compromise in timekeeping precision. The caliber's immaculate finishing and decorations in Côtes de Genève and circular graining may be admired through the watch's sapphire crystal caseback.

▲ NAUTILUS TRAVEL TIME CHRONOGRAPH
This sophisticated dual time zone wristwatch balances the bold masculinity of its 40.5mm stainless steel case with the elegance of refined dial architecture.

The Annual Calendar Chronograph owes its visual sobriety to Patek Philippe's ingenious construction of a complex mono-counter at 6 o'clock.

The manufacture's Annual Calendar Chronograph is an equally distinguished recipient of Patek Philippe's mastery of design and dial architecture, presenting a wealth of complexity and information within an impressively uncluttered décor. Displayed within the superb contrast of a two-tone dial in ebony black and silvery opaline, the 456-part CH 28-520 IRM QA 24H caliber's numerous indications present themselves with an ease and clarity fundamental to the nature of the timepiece. Day, date and month apertures at 10, 12 and 2 o'clock take the notion of contrast to a three-dimensional level, rising from their clean white backgrounds and framed with outstanding relief by their contoured borders that echo the multi-layer aesthetic of the dial's eight hour markers. The aperture frames and the hour markers are crafted in black galvanized 18-karat white-gold. Vivid red accents contribute another touch of brilliant contrast to the design, as the flyback chronograph's unmistakable central seconds hand is matched in hue not only by the 60-minute counter's distinct stem at 6 o'clock, but also by the date's "1" numeral, which initiates each month with an exciting splash of color. The sophisticated calendar requires only one adjustment per year, as February becomes March. The 40.5mm stainless steel Annual Calendar Chronograph owes its visual sobriety in large part to Patek Philippe's ingenious construction of a complex mono-counter at 6 o'clock. The four-function sub-dial frames its dual-scale minute counter (0 to 30 and 30 to 60) with the contrast of a 12-hour circle of opposing colors, read via the long black stem-shaped hand. Finally, a discreet day/night indicator enlivens the counter with its subtle inclusion at the bottom of the central subdial. Complete with a −/+ power-reserve indicator at 12 o'clock, the Patek Philippe Annual Calendar Chronograph is worn on the manufacture's signature "drop-links" bracelet, whose five rows of supple stainless steel connectors enhance and affirm the sculptural dimensions of this multi-complicated timepiece.

▲ **ANNUAL CALENDAR CHRONOGRAPH**

The self-winding Annual Calendar Chronograph presents its tremendous mechanical complexity within a thoroughly legible arrangement.

PATEK PHILIPPE

LADIES COMPLICATIONS   REF. 7121/1J-001

Movement: manual-winding 215 PS LU caliber; Ø 21.9mm, thickness: 3mm; 44-hour power reserve; 157 components; 18 jewels; 28,800 vph; Gyromax balance.
Functions: hours, minutes; small seconds on the moonphase at 6.
Case: yellow gold; Ø 33mm; bezel set with 66 diamonds (approx. 0.52 carat); water resistant to 3atm.
Dial: grained silvery white; gold Breguet numeral appliqués.
Bracelet: yellow gold; fold-over clasp.
Suggested price: $53,600

LADIES COMPLICATIONS   REF. 4968G-010

Movement: manual-winding 215 PS LU caliber; Ø 21.9mm, thickness: 3mm; 44-hour power reserve; 157 components; 18 jewels; 28,800 vph; Gyromax balance.
Functions: hours, minutes; small seconds on the moonphase at 6.
Case: white gold; Ø 33.3mm; bezel and case set with 273 graduated size diamonds in spiral (approx. 2.12 carats); water resistant to 3atm.
Dial: white mother-of-pearl; engraved spiral decoration; gold ruthenium-black numeral appliqués.
Strap: shiny taupe alligator leather with square scales, hand stitched; prong buckle set with 32 diamonds (approx. 0.25 carat).
Suggested price: $58,600

MEN CALATRAVA   REF. 5153G-010

Movement: automatic-winding 324 S C caliber; Ø 27mm, thickness: 3.3mm; 35-45-hour power reserve; 213 components; 29 jewels; 28,800 vph; six bridges; Gyromax balance; Patek Philippe Hallmark.
Functions: hours, minutes, seconds; date at 3.
Case: white gold; Ø 38mm; sapphire crystal caseback protected by hinged dust cover; water resistant to 3atm.
Dial: silvery opaline with hand-guilloché center; white-gold hour marker appliqués.
Strap: shiny black alligator leather with square scales, hand-stitched; fold-over clasp.
Suggested price: $37,000

MEN GRAND COMPLICATIONS   REF. 5140P-013

Movement: automatic-winding ultra-thin 240 Q caliber; Ø 27.5mm, thickness: 3.88mm; 38-48 hour-power reserve; 275 components; 27 jewels; 21,600 vph; eight bridges; Gyromax balance; Patek Philippe Hallmark; Patent: CH 595 653.
Functions: hours, minutes; perpetual calendar: date, day, month, leap year by hands; moonphase; day/night indicator; 24-hour dial.
Case: platinum; Ø 37.2mm; interchangeable full sapphire crystal caseback; water resistant to 3atm.
Dial: ebony-black sunburst; diamond hour markers.
Strap: shiny black alligator leather with square scales, hand-stitched; fold-over clasp.
Suggested price: $115,700

MEN GRAND COMPLICATIONS   REF. 5140R-011

Movement: automatic-winding ultra-thin 240 Q caliber; Ø 27.5mm, thickness: 3.88mm; 38-48 hour-power reserve; 275 components; 27 jewels; 21,600 vph; eight bridges; Gyromax balance; Patek Philippe Hallmark; Patent: CH 595 653.
Functions: hours, minutes; perpetual calendar: date, day, month, leap year by hands; moonphase; day/night indicator; 24-hour dial.
Case: rose gold; Ø 37.2mm; interchangeable full sapphire crystal caseback; water resistant to 3atm.
Dial: silvery-opaline; rose-gold hour marker appliqués.
Strap: shiny brown alligator leather with square scales, hand-stitched; fold-over clasp.
Suggested price: $91,000

MEN GRAND COMPLICATIONS   REF. 5204P-011

Movement: manual-winding CHR 29-535 PS Q caliber; Ø 32mm, thickness: 8.7mm; 55-65 hour power reserve; 496 components; 34 jewels; 28,800 vph; 12 bridges; Gyromax balance; Patek Philippe Hallmark.
Functions: hours, minutes; small seconds at 9; date at 4:30; split-seconds chronograph: 30-minute counter at 3; perpetual calendar: day and month at 12; leap year, day/night indicator; moonphase at 6.
Case: platinum; Ø 40mm; interchangeable full sapphire crystal caseback; water resistant to 3atm.
Dial: ebony black opaline; gold hour marker appliqués with luminescent coating; 18K gold plate.
Strap: shiny black alligator leather with square scales, hand-stitched; fold-over clasp.
Suggested price: $317,500

MEN GRAND COMPLICATIONS   REF. 5270G-013

Movement: manual-winding CH 29-535 PS Q caliber; Ø 32mm, thickness: 7mm; 55-65 hour power reserve; 456 components; 33 jewels; 28,800 vph.
Functions: hours, minutes; small seconds at 9; date at 6; chronograph: 30-minute counter at 3; perpetual calendar: day and month at 12; leap year at 4:30; moonphase at 6; day/night indicator at 7:30; tachometer.
Case: white gold; Ø 41mm; interchangeable full sapphire crystal caseback; water resistant to 3atm.
Dial: silvery opaline; gold hour marker appliqués.
Strap: matte black alligator leather with square scales, hand-stitched; fold-over clasp.
Suggested price: $176,300

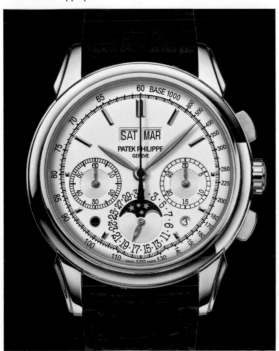

MEN GRAND COMPLICATIONS   REF. 5271P-001

Movement: manual-winding CH 29-535 PS Q caliber; Ø 32mm, thickness: 7mm; 55-65-hour power reserve; 456 components; 33 jewels; 28,800 vph; Gyromax balance.
Functions: hours, minutes; small seconds at 9; date at 4:30; chronograph: 30 minute counter at 3; perpetual calendar: day and month at 12; leap year, day/night indicator; moonphase at 6; tachometer.
Case: platinum; Ø 41mm, bezel and lugs set with 58 baguette diamonds (3.63 carats); interchangeable full sapphire crystal caseback; water resistant to 3atm.
Dial: black lacquer; gold hour marker appliqués; one baguette diamond at 12.
Strap: shiny black alligator leather with square scales, hand-stitched; fold-over clasp set with 22 baguette diamonds (approx. 0.97 carat).
Suggested price: $280,200

PATEK PHILIPPE

MEN GRAND COMPLICATIONS   REF. 5304R-001

Movement: automatic-winding R 27 PS QR LU caliber; Ø 28mm, thickness: 7.23mm; 38-48-hour power reserve; 517 components; 41 jewels; 21,600 vph; Patek Philippe Hallmark.
Functions: hours, minutes; minute repeater: chime with two gongs activated by slide piece in case; perpetual calendar with retrograde date hand: day, month and leap year apertures; moonphase by hand; moon age.
Case: rose gold; Ø 43mm; sapphire crystal caseback.
Dial: sapphire crystal.

Strap: shiny black alligator leather with square scales, hand-stitched; fold-over clasp.
Price: available upon request.

MEN GRAND COMPLICATIONS   REF. 5217P-001

Movement: manual-winding RTO 27 PS QR caliber; Ø 28mm, thickness: 8.61mm; 38-48-hour power reserve; 506 components; 28 jewels; 21,600 vph; Gyromax balance; Breguet spiral; Patek Philippe Hallmark.
Functions: hours, minutes; minute repeater: chime with two gongs activated by slide piece in case; tourbillon and moonphase at 6; retrograde perpetual calendar: day, month, leap year in apertures.
Case: platinum; Ø 39.5mm; bezel and lugs set with 56 baguette diamonds (approx. 3.54 carats); interchangeable full sapphire crystal caseback.

Dial: black lacquer; diamond hour markers.
Strap: shiny black alligator leather with square scales, hand-stitched; fold-over clasp set with 22 baguette diamonds (approx. 0.97 carat).
Price: available upon request.

MEN GRAND COMPLICATIONS   REF. 5496P-014

Movement: automatic-winding 324 S QR caliber; Ø 28mm, thickness: 5.35mm; 35-45-hour power reserve; 361 components; 30 jewels; 28,800 vph; Gyromax balance; nine bridges; Patek Philippe Hallmark.
Functions: hours, minutes, sweep seconds; retrograde perpetual calendar with retrograde date hand: day, month and leap year in apertures; moonphase.
Case: platinum; Ø 39.5mm; interchangeable full sapphire crystal caseback; water resistant to 3atm.
Dial: honey brown; gold hour marker appliqués.

Strap: shiny brown alligator leather with square scales, hand-stitched; fold-over clasp.
Suggested price: $115,700

MEN GRAND COMPLICATIONS   REF. 5940G-001

Movement: automatic-winding ultra-thin 240 Q caliber; Ø 27.5mm, thickness: 3.88mm; 38-48-hour power reserve; 275 components; 27 jewels; 21,600 vph; eight bridges; Gyromax balance; 22K gold off-center mini rotor; Patek Philippe Hallmark; CH 595 653.
Functions: hours, minutes; perpetual calendar: day, date, month, leap year by hands; moonphase; day/night indicator.
Case: white gold; 37x44.6mm; interchangeable full sapphire crystal caseback; water resistant to 3atm.
Dial: velvety silvery white; gold numeral appliqués.
Strap: shiny black alligator leather with square scales, hand-stitched; prong buckle.
Suggested price: $93,800

MEN GRAND COMPLICATIONS   REF. 5950/1A-011

Movement: manual-winding CHR 27-525 PS caliber; Ø 27.3mm, thickness: 5.25mm; 48-hour power reserve; 252 components; 27 jewels; 21,600 vph; Gyromax balance; 12 bridges; Patek Philippe Hallmark.
Functions: hours, minutes; small seconds; chronograph: split seconds monopusher chronograph: 60-minute counter.
Case: steel; 37x44.6mm; interchangeable full sapphire crystal caseback; water resistant to 3atm.
Dial: rose gold, sunburst; decorative gold-filled engravings.
Bracelet: steel; fold-over clasp.
Price: available upon request.

MEN GRAND COMPLICATIONS   REF. 5951P-012

Movement: manual-winding CHR 27-525 PS Q caliber; Ø 27.3mm, thickness: 7.3mm; 400 components; 27 jewels; 21,600 vph; Gyromax balance; 12 bridges; Patek Philippe Hallmark.
Functions: hours, minutes; split-seconds chronograph: 60-minute counter, small seconds; perpetual calendar: date by hand, day, month, day/night indicator, leap year indicator; moonphase.
Case: platinum; 37x45mm; interchangeable full back and sapphire crystal caseback; water resistant to 3atm.
Dial: 18K gold plate; sunburst ring frame with decorative gold-filled engravings.
Strap: shiny black alligator leather with square scales, hand-stitched; prong buckle.
Price: available upon request.

LADIES CALATRAVA   REF. 4895R-001

Movement: manual-winding caliber 215; Ø 21.9mm, thickness: 2.55mm; 44-hour power reserve; 130 components; 18 jewels; 28,800 vph; Gyromax balance; five bridges; Patek Philippe Hallmark.
Functions: hours, minutes.
Case: rose gold; Ø 34mm; set with 162 baguette diamonds (approx. 5.62 carats) set in elegant draped pattern; sapphire crystal caseback.
Dial: black lacquer; gold hour marker appliqués.
Strap: shiny seamless black alligator leather; prong buckle set with 20 baguette diamonds (approx. 0.72 carat).
Suggested price: $225,400

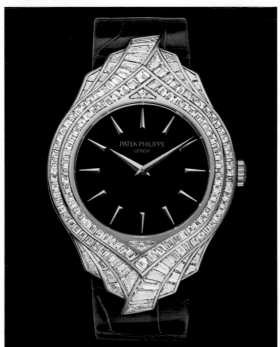

MEN GRAND COMPLICATIONS   REF. 5078R-001

Movement: automatic-winding R 27 PS caliber; Ø 28mm, thickness: 5.05mm; 43-48-hour power reserve; 342 components; 39 jewels; 21,600 vph; Gyromax balance; Patek Philippe Hallmark.
Functions: hours, minutes; small seconds at 6; minute repeater: chime with two gongs activated by slide piece in case.
Case: rose gold; Ø 38mm; interchangeable full sapphire crystal caseback.
Dial: authentic enamel.
Strap: shiny chocolate brown alligator leather with square scales, hand-stitched; prong buckle.
Price: available upon request.

PATEK PHILIPPE

MEN NAUTILUS — REF. 5980.1AR.001

Movement: automatic-winding CH 28-520 C caliber; Ø 30mm, thickness: 6.63mm; 45-55 hour power reserve; 327 components; 35 jewels; 28,800 vph; 13 bridges; Gyromax balance; Breguet spiral; Patek Philippe Hallmark.
Functions: hours, minutes; date at 3; chronograph: 12-hour and 60-minute mono-counter at 6, central seconds hand.
Case: rose gold and steel; Ø 40.5mm; screw-down crown; sapphire crystal caseback; water resistant to 12atm.
Dial: blue gradient; gold hour marker appliqués with luminescent coating.
Bracelet: rose gold and steel; Nautilus fold-over clasp.
Price: available upon request.

MEN COMPLICATIONS — REF. 5170G.001

Movement: manual-winding CH 29-535 PS caliber; Ø 29.6mm, thickness: 5.35mm; 65-hour power reserve; 269 components; 11 jewels; 28,800 vph; eleven bridges; Gyromax balance; Patek Philippe Hallmark.
Functions: hours, minutes; small seconds at 9; chronograph: 30-minute counter at 3, central seconds hand.
Case: white gold; Ø 39mm; sapphire crystal caseback; water resistant to 3atm.
Dial: silvery white; gold numeral appliqués.
Strap: shiny black hand-stitched alligator leather with square scales; fold-over clasp.
Price: available upon request.

MEN COMPLICATIONS — REF. 5205R.010

Movement: automatic-winding 324 S QA LU 24H caliber; Ø 32.6mm, thickness: 5.78mm; 35-45-hour power reserve; 347 components; 34 jewels; 28,800 vph; ten bridges; Gyromax balance; Patek Philippe Hallmark.
Functions: hours, minutes, seconds; annual calendar: month, day and date in apertures; 24-hour dial and moonphase at 6.
Case: rose gold; Ø 40mm; sapphire crystal caseback; water resistant to 3atm.
Dial: black lacquer; gold hour marker appliqués.
Strap: shiny black hand-stitched alligator leather with square scales.
Price: available upon request.

MEN COMPLICATIONS — REF. 5396.1R.010

Movement: automatic-winding 324 S QA LU 24H caliber; Ø 32.6mm, thickness: 5.78mm; 35-45-hour power reserve; 347 components; 34 jewels; 28,800 vph; ten bridges; Gyromax balance; Patek Philippe Hallmark.
Functions: hours, minutes, seconds; annual calendar: month and day at 12, date at 6; 24-hour dial and moonphases at 6.
Case: rose gold; Ø 38.5mm; sapphire crystal caseback; water resistant to 3atm.
Dial: silvery opaline; gold hour marker appliqués.
Bracelet: gold; fold-over clasp.
Price: available upon request.

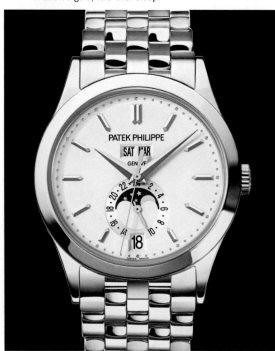

LADIES GONDOLO
REF. 7099G.001

Movement: manual-winding 25-21 REC caliber; 24.6 x 21.5mm, thickness: 2.57mm; 44-hour power reserve; 142 components; 18 jewels; 28,800 vph; seven bridges; Gyromax balance; Patek Philippe Hallmark.
Functions: hours, minutes.
Case: white gold; 29.6 x 38.9mm; set with 480 diamonds (approx. 3.31 carats), gridless setting; water resistant to 3atm.
Dial: hand-guilloché gold set with 367 diamonds (approx. 0.56 carat); gold cabochon hour markers.
Strap: electric blue brushed satin.
Price: available upon request.

LADIES COMPLICATIONS
REF. 7130R.001

Movement: automatic-winding 240 HU caliber; Ø 32mm, thickness: 3.88mm; 48-hour power reserve; 239 components; 21,600 vph; eight bridges; Gyromax balance; Patek Philippe Hallmark.
Functions: hours, minutes; 24-hour and day/night indication for the 24 time zones; world time.
Case: rose gold; Ø 36mm; set with 62 diamonds (approx. 0.82 carat); sapphire crystal caseback; water resistant to 3atm.
Dial: ivory-opaline hand guilloché.
Strap: shiny dark chestnut hand-stitched alligator leather with square scales; prong buckle set with 27 diamonds (approx. 0.21 carat).
Price: available upon request.

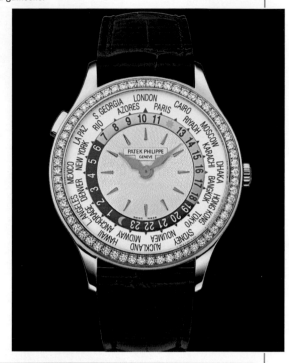

LADIES COMPLICATIONS
REF. 7134G.001

Movement: manual-winding 215 PS FUS 24H caliber; Ø 21.9mm, thickness: 3.35mm; 44-hour power reserve; 1/8 components; 18 jewels; 28,800 vph; six bridges; Gyromax balance; Patek Philippe Hallmark; CH 215 PS FUS 24H caliber.
Functions: hours, minutes; small seconds at 6; dual time zone mechanism indicating local and home time: 24-hour "home" time indicator at 12.
Case: white gold; Ø 35mm; set with 112 diamonds (approx. 0.59 carat); sapphire crystal caseback; water resistant to 3atm.
Dial: brown sunburst; gold numeral appliqués.
Strap: shiny taupe hand-stitched alligator leather with square scales.
Price: available upon request.

LADIES NAUTILUS
REF. 7014.1R.001

Movement: automatic-winding 324 S C caliber; Ø 27mm, thickness: 3.3mm; 35-45-hour power reserve; 213 components; 29 jewels; 28,800 vph; six bridges; Gyromax balance; Patek Philippe Hallmark.
Functions: hours, minutes, seconds; date at 6.
Case: rose gold; Ø 33.6mm; bezel set with 56 baguette diamonds (approx. 2.42 carats); sapphire crystal caseback; water resistant to 6atm.
Dial: golden brown sunburst; gold numeral appliqués with luminescent coating and diamond hour markers.
Bracelet: gold; set with 146 baguette diamonds (approx. 8.76 carats); Nautilus fold-over clasp.
Price: available upon request.

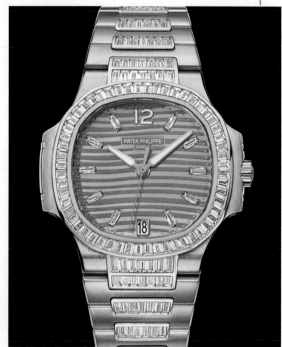

P.

PERRELET
1777

TIME'S TURBINES

WHEN ABRAHAM-LOUIS PERRELET INVENTED A WATCHMAKING MECHANISM WOUND AUTOMATICALLY BY WAY OF AN OSCILLATING WEIGHT, THE BRILLIANT SWISS HOROLOGER REVOLUTIONIZED THE POSSIBILITIES OF TIMEKEEPING. Honoring his 1777 creation, Perrelet endows two stunning wristwatches with iconic turbines that harness the power and fascination of 21st-century aeronautical engineering.

The Turbine Pilot plays on its three-dimensional construction to showcase its flight-inspired design and dynamism. A perfectly sculpted black turbine, composed of 12 titanium blades, reveals through numerous apertures the yellow aviation-themed stripes of the timepiece's under-dial, creating a riveting effect when the module is in motion. Connected to the hollowed and decorated oscillating weight, visible through the watch's transparent caseback, the turbine brings the 48mm stainless steel timepiece to life with every movement of the wrist, evoking the might of a jet's engines. The masculine design is further accentuated by the bold lines of its three luminous hands indicating the hours, minutes and seconds with the precision of the brand's in-house P-331 caliber. While an integrated crown at 9 o'clock may be used to set the time, a secondary crown, at 3 o'clock, activates the Turbine Pilot's graduated bidirectional rotating ring. On the bezel, a circular aviation slide rule adds the finishing touch to the timepiece, whose design brilliantly combines multi-layered architecture with the wealth of information provided by a true aeronautical instrument. Robust and imbued with the spirit of high-powered flight, the Turbine Pilot, available with or without black PVD coating on the case, completes its striking aesthetic effect with a strap in black rubber or calf leather.

A simple movement of the wrist activates the Turbine Skeleton's 10-blade turbine, through which the skeletonized architecture gains a unique and animated visual appeal.

Beneath Perrelet's emblematic turbine mechanism lies a revelation of the watch-maker's exceptional finesse and design expertise. The Turbine Skeleton graces its wearer with a superb view of the P-381 caliber's precise inner workings, imbuing the openworked concept with a jolt of energy and imagination. A simple movement of the wrist activates the full speed of the 10-blade aluminum turbine, through which the skeletonized architecture gains a unique and animated visual appeal. The Turbine Skeleton is housed in a 44mm stainless steel case with a bezel in black PVD coating or 18-karat rose gold. The ingenious, discreet construction of the crown preserves the Turbine Skeleton's contemporary ergo-nomics. A revelation of Perrelet's mastery of elegant transparency and imaginative architecture, the Turbine Skeleton speaks to the brand's adventurous DNA and bold approach to horological challenges.

▶ **TURBINE SKELETON**

This self-winding wristwatch's delicately openworked in-house caliber is revealed beneath a 10-blade turbine that mirrors the high-speed motion of the caseback's oscillating weight.

◀ **TURBINE PILOT**

The slightest motion of the wrist activates the turbine mechanism and brings to life the Turbine Pilot's high-powered aviation theme.

PERRELET

FIRST CLASS OPEN HEART   REF. A1087/2

Movement: automatic-winding in-house P-391 caliber.
Functions: hours, minutes, seconds.
Case: stainless steel; Ø 42.5mm, thickness: 10.7mm; antireflective sapphire crystal; transparent caseback; water resistant to 5atm.
Dial: black; openworked at 6; Arabic numerals.
Strap: black alligator leather; stainless steel folding clasp buckle.
Suggested price: $2,700

FIRST CLASS LADY OPEN HEART   REF. A2067/1

Movement: automatic-winding in-house P-391 caliber.
Functions: hours, minutes, seconds.
Case: stainless steel; Ø 35mm, thickness: 10mm; antireflective sapphire crystal; transparent caseback; water resistant to 5atm.
Dial: white; openworked at 6; Arabic numerals.
Strap: black alligator leather; stainless steel folding clasp buckle.
Suggested price: $2,700

TURBINE PILOT   REF. A1086/1

Movement: automatic-winding in-house P-331 caliber.
Functions: hours, minutes, seconds; circular aviation slide rule; countdown.
Case: stainless steel with black PVD coating; Ø 48mm, thickness: 13.65mm; antireflective sapphire crystal; transparent caseback; water resistant to 5atm.
Dial: black turbine (12 aluminum blades); black under-dial with yellow stripes; top sapphire dial; bidirectional rotating ring; luminous Arabic numerals, hour markers and hands.
Strap: black rubber; stainless steel pin buckle with black PVD coating.
Suggested price: $7,200

TURBINE YACHT   REF. A1088/1

Movement: automatic-winding in-house P-331 caliber.
Functions: hours, minutes, seconds; wind rose.
Case: stainless steel with black PVD coating; Ø 47mm, thickness: 15.45mm; antireflective sapphire crystal; transparent caseback; water resistant to 30atm.
Dial: black turbine (11 aluminum blades); under-dial with blue and light blue stripes and shiny decorating appliqué; bidirectional rotating ring; luminous Arabic numerals, hour markers and hands.
Strap: blue rubber; stainless steel pin buckle with black PVD coating.
Suggested price: $7,200

TURBINE SKELETON
REF. A1081/1A

Movement: automatic-winding in-house P-381 caliber.
Functions: hours, minutes, seconds.
Case: stainless steel with black PVD coating; Ø 44mm, thickness: 13.3mm; antireflective sapphire crystal; transparent caseback; water resistant to 5atm.
Dial: black turbine (10 aluminum blades); skeletonized under-dial; luminous Arabic numerals, hour markers and hands.
Strap: black bi-material (PU/calksin) with gray stitching; stainless steel pin buckle with black PVD coating.
Suggested price: $7,600

TURBINE CHRONO
REF. A1075/1

Movement: automatic-winding Perrelet exclusive chronograph P-361 caliber.
Functions: hours, minutes and chronograph seconds; sapphire central 60-minute chronograph counter; date at 6.
Case: stainless steel with black PVD coating; Ø 47mm, thickness: 16mm; stainless steel bezel; antireflective sapphire crystal; transparent caseback; water resistant to 5atm.
Dial: black turbine (12 aluminum blades); black under-dial; white ring; luminous Arabic numerals, hour markers and hands.
Strap: black rubber; stainless steel pin buckle with black PVD coating.
Suggested price: $8,650

DIAMOND FLOWER
REF. A3032/2

Movement: automatic-winding Perrelet exclusive double rotor P-181 caliber.
Functions: hours, minutes, seconds.
Case: 18K 4N rose gold; Ø 36.5mm, thickness: 12.3mm; antireflective sapphire crystal; transparent caseback; water resistant to 5atm.
Dial: black; Roman numerals and petal-shaped hour markers.
Strap: black alligator leather; stainless steel folding clasp buckle with 18K 4N rose gold.
Suggested price: $17,500

TOURBILLON
REF. A3037/1

Movement: automatic-winding in-house P-371 caliber.
Functions: hours, minutes; small seconds on tourbillon carriage at 12.
Case: stainless steel with black PVD coating; Ø 46mm, thickness: 13.4mm; 18K 4N rose-gold bezel and back; antireflective sapphire crystal; transparent caseback; water resistant to 5atm.
Dial: transparent sapphire turbine (10 blades); black under-dial; 18K 4N rose-gold top rotor ring; luminous Arabic numerals, hour markers and hands.
Strap: black rubber; stainless steel pin buckle with black PVD coating.
Suggested price: $78,000

PIAGET

THE LINE OF REFINEMENT

PIAGET EXPRESSES HAUTE HOROLOGY WITHIN IMPOSSIBLY SMALL DIMENSIONS, and creates a ladies' collection illuminated by the diamonds that inspired it.

A tour-de-force of synergic virtuosity, the Altiplano expands the possibilities of mechanical watchmaking thanks to Piaget's daring reinvention of horological architecture. The world's thinnest mechanical wristwatch, this 3.65mm-thick timepiece owes its record-setting dimension to the brand's all-inclusive expertise and rejection of established boundaries. Piaget's two integrated manufactures come together to unite the watch's case and movement into one inseparable work of genius. The utilization of the platinum caseback as a housing base for both the caliber and case permits an exceptional reduction of width with no compromise in performance, and the Swiss watchmaker transformed other challenges into groundbreaking opportunities. The Altiplano's remarkable configuration required a reversal of the hand-wound 900P caliber's architecture—this delightful quirk treats the wearer to a rare dial-side exhibition of the finely finished bridges and gear trains. The off-centered positioning of the hours and minutes subdial, while pleasing in its harmonious asymmetry, allows the mechanical construction to be contained within the balance, preserving the timepiece's unprecedented thinness. Even the barrel joins the record-setting effort, as its specially designed single-bridge suspension maintains the slim silhouette while still providing the movement with a 48-hour power reserve. This crowning achievement of more than 50 years of devotion to the world of ultra-thin haute horology is presented in white or pink gold and worn on a black alligator strap. The ultra-thin Altiplano is a colossal masterpiece of infinitesimal dimension.

The Limelight Diamonds line of wristwatches embodies timekeeping finesse, shimmering luxury and aesthetic refinement inspired by diamond solitaires.

Piaget extends its watchmaking elegance to the feminine wrist with a collection of timepieces as radiant as the woman who wears it. The Limelight Diamonds line of wristwatches presents a mesmerizing union of timekeeping finesse, shimmering luxury and aesthetic refinement, all inspired by the scintillation of diamond solitaires.

A sparkling duo of oval wristwatches provides a striking horizontal dimension to Piaget's luxurious adornment of the feminine wrist. Designed with a choice of dials in black lacquer or white gold with sparkling diamond pavé, the Limelight Diamonds' horizontal-oval variations shine against a dramatic black satin bracelet and white-gold buckle set with a brilliant-cut diamond.

Designed to evoke the prismatic geometry of an emerald-cut diamond, two faceted white-gold variations adorn the wrist with their play of sharp lines and the slender grace of their outlines. On one interpretation, a dial in black lacquer echoes its satin bracelet, a ribbon of rich darkness flowing seamlessly around the wrist and through a contour enlivened by 1.1 carats of brilliant-cut diamonds. Also presented with the embellishment of a delicate pavé diamond-setting on a white-gold dial, the emerald-shaped Limelight Diamonds wristwatches celebrate the unique beauty of each passing moment.

▲ LIMELIGHT DIAMOND COLLECTION
Inspired by diamond solitaires, these four ladies' wristwatches are luxurious embodiments of Piaget's graceful artistry and imagination.

◄ ALTIPLANO 900P
This 38mm hand-wound timepiece achieves its record-setting thinness of 3.65mm thanks to an innovative reverse configuration of the movement and integration of the platinum caseback into the caliber itself.

PIAGET

PIAGET EMPERADOR COUSSIN XL   REF. GOA38019

Movement: automatic-winding 1290P caliber; ultra-thin; thickness: 4.8mm; pink-gold colored platinum oscillating weight.
Functions: hours, minutes; minute repeater.
Case: 18K pink gold; Ø 48mm, thickness: 9.4mm; pink-gold colored platinum oscillating weight visible through caseback.
Dial: sapphire crystal; inertia wheel underlined with gilded opening; gilded hour markers.
Strap: brown alligator leather.

Price: available upon request.

PIAGET EMPERADOR COUSSIN XL   REF. GOA38058

Movement: automatic-winding 1270P caliber; ultra-thin; thickness: 5.5mm; pink-gold colored platinum oscillating weight.
Functions: hours, minutes, seconds; tourbillon; power reserve indicator on caseback.
Case: 18K pink gold; Ø 46.5mm, thickness: 10.4mm; set with 238 diamonds (2 carats).
Dial: sapphire crystal; tourbillon and micro rotor underlined with polished red gold; gilded hour markers; platinum oscillating weight.
Strap: brown alligator leather.
Note: numbered edition.

Price: available upon request.

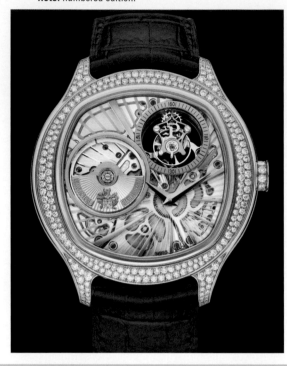

PIAGET EMPERADOR TOURBILLON   REF. GOA38041

Movement: automatic-winding Piaget 1270P caliber, ultra-thin; platinum oscillating weight.
Functions: hours, minutes, seconds; tourbillon.
Case: white gold; Ø 46.5mm, thickness: 10.4mm; sapphire crystal caseback; water resistant to 3atm.
Dial: sapphire crystal; tourbillon and micro-rotor underlined with polished white gold; silvered hands.
Strap: black alligator leather; folding clasp.

Price: available upon request.

PIAGET EMPERADOR COUSSIN XL TOURBILLON   REF. GOA37039

Movement: automatic-winding 1270P caliber; ultra-thin; Ø 34.9mm, thickness: 5.5mm; 40-hour power reserve; 35 jewels; 21,600 vph; circular Côtes de Genève; circular-grained plate and bridges; hand-beveled and hand-drawn plate; hand-drawn and sunburst satin-brushed bridges; blued screws on bridges; circular satin-brushed wheels; sunburst satin-brushed barrel cover; platinum oscillating weight.
Functions: hours, minutes, seconds; tourbillon; power reserve indicator on caseback.
Case: 18K white gold; set with 874 brilliant-cut diamonds (5.8 carats), 92 baguette-cut diamonds (2.9 carats), 44 emerald-cut diamonds (8.2 carats); gold crown set with one brilliant-cut diamond (0.3 carat) and eight baguette-cut diamonds (0.2 carat); sapphire crystal caseback.
Dial: sapphire crystal; tourbillon and micro-rotor underlined with white gold and 107 brilliant-cut diamonds (0.2 carat); slate-gray hour markers and hands.
Strap: black alligator leather; folding clasp set with 24 baguette-cut diamonds (1.7 carats).
Price: available upon request.

PIAGET GOUVERNEUR   REF. GOA37111

Movement: automatic-winding 800P caliber; black oscillating weight.
Functions: hours, minutes, seconds; date at 6.
Case: white gold; Ø 43mm, thickness: 9mm; sapphire crystal caseback.
Dial: silvered guilloché; white-gold hour marker appliqués; date underlined with white gold.
Strap: black alligator leather; white-gold ardillon buckle.
Price: available upon request.

PIAGET GOUVERNEUR   REF. GOA37110

Movement: automatic-winding 800P caliber; pink-gold colored oscillating weight.
Functions: hours, minutes, seconds; date at 6.
Case: red gold; Ø 43mm, thickness: 9mm; sapphire crystal caseback.
Dial: silvered guilloché; pink-gold hour marker appliqués; date underlined with polished pink gold.
Strap: brown alligator leather; red-gold ardillon buckle.
Price: available upon request.

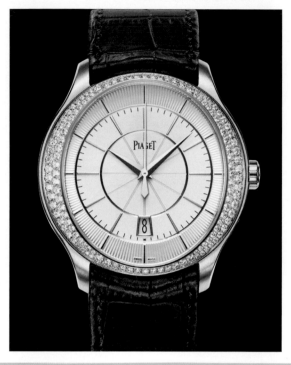

PIAGET GOUVERNEUR   REF. GOA38114

Movement: manual-winding Piaget 642P caliber; ultra-thin.
Functions: hours, minutes, seconds; moonphase at 6.
Case: white gold; Ø 43mm; sapphire crystal caseback; water resistant to 3atm.
Dial: silvered guilloché; applied white-gold hour markers and moons; carriage underlined with satin-brushed white gold.
Strap: black alligator leather; white-gold folding clasp.
Price: available upon request.

PIAGET GOUVERNEUR   REF. GOA39116

Movement: manual-winding Piaget 642P caliber, ultra-thin.
Functions: hours, minutes; moonphase at 6.
Case: red gold; Ø 43mm; set with 128 diamonds (1.40 carats); water resistant to 3atm.
Dial: silvered guilloché; pink-gold hour markers and moons; tourbillon carriage underlined with satin-brushed pink gold.
Strap: brown alligator leather; red-gold folding clasp.
Price: available upon request.

PIAGET

PIAGET ALTIPLANO — REF. GOA38130

Movement: automatic-winding Piaget 1205P caliber, ultra-thin; pink-gold oscillating weight.
Functions: hours, minutes; small seconds at 5; date at 9.
Case: white gold; Ø 40mm, thickness: 6.36mm; sapphire crystal caseback; water resistant to 3atm.
Dial: silvered; black hour markers.
Strap: black alligator leather; ardillon buckle.
Price: available upon request.

PIAGET ALTIPLANO — REF. GOA38131

Movement: automatic-winding Piaget 1205P caliber, ultra-thin; pink-gold oscillating weight.
Functions: hours, minutes; small seconds at 5; date at 9.
Case: red gold; Ø 40mm, thickness: 6.36mm; sapphire crystal caseback; water resistant to 3atm.
Dial: silvered; black hour markers.
Strap: brown alligator leather; ardillon buckle.
Price: available upon request.

PIAGET ALTIPLANO — REF. GOA40030

Movement: manual-winding 883P caliber; ultra-thin.
Functions: hours, minutes; small seconds at 6; flyback chronograph: 30-minute counter at 3, central seconds hand; second time zone at 9.
Case: red gold; Ø 41mm, thickness: 8.24mm; sapphire crystal caseback; water resistant to 3atm.
Dial: silvered; black hour markers.
Strap: brown alligator leather; red-gold ardillon buckle.
Price: available upon request.

PIAGET ALTIPLANO — REF. GOA37132

Movement: automatic-winding 1200S caliber; ultra-thin; thickness: 2.4mm; 44-hour power reserve; 26 jewels; finishing: sunburst satin-brushed plate and bridges, hand-drawn and hand-beveled bridges and mainplate, circular and sunburst satin-brushed wheels, black screws, "P" fixed to the regulator-assembly as Piaget signature, black platinum oscillating weight.
Functions: hours, minutes.
Case: 18K white gold; Ø 38mm; sapphire crystal caseback.
Dial: skeletonized.

Strap: black alligator leather; white-gold ardillon buckle.
Price: available upon request.

PIAGET ALTIPLANO 900P — REF. G0A39110

Movement: manual-winding Piaget 900P caliber; ultra-thin; 48-hour power reserve; 20 jewels; finishing: circular satin-brushed caseback, sunburst satin-brushed bridges, beveled bridges, sunburst or circular satin-brushed wheels, slate gray-colored screws, dedicated index-assembly with Piaget "P" signature.
Functions: off-centered hours, minutes at 10.
Case: 18K pink gold; Ø 38mm, thickness: 3.65mm; merged with caliber.
Dial: partially skeletonized.
Strap: slate gray alligator leather; pink-gold pin buckle.
Price: available upon request.

PIAGET ALTIPLANO 900P — REF. G0A39111

Movement: manual-winding 900P caliber; ultra-thin; 48-hour power reserve; 20 jewels; finishing: circular satin-brushed caseback, black-colored sunburst satin-brushed bridges, beveled bridges, sunburst or circular satin-brushed wheels, black colored screws, dedicated index-assembly with Piaget "P" signature.
Functions: off-centered hours, minutes at 10.
Case: 18K white gold; Ø 38mm, thickness: 3.65mm; merged with caliber.
Dial: partially skeletonized.
Strap: black alligator leather; white-gold pin buckle.
Price: available upon request.

PIAGET ALTIPLANO 900P — REF. G0A39112

Movement: manual-winding Piaget 900P caliber; ultra-thin; 48-hour power reserve; 20 jewels; finishing: circular satin-brushed caseback, sunburst satin-brushed bridges, beveled bridges, sunburst or circular satin-brushed wheels, slate gray-colored screws, dedicated index-assembly with Piaget "P" signature.
Functions: off-centered hours, minutes at 10.
Case: 18K white gold; Ø 38mm, thickness: 3.65mm; set with 78 brilliant-cut diamonds (0.71 carat); merged with caliber.
Dial: partially skeletonized.
Strap: black alligator leather; white-gold pin buckle.
Price: available upon request.

PIAGET ALTIPLANO 900P HIGH JEWELLERY — REF. G0A39120

Movement: manual-winding Piaget 900P caliber; ultra-thin; 48-hour power reserve; 20 jewels; finishing: black-colored circular satin-brushed caseback, sunburst satin-brushed bridges, beveled bridges, sunburst or circular satin-brushed wheels, diamond-set or black-colored screws, dedicated index-assembly with Piaget "P" signature.
Functions: off-centered hours, minutes at 10.
Case: 18K white gold; Ø 38mm, thickness: 3.65mm; set with 38 baguette-cut diamonds (1.36 carats) and 267 brilliant-cut diamonds (1.86 carats); merged with caliber.
Dial: set with 33 baguette-cut diamonds (1.141 carats).
Strap: black alligator leather; triple folding clasp set with 23 brilliant-cut diamonds (0.05 carat).
Price: available upon request.

PIAGET ALTIPLANO   REF. G0A40108

Movement: automatic-winding 534P caliber.
Functions: hours, minutes.
Case: pink gold; Ø 34mm, thickness: 7.9mm; set with 68 brilliant-cut diamonds (0.6 carat); water resistant to 3atm.
Dial: white; slate gray hour markers.
Bracelet: 18 pink gold; integrated folding clasp.
Price: available upon request.

PIAGET ALTIPLANO   REF. G0A40114

Movement: automatic-winding 534P caliber.
Functions: hours, minutes.
Case: pink gold; Ø 38mm, thickness: 7.9mm; set with 78 brilliant-cut diamonds (0.7 carat); water resistant to 3atm.
Dial: white; slate gray hour markers.
Bracelet: 18K pink gold; integrated folding clasp.
Price: available upon request.

PIAGET ALTIPLANO   REF. G0A40109

Movement: automatic-winding 534P caliber.
Functions: hours, minutes.
Case: white gold; Ø 34mm, thickness: 7.8mm; set with 68 brilliant-cut diamonds (0.6 carat); water resistant to 3atm.
Dial: white; slate gray hour markers.
Bracelet: 18K white gold; integrated folding clasp.
Price: available upon request.

PIAGET ALTIPLANO   REF. G0A40112

Movement: automatic-winding 534P caliber.
Functions: hours, minutes.
Case: white gold; Ø 38mm, thickness: 7.9mm; set with 78 brilliant-cut diamonds (0.7 carat); water resistant to 3atm.
Dial: white; slate gray hour markers.
Bracelet: 18K white gold; integrated folding clasp.
Price: available upon request.

PIAGET LIMELIGHT DIAMONDS   REF. G0A39200

Movement: quartz 56P caliber.
Functions: hours, minutes.
Case: white gold; 15x31mm, thickness: 6.5mm; emerald-shaped; set with 34 brilliant-cut diamonds (1.1 carats); water resistant to 3atm.
Dial: black lacquer.
Strap: black satin; white-gold ardillon buckle set with one diamond (0.01 carat).
Price: available upon request.

PIAGET LIMELIGHT DIAMONDS   REF. G0A39201

Movement: quartz 56P caliber.
Functions: hours, minutes.
Case: white gold; 15x31mm, thickness: 6.5mm; emerald-shaped; set with 34 brilliant-cut diamonds (1.1 carats); water resistant to 3atm.
Dial: set with 84 brilliant-cut diamonds (0.5 carat).
Strap: black satin; white-gold ardillon buckle set with one diamond (approx. 0.01 carat).
Price: available upon request.

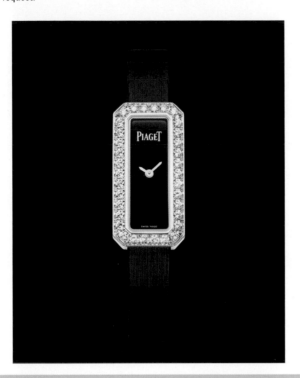

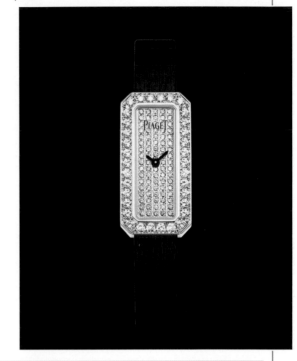

PIAGET LIMELIGHT DIAMONDS   REF. G0A39202

Movement: quartz 56P caliber.
Functions: hours, minutes.
Case: white gold; 28x23mm, thickness: 6.7mm; set with 30 brilliant-cut diamonds (0.9 carat).
Dial: black lacquer.
Strap: black satin; white-gold ardillon buckle set with one brilliant-cut diamond (0.01 carat).
Price: available upon request.

PIAGET LIMELIGHT DIAMONDS   REF. G0A39203

Movement: quartz 56P caliber.
Functions: hours, minutes.
Case: white gold; 28x23mm, thickness: 6.7mm; sct with 30 brilliant-cut diamonds (0.9 carat).
Dial: set with 111 brilliant-cut diamonds (0.6 carat).
Strap: black satin; white-gold ardillon buckle set with one brilliant-cut diamond (approx. 0.01 carat).
Price: available upon request.

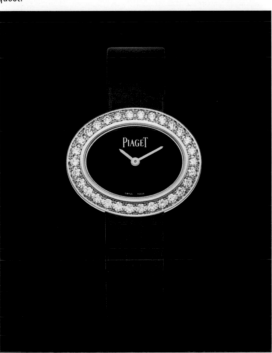

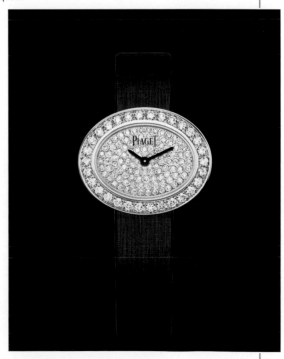

PIAGET

LIMELIGHT GALA – 38MM   REF. GOA39166

Movement: quartz Piaget 690P caliber.
Functions: hours, minutes.
Case: white gold; Ø 38mm, thickness: 7.7mm; set with 62 diamonds (2.8 carats); water resistant to 3atm.
Dial: silvered; black Roman numeral hour markers.
Strap: black satin; white-gold ardillon buckle set with one diamond (0.01 carat).
Price: available upon request.

LIMELIGHT GALA – 32MM   REF. GOA38161

Movement: quartz 690P Piaget caliber.
Functions: hours, minutes.
Case: pink gold; Ø 32mm, thickness: 7.4mm; set with 62 diamonds (1.8 carats); water resistant to 3atm.
Dial: silvered; black Roman numeral hour markers.
Strap: white satin; pink-gold ardillon buckle set with one diamond (0.01 carat).
Price: available upon request.

LIMELIGHT GALA – 38MM   REF. GOA38166

Movement: quartz 690P caliber.
Functions: hours, minutes.
Case: 18K white gold; Ø 38mm, thickness: 7.7mm; set with 62 brilliant-cut diamonds (2.8 carats); water resistant to 3atm.
Dial: paved with 336 brilliant-cut diamonds (1.7 carats); white-gold hour markers.
Strap: black satin; ardillon buckle set with 15 brilliant-cut diamonds (0.1 carat).
Price: available upon request.

28. PIAGET LIMELIGHT GALA – 38MM   REF. GOA38167

Movement: quartz 690P Piaget caliber.
Functions: hours, minutes.
Case: pink gold; Ø 38mm, thickness: 7.7mm; set with 62 brilliant-cut diamonds (2.8 carats); water resistant to 3atm.
Dial: fully pavé with 336 brilliant-cut diamonds (1.7 carats); pink-gold hour markers.
Strap: white satin; ardillon buckle set with 15 diamonds (0.1 carat).
Price: available upon request.

TRADITION 34MM   REF. G0A37045

Movement: manual-winding 430P caliber; ultra-thin.
Functions: hours, minutes.
Case: 18K white gold; Ø 34mm, thickness: 5.6mm; set with 52 brilliant-cut diamonds (0.8 carat); water resistant to 3atm.
Dial: silvered; set with 12 diamond hour markers (0.1 carat).
Bracelet: white-gold; hand-manufactured; integrated clasp.
Price: available upon request.

TRADITION 26MM   REF. G0A37044

Movement: manual-winding 430P caliber; ultra-thin.
Functions: hours, minutes.
Case: 18K pink gold; Ø 26mm, thickness: 5.6mm; set with 42 brilliant-cut diamonds (approx. 0.6 carat).
Dial: diamond pavé, fully set with 290 diamonds (1 carat) and 12 garnet dot hour markets (0.1 carat).
Bracelet: pink gold; hand-manufactured; integrated clasp.
Price: available upon request.

PIAGET DANCER   REF. G0A38056

Movement: manual-winding Piaget 430P caliber; ultra-thin.
Functions: hours, minutes.
Case: pink gold; Ø 38mm, thickness: 6.9mm; set with 36 diamonds (0.7 carat); sapphire crystal caseback; water resistant to 3atm.
Dial: silvered; applied pink-gold baton-shaped hour markers and black hour markers.
Bracelet: pink gold; integrated clasp.
Price: available upon request.

PIAGET DANCER 38MM   REF. G0A38046

Movement: manual-winding Piaget 430P caliber; ultra-thin.
Functions: hours, minutes.
Case: white gold; Ø 28mm, thickness: 6.9mm; set with 36 brilliant-cut diamonds (0.7 carat); water resistant to 3atm.
Dial: silvered; white-gold baton-shaped hour marker appliqués and black hour markers.
Bracelet: white gold; integrated clasp.
Price: available upon request.

Poiray

PARIS

SLEEPING BEAUTY AWAKENS

▲ **MA PREMIERE** (*top two left*) **AND MA PREMIERE GRAND MODELE** (*top two right*)

Thanks to their many dials and interchangeable straps, the Ma Première and Ma Première Grand Modèle collections bring to the feminine wrist a nearly infinite number of stylistic combinations, each as youthful and colorful as the next.

▲ **BENJAMIN LOBEL** (*above left*) **AND MANUEL MALLEN** (*above right*)

Benjamin Lobel and Manuel Mallen have brought the effervescent spirit of Poiray back to life 40 years after the founding of the Parisian brand.

POIRAY CELEBRATES ITS 40TH ANNIVERSARY WITH A REBIRTH OF THE BOLD SPIRIT AND URBAN-CHIC CODES that earned it esteem amongst its legendary neighbors in Paris's Place Vendôme.

The French watchmaker expertly plays off of Art Deco sensibilities while incorporating a personalized touch of daring modernity in its creations. It was 30 years ago that the brand presented to the world the now iconic vision of the Ma Première Watch, a timepiece renowned for its modern feminine elegance and groundbreaking interchangeable strap. Exploring refined sensuality with its infusion of fluid curvature within the sophisticated appeal of straight lines, the Ma Première has, from its beginning, communicated a timeless balance of contemporary relevance and nostalgic authenticity.

The resolutely youthful brand, now under the visionary leadership of AMS Industries shareholders Benjamin Lobel and Manuel Mallen, resurfaces from years of inactivity with a resurrected vitality full of colors and fresh visual accents, devoted to providing watchmaking enthusiasts with creations as stunning as they are accessible. A wide variety of dials brilliantly complements the joyful essence of a new collection that juxtaposes its lively spirit with undeniable notes of classical elegance.

A new feminine collection honors the brand's renaissance with an array of unique identities sure to fascinate the multi-faceted personalities of the modern woman. In collaboration with trend-setting bracelet designer Hipanema, Poiray adorns its wristwatches with straps—interchangeable of course—that hold nothing back in the quest to showcase the vibrancy of their appealing dials and cases.

In collaboration with trend-setting bracelet designer Hipanema, Poiray adorns its wristwatches with straps that showcase the vibrancy of their stunning dials and cases.

MA PREMIERE
Rose-gold bezel and rose-lined dial.

The Ma Première line of timepieces boasts a variety of design combinations that epitomizes Poiray's endless creativity, always boasting the collection's emblematic rectangular case architecture. Presented in rose gold, stainless steel with or without diamonds on the bezel, or yellow gold, with straps ranging from "shiny chocolate" to "pink fluorescent," "navy blue techno satin" and even an interlaced "double" strap, the collection playfully enlivens the appeal of its distinctive dials. The faces, in silver, lined gray, white mother-of-pearl or off-white, confirm their unique personalities with varied combinations of Roman numerals and markers—or even, on some models, nothing at all.

The Ma Première Grand Modèle line boasts variations that make the most of their more generous dimensions by including a full set of classic Roman or Arabic numerals around the radiant silver dial. Here, too, the freedom of interchangeable straps can completely change the aesthetic effect of the timepiece. While a charcoal-gray lizard strap grants any model a sense of luxurious elegance, one in taupe satin might befit a more understated mood, and of course a glossy red fluorescent calf strap brings about a brilliant contrast of classicism and delightful exuberance.

The Ma Mini timepieces make of their reduced dimensions a playground for refinement, visual delicacy and bold juxtapositions of colors. Housed in stainless steel or rose-gold cases, with lined dials that echo the accents of their respective frames, the two watches accentuate the sober allure of their minimalist architectures with superb ostrich straps in cognac brown or charcoal gray.

▲ MA PREMIERE AND MA PREMIERE GRAND MODÈLE

Thanks to their many dials and interchangeable straps, the Ma Première and Ma Première Grand Modèle collections bring to the feminine wrist a nearly infinite number of stylistic combinations, each as youthful and colorful as the next.

▼ MA MINI

The Ma Mini presents the joyful elegance of the Ma Première collection in a size perfectly suited for the most slender of wrists.

Poiray's presentation of its newest ladies' wristwatches is a dazzling exhibition of the brand's renewed devotion to the fusion of fresh visual accents and contemporary refinement. The Parisian watchmaker thus celebrates its long-due awakening with a statement of contemporary youthfulness and sensuality.

Poiray extends the celebration of the Ma Première's 30th anniversary with five models suited for men's wrists. The stainless steel Ma Première XL translates the brand's iconic curved rectangular case into a declaration of tasteful masculinity.

A self-winding mechanical model invigorates the silvered dial's 11 Roman numerals with the sophisticated touch of a date aperture at 6 o'clock and third central hand indicating the sweeping seconds. The automatic Ma Première XL is joined by the presentation of a quartz model, also in stainless steel with a silvered dial, fitted with an interchangeable alligator bracelet.

Poiray's renaissance can be seen in every one of its fresh and colorful timepieces as the brand revives the Parisian-chic spirit that made it famous four decades ago. Lively, inventive and always daring to stand out with grace and elegance, the house's creations adorn the wrists of horological enthusiasts with a timeless sense of originality.

▼ MA PREMIERE XL

This masculine interpretation of Poiray's iconic Ma Première codes of design is available as a quartz or self-winding mechanical version, both worn on elegant interchangeable alligator straps.

RICHARD MILLE'S EXPANDING UNIVERSE

Without a doubt, Richard Mille's watches are revolutionary timekeeping devices. **EACH MODEL EXPRESSES AN INDIVIDUALISTIC AND IDIOSYNCRATIC VIEW OF LIFE AND THE PLEASURE INHERENT IN BEAUTY, ART AND CREATION**. Mille's timepieces stand at a figurative crossroads, where life meets time.

The phenomenal artist Pharrell Williams, a future collaborator and a friend of Richard Mille the brand and Richard Mille the man, put it this way: "I was honored to work with Richard because of his work, the work that he puts into the concept... I bow down to him—what a genius. Nothing short of Isaac Newton or Leonardo da Vinci. He offers you insights on something you take for granted and it is deeper than the concept, or the beauty that goes into the watches."

RM 19-02 FLYING TOURBILLON FLEUR

The continuous reinvention of time—with the development of new concepts, materials and views of watchmaking—has been a hallmark of the brand's identity since the introduction of its very first timepiece, the RM 001. This continuous progression of ideas culminates in 2015 with a daring piece of haute jewelry and mechanical wizardry: the RM 19-02 Flying Tourbillon Fleur. This watch taps into the values of the past and updates them for women in the 21st century.

We are all familiar with the centuries of Swiss fascination with the art of fine horology, but the refined and equally age-old Swiss tradition of mimetic mechanical objects has gained much less recognition. These manmade marvels imitate nature, thus blurring the dividing line between artistic creativity and life itself. This idea of capturing the substance of life using mechanical means was born during the Enlightenment, motivated by philosophers' attempts to comprehend the mysterious inner workings of nature. In this vein, exquisite miniature animal, insect and flower automatons of all kinds were created in precious metals and lacquer work to amuse and delight royal patrons in Europe and around the globe.

The new RM 19-02 Flying Tourbillon Fleur epitomizes these traditions of horological artistry in a vibrant expression of watchmaking distinctive to Richard Mille's vision of modern timekeeping. For the creation of this timepiece, Richard Mille chose the magnolia flower as a guiding concept. The magnolia evolved millions of years ago, before even the emergence of bees, flowering in an endless cycle of birth and regeneration. The magnolia's delicate appearance belies its strength and resilience in difficult environments.

At the lower left of the dial on the RM 19-02 Flying Tourbillon Fleur we see the magnolia surrounding a flying tourbillon escapement with five delicate and colored petals, hand-crafted by Olivier Vauche, famous name in the world of Swiss engravers. Working either in passing, or on demand using the pusher at 9 o'clock, the magnolia opens and closes with rhythmic regularity in a delicate kinetic ballet. However, closer observation reveals an exquisite, extreme fidelity to nature. The magnolia does not merely open—the entire flying tourbillon with its stone-set stamen actually moves upwards 1mm when fully opened, exactly copying the way the flower arches its stamen upwards to increase its chances of pollination. Attention to details such as these exemplify the Richard Mille approach to watchmaking artistry on every level.

Within, a complex mechanism comprising five levers surrounds the underside of the petals, and another system combined with a long pinion is used to raise the flying tourbillon and stamen upwards within the flower's circumference—all using energy supplied by a separate, second winding barrel. The RM 19-02 Fleur is limited to a production of 30 pieces worldwide.

On the Flying Tourbillon Fleur, the entire tourbillon actually moves upwards 1mm when fully opened, copying the way the flower arches its stamen upwards to increase its chances of pollination.

◄ **RM 19-02**
FLYING TOURBILLON FLEUR
This exquisite women's model combines a lifelike magnolia theme with a complex tourbillon mechanism.

CHANTILLY ARTS & ELEGANCE

Richard Mille's fascination with the latest developments in art, culture, sports and racing leads to technically sophisticated timepieces that represent a rich interplay of mechanical and visual disciplines. In the same manner, Richard Mille has worked hard to shape the brand identity and bring it closer in line with synergistic outside events. This now includes an entire series of happenings around the globe, such as the biannual Le Mans Classic, the Lacoste Ladies Open, the Richard Mille invitational, les Voiles de Saint Barth and a host of others. One of the latest affairs to join this distinguished roster is the Chantilly Arts & Elegance event, a rival to the prestigious automobile shows of Pebble Beach and the Villa d'Este that takes place at the magnificent Château de Chantilly in France. Attended by glitterati from all over the globe, this event welcomed Richard Mille brand ambassador Natalie Portman and her husband Benjamin Millepied, despite their current grueling schedules on two different productions at opposite ends of the map. Center stage, however, belonged to the more than 400 cars that were assembled for the event, along with a large number of the most rare and extraordinary cars that exist, such as the Bugatti Atalante C. The inaugural celebration not only revived the tradition of the automobile concours d'elegance, it is also a festival of all art forms. This concept linked such attractions as a major exhibition devoted to Botticelli and Fra Angelico, a recital by Irina Lankova on a Pleyel grand piano deigned by the Peugeot design lab, a fashion show and guided tours of the chateau's architectural highpoints. This exceptional event brings together all aspects of the brand's essence, and is to become a recurring event each year.

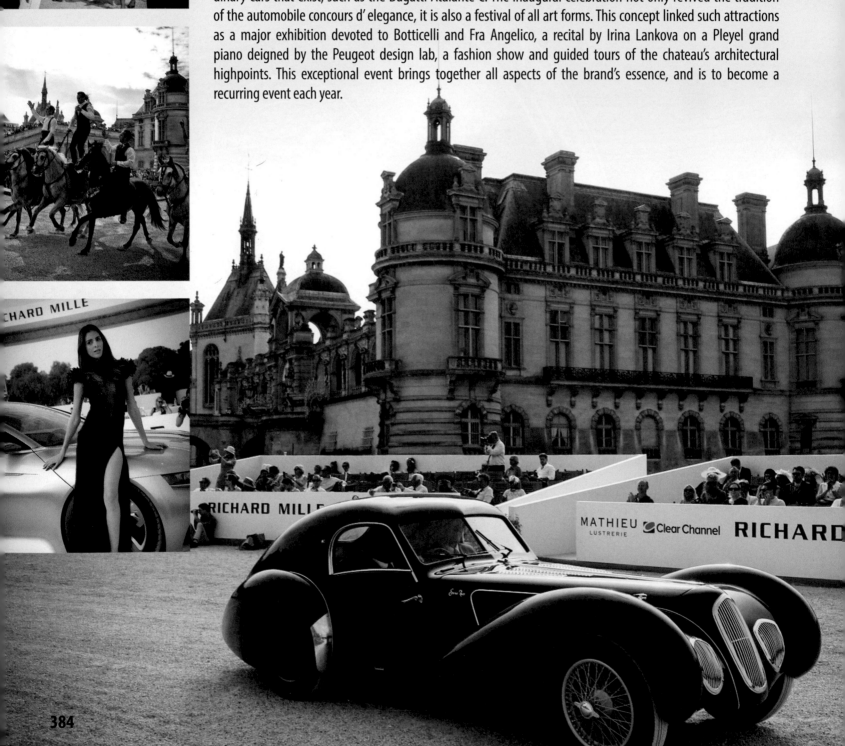

www.chantillyartsetelegance.com

◄ **RICHARD MILLE, NATALIE PORTMAN AND BENJAMIN MILLEPIED**

The Chantilly Arts & Elegance event, a prestigious automobile show, takes place at the Château de Chantilly in France.

▶ **LES VOILES DE SAINT-BARTH**

Les Voiles de Saint-Barth gives top sailors the chance to compete in the area between the Caribbean Sea and the Atlantic Ocean.

LES VOILES DE SAINT-BARTH

At the other end of the spectrum is Les Voiles de Saint-Barth, a boating event nestled between the Caribbean Sea and the Atlantic Ocean. According to Patrick Demarchelier, the godfather of the event's first iteration five years ago, St. Barth "is an ideal place for sailing, with very good wind conditions and trade winds blowing between 10 to 20 knots." Every year, St. Barth grows ever more important as the venue of choice for professional sailors as well as gentlemen sailo rs of all persuasions (and a handful of ladies); all line up side by side at the start line of one of the most beautiful and exclusive sailing events in the world. More than 70 boats, from classic to fast multi-hull and super yachts with nearly a thousand sailors, compete during a week that marks the kickoff to the Mediterranean yachting season. Begun in 2010, Les Voiles de Saint-Barth has quickly established itself as "the place to be" for some of the world's great names from top European sailing crews and sailors from TP52s, the America's Cup, and the Volvo Ocean Race.

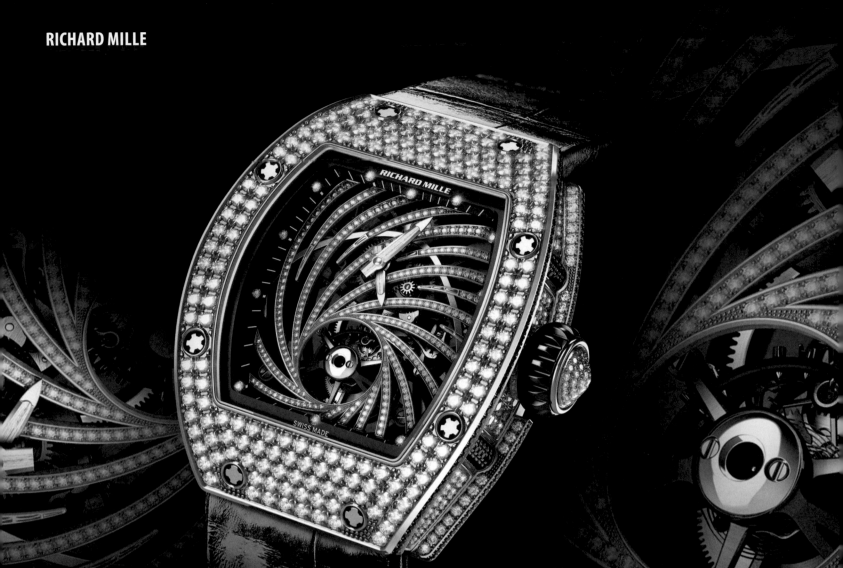

RM 51-02 TOURBILLON DIAMOND TWISTER

A myriad of natural forms, many seen on St. Barth, echo the new RM 51-02 Tourbillon Diamond Twister, a high jewelry tourbillon that takes its cues from the swirling forms of twisting spirals. The pattern recurs in waves on the beach, seashells, plants, and an x-ray of organic structures within the human ear, as well as in cloud patterns, storms, flowers and trees. This is not, however, the only artistic inspiration and point of reference behind the RM 51-02; in the world of philosophy, the spiral connotes the pathways one follows through life and inner consciousness. Even in the extreme reaches of space, this form can also be observed in the spiraling vortexes of the myriad galaxies found in the Milky Way and in the birth of stars. And of course, the very word tourbillon, French for "whirlwind," refers poetically to the spiraling, twirling motion described by this elegant form of escapement found in many watches today. All of these ideas found expression in a spray of diamonds emanating outwards in 14 rays from the periphery of the tourbillon escapement at 6 o'clock.

The baseplate of this manual-winding tourbillon has been crafted in black onyx, a variety of cryptocrystalline quartz

chalcedony composed of silicium dioxide. Onyx varieties with rectilinear black and white parallel stripes are actually a part of the agate family, and only the completely black variety is true black onyx. In keeping with the technically sophisticated nature of all watches created by the brand, the RM 51-02 has a free sprung balance and skeletonized bridges in PVD-treated grade-5 titanium, with various hand-finishing techniques such as anglage and black polish used throughout the movement. An additional security system in the form of a torque-limiting crown prevents any possibility of accidental overwinding that might damage the winding stem or exert extreme pressure on the mainspring barrel.

Each spiral ray of the Diamond Twister is perfectly set with a single row of diamonds; the case is set with white diamonds, with black diamonds to accentuate case details. As a final flourish, and with an eye for detail typical of Richard Mille's fastidious approach, the crown has also been set with 3 rows of diamonds to complete the brilliant richness of this shimmering new timepiece. The RM 51-02 Diamond Twister will be available in an edition of 30 pieces worldwide.

OPEN LINK

Richard Mille continues to develop and enlarge the women's collections, this year with the addition of the Open Link bracelet, to complement the brand's large offerings of straps in all kinds of leather, silk and rubber. Each piece of this new bracelet is fitted and finished by hand. It offers women a very light, airy and flexible type of bracelet with a more casual and informal expressivity. It too is designed to be fully compatible with the RM 07-01 and RM 037, and fully fits with the brand's previously mentioned aim of offering an exceptional variety of watches and accessories—created in the highest quality available in the world—to its customers.

The extension of the collection into new territory, the rise in stature of the venues on the Richard Mille event calendar and the ever increasing connections with partners such as Rafael Nadal, the Lotus F1 team, Bubba Watson, Pablo Mac Donough, Michelle Yeoh, Yohan Blake, Sebastien Loeb, Natalie Portman, Cristie Kerr, Romain Grosjean, Diana Luna, Jackie Chan and many others, ensure that Richard Mille's universe is at the heart of the watchmaking galaxy.

▶ **OPEN LINK**

The Open Link bracelet joins Richard Mille's wide range of straps in leather, silk and rubber.

◀ **RM 51-02 TOURBILLON DIAMOND TWISTER**

This high jewelry tourbillon takes its cues from the swirling forms of twisting spirals.

![Roger Dubuis logo]

ROGER DUBUIS
HORLOGER GENEVOIS

A FRESH TRADITION

In paying tribute to haute horology's superb legacy, Roger Dubuis's Hommage collection transforms a fascinating past into **THE INSPIRATION FOR THE ART FORM'S EXHILARATING FUTURE**.

A resounding union of science and hand-crafted artistry, the Hommage Double Flying Tourbillon honors traditional watchmaking with a contemporary voice of technical expertise.

Past and present come together on the dial to exemplify the comprehensive pursuit of excellence of the celebrated Swiss horologer. The timepiece's two flying tourbillons, at 5 and 7 o'clock, pierce an exquisitely decorated foreground, invigorating the design with a sophisticated dynamism. The delicacy of the dial, achieved with the centuries-old tradition of guilloché, captures the rich history of haute horology with every meticulously carved line of its stunning motifs. First incorporated into the decoration of timepieces in 1786, the art of guilloché consists of a combination of intricate engravings into the surface, by way of a hand-guided rose engine, helping to construct a pattern composed of lines thinner than one tenth of a millimeter. The resulting array of visual effects endows the Hommage Double Flying Tourbillon with an interplay of light befitting the mechanism oscillating beneath. Honored with the exclusive Poinçon de Genève, the watch's 452-component RD100 caliber is a magnificent demonstration of Roger Dubuis's endless virtuosity. While the movement drives a deliberately simple display of the time, the 1,200 hours required for its manufacturing are a testament to the rigorous standards of the watchmaker. The Hommage Double Flying Tourbillon unites artisanal traditions and modern micro-mechanical savoir-faire, taking its wearer on a voyage through the heritage of haute horology.

The carriage of Roger Dubuis's flying tourbillon, redesigned to ensure ideal inertia, equilibrium and shock resistance, exhibits the devotion to excellence that earned the watch its Poinçon de Genève certification.

The Hommage Minute Repeater Tourbillon Automatic pays tribute to the royal couple of watchmaking complications: the tourbillon and minute repeater.

Adorned with a guilloché sunray décor, the watch's central dial permits an exhibition of the caliber's fascinating components, due to a reduction in its size and thus a better view of the face's openworked periphery. In doing so, Roger Dubuis enchants the wearer with both sight and sound of the complication's striking mechanism throughout the melodious performance. The exposure of the RD104 caliber's flying tourbillon further enlivens the vibrant multi-dimensional tableau of precisely interconnected components. Housed within a radiant pink-gold case boasting a sliding minute-repeater activating lever at 8 o'clock, the Hommage Minute Repeater Tourbillon Automatic boasts a sophisticated double micro-rotor for optimal winding performance. The flying tourbillon's carriage, redesigned to ensure ideal inertia, equilibrium and shock resistance, exhibits the devotion to excellence that earned the watch its well-deserved Poinçon de Genève certification. A daring yet graceful juxtaposition of age-old techniques and contemporary design sensibilities, Roger Dubuis's multi-complication timepiece is a worthy new chapter in the elegant history of haute horology.

▲ **HOMMAGE MINUTE REPEATER TOURBILLON AUTOMATIC**
This self-winding wristwatch with double micro-rotor reveals the visual spectacle behind haute horology's most revered sonorous complication.

◄ **HOMMAGE DOUBLE FLYING TOURBILLON**
This pink-gold timepiece combines the sophistication of a double tourbillon with the timeless delicacy of artisanal guilloché craftsmanship.

In stripping the timepiece down to its most fundamental essentials, Roger Dubuis expands the scope of fine watchmaking and expands the realm of micro-mechanical architecture.

Rather than using the technique of skeletonization for the sole purpose of transparency and enhanced visibility, the manufacture makes of it an inspiring starting block in the creation of a magnificent sculptural piece. The Excalibur Spider Skeleton Double Flying Tourbillon, in its masterful use of negative space and minimalist design codes, creates a three-dimensional tableau that echoes the fascinating aesthetic principles of some of the world's finest architectural masterpieces. Stripped of their superfluous matter, the piece's components lay bare the complex tenets of haute horology and showcase an astounding degree of finesse and textural relief. The 47mm titanium timepiece creates a dynamic blend of delicate craftsmanship and sporty personality.

A bold star, expanding like a web from the center of the barrel at 12 o'clock, leads the eye to two apertures on the lower half of the watch, where the RD01SQ caliber's two flying tourbillons perform their full revolutions over the course of 60 seconds. Their carriages, in the shapes of Celtic crosses, further demonstrate Roger Dubuis's dedication to artful skeletonization. Adjusted in six positions and enhanced with a tourbillon differential, the hand-wound 301-part movement boasts a level of precision and reliability befitting its certification under the strict standards of the distinguished Poinçon de Genève. Speedometer-type rings around the tourbillons pay tribute to the sporting world. Fiery red aluminum accents on the dial, crown, flange and caseband play off the cool tones of the titanium to emphasize the multi-layered identity of the design. Circles and straight lines work smoothly off one another to enliven the architecture with every angle and curve.

The Excalibur Spider Skeleton Double Flying Tourbillon hides nothing, instead exposing every chamfered angle, every gear and every bridge in its full beauty and revealing the heart of the movement's finely tuned choreography. The 188-piece limited edition is mounted on a black rubber strap with black DLC titanium clasp, in line with the sporty feel of the overall design. The Excalibur Spider Double Flying Tourbillon oscillates at a frequency of 21,600 vph and boasts a power reserve of 50 hours.

**EXCALIBUR SPIDER SKELETON
DOUBLE FLYING TOURBILLON**

This titanium wristwatch is fully skeletonized
to reveal its numerous internal components as well as two flying tourbillons.

ROGER DUBUIS

VELVET   REF. RDDBVE0001

Movement: automatic-winding RD821 caliber; 11½ lines; 48-hour power reserve; 172 components; 33 jewels; Poinçon de Genève.
Functions: hours, minutes.
Case: white gold; Ø 36mm; bezel set with diamonds.
Dial: silver.
Bracelet: white gold; set with diamonds.
Note: total diamond weight: approx. 3.21 carats.
Suggested price from: $73,900

VELVET   REF. RDDVE00020

Movement: automatic-winding RD821 caliber; 11½ lines; 48-hour power reserve; 172 components; 33 jewels; Poinçon de Genève.
Functions: hours, minutes.
Case: pink gold; Ø 36mm; bezel, lugs and decor set with diamonds.
Dial: white mother-of-pearl.
Strap: brown genuine alligator leather.
Note: total diamond weight: approx. 1.77 carats.
Suggested price from: $42,600

VELVET   REF. RDDBVE0003

Movement: automatic-winding RD821 caliber; 11½ lines; 48-hour power reserve; 172 components; 33 jewels; Poinçon de Genève.
Functions: hours, minutes.
Case: pink gold; Ø 36mm; fully paved with diamonds.
Dial: fully pavé with diamonds; sapphire crystal with metal-finish Roman numerals.
Bracelet: pink gold; fully pavé with diamonds.
Note: total diamond weight: approx. 9.56 carats.
Suggested price from: $146,500

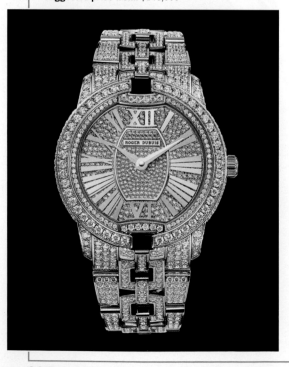

HOMMAGE   REF. RDDBHO0563

Movement: manual-winding RD100 caliber; 16 lines; 50-hour power reserve; 452 components; 52 jewels; Poinçon de Genève.
Functions: hours, minutes; double flying tourbillon with differential.
Case: pink gold; Ø 45mm; sapphire crystal; caseback metalized with Mr. Roger Dubuis's signature.
Dial: rhodium-plated; hand-guilloché; pink-gold Roman numeral appliqués.
Strap: brown genuine alligator leather.
Suggested price from: $328,500

HOMMAGE TRIBUTE TO MR. ROGER DUBUIS   REF. RDDBHO0568

Movement: manual-winding RD540 caliber; 15 lines; 60-hour power reserve; 493 components; 28 jewels; Poinçon de Genève.
Functions: hours, minutes; instantaneous large date at 12; flying tourbillon at 7:30; power reserve indicator at 4:30.
Case: pink gold; Ø 45mm; caseback engraved with Mr. Roger Dubuis's signature.
Dial: white lacquered; pink-gold ring.
Strap: brown genuine alligator leather.
Note: limited edition of 208 pieces.
Suggested price from:
$177,500

HOMMAGE   REF. RDDBHO0567

Movement: automatic-winding RD680 caliber; 13¾ lines; 52-hour power reserve; 261 components; 44 jewels; Poinçon de Genève.
Functions: hours, minutes; small seconds at 9; chronograph: 30-minute counter at 3, central seconds hand.
Case: white gold; Ø 42mm; sapphire crystal; caseback metalized with Mr. Roger Dubuis's signature.
Dial: guilloché; charcoal gray flange; black Roman numeral appliqués.
Strap: black genuine alligator leather.
Suggested price from:
$48,500

HOMMAGE   REF. RDDBHO565

Movement: automatic winding RD620 caliber; 13¾ lines; 52-hour power reserve; 184 components; 35 jewels; Poinçon de Genève.
Functions: hours, minutes; small seconds at 9.
Case: pink gold; Ø 42mm; sapphire crystal; caseback metalized with Mr. Roger Dubuis's signature.
Dial: guilloché; charcoal gray flange; pink-gold Roman numeral appliqués.
Strap: brown genuine alligator leather.
Suggested price from: $30,800

EXCALIBUR 36   REF. RDDBEX0275

Movement: automatic-winding RD821 caliber; 11½ lines; 48-hour power reserve; 172 components; 33 jewels; Poinçon de Genève.
Functions: hours, minutes; small seconds at 6.
Case: pink gold; Ø 36mm; bezel set with diamonds.
Dial: rhodium-plated satin sunburst.
Strap: gray genuine alligator leather.
Note: total diamond weight: approx. 0.99 carat.
Suggested price from: $31,900

ROGER DUBUIS

EXCALIBUR 36   REF. RDDBEX0376

Movement: automatic-winding RD821 caliber; 11½ lines; 48-hour power reserve; 172 components; 33 jewels; Poinçon de Genève.
Functions: hours, minutes; small seconds at 6.
Case: stainless steel; Ø 36mm; bezel set with diamonds.
Dial: black satin sunburst.
Bracelet: stainless steel.
Note: total diamond weight: approx. 0.99 carat.
Suggested price from: $23,700

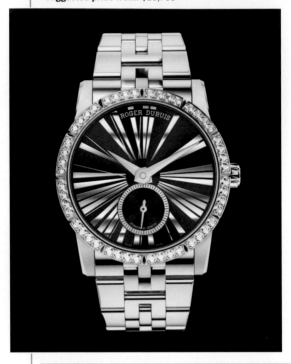

EXCALIBUR 36   REF. RDDBEX0381

Movement: automatic-winding RD821 caliber; 11½ lines; 48-hour power reserve; 172 components; 33 jewels; Poinçon de Genève.
Functions: hours, minute; small seconds at 6.
Case: pink gold; Ø 36mm; bezel set with diamonds.
Dial: semi-matte white varnish.
Bracelet: pink gold set with diamonds.
Note: total diamond weight: approx. 5.24 carats.
Suggested price from: $85,200

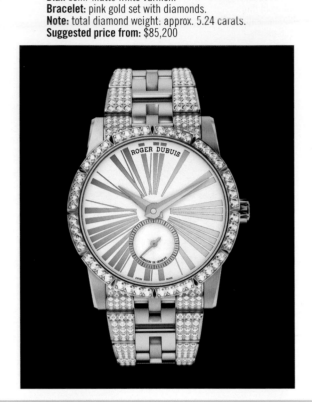

EXCALIBUR 42   REF. RDDBEX0351

Movement: automatic-winding RD620 caliber; 13¾ lines; 52-hour power reserve; 184 components; 35 jewels; Poinçon de Genève.
Functions: hours, minutes; small seconds at 9.
Case: pink gold; Ø 42mm.
Dial: silver satin sunburst.
Strap: black genuine alligator leather.
Suggested price from: $29,600

EXCALIBUR 42   REF. RDDBEX0390

Movement: automatic-winding RD681 caliber; 13¾ lines; 52-hour power reserve; 280 components; 44 jewels; Poinçon de Genève.
Functions: hours, minutes; small seconds at 9; date at 6; chronograph: 30-minute counter at 3, central seconds hand.
Case: pink gold; Ø 42mm.
Dial: ivory-colored satin sunburst.
Strap: brown genuine alligator leather.
Suggested price from: $45,900

EXCALIBUR 42   REF. RDDBEX0392

Movement: manual-winding RD505SQ caliber; 16 lines; 60-hour power reserve; 165 components; 19 jewels; Poinçon de Genève.
Functions: hours, minutes; flying tourbillon at 7:30.
Case: pink gold; Ø 42mm.
Dial: skeletonized.
Strap: brown genuine alligator leather.
Suggested price from: $169,000

EXCALIBUR 42   REF. RDDBEX0418

Movement: manual-winding RD505SQ caliber; 16 lines; 60-hour power reserve; 165 components; 19 jewels; Poinçon de Genève.
Functions: hours, minutes; flying tourbillon between 6 and 7.
Case: pink gold; Ø 42mm.
Dial: skeletonized; brilliant-cut diamonds on flange.
Strap: mahogany brown genuine alligator leather.
Note: total diamond weight: approx. 4.47 carats.
Suggested price from: $260,000

EXCALIBUR 45   REF. RDDBEX0395

Movement: manual-winding RD01SQ caliber; 16¾ lines; 48-hour power reserve; 319 components; 28 jewels; Poinçon de Genève.
Functions: hours, minutes; double tourbillon with differential.
Case: pink gold; Ø 45mm.
Dial: skeletonized.
Strap: brown genuine alligator leather.
Suggested price from: $328,500

EXCALIBUR 48   REF. RDDBEX0425

Movement: manual-winding RD101 caliber; 16¾ lines; 40-hour power reserve; 590 components; 113 jewels; Poinçon de Genève; four balance springs; five differentials.
Functions: hours, minutes; power reserve indicator at 9.
Case: titanium black DLC; Ø 48mm.
Dial: black interior flange; black satin circular exterior flange; titanium black DLC appliqués.
Strap: black genuine alligator leather.
Suggested price from: $447,500

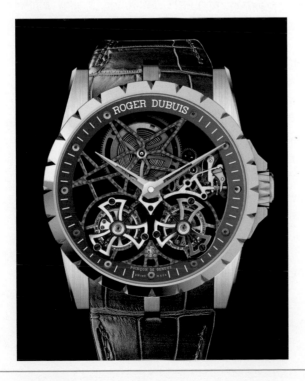

ROLEX

PERPETUAL EXCELLENCE

Whether counteracting the adverse effects of magnetism or challenging the limits of ceramic material, a duo of innovative Perpetual Oyster timepieces epitomizes Rolex's status as **A PREEMINENT LEADER IN THE FIELD OF HAUTE HOROLOGY**.

Beneath its bold harmony of colors and purity of design, the Oyster Perpetual Milgauss possesses a sophisticated caliber that combats one of watchmaking's most notorious challenges: magnetism. Rolex's 1954 invention of a ferromagnetic shield surrounding the movement provided a groundbreaking line of defense against the adverse effects of magnetic fields on the performance of the regulating organ. The Oyster Perpetual Milgauss goes a step further, endowing its self-winding 3131 caliber with an array of innovative materials and components. Produced entirely in-house, the movement's escape wheel is made of a nickel-phosphorous alloy whose paramagnetic qualities provide exceptional resistance to magnetic interference. The oscillator's blue Parachrom hairspring, constructed in an alloy of niobium and zirconium, boasts optimal stability in the face of shocks and extreme temperatures, as well as, of course, a remarkable insensitivity to magnetic fields. Visually, the watchmaker crafts a much-deserved celebration of these engineering accomplishments with a clever nod to the electromagnetic fields the timepiece conquers. A lightning-bolt-shaped orange seconds hand stands out vibrantly against the dial's rich "Z blue," named for the zirconium that gives it its deep, mesmerizing hue. As robust on the outside as the inside, the Oyster Perpetual Milgauss is housed within a 40mm case composed of 904L stainless steel superalloy and boasts an additional internal magnetic shield that further protects the 28,800vph movement from its environment.

◄ **OYSTER PERPETUAL MILGAUSS**
This timepiece's lightning-bolt-shaped seconds hand hints at the caliber's and case's numerous paramagnetic innovations.

◀ OYSTER PERPETUAL GMT-MASTER II

A highly demanding and innovative process allows Rolex to adorn this GMT timepiece with a rich two-tone red and blue ceramic bezel.

Achieved in two stages, the Oyster Perpetual GMT-Master II's sharp two-tone bezel provides an intuitive indication of the day/night status of the second time zone.

The Oyster Perpetual GMT-Master II presents a secondary 24-hour time zone enlivened by the vibrant colors of its innovative bezel. Achieved in two highly demanding stages, the bezel's sharp two-tone Cerachrom-insert aesthetics adorn the timepiece's arrow-tipped red stem with an intuitive indication of the day/night status of the GMT function's chosen location. Firstly, a red ceramic disc is created via a secret method; this is a feat in itself, given the difficulty of creating the shade, for which no stable mineral pigments exist that can withstand the extremely high temperatures of the ceramic process. Next, the core of every grain's chemical composition is altered on exactly half the bezel, transforming the red to a profound blue between the engraved numerals 18 and 6. The watch's self-winding 3186 caliber additionally drives a display of the hours, minutes and running seconds against a black-lacquer dial that provides the contrast needed for ideal clarity. Rolex's devotion to legibility is exemplified at 3 o'clock, where a Cyclops lens amplifies the date indication by 2.5 times, providing a prominent display while preserving the uncluttered appeal of the architecture. The 40mm 18-karat white-gold timepiece has another trick up its sleeve, one that further enhances the watch's utility. The bezel, coated with platinum by way of magnetron sputtering, may be rotated in both directions around the periphery of the dial for the added function of indicating of a third time zone with ease.

OYSTER PERPETUAL GMT-MASTER II   REF. 116719 BLRO-78209

Movement: automatic-winding Manufacture Rolex 3186 caliber; 48-hour power reserve; 31 jewels; 28,800 vph; paramagnetic blue Parachrom hairspring with Breguet overcoil; large balance wheel with variable inertia; high-precision regulating via four gold Microstella nuts; traversing balance bridge; COSC-certified.
Functions: hours, minutes, seconds; date at 3; GMT: 24-hour display via additional hand, second time zone via independent rapid setting of hour hand; stop seconds for precise time setting.
Case: 18K white gold, satin and polished finish; Ø 40mm; bidirectional rotatable 24-hour graduated bezel with two-color Cerachrom insert in red and blue ceramic, engraved numerals and graduations coated with platinum via magnetron sputtering (PVD); screw-down winding crown with triplock triple waterproofness system; screw-down caseback with Rolex fluting; scratch-resistant sapphire crystal; water resistant to 10atm.
Dial: black lacquer; highly legible Chromalight hour marker appliqués in 18K white gold; 18K white-gold chromalight hands; red 24-hour hand.
Bracelet: 18K white gold; polished center links and satin-finished outer links with polished edges; Oysterlock folding safety clasp.

OYSTER PERPETUAL SEA-DWELLER 4000   REF. 116600-97400

Movement: automatic-winding Manufacture Rolex 3135 caliber; 48-hour power reserve; 31 jewels; 28,800 vph; paramagnetic blue Parachrom hairspring with Breguet overcoil; large balance wheel with variable inertia; high-precision regulating via four gold Microstella nuts; traversing balance bridge; COSC-certified.
Functions: hours, minutes, seconds; date at 3; stop seconds for precise time setting.
Case: 904L stainless steel superalloy, satin finish; Ø 40mm; unidirectional rotatable 60-minute graduated bezel with black Cerachrom insert in ceramic, engraved numerals and graduations coated with platinum in magnetron sputtering (PVD); helium valve; screw-down winding crown, triplock triple waterproofness system; scratch-resistant sapphire crystal; water resistant to 122atm.
Dial: black, satin finish; highly legible Chromalight appliqués (long-lasting luminescence) in 18K white gold; 18K white-gold Chromalight hands.
Bracelet: 904L stainless steel superalloy; satin-finished, polished edges; Oysterlock folding safety clasp; Rolex Glidelock extension system; flip-lock exension link.

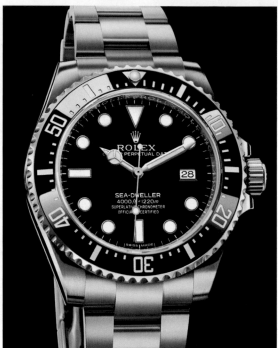

OYSTER PERPETUAL SKY-DWELLER   REF. 326935-72415

Movement: automatic-winding Manufacture Rolex 9001 caliber; 72-hour power reserve; 40 jewels; 28,800 vph; paramagnetic blue Parachrom hairspring with Breguet overcoil; large balance wheel with variable inertia; high-precision regulating via four gold Microstella nuts; traversing balance bridge; COSC-certified.
Functions: hours, minutes, seconds; 24-hour display on off-centered disc; second time zone via independent rapid-setting of hour hand; instantaneous annual calendar at 3 with Saros system and unrestricted birectional rapid-setting of date; month display via 12 apertures around circumference of dial; stop seconds for precise time setting.
Case: 18K Everose gold, polished finish; Ø 42mm; fluted bidirectional rotatable bezel with Ring Command for function setting; screw-down crown, Twinlock double waterproofness system; screw-down caseback with Rolex fluting; scratch-resistant sapphire crystal; water resistant to 10atm.
Dial: sundust, sunray finish; 18K pink-gold Roman numeral hour marker appliqués; 18K pink-gold hands with phosphorescent material.
Bracelet: 18K Everose gold; polished center links, satin-finished outer links with polished edges; folding Oysterclasp.

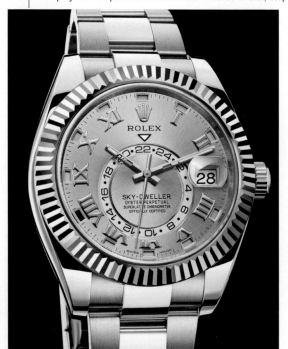

OYSTER PERPETUAL SKY-DWELLER   REF. 326139

Movement: automatic-winding Manufacture Rolex 9001 caliber; 72-hour power reserve; 40 jewels; 28,800 vph; paramagnetic blue Parachrom hairspring with Breguet overcoil; large balance wheel with variable inertia; high-precision regulating via four gold Microstella nuts; traversing balance bridge; COSC-certified.
Functions: hours, minutes, seconds; 24-hour display on off-centered disc; second time zone via independent rapid-setting of hour hand; instantaneous annual calendar at 3 with Saros system and unrestricted birectional rapid-setting of date; month display via 12 apertures around circumference of dial; stop seconds for precise time setting.
Case: 18K white gold, polished finish; Ø 42mm; fluted, bidirectional rotatable bezel with Ring Command for function setting; screw-down crown, Twinlock double waterproofness system; screw-down caseback with Rolex fluting; scratch-resistant sapphire crystal; water resistant to 10atm.
Dial: black, satin finish; 18K white-gold Arabic numeral hour marker appliqués; 18K white-gold hands with phosphorescent material.
Strap: black Mississippiensis alligator leather; 18K white-gold folding Oysterclasp.

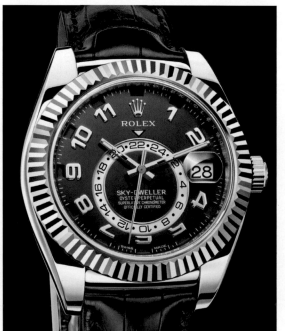

OYSTER PERPETUAL COSMOGRAPH DAYTONA   REF. 116576 TBR-78596

Movement: automatic-winding Manufacure Rolex 4130 caliber; 72-hour power reserve; 44 jewels; 28,800 vph; paramagnetic blue Parachrom hairspring with Breguet overcoil; large balance wheel with variable inertia; high-precision regulating via four gold Microstella nuts; traversing balance bridge; COSC-certified.
Functions: hours, minutes; small seconds at 6; chronograph: 12-hour counter at 9, 30-minute counter at 3, central chronograph seconds hand; stop seconds for precise time setting.
Case: 950 platinum, polished finish; Ø 40mm; bezel set with 36 baguette-cut diamonds; screw-down winding crown, Triplock triple waterproofness system; screw-down caseback with Rolex fluting; scratch-resistant sapphire crystal; water resistant to 10atm.
Dial: fully pavé with 437 diamonds; ice blue counters with 18K white-gold border; highly legible Chromalight hour marker appliqués in blued 18K white gold; blued 18K white-gold hands.
Bracelet: 950 platinum; polished center links, satin-finished outer links with polished edges; Oysterlock folding safety clasp.

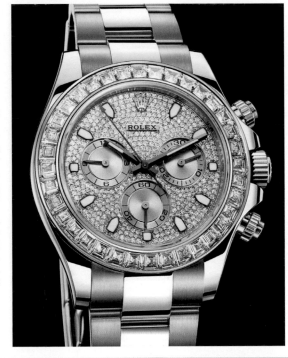

OYSTER PERPETUAL DATEJUST PEARLMASTER 34   REF. 81348 SARO-72848

Movement: automatic-winding Manufacture Rolex 2236 caliber; 55-hour power reserve; 31 jewels; 28,800 vph; Syloxi hairspring in silicon with patented geometry; balance wheel with variable inertia; high-precision regulating via two gold Microstella nuts; traversing balance bridge; high-performance Paraflex shock absorbers; COSC-certified.
Functions: hours, minutes, seconds; date at 3; stop seconds for precise time setting.
Case: 18K yellow gold, polished finish; Ø 34mm; bezel set with 12 baguette-cut pink sapphires and 24 baguette-cut light pink sapphires; screw-down winding crown, Twinlock double waterproofness system; screw-down caseback with Rolex fluting; scratch-resistant sapphire crystal; water resistant to 10atm.
Dial: 18K yellow gold pavé with 455 diamonds; 18K yellow-gold Roman numeral hour marker appliqués; 18K yellow-gold hands.
Bracelet: 18K yellow gold, polished finish; concealed folding Crownclasp.

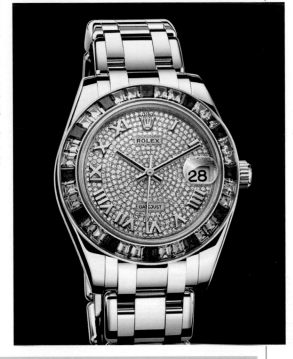

MILGAUSS   REF. 116400 GV-72400

Movement: automatic-winding Manufacture Rolex 3131 caliber; 48-hour power reserve; 31 jewels; 28,800 vph; paramagnetic blue Parachrom hairspring with Breguet overcoil; large balance wheel with variable inertia; Paramagnetic nickel-phosphorus escape wheel; high-precision regulating via four gold Microstella nuts; traversing balance bridge; COSC-certified.
Functions: hours, minutes, seconds; stop seconds for precise time setting.
Case: 904L stainless steel superalloy, polished finish; Ø 40mm; smooth bezel; screw-down winding crown, Triplock double waterproofness system; scratch-resistant green sapphire crystal; water resistant to 10atm.
Dial: Z blue; highly legible Chromalight hour marker appliqués in 18K white gold; 18K white-gold Chromalight hands; orange lightning-bolt-shaped seconds hand.
Bracelet: 904L stainless steel superalloy; polished center links; satin-finished outer links with polished edges; folding Oysterclasp.

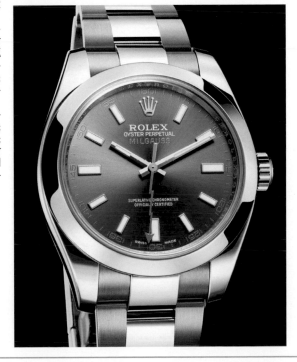

OYSTER PERPETUAL   REF. 116000-70200

Movement: automatic-winding 3130 caliber; 48-hour power reserve; 31 jewels; 28,800 vph; paramagnetic blue Parachrom hairspring with Breguet overcoil; large balance wheel with variable inertia; high-precision regulating via four gold Microstella nuts; traversing balance bridge; COSC-certified.
Functions: hours, minutes, seconds; stop seconds with precise time setting.
Case: 904L stainless steel superalloy, satin finished; Ø 36mm; domed bezel; screw-down crown, Twinlock double waterproofness system; screw-down caseback with Rolex fluting; scratch-resistant sapphire crystal; water resistant to 10atm.
Dial: red grape, sunray finish; 18K white-gold hour marker appliqués with phosphorescent material.
Bracelet: 904L stainless steel superalloy; satin finished, polished edges; folding Oysterclasp.

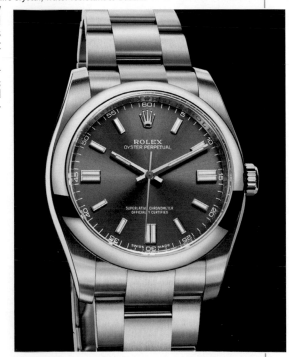

OYSTER PERPETUAL CHRONOGRAPH DAYTONA   REF. 116506-78596

Movement: automatic-winding Manufacture Rolex 4130 caliber; 72-hour power reserve; 44 jewels; 28,800 vph; paramagnetic blue Parachrom hairspring; Breguet overcoil; large balance wheel with variable inertia; high-precision regulating via four gold Microstella nuts; traversing balance bridge; bidirectional self-winding via PERPETUAL rotor on ball bearing; COSC-certified.
Functions: hours, minutes; small seconds at 6; chronograph: 12-hour counter at 9, 30-minute counter at 3, central seconds hand; stop seconds for precise time setting.
Case: 950 platinum, polished finish; Ø 40mm; chestnut brown monobloc Cerachrom in ceramic, engraved numerals and graduations coated with platinum via magnetron sputtering; screw-down winding crown, Triplock triple water resistance system; scratch-resistant sapphire crystal; water resistant to 10atm.

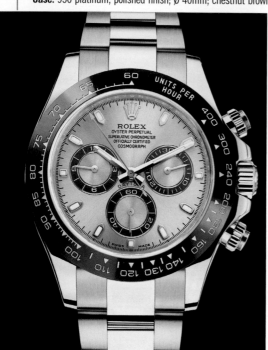

Dial: ice blue; highly legible Chromalight hour marker appliqués in 18K white gold; chestnut brown lacquer counters with 18K white-gold border; 18K white-gold Chromalight hands.
Bracelet: 950 platinum; polished center links; satin-finished outer links with polished edges; folding Oysterlock safety clasp; Easylink 5mm comfort extension link.

OYSTER PERPETUAL GMT-MASTER II   REF. 116710BLNR-78200

Movement: automatic-winding Manufacture Rolex 3186 caliber; 48-hour power reserve; 31 jewels; 28,800 vph; paramagnetic blue Parachrom hairspring; Breguet overcoil; large balance wheel with variable inertia; high-precision regulating via four gold Microstella nuts; traversing balance bridge; bidirectional self-winding via Perpetual rotor; COSC-certified.
Functions: hours, minutes, seconds; date at 3; 24-hour display via additional hand, second time zone with independent rapid-setting of hour hand; stop seconds for precise time setting.
Case: 904L stainless steel superalloy, satin and polished finish; Ø 40mm; bidirectional rotatable 24-hour graduated bezel with two-color blue and black Cerachrom insert in ceramic, engraved numerals and graduations coated with platinum via magnetron sputtering; screw-down crown, TRIPLOCK triple water resistance system; scratch-resistant sapphire crystal; water resistant to 10atm.

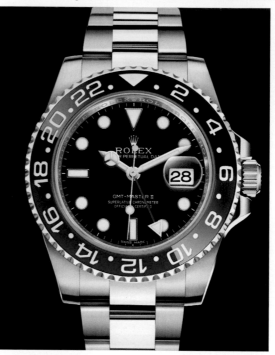

Dial: black lacquer; highly legible Chromalight appliqué hour markers and hands in 18K white gold; blue 24-hour hand.
Bracelet: 904L stainless steel superalloy, polished center links, satin-finished outer links with polished edges; folding Oysterlock safety clasp; Easylink 5mm comfort extension link.

OYSTER PERPETUAL YACHT-MASTER II   REF. 1166880-78210

Movement: automatic-winding Manufacture Rolex 4161 caliber; 72-hour power reserve; 42 jewels; 28,800 vph; paramagnetic blue Parachrom hairspring; Breguet overcoil; large balance wheel with variable inertia; high-precision regulating via four gold Microstella nuts; traversing balance bridge; bidirectional self-winding via Perpetual rotor; COSC-certified.
Functions: hours, minutes; small seconds at 6; programmable regatta countdown with mechanical memory; retrograde minute hand; on-the-fly synchronization of countdown seconds and minute hands; stop seconds for precise time setting.
Case: 904L stainless steel superalloy, satin and polished finish; Ø 44mm; bidirectional 90° rotatable Ring Command bezel, blue Cerachrom insert in ceramic, engraved numerals and inscription coated with platinum via magnetron sputtering; screw-down crown, Triplock triple water resistance system; screw-down caseback with Rolex fluting; scratch-resistant sapphire crystal; water resistant to 10atm.

Dial: matte white lacquer; blue lacquer small seconds counter with 18K white-gold border; highly legible Chromalight hour marker appliqués in 18K white gold with blue PVD coating; Chromalight hands in blued 18K gold; red seconds hand.
Bracelet: 904 stainless steel superalloy, polished center links, satin-finished outer links with polished edges; folding Oysterlock safety clasp; Easylink 5mm comfort extension link.

OYSTER PERPETUAL DAY-DATE SERTIE   REF. 118395 BR-73205

Movement: automatic-winding Manufacture Rolex 3155 caliber; 48-hour power reserve; 31 jewels; 28,800 vph; paramagnetic blue Parachrom hairspring; Breguet overcoil; large balance wheel with variable inertia; high-precision regulating via four gold Microstella nuts; traversing balance bridge; bidirectional self-winding via Perpetual rotor; COSC-certified.
Functions: hours, minutes, seconds; day at 12; date at 3; stop seconds for precise time setting.
Case: 18K Everose gold, polished finish; Ø 36mm; 18K white-gold bezel, set with 60 baguette-cut diamonds; screw-down crown, Twinlock double water resistance system; screw-down caseback with Rolex fluting; scratch-resistant sapphire crystal; water resistant to 10atm.

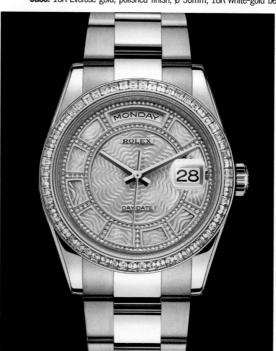

Dial: carousel of pink mother-of-pearl; 18K white-gold set with 217 diamonds; 18K white-gold hands.
Bracelet: 18K Everose gold; polished center links, satin-finished outer links with polished edges; concealed folding Crownclasp.

OYSTER PERPETUAL LADY-DATE JUST PEARLMASTER WHITE GOLD   REF. 80319

Movement: automatic-winding Manufacture Rolex 2235 caliber; 48-hour power reserve; 31 jewels; 28,800 vph; hairspring with Breguet overcoil; balance wheel with variable inertia; high-precision regulating via two gold Microstella nuts; traversing balance bridge; bidirectional self-winding via Perpetual rotor; COSC-certified.
Functions: hours, minutes, seconds; date at 3; stop seconds for precise time setting.
Case: 18K white gold, polished finish; Ø 29mm; 18K white-gold bezel set with 12 diamonds; screw-down winding crown, TWINLOCK double water resistance system; screw-down caseback with Rolex fluting; scratch-resistant sapphire crystal; water resistant to 10atm.
Dial: white; white gold Roman numeral hour markers.
Bracelet: 18K white gold, polished finish; concealed folding Crownclasp.

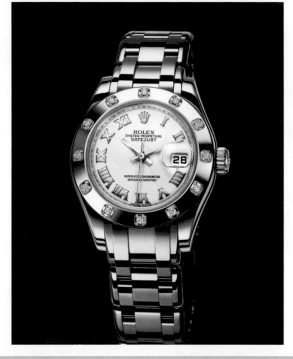

OYSTER PERPETUAL LADY-DATE JUST PEARLMASTER   REF. 80285-74945 BR

Movement: automatic-winding Manufacture Rolex 2235 caliber; 48-hour power reserve; 31 jewels; 28,800 vph; hairspring with Breguet overcoil; balance wheel with variable inertia; high-precision regulating via two gold Microstella nuts; traversing balance bridge; bidirectional self-winding via Perpetual rotor; COSC-certified.
Functions: hours, minutes, seconds; date at 3; stop seconds for precise time setting.
Case: 18K Everose gold, polished finish; Ø 29mm; 18K white-gold bezel set with 34 brilliant-cut diamonds; screw-down winding crown, Twinlock double water resistance system; screw-down caseback with Rolex fluting; scratch-resistant sapphire crystal; water resistant to 10atm.
Dial: white mother-of-pearl with a pink-gold color lotus flower motif; 18K pink-gold Roman numeral hour markers, large "VI" in 18K pink gold set with 11 diamonds; 18K pink-gold hands.
Bracelet: 18K Everose gold center and outer links; intermediate links in 18K white-gold set with 226 brilliant-cut diamonds, polished finish; concealed folding Crownclasp.

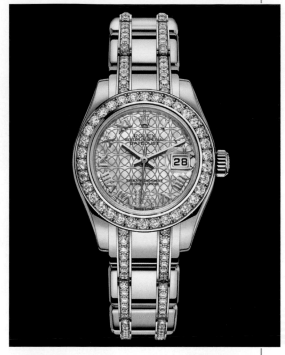

OYSTER PERPETUAL DAY-DATE   REF. 118138

Movement: automatic-winding Manufacture Rolex 3155 caliber; 48-hour power reserve; 31 jewels; 28,800 vph; paramagnetic blue Parachrom hairspring; Breguet overcoil; large balance wheel with variable inertia; high-precision regulating via four gold Microstella nuts; traversing balance bridge; bidirectional self-winding via Perpetual rotor; COSC-certified.
Functions: hours, minutes, seconds; day at 12; date at 3; stop seconds for precise time setting.
Case: 18K yellow gold, polished finish; Ø 36mm; fluted bezel; screw-down crown, Twinlock double water resistance system; scratch-resistant sapphire crystal; screw-down caseback with Rolex fluting; water resistant to 10atm.
Dial: green, sunray finish; 18K yellow-gold hour marker appliqués and hands with phosphorescent material.
Strap: green Alligator mississippiensis leather; adjustable folding Crownclasp in 18K gold.

OYSTER PERPETUAL DAY-DATE   REF. 118139

Movement: automatic-winding Manufacture Rolex 3155 caliber; 48-hour power reserve; 31 jewels; 28,800 vph; paramagnetic blue Parachrom hairspring; Breguet overcoil; large balance wheel with variable inertia; high-precision regulating via four gold Microstella nuts; traversing balance bridge; bidirectional self-winding via Perpetual rotor; COSC-certified.
Functions: hours, minutes, seconds; day at 12; date at 3; stop seconds for precise time setting.
Case: 18K white gold, polished finish; Ø 36mm; fluted bezel; screw-down crown, Twinlock double water resistance system; scratch-resistant sapphire crystal; screw-down caseback with Rolex fluting; water resistant to 10atm.
Dial: cherry, sunray finish; 18K white-gold hour marker appliqués and hands with phosphorescent material.
Strap: Bordeaux Alligator mississippiensis leather; adjustable folding Crownclasp in 18K gold.

TAG Heuer

SWISS AVANT-GARDE SINCE 1860

AMAZING RACE

With an aesthetic remarkable for its understated force, TAG Heuer presents models whose intuitive dials belie **THE MECHANICAL SOPHISTICATION WITHIN**.

The TAG Heuer Carrera Calibre 1887 is a powerful demonstration of past and present uniting for a common objective. The decisively sporty 45mm timepiece showcases TAG Heuer's mastery of contemporary motoring aesthetics within a design that pays tribute to classic mechanical stopwatches. Distinguished by its evocative positioning of the crown and chronograph pushers at the top of its fine-brushed titanium case, the self-winding timepiece invigorates its sunray-finished dial with a resonant play of multi-dimensional relief. The chronograph's 30-minute and 12-hour counters, along with 12 Arabic numerals, rise from the two-tone anthracite dial, echoing the visual notes of a racecar's dashboard indicators. At 6 o'clock, a date aperture coexists with the movement's subdial-free small-seconds hand. Driving the 28,800vph choreography, the Calibre 1887 pays tribute to Edouard Heuer, the brand's founder, who patented his acclaimed "oscillating pinion" in the movement's namesake year. The 39-jewel caliber, winner of the Grand-Prix d'Horlogerie de Genève's prestigious "Petite Aiguille" in 2010, is displayed through the asymmetrical case's smoked-sapphire caseback.

► **TAG HEUER CARRERA CALIBRE 1887**
This high-precision self-winding chronograph combines a contemporary reflection of racing instruments with the nostalgia of vintage stopwatches.

The Aquaracer 300M Calibre 5 combines horological elegance with a design suited for aquatic races and diving adventures.

The Swiss watchmaker builds upon its celebrated tradition of yachting timepieces with a rugged, youthful entrant into its iconic Aquaracer collection. The Aquaracer 300M Calibre 5 combines haute horology's understated elegance with a robust design suited for the most intense aquatic races and diving adventures. Housed in a polished steel case, the self-winding wristwatch asserts its sporting pedigree with a remarkable underwater resistance of 300m. Its H-shaped bracelet, fitted with a diving extension and safety buttons, extends the striking monochromatic theme of the timepiece and plays off the design's sharp lines and geometry, exemplified by the unidirectional rotating bezel's six finely polished studs. The shock-resistant watch boasts high level of clarity thanks to the vivid contrast of its luminescent components against a deep black dial with horizontal streak patterns. A statement of masculine refinement, the Aquaracer 300M Calibre 5 breathes new life into a line of TAG Heuer timepieces that has embodied the aquatic sporting experience for more than seven decades.

Designed in collaboration with five-time Grand Slam tennis champion Maria Sharapova, the TAG Heuer Carrera Lady Calibre 9 is a revelation of feminine strength and athletic luxury. Like Sharapova herself, the self-winding wristwatch blends its attention to aesthetic detail with a resilient spirit of high-end performance. Powered by TAG Heuer's new Calibre 9, the 28mm steel timepiece indicates the hours, minutes, seconds and date with outstanding precision and reliability. A mother-of-pearl dial provides a shimmering interplay of light and colors, further embellished by a setting of 12 diamonds that reflects the sparkling spectacle of the bezel's 56 additional precious stones. Equally stunning under bright lights or in an intimate setting, the Carrera Lady Calibre 9 takes on feminine horology with exquisite sophistication.

▲ **AQUARACER 300M CALIBRE 5**
Resistant to a depth of 300 meters below the surface, this robust sporting timepiece brings a tasteful elegance to the world of aquatic adventure.

▶ **TAG HEUER CARRERA LADY CALIBRE 9**
A diamond-adorned bezel and mother-of-pearl dial confirm the decisive sensuality of this self-winding feminine wristwatch.

TAG HEUER CARRERA CALIBRE 1887 CHRONOGRAPH   REF. CAR2C12.FC6327

Movement: automatic-winding TAG Heuer caliber 1887.
Functions: hours, minutes; small seconds and date at 6; chronograph: 30-minute counter at 9, 12-hour counter at 3, central seconds hand.
Case: polished, fine-brushed and sandblasted steel and titanium; Ø 45mm; black titanium carbide coated steel fixed bezel; curved scratch-resistant antireflective sapphire crystal; scratch-resistant smoked sapphire caseback; water resistant to 10atm.
Dial: light gray interior; anthracite exterior with sunray effect; hand-applied Arabic numerals; polished hour and minute hands with luminescent material; red tip on chronograph seconds hand; red tip on chronograph hour and minute hands; hand-applied TAG Heuer logo; "CARRERA – CAL. 1887" lettering.
Strap: "soft-touch" black alligator leather; grade-2 black titanium folding clasp with safety pushbuttons.
Price: available upon request.

TAG HEUER CARRERA CALIBRE 1887 CHRONOGRAPH   REF. CAR2A10.BA0799

Movement: automatic-winding TAG Heuer caliber 1887.
Functions: hours, minutes; small seconds at 9; date at 3; chronograph: 12-hour counter at 6, 30-minute counter at 12, central seconds hand.
Case: polished and fine-brushed steel; Ø 43mm; ceramic bezel with tachometer scale; curved scratch-resistant antireflective sapphire crystal; scratch-resistant sapphire caseback; water resistant to 10atm.
Dial: black; hand-applied Arabic numerals, polished hour and minute hands with luminescent material, red tip on chronograph seconds hand; red tip on chronograph hour and minute hands; hand-applied TAG Heuer logo; "CARRERA CAL. 1887" lettering.
Bracelet: three-row multifaceted steel; finishing: alternated polished and fine-brushed central row and fine-brushed lateral rows with polished edges; steel folding clasp with safety pushbuttons.
Price: available upon request.
Also available: black dial with black alligator leather strap; anthracite dial with steel bracelet; anthracite dial with anthracite alligator leather strap.

TAG HEUER CARRERA CALIBRE 7 TWIN-TIME   REF. WAR2012.BA0723

Movement: automatic-winding TAG Heuer caliber 7 Twin-Time.
Functions: hours, minutes, seconds; date at 3; GMT by hand.
Case: polished steel; Ø 41mm; polished steel fixed bezel; polished crown with TAG Heuer logo; curved scratch-resistant antireflective sapphire crystal; scratch-resistant sapphire caseback; water resistant to 10atm.
Dial: anthracite with sunray effect; hand-applied polished and fine-brushed hour markers; hour and minute hands with luminescent markers; polished GMT hand with red touch; hand-applied TAG Heuer logo; "CARRERA - CALIBRE 7 TWIN-TIME automatic" lettering.
Bracelet: three-row multifaceted steel; finishing: alternated polished and fine-brushed central row and fine-brushed lateral rows with polished edges; steel folding clasp with safety pushbuttons.
Price: available upon request.
Also available: anthracite dial with anthracite alligator leather strap; black dial with steel bracelet; black dial with black alligator leather strap; silver dial with steel bracelet; silver dial with brown alligator leather strap.

TAG HEUER CARRERA CALIBRE 5 STEEL & ROSE GOLD   REF. WAR215D.BD0784

Movement: automatic-winding TAG Heuer caliber 5.
Functions: hours, minutes, seconds; date at 3.
Case: polished steel; Ø 39mm; solid 18K 5N rose-gold fixed bezel; solid 18K 5N rose-gold crown with TAG Heuer logo; curved scratch-resistant antireflective sapphire crystal; scratch-resistant sapphire caseback; water resistant to 10atm.
Dial: silver opalin; hand-applied polished and fine-brushed rose-gold plated hour markers, rose-gold plated hour and minute hands with luminescent material; hand-applied TAG Heuer logo; "CARRERA - CALIBRE 5 automatic" lettering.
Bracelet: three-row multifaceted steel and polished 18K 5N rose gold capped; alternated polished and fine-brushed central row and fine-brushed lateral rows with polished edges; steel folding clasp with safety pushbuttons.
Price: available upon request.
Also available: silver dial with brown alligator leather strap; anthracite dial with steel and rose-gold bracelet; anthracite dial with anthracite alligator leather strap.

AQUARACER 300M CALIBRE 16 CHRONOGRAPH   REF. CAY2110.BA0925

Movement: automatic-winding TAG Heuer caliber 16.
Functions: hours, minutes; small seconds at 9; date at 3; chronograph: 30-minute counter at 12, 12-hour counter at 6, central seconds hand.
Case: fine-brushed and polished steel; Ø 43mm; unidirectional turning steel bezel: engraved numbers, luminescent dot at 12 and polished chamfer; polished steel screw-down crown; scratch-resistant antireflective sapphire crystal; screw-down caseback with diving bell engraving; water resistant to 30atm.
Dial: black with horizontal lines; hand-applied faceted hour markers with luminescent

material; faceted hour and minute hands with luminescent material; chronograph seconds hand with a yellow triangle-shaped tip; hand-applied "TAG Heuer" logo; "AQUARACER - CALIBRE 16" lettering at 3.
Bracelet: fine-brushed and polished steel H-shaped links; fine-brushed steel folding clasp with safety pushbuttons and diving extension.
Price: available upon request.
Also available: blue dial with steel bracelet; silver dial with steel bracelet.

AQUARACER 300M CALIBRE 5   REF. WAY2110.BA0910

Movement: automatic-winding TAG Heuer caliber 5.
Functions: hours, minutes, seconds; date at 3.
Case: fine-brushed and polished steel; Ø 40.5mm; unidirectional turning bezel: engraved numbers, luminescent dot at 12 and polished chamfer; polished steel screw-down crown; scratch-resistant antireflective sapphire crystal; screw-down caseback with diving bell engraving; water resistant to 30atm.
Dial: black with horizontal lines; hand-applied faceted hour markers with luminescent material; faceted hour and minute hands with luminescent material; seconds hand with

triangle-shaped tip and luminescent material; protruded "TAG Heuer" logo at 12; "AQUARA-CER – CALIBRE 5 – 300 m/1000 ft" lettering.
Bracelet: fine-brushed and polished steel H-shaped links; fine-brushed steel folding clasp with safety pushbuttons and diving extension.
Price: available upon request.
Also available: black dial with black rubber strap; silver dial with steel bracelet; blue dial with steel bracelet; anthracite dial with steel bracelet ("sunray" effect dial for blue and anthracite versions).

AQUARACER 300M CALIBRE 5 STEEL & ROSE GOLD   REF. WAY2150.BD0911

Movement: automatic-winding TAG Heuer caliber 5.
Functions: hours, minutes, seconds; date at 3.
Case: fine-brushed and polished steel; Ø 40.5mm; unidirectional turning bezel: engraved numbers, luminescent dot at 12; polished chamfer and fine-brushed solid 5N 18K rose gold ring; polished steel screw-down crown; scratch-resistant antireflective sapphire crystal; screw-down caseback with diving bell engraving; water resistant to 30atm.
Dial: silver with horizontal lines; hand-applied rose-gold plated hour markers with lumines-

cent material; rose-gold plated faceted hour and minute hands with luminescent material; seconds hand with triangle-shaped tip and luminescent material; protruded rose-gold colored "TAG Heuer" logo at 12; "AQUARACER – CALI-BRE 5 – 300 m/1000 ft" lettering.
Bracelet: fine-brushed and polished steel and 5N 18K rose-gold capped H-shaped links; fine-brushed steel folding clasp with safety pushbuttons and diving extension.
Price: available upon request.
Also available: steel and 3N 18K yellow-gold.

LINK CALIBRE 16 CHRONOGRAPH   REF. CAT2010.BA0952

Movement: automatic-winding TAG Heuer caliber 16.
Functions: hours, minutes; small seconds at 9; date at 3; chronograph: 30-minute counter at 12, 12-hour counter at 6, central seconds hand.
Case: polished and fine-brushed steel; Ø 43mm; polished "cushion-shaped" fixed bezel with black tachometer; polished steel pushbuttons and screw-down crown; curved scratch-resistant antireflective sapphire crystal; screw-down caseback with engraved decoration and TAG Heuer logo; water resistant to 10atm.
Dial: black with vertical streak effect; hand-applied curved, faceted and polished hour markers;

faceted polished hour and minute hands; lumines-cent material on minute and hour hands and on flange; hand-applied monochrome TAG Heuer logo; "LINK – CALIBRE 16" lettering.
Bracelet: fine-brushed steel with polished edges; steel folding clasp with safety pushbuttons.
Price: available upon request.
Also available: silver dial with steel brace-let; anthracite dial with steel bracelet.

TAG HEUER FORMULA 1 CALIBRE 6 — REF. WAZ2110.BA0875

Movement: automatic-winding TAG Heuer caliber 6.
Functions: hours, minutes; small seconds at 6; date at 3.
Case: polished and fine-brushed steel; Ø 41mm; unidirectional polished and fine-brushed steel turning bezel; polished steel "Easy Grip" screw-down crown with raised fine-brushed TAG Heuer shield with black line; sapphire crystal; circular fine-brushed screw-down caseback with special checkered decoration; water resistant to 20atm.
Dial: black; black small seconds counter with azurage; polished hand-applied hour markers and oversized "12" numeral with luminescent material; polished hour and minute hands with luminescent material; small seconds hand with red tip; monochrome "TAG Heuer" logo; "FORMULA 1" lettering at 12; printed minuterie with a red touch on flange.
Bracelet: fine-brushed steel; three rows; fine-brushed steel double safety clasp.
Price: available upon request.
Also available: black dial with black rubber strap, white dial with steel bracelet.

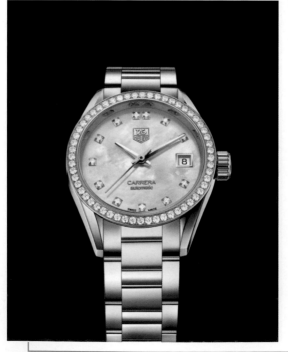

MONACO CALIBRE 12 CHRONOGRAPH — REF. CAW2111.FC6183

Movement: automatic-winding TAG Heuer caliber 12.
Functions: hours, minutes; small seconds at 3; date at 6; chronograph: 30-minute counter at 9, central seconds hand.
Case: polished and fine-brushed steel; Ø 39mm; polished crown; polished steel push-buttons; sapphire crystal; sapphire caseback; water resistant to 10atm.
Dial: blue; faceted polished hour and minute hands with luminescent material; hand-applied hour markers; "MONACO" – "AUTOMATIC CHRONOGRAPH" – "CALIBRE 12" lettering; monochrome TAG Heuer logo.

Strap: blue alligator leather; folding buckle with safety pushbuttons.
Note: modeled after Steve McQueen's chronograph in 1970 movie *Le Mans*.
Price: available upon request.
Also available: black dial with black alligator leather strap.

TAG HEUER CARRERA LADY CALIBRE 9 — REF. WAR2415.BA0770

Movement: automatic-winding TAG Heuer caliber 9.
Functions: hours, minutes, seconds; date at 3.
Case: polished steel; Ø 28mm; polished steel fixed bezel set with 56 Top Wesselton diamonds (0.55 carat); polished steel crown; scratch-resistant antireflective sapphire crystal; scratch-resistant sapphire caseback; water resistant to 10atm.
Dial: white mother-of-pearl; 12 Top Wesselton diamonds (0.1 carat); faceted and polished hour and minute hands; polished seconds hand; hand-applied date window at 3; polished and protruded TAG Heuer logo at 12; "CARRERA – automatic" lettering.
Bracelet: polished steel "H-shaped" links; steel folding clasp with safety pushbuttons.
Price: available upon request.

TAG HEUER CARRERA LADY STEEL & ROSE GOLD — REF. WAR1352.BD0774

Movement: quartz.
Functions: hours, minutes; date at 3.
Case: polished steel; Ø 32mm; 5N 18K solid rose-gold fixed bezel; 5N 18K solid rose-gold crown; scratch-resistant antireflective sapphire crystal; water resistant to 10atm.
Dial: white mother-of-pearl; 12 Top Wesselton diamond hour markers (0.1 carat); faceted and polished rose-gold plated hour and minute hands; polished and protruded TAG Heuer logo at 12; "CARRERA" lettering.
Bracelet: polished steel and 5N 18K rose-gold capped H-shaped links; steel folding clasp with safety pushbuttons.
Price: available upon request.

AQUARACER LADY STEEL & YELLOW GOLD   REF. WAY1351.BD0917

Movement: quartz.
Functions: hours, minutes, seconds; date at 3.
Case: fine-brushed and polished steel; Ø 32mm; unidirectional turning bezel: engraved numbers, luminescent dot at 12, polished chamfer and polished solid 3N 18K yellow gold ring; polished steel screw-down crown; scratch-resistant antireflective sapphire crystal; screw-down caseback with diving bell engraving; water resistant to 30atm.
Dial: white mother-of-pearl; 11 Top Wesselton diamond hour markers (0.11 carat); faceted and polished yellow-gold plated hour and minute hands with luminescent material; polished yellow-gold plated second hand; polished and protruded "TAG Heuer" logo at 12; "AQUARACER – 300m /1000ft" lettering.
Bracelet: fine-brushed and polished steel and 3N 18K yellow-gold capped H-shaped links; fine-brushed steel folding clasp with safety pushbuttons and diving extension.
Price: available upon request.

AQUARACER LADY   REF. WAY1414.BA0920

Movement: quartz.
Functions: hours, minutes, seconds; date at 3.
Case: fine-brushed and polished steel; Ø 27mm; unidirectional turning polished steel bezel set with 30 Top Wesselton diamonds (0.36 carat); polished steel screw-down crown; scratch-resistant antireflective sapphire crystal; screw-down caseback with diving bell engraving; water resistant to 30atm.
Dial: mother-of-pearl; 11 Top Wesselton diamond hour markers (0.08 carat); faceted hour and minute hands with luminescent material; TAG Heuer logo at 12; "AQUARACER – 300m/1000ft" lettering.
Bracelet: fine-brushed and polished steel; H-shaped links; fine-brushed steel folding clasp with safety pushbuttons.
Price: available upon request.

TAG HEUER FORMULA 1 LADY CALIBRE 5   REF. WAU2212.BA0859

Movement: automatic-winding TAG Heuer caliber 5.
Functions: hours, minutes, seconds; date at 6.
Case: polished steel; Ø 37mm; polished steel and black ceramic fixed bezel set with 48 diamonds (0.35 carat); polished steel screw-down crown and crown protectors; sapphire caseback; water resistant to 20atm.
Dial: black; set with 11 Wesselton diamond hour markers and 38 Wesselton diamonds in central ring (0.18 carat); polished hour and minute hands with luminescent material; protruded monochrome TAG Heuer logo; "TAG HEUER – FORMULA 1 – AUTOMATIC" lettering.
Strap: five-row alternating polished steel and black ceramic; polished steel butterfly folding clasp with safety pushbuttons.
Price: available upon request.
Also available: white ceramic.

TAG HEUER FORMULA 1 LADY   REF. WAH1313.BA0868

Movement: quartz.
Functions: hours, minutes, seconds; date at 3.
Case: polished steel; Ø 32mm; polished fixed steel and white ceramic bezel set with 48 Wesselton diamonds (0.35 carat) and black engraved minute markers; polished steel screw-down crown, crown protectors and screw-down caseback; water resistant to 20atm.
Dial: white; 12 Wesselton diamonds (0.09 carat); faceted hour and minute hands with luminescent material; protruded monochrome TAG Heuer logo; "TAG HEUER – FORMULA 1" lettering.
Bracelet: five-row alternating steel and white ceramic; polished steel butterfly folding clasp and safety pushbuttons.
Price: available upon request.
Also available: black ceramic.

VACHERON CONSTANTIN
Manufacture Horlogère. Genève, depuis 1755.

OPEN INTRICACIES

Vacheron Constantin unveils two timepieces representative of the watchmaker's extraordinary range of expertise and passion for transparency and intricate details. **BLENDING ART AND ENGINEERING, FUNCTION AND AESTHETIC BEAUTY, THE 260-YEAR-OLD HOUSE DEMONSTRATES A COURAGE ACHIEVABLE ONLY BY A TRUE MASTER OF THE CRAFT.** The Malte Tourbillon Openworked and Métiers d'Art Mécaniques Ajourées High Jewellery boldly bare their most elusive secrets in a tour de force that transcends the multitude of skills involved in their creation.

The Swiss manufacture's Malte Tourbillon Openworked, anointed with the exclusive Hallmark of Geneva, presents its wearer with a stunning spectacle of depth and dimensions. Within the graceful frame of its tonneau-shaped platinum case, the hand-wound timepiece explores the sophisticated beauty of watchmaking. A masterpiece of exquisite craftsmanship, the Malte Tourbillon Openworked achieves its splendor, not through adding superfluous displays of skill, but rather by removing the obstacles that conceal the mesmerizing heartbeat of a fine timekeeping instrument. The caliber, boasting 246 hand-drawn and chamfered components, is showcased via a skeletonized architecture that required more than 500 hours to perfect. An imposing tourbillon carriage, occupying nearly the entire lower half of the face, strikes a powerful counter-balance to the upper quadrants' exhibition of the 2790 SQ caliber's dynamic gears and superb finishes. At 2 o'clock, a hand-guided date counter is instantly legible, while preserving the dial's depth and three-dimensional effect.

The tourbillon at 6 o'clock dominates the face of this sculptural work of art with weightless aesthetics and vibrant energy. A ballet of sharp lines and fluid curves, of lights and shadows, the 18,000vph timepiece acts as a breathtaking tribute to Jean-Marc Vacheron's passion for the openwork concept—a fascination that began with his very first creation in 1755. A slate-colored opaline ring frames the dial with refined sobriety, graced by a single slender Roman numeral drawing the eye back to the construction's upper level in a masterful display of spatial artistry.

Each new inspection of the face of the Malte Tourbillon Openworked yields a wealth of delicate details and artisanal finishes. Vacheron Constantin thus dazzles the world of haute horology with a creation more enthralling with each reflected ray of light, with each movement of the wrist—and ultimately, with every pulse of its superb caliber.

Vacheron Constantin dazzles the world of haute horology with a creation that grows more enthralling with every pulse of its superb caliber.

◀ **MALTE TOURBILLON OPENWORKED**
A large tourbillon at 6 o'clock adds a complicated layer to this wristwatch's stunning play of depth and three-dimensional space..

Yet it is with its openworked movement that the manually-wound timepiece makes its most striking artistic statement. Hand-engraved and finished with meticulous precision, the 127-component 4400 SQ caliber brings its inner beauty to the forefront, presented without obstruction beneath two skeleton-ized hands indicating the hours and minutes. Using an ingenious array of age-old tech-niques, Vacheron Constantin's expert artisans strike an inspiring balance of aesthetic delight and flawless functionality. Several hundred hours were required to remove nearly half of the base caliber's material in the quest for a sculp-tural work of brilliance, depth and weightlessness. Of course, we must not forget the devotion to performance of the legendary Swiss manufacture. The 2.8mm-thick movement, while hypnotic in its visual beauty, operates with a precision worthy of the Hallmark of Geneva's strict standards of complete excel-lence, oscillating at a frequency of 28,800 vph with a generous 65-hour power reserve. The 40mm wristwatch is worn on a black hand-sewn Mississippiensis alligator strap boasting an 18-karat white-gold buckle adorned with 12 additional baguette-cut diamonds.

Vacheron Constantin continues its tradition of architectural transparency with a timepiece that sees its core transformed into a canvas for technical dexterity and artistic audacity. The Métiers d'Art Mécaniques Ajourées High Jewellery, honored with the Hallmark of Geneva, begins its story with the shimmer of 42 baguette-cut diamonds on the 18-karat white-gold case's bezel. Playing off the luster of the numerous precious stones, the timepiece boasts a dial embellished by the inimitable impact of a deep opaque black external ring in Grand Feu enamel. The extremely unforgiving process—which requires successive high-temperature firings compromised by even the slightest imperfection or dust particle—is made even more challenging by the choice of color, as darker hues expose the smallest of flaws. Evoking the aesthetics of a large railroad-station clock, 12 Roman numerals rise from the struc-ture and accentuate the watch's decisive three-dimensional personality.

Juxtaposing the shimmer of its precious stones with a splendidly finished caliber and Grand Feu enamel, the Métiers d'Art Mécaniques Ajourées High Jewellery communicates the full richness of the horological arts.

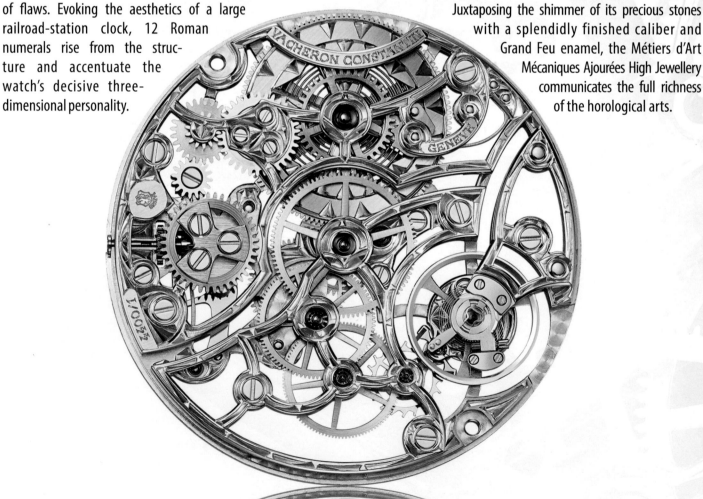

VACHERON CONSTANTIN

◀ **MÉTIERS D'ART MÉCANIQUES AJOURÉES HIGH JEWELLERY**

Finished with the legendary manufacture's emblematic Maltese Cross at 12 o'clock, this openworked handwound timepiece embellishes its sublime engraving craftsmanship with an external ring in opaque black Grand Feu enamel.

VACHERON CONSTANTIN

PATRIMONY ULTRA-THIN CALIBRE 1731
REF. 30110/00R-9793

Movement: manual-winding 1731 caliber; Ø 32.8mm, thickness: 3.9mm; 65-hour power reserve; 265 components; 36 jewels; 21,600 vph.
Functions: hours, minutes; small seconds at 8; minute repeater.
Case: 5N 18K pink gold; Ø 41mm, thickness: 8.09mm; sapphire crystal caseback.
Dial: silvered opaline; convex exterior; 5N 18K pink-gold hour markers and pearl minute-track.
Strap: black Mississippiensis alligator leather; hand-stitched; saddle-finish; large square scales; 5N 18K pink-gold buckle with polished half Maltese cross.

Note: delivered with resonator of sound "La Musique du Temps" enhancing the sound and harmony notes of Vacheron Constantin minute repeaters; Hallmark of Geneva certified timepiece.
Price: available upon request.

PATRIMONY RETROGRADE DAY & DATE
REF. 86020/000G-9508

Movement: automatic-winding Vacheron Constantin 2460 R31R7 caliber; Ø 27.2mm, thickness: 5.4mm; approx. 40-hour power reserve; 283 components; 27 jewels; 28,800 vph.
Functions: hours, minutes; retrograde day at 6; retrograde date on an arc between 9 and 3.
Case: 18K white gold; Ø 42.5mm, thickness: 10.07mm; sapphire crystal caseback, snap-on; water resistant to 3atm.
Dial: silvered opaline; convex external zone; circular-grained minute track; applied gold hour markers and baton-shaped hands.
Strap: black Mississippiensis alligator leather, hand-stitched, saddle finish, large square scales; 18K white-gold buckle with polished half Maltese cross.
Note: Hallmark of Geneva certified timepiece.
Suggested price: $49,600
Also available: 5N 18K pink gold.

TRADITIONNELLE SMALL SECONDS
REF. 82172/000R-9382

Movement: manual-winding Vacheron Constantin 4400 AS caliber; Ø 28.6mm, thickness: 2.8mm; approx. 65-hour power reserve; 127 components; 21 jewels; 28,800 vph.
Functions: hours, minutes; small seconds at 6.
Case: 5N 18K pink gold; Ø 38mm; screw-down sapphire crystal caseback; water resistant to 3atm.
Dial: silvered opaline; 12 gold applied hour markers and dauphine-shaped hands; black-painted minute tracks.
Strap: brown Mississippiensis alligator leather, hand-stitched, saddle finish, large square scales; 5N 18K pink-gold buckle with polished half Maltese cross.
Note: Hallmark of Geneva certified timepiece.
Suggested price: $20,900
Also available: platinum 950 with dark gray dial; 5N 18K pink gold with diamond-set hour markers; 18K white gold with or without diamond-set hour markers.

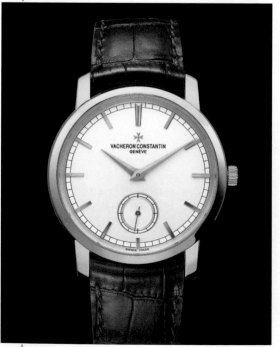

TRADITIONNELLE WORLD TIME
REF. 86060/000R-9640

Movement: automatic-winding Vacheron Constantin 2460 WT caliber; Ø 36.6mm, thickness: 7.55mm; 40-hour power reserve; 255 components; 27 jewels; 28,800 vph.
Functions: hours, minutes, seconds; world-time indication with day/night zone (37 cities).
Case: 5N 18K pink gold; Ø 42.5mm; sapphire crystal caseback closed with screws; water resistant to 3atm.
Dial: three dials; inner ring: sapphire with day/night indication and inked and engraved 24-hour indications; middle ring: metal with "Lambert Projection" map and transferred city names; external ring: metal with transferred minute-track and gold applied hour markers; gold hands.
Strap: brown Mississippiensis alligator leather, hand-stitched, saddle finish, large square scales; 5N 18K pink-gold triple-blade deployant half Maltese cross buckle.
Note: Hallmark of Geneva certified timepiece.
Suggested price: $52,600

TRADITIONNELLE SMALL SECONDS   REF. 82172/000P-9811

Movement: manual-winding Vacheron Constantin 4400 AS caliber; Ø 28.6mm, thickness: 2.8mm; 65-hour power reserve; 127 components; 21 jewels; 28,800 vph.
Functions: hours, minutes; small seconds at 6.
Case: 950 platinum; Ø 38mm, thickness: 7.7mm; transparent caseback; water resistant to 3atm.
Dial: slate gray opaline; white painted markers.
Strap: black Mississippiensis alligator leather with alligator leather inner shell: hand-stitched, saddle-finish, large square scales; polished 950 platinum half Maltese cross buckle.
Note: Hallmark of Geneva certified timepiece.
Suggested price: $35,700

TRADITIONNELLE CALIBRE 2253   REF. 88172/000R-X0001

Movement: manual-winding Vacheron Constantin 2253 caliber; Ø 32mm, thickness: 9.6mm; approx. 336-hour power reserve; 457 components; 30 jewels; 18,000 vph.
Functions: hours, minutes; small seconds on tourbillon at 6; equation of time; sunset/sunrise time chosen by the client; perpetual calendar: date at 3, day of the week at 9, month at 12, leap year at 1; power reserve indicator on caseback.
Case: 5N 18K pink gold; Ø 44mm, thickness: 15.71mm; screw-down sapphire crystal caseback; water resistant to 3atm.
Dial: silvered opaline; black-painted minute tracks; applied gold hour markers and dauphine-shaped hands.
Strap: brown Mississippiensis alligator leather; hand-stitched; saddle finish; large square scales; 5N 18K pink-gold triple-blade deployant half Maltese cross buckle.
Note: Hallmark of Geneva certified timepiece.
Price: available upon request.

PATRIMONY AUTOMATIC   REF. 85180/000G-9230

Movement: automatic-winding 2450 caliber; Ø 25.6mm, thickness: 3.6mm; 27 jewels; 28,800 vph.
Functions: hours, minutes, seconds; date at 6.
Case: 18K white gold; Ø 40mm; water resistant to 3atm.
Dial: clear opalescent silvered sunray; convex exterior; beaded minute track; 18K gold hour markers;
Strap: black Mississippiensis alligator leather; hand-stitched; 18K white-gold ardillon buckle.
Suggested price: $27,800

PATRIMONY PERPETUAL CALENDAR   REF. 43175/000R-9687

Movement: automatic-winding Vacheron Constantin 1120 QP caliber; Ø 29.6mm, thickness: 4.05mm; 40-hour power reserve; 276 components; 36 jewels; 19,800 vph.
Functions: hours, minutes; perpetual calendar: day at 9, date at 3, 48-month counter with leap year cycle at 12; moonphase at 6.
Case: 5N 18K pink gold; Ø 41mm; sapphire crystal caseback snap-on; water resistant to 3atm.
Dial: silvered opaline; convex external zone; circular-grained minute track, applied gold hour markers and baton-shaped hands.
Strap: brown Mississippiensis alligator leather, hand-stitched, saddle finish, large square scales; 5N 18K pink-gold triple-blade deployant half Maltese cross buckle.
Note: Hallmark of Geneva certified timepiece.
Suggested price: $83,000

VACHERON CONSTANTIN

PATRIMONY – SMALL MODEL   REF. 85515/CA1G-9841

Movement: manual-winding 2450 SC caliber; Ø 26.6mm, thickness: 3.6mm; 40-hour power reserve; 196 components; 27 jewels; 28,800 vph; gold hand-guilloché oscillating weight.
Functions: hours, minutes, seconds; date at 6.
Case: 18K white gold; Ø 36mm, thickness: 9.15mm; bezel set with 68 round-cut diamonds (approx. 0.78 carat); sapphire crystal caseback; water resistant to 3atm.
Dial: silvered opaline; convex exterior; minute track set with 48 round-cut diamonds (approx. 0.16 carat); 18K white-gold hour markers and leaf-shaped hands.

Bracelet: 18K white gold with folding clasp.
Suggested price: $59,900

PATRIMONY LADY GOLD BRACELET   REF. 86615/CA2R-9839

Movement: automatic-winding 2460 SC Vacheron Constantin caliber; Ø 26.2mm, thickness: 3.6mm; 40-hour power reserve; 182 components; 27 jewels; 28,800 vph.
Functions: hours, minutes, seconds.
Case: 18K 5N pink gold; Ø 36mm, thickness: 9.15mm; bezel, lugs and crown set with 77 round-cut diamonds (approx. 1 carat); sapphire crystal caseback; water resistant to 3atm.
Dial: gold; fully paved with 606 round-cut diamonds (approx. 1.8 carats); convex external zone; applied gold hour markers and leaf-shaped hands.

Bracelet: polished 5N 18K pink gold; 5N 18K pink-gold triple-blade deployant buckle; external links set with 92 round-cut diamonds (approx. 0.63 carat).
Note: Hallmark of Geneva certified timepiece.
Suggested price: $102,500

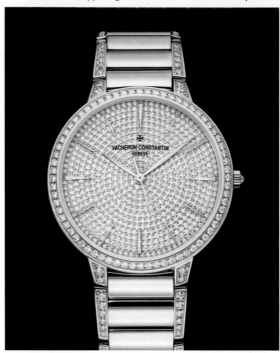

PATRIMONY – LADY MANUAL WINDING   REF. 81530/000R-9682

Movement: manual-winding 1400 caliber; Ø 20.65mm, thickness: 2.6mm; 40-hour power reserve; 98 components; 20 jewels; 28,800 vph.
Functions: hours, minutes.
Case: 5N 18K pink gold; Ø 36mm; caseband set with 62 brilliant-cut diamonds (approx. 0.39 carat); sapphire crystal caseback; water resistant to 3atm.
Dial: silvered opaline; convex exterior with circular grained minute track; 18K gold hour marker appliqués.
Strap: warm gray Mississippiensis alligator leather; stitched-tip; square scales; 5N 18K pink-gold buckle with polished half Maltese cross.
Note: delivered with second anthracite satin strap; Hallmark of Geneva certified timepiece.
Suggested price: $26,300
Also available: dark blue strap.

TRADITIONNELLE LADY MANUAL-WINDING   REF. 81590/000G-9848

Movement: manual-winding Vacheron Constantin 1400 caliber; Ø 20.65mm, thickness: 2.6mm; 40-hour power reserve; 98 components; 20 jewels; 28,800 vph.
Functions: hours, minutes.
Case: 18K white gold; Ø 33mm, thickness: 7.65mm; bezel set with 54 round-cut diamonds (approx. 0.88 carat); sapphire crystal caseback; water resistant to 3atm.
Dial: silvered opaline; gray painted minute track; applied gold hour markers and dauphine-shaped hands.
Strap: dark blue Mississippiensis alligator leather; stiched-tip; square scales; 18K white-gold buckle with polished half Maltese cross.
Note: Hallmark of Geneva certified timepiece.
Suggested price: $27,900

TRADITIONNELLE HIGH JEWELLERY REF. 81760/000G-9862

Movement: manual-winding Vacheron Constantin 1400 caliber; Ø 20.65mm, thickness: 2.6mm; 40-hour power reserve; 98 components; 20 jewels; 28,800 vph.
Functions: hours, minutes.
Case: 18K white gold; Ø 35mm, thickness: 8.34mm; fully paved with 124 baguette-cut diamonds (approx. 9.3 carats); crown set with 16 baguette-cut diamonds (approx. 0.22 carat); sapphire crystal caseback; water resistant to 3atm.
Dial: 18K gold; fully paved with 156 baguette-cut diamonds (approx. 6 carats); gold dauphine-shaped hands.
Strap: black satin; stitched tip; 18K white-gold half Maltese cross buckle set with 12 baguette-cut diamonds (approx. 0.74 carat).
Note: Hallmark of Geneva certified timepiece.
Price: available upon request.
Also available: Ø 40mm with Vacheron Constantin 4400 caliber.; Ø 30mm with quartz movement.

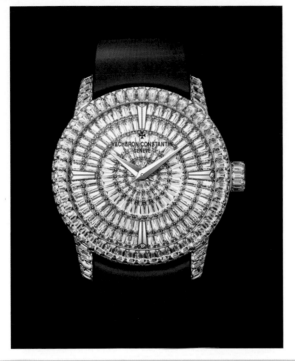

MALTE LADY REF. 25530/000R-9802

Movement: quartz; 1202 caliber; 13x15.7mm, thickness: 2.1mm; 33 components; 4 jewels; 32,768Hz.
Functions: hours, minutes.
Case: 5N 18K pink gold; 28.3x38.7mm, thickness: 7.28mm; bezel set with 50 round-cut diamonds (approx. 0.96 carat); water resistant to 3atm.
Dial: silvered, sand-blasted; 18K gold center paved with 142 round-cut diamonds (approx. 0.59 carat); 10 applied gold baton-shaped and 2 applied gold Roman numeral hour markers; gold lance-shaped hands.
Strap: gray satin; stitched-tip; 5N 18K pink-gold half Maltese cross buckle set with 21 round-cut diamonds (approx. 0.08 carat).
Suggested price: $35,300

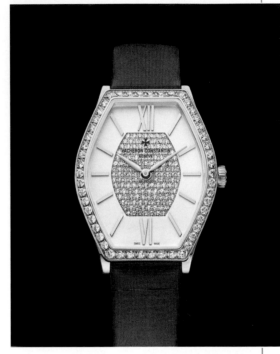

MALTE SMALL SECONDS REF. 82230/000G-9962

Movement: manual-winding Vacheron Constantin 4400 AS caliber; Ø 28.6mm, thickness: 2.8mm; 65-hour power reserve; 127 components; 21 jewels; 28,800 vph.
Functions: hours, minutes; small seconds at 6.
Case: 18K white gold; 36.7x47.61mm, thickness: 9.1mm; sapphire crystal caseback; water resistant to 3atm.
Dial: silvered sandblasted; two 18K white-gold applied Roman numerals at 12 and 6.
Strap: black Mississippiensis alligator leather: hand-stitched, saddle-finished, large square scales; 18K white-gold buckle with polished half Maltese cross.
Note: Hallmark of Geneva certified timepiece.
Suggested price: $26,800

MALTE TOURBILLON REF. 30130/000R-9754

Movement: manual-winding 2795 caliber; 27.37x29.3mm, thickness: 6.1mm; 45-hour power reserve; 169 components; 27 jewels; 18,000 vph.
Functions: hours, minutes; small seconds on the tourbillon at 6.
Case: 5N 18K pink gold; 38x48.24mm, thickness: 12.73mm; screw-down sapphire crystal caseback; water resistant to 3atm.
Dial: sand-blasted silvered; black painted minute tracks; ten baton-shaped hour marker appliqués and two Roman numeral appliqués at 12 and 6 in 5N 18K pink gold.
Strap: brown Mississippiensis alligator leather; large square scales; hand-stitched; saddle-finish; 5N 18K pink-gold triple-blade folding clasp with polished half Maltese cross.
Price: available upon request.

VACHERON CONSTANTIN

HISTORIQUES AMERICAN 1921 — REF. 82035/000R-9359

Movement: manual-winding 4400 caliber; Ø 28mm, thickness: 2.8mm; 65-hour power reserve; 21 jewels; 28,800 vph.
Functions: hours, minutes; small seconds at 3.
Case: 5N 18K rose gold; Ø 40mm; antireflective sapphire crystal; screw-down transparent caseback; water resistant to 3atm.
Dial: sandblasted finishing; black Arabic numerals; railway minute track; oxidized black 18K gold hands; 5N 18K pink-gold polished Maltese cross.
Strap: brown alligator leather; square scales; hand-stitched; saddle finish; 5N 18K pink-gold buckle with polished half Maltese cross.
Suggested price: $36,800

HISTORIQUES TOLEDO 1951 — REF. 86300/000R-9826

Movement: automatic-winding 2460 SC caliber; Ø 26.2mm, thickness: 3.6mm; 40-hour power reserve; 182 components; 27 jewels; 28,800 vph; 22K gold rotor.
Functions: hours, minutes, seconds.
Case: 5N 18K pink gold; 36.4x43mm, thickness: 8.9mm; water resistant to 3atm.
Dial: 18K gold, silvered opaline; hand-guilloché center; 5N 18K pink-gold Arabic numeral appliqué hour markers and pearl minute track.
Strap: brown Mississippiensis alligator leather; hand-stitched; saddle finish; large square scales; 5N 18K pink-gold buckle with polished half Maltese cross.
Suggested price: $39,700

HISTORIQUES ARONDE 1954 — REF. 81018/000R-9657

Movement: manual-winding 1400 AS caliber; Ø 20.65mm, thickness: 2.6mm; 40-hour power reserve; 20 jewels; 28,800 vph.
Functions: hours, minutes; small seconds at 6.
Case: 5N 18K pink gold; 31.2x44.5mm; water resistant to 3atm.
Dial: opaline silvered; hand-guilloché.
Strap: brown Mississippiensis alligator leather; stitched-tip; square-scaled; 5N 18K pink-gold buckle with polished half Maltese cross.
Suggested price: $32,000

1972 PRESTIGE — REF. 33172/000G-9775

Movement: manual-winding 1003 caliber; Ø 21.1mm, thickness: 1.64mm 31-hour power reserve; 117 components; 18 jewels; 18,000 vph; ultra-thin; 18K gold.
Functions: hours, minutes.
Case: 18K white gold; 25x47mm, thickness: 8.72mm; caseback engraved with "Prestige de la France"; water resistant to 3atm.
Dial: gray sunbrushed with transferred chevron pattern.
Strap: brown Mississippiensis alligator leather; alligator leather inner shell; stitched-tip; large square scales; 18K white-gold buckle with polished half Maltese cross.
Note: limited boutique edition of 40 pieces.
Suggested price: $41,900

OVERSEAS CHRONOGRAPH   REF. 49150/000A-9745

Movement: automatic-winding 1137 caliber; Ø 26.2mm, thickness: 6.6mm; 40-hour power reserve; 183 components; 27 jewels; 21,600 vph.
Functions: hours, minutes; small seconds at 6; large date at 12; column-wheel chronograph: 12-hour counter at 9, 30-minute counter at 3, central chronograph sweep seconds hand.
Case: stainless steel; Ø 42mm, thickness: 12.45mm; screw-down crown and pushbuttons; solid caseback stamped with "Overseas" medallion; water resistant to 15atm.
Dial: lacquered shiny blue with white painted markers; blue snailed counters with rhodiumized diamond-polish filets; 18K white-gold hands and hour markers with white luminescent material.
Strap: dark blue rubber; stainless steel triple-blade folding clasp, double security with buttons.
Note: comes with second dark blue Mississippiensis alligator leather strap: hand-stitched, saddle-finish, large square scales.
Suggested price: $21,500

OVERSEAS CHRONOGRAPH   REF. 49150/000R-9454

Movement: automatic-winding 1137 caliber; Ø 26.2mm, thickness: 6.6mm; approx. 40-hour power reserve; 183 components; 37 jewels; 21,600 vph.
Functions: hours, minutes; small seconds at 6; large date at 12; column-wheel chronograph: 12-hour counter at 9, 30-minute counter at 3 and central chronograph hand.
Case: 5N 18K pink gold; Ø 42mm, thickness: 12.4mm; screw-down crown and pushbuttons; screw-down solid caseback stamped with the "Overseas" medallion; anti-magnetic protection certified to 25,000 A/m; water resistant to 15atm.
Dial: silvered "Overseas" pattern; black-painted indications; snailed counters; 5N 18K pink-gold hour markers and hands with white luminescent coating.
Strap: brown Mississippiensis alligator leather, hand-stitched, large square scales; 5N 18K pink-gold triple-blade deployant half Maltese cross buckle with double security pushbuttons; delivered with an additional dark brown vulcanized rubber strap.
Suggested price: $48,400

OVERSEAS DUALTIME AUTOMATIC   REF. 47450-000W-9511

Movement: automatic-winding 1222 SC caliber; Ø 26.6mm, thickness: 4.85mm; 40-hour power reserve; 34 jewels; 28,800 vph.
Functions: hours, minutes, seconds; power reserve indicator at 9; second time zone with day/night indicator.
Case: stainless steel; titanium bezel; screw-down caseback; water resistant to 15atm.
Dial: slate gray; circular satin finish; painted minute track; twelve 18K white-gold hour marker appliqués with luminescent material.
Strap: black rubber; triple-blade lobster clasp with double stainless steel safety clasp.
Note: delivered with second dark gray hand-stitched square-scaled alligator leather strap.
Suggested price: $19,300

OVERSEAS DATE SELF-WINDING   REF. 47040/B01A-9093

Movement: automatic-winding 1226 SC caliber; Ø 26.6mm, thickness: 3.25mm; 40-hour power reserve; 143 components; 36 jewels; 28,800 vph.
Functions: hours, minutes, seconds; date at 4:30.
Case: stainless steel; polished bezel; screwed-down crown; solid caseback stamped with "Overseas" medallion; water resistant to 15atm.
Dial: silvered opaline with "Overseas" pattern; 18K white-gold hands and hour markers with white luminescent material.
Bracelet: stainless steel; polished and satin-finished half Maltese cross links; stainless steel triple-blade folding clasp, double security with buttons.
Suggested price: $15,200

VULCAIN

MANUFACTURE DEPUIS 1858

FLYING IN THE FACE OF TRADITION

SHOWCASING ITS BRILLIANT HERITAGE AND BOUNDLESS IMAGINATION THROUGHOUT ITS COLLECTIONS, Vulcain presents three mechanical timepieces of exquisite personality and tasteful technical complexity.

With its presentation of the First Lady Automatic, Vulcain reignites a love affair with feminine watchmaking that began in the dawn of the 20th century.

The self-winding wristwatch exudes a 1920s visual elegance enriched by a bold composition of colors and radiant materials. Housed in a refined 18-karat pink-gold oval case, the First Lady Automatic's charcoal-gray mother-of-pearl dial with guilloché decoration sets off the warmth of its golden hands and indexes with the sparkle of 39 diamonds in the Roman numerals at 12 and 6 o'clock. An additional 82 diamonds, lining the entirety of the watch's case and slender lugs, lend even more vitality to the sumptuous face. The heartbeat of the First Lady Automatic keenly mirrors the timepiece's exceptional attention to detail and standard of excellence. Animating two openworked hour and minute hands, a central seconds baton and a subtle date window at 3 o'clock, the 25-jewel V-61 caliber is prominently displayed through a sapphire crystal caseback. There, its elegant owner may admire an intimate spectacle: a skeletonized bidirectional oscillating weight with an intricate floral motif.

▶ **FIRST LADY AUTOMATIC**
This diamond-set ladies' wristwatch with guilloché mother-of-pearl dial extends its delicate visual grace to the stunning finishes of its caliber, which bears a skeletonized floral-motif oscillating weight.

Vulcain embodies a daring approach to haute horology, combining mechanical virtuosity with unique design codes that present a stunning vision of timekeeping.

The Swiss manufacture perpetuates its impressive aeronautical heritage—one marked by the equipping of local and American pilots as early as the 1950s—with a timepiece as sporty and masculine as it is authentically "Aviator."

The comprehensive dial of the Aviator Instrument Chronograph owes its remarkable legibility in large part to an ingeniously layered architecture and contrast of colors. A nod to the pilot's cockpit at 9 o'clock, complementing the watch's two chronograph counters, sweeping chronograph seconds stem and luminous principal hands, definitively confirms the timepiece's suitability for the wrist of an airborne adventurer. Indicated through two small openings, the self-winding V-59 caliber's running seconds are represented by way of a unique module that pays tribute to the aesthetics of an "alarm flag" found in cockpits' radio-altimeter instruments. The integration of a discreet date window within the 12-hour counter at 6 o'clock perfectly preserves the uncluttered refinement of the dial. The Aviator Instrument Chronograph extends its dynamic character to the caseback, where the owner is treated to a stunning view of the movement's detailed finishes through the openworked construction of its oscillating weight.

Vulcain has never shied away from a daring approach to haute horology, combining mechanical virtuosity with unique design codes that present the keeping of time in its most stunning manifestation.

The 50s Presidents Watch Manual contrasts the classicism of its form and refinement of its sophisticated movement with a fearless exhibition of colors. Framed by a ring of 80 shimmering diamonds on its 42mm steel case, the hand-wound wristwatch enlivens the spirit of haute horology with an attention-getting raspberry-toned dial. The colorful vibrancy is fittingly echoed by a shiny raspberry-colored Louisiana alligator leather strap. The 199-component Vulcain Cricket V-11 caliber, equipped with a double barrel and Exactomatic system, complements a classical three-hand-and-date configuration with Vulcain's legendary alarm complication. Indicated by an arrow-tipped baton set against understated numerals in the chapter ring, the caliber's alarm honors the watchmaker's extraordinary tradition within an exhilarating visual exposition.

▲ **AVIATOR INSTRUMENT CHRONOGRAPH**

A unique cockpit-inspired illustration of the running seconds leaves little doubt as to the high-flying personality of this self-winding chronograph.

▲ **50S PRESIDENTS WATCH MANUAL**

This daring spectacle of colors boasts a modern variation of Vulcain's groundbreaking Cricket alarm caliber.

VULCAIN

NAUTICAL SEVENTIES REF. 100159.081L

Movement: manual-winding Vulcain Cricket Manufacture V-10 caliber; 12 lines; 42-hour power reserve; 165 components; 25 jewels; 18,000 vph; twin barrels; equipped with Exactomatic system; angle of lift: 48°; decoration: nickel coating, blued screws.
Functions: hours, minutes, seconds; alarm: duration circa 20 seconds.
Case: 316L steel; Ø 42mm, thickness: 17.6mm; hesalite glass; screw-down crown at 4; triple caseback serving as resonance chamber and enabling use of alarm function; water resistant to 3atm.
Dial: orange re-edition of 1970s model; fixed with decompression table indication and 60-minute graduated rotating inner bezel ring.
Strap: black and orange water repellent leather; steel pin buckle, option of folding clasp.
Note: limited edition of 300 pieces.
Suggested price: $5,400
Also available: blue (ref. 100159.082L); green (ref. 100159A97.BAC116).

FIRST LADY AUTOMATIC REF. 61S164N2S.BAL412

Movement: automatic-winding Vulcain Automatic V-61 caliber; 11½ lines; 42-hour power reserve; 93 components; 25 jewels; 28,800 vph; angle of lift: 47°; decoration: rhodium coating, Côtes de Genève motifs, skeletonized rotor, blued screws.
Functions: hours, minutes, seconds; date at 3.
Case: 316L steel; 37.6x32.1mm, thickness: 9.2mm; set with 82 TW VS1-2 diamonds (approx. 1.07 carats); crown with cabochon; sapphire crystal caseback; water resistant to 3atm.
Dial: silver mother-of-pearl; rhodium hour markers set with 39 TW VS1-2 diamonds (approx. 0.056 carat).
Strap: pearl white Louisiana alligator leather; steel pin buckle.
Suggested price: $8,850
Also available: charcoal gray (ref. 61S164N1S.BAL413); chocolate brown (ref. 61S164N4S.BAL407).

AVIATOR INSTRUMENT CHRONOGRAPH DLC REF. 590863A07.BFC011

Movement: automatic-winding Vulcain Automatic V-59 caliber; 13¼ lines; 48-hour power reserve; 27 jewels; 247 components; angle of lift: 49°; decoration: nickel coating, skeletonized rotor.
Functions: hours, minutes; small seconds at 9; date at 6; chronograph: 12-hour counter at 6, 30-minute counter at 3, central chronograph seconds hand.
Case: DLC-coated 316L steel; Ø 44.6mm, thickness: 15.4mm; black pushbutton; anti-reflective sapphire crystal; water resistant to 10atm.
Dial: black; rhodiumed appliqués with C3 SuperLumiNova.
Strap: brown leather; steel folding clasp.
Note: limited edition of 100 pieces.
Suggested price: $4,600

50S PRESIDENTS WATCH CRICKET PRESIDENT 39MM REF. 100153.297L

Movement: manual-winding Vulcain Cricket Manufacture V-10 caliber; 12 lines; 42-hour power reserve; 25 jewels; 165 components; 18,000 vph; angle of lift: 48°; equipped with Exactomatic system; decoration: nickel coating, blued screws, skeletonized ratchet.
Functions: hours, minutes, seconds; alarm: circa 20 seconds.
Case: 316L steel; Ø 39mm, thickness: 12.4mm; antireflective sapphire crystal; caseback revealing stylized V for Vulcain; water resistant to 5atm.
Dial: blue sunray; rhodium hour markers.
Strap: Louisiana alligator leather; steel pin buckle, option of steel folding clasp.
Suggested price: $5,400
Also available: steel with silver dial (ref. 100153.295L); steel with charcoal gray dial (ref. 100153.296L).

HERITAGE PRESIDENTS 39MM
REF. 100653.290LF

Movement: manual-winding Vulcain Cricket Manufacture V-10 caliber; 12 lines; 42-hour power reserve; 25 jewels; 165 components; 18,000 vph; angle of lift: 48°; equipped with Exactomatic system; decoration: nickel coating, blued screws, skeletonized ratchet.
Functions: hours, minutes; seconds; alarm: circa 20 seconds.
Case: two-tone 5N 18K pink gold and 316L steel; Ø 39mm, thickness: 12.4mm; antireflective sapphire crystal; caseback revealing stylized V for Vulcain; water resistant to 5atm.
Dial: silver; re-edition of 1950 original; pink-gold hour markers.
Strap: brown Louisiana alligator leather; steel pin buckle, option of steel folding clasp.
Note: limited edition of 500 pieces.
Suggested price: $9,150
Also available: charcoal gray sunray dial (ref. 100653.291L).

50S PRESIDENTS AUTOMATIC
REF. 210550.280L

Movement: automatic-winding Vulcain Automatic Cricket Manufacture V-21 caliber; 12 lines; 42-hour power reserve; 36 jewels; 271 components; 18,000 vph; angle of lift: 48°; double barrel; equipped with Exactomatic system; decoration: rhodium coating, Côtes de Genève motifs, blued screws.
Functions: hours, minutes, seconds; date at 6; alarm, circa 20 seconds.
Case: 5N 18K pink gold; Ø 42mm, thickness: 14.6mm; antireflective sapphire crystal; caseback revealing stylized V for Vulcain.
Dial: charcoal gray; pink-gold hour markers.
Strap: black Louisiana alligator leather; 5N 18K pink-gold pin buckle.
Suggested price: $26,250
Also available: silver dial (ref. 210550.279L).

AVIATOR GMT PILOT
REF. 100108.333C

Movement: manual-winding Vulcain Cricket Manufacture V-10 caliber; 12 lines; 42-hour power reserve; 25 jewels; 165 components; 18,000 vph; angle of lift: 48°; equipped with Exactomatic system; decoration: nickel coating, blued screws, skeletonized ratchet.
Functions: hours, minutes, seconds; alarm; world time.
Case: 316L steel; Ø 42mm, thickness: 13.4mm; screw-down crown at 4; sapphire crystal; triple caseback acting as resonance chamber; water resistant to 10atm.
Dial: matte black; gold-toned SuperLumiNova numerals.
Strap: dark brown vintage-style calfskin; steel folding clasp, option of pin buckle.
Suggested price: $4,950
Also available: steel with silver ruthenium dial on black Lousiana alligator leather strap (ref. 100108.335L).

TOURBILLON
REF. 620565Q18.BGK101

Movement: manual-winding Vulcain Tourbillon V-62 caliber; 13¼ lines; 5 day power reserve; 37 jewels, 264 components; 28,800 vph; double barrel; angle of lift: 54°; decoration: charcoal gray-coated finish, Côtes de Genève motifs, tourbillon bridge representing stylized V for Vulcain, blued screws.
Functions: hours, minutes; 60-seconds tourbillon at 9; power reserve indicator at 5; retrograde date at 1:30.
Case: 5N 18K pink gold; Ø 42mm, thickness: 12.5mm; antireflective sapphire crystal; water resistant to 5atm.
Dial: charcoal gray; pink hour markers; circular semi-skeletonized satin-like and locked polished angles.
Strap: black hand-sewn Louisiana alligator leather; 5N 18K pink-gold three-strip ergonomic folding clasp.
Note: limited edition of 25 pieces.
Suggested price: $102,500
Also available: silver dial (ref. 620565Q28. BGK101).

ZENITH
SWISS WATCH MANUFACTURE
SINCE 1865

150 YEARS OF INSATIABLE ADVENTURE

A CENTURY AND A HALF AFTER ITS FOUNDING BY 22-YEAR-OLD VISIONARY Georges Favre-Jacot, Zenith once again displays the daring spirit that has guided the manufacture throughout its remarkable history.

In celebrating its 150th anniversary, the Swiss watchmaker honors a legacy that boasts an incredible 300 patents, 600 movement variations and more than 2,300 prizes in the field of precision timekeeping. But more than accolades and records, Zenith pays tribute to a tradition of excellence born from the exuberant ambitions of a young virtuoso in Switzerland's now renowned small town of Le Locle. And what better way to commemorate the occasion than with the iconic caliber brought to life by the manufacture just six months before humankind's first triumphant step on the surface of the moon? The world's first integrated automatic chronograph movement, the El Primero first dazzled the world of haute horology in 1969 with its unprecedented frequency of 36,000 vph.

Today, the hand-wound El Primero 4810 caliber animates the stunning limited edition Academy Georges Favre-Jacot, bringing the wearer close to a contemporary 575-component interpretation of haute horology's legendary fusée-and-chain mechanism. Showcased prominently on the upper half of the 18-karat rose-gold timepiece's dial, the movement's fusée-and-chain transmission permits a stabilization of the energy transmitted by the barrel to the silicon escape wheel regardless of the barrel's state of winding. The fruit of two years of research and development, the transmission accomplishes this regulation of force as the barrel, at 11 o'clock, and helical fusée, at 1 o'clock, are interconnected by an 18cm chain that wraps itself around the barrel during the course of the timepiece's 50-hour power reserve. A simple winding of the crown, however, activates the entire mechanism in reverse, causing it to turn counter-clockwise for the chain to once again wrap itself around the fusée. This modern high-performance take on the historic invention is contained within a design that exudes an air of 19th-century elegance. A small seconds subdial at 7 o'clock and power reserve indicator at 5 o'clock complete the fascinating architecture on a grained silver-toned dial.

▲ Head of LVMH Watches Jean-Claude Biver and son with the Rolling Stones: Ronnie Wood, Mick Jagger, Keith Richards and Charlie Watts.

The limited edition El Primero Chronomaster 1969 Tribute to the Rolling Stones infuses the original El Primero model with a jolt of rock and roll.

The 1960s upended the status quo all over the world, bringing the counter-culture to the mainstream and effecting fundamental changes in the realm of politics, technology—and, of course, rock and roll. The year 1962 marked the beginning of the Rolling Stones' musical career. But the rock legends were not the only stars to emerge in that unforgettable decade... In 1969, the El Primero was born. The two icons in their respective fields would join forces roughly a half century later. The El Primero Chronomaster 1969 Tribute to the Rolling Stones infuses the authentic design codes of the original El Primero model with a jolt of rock and roll and watch-making modernity. Revealing the heartbeat of its El Primero 4061 caliber through an aperture between 9 and 11 o'clock, the 36,000vph timepiece complements its central red chronograph hand with two counters depicting the complication's 30-minute and 12-hour increments. While the former, at 3 o'clock, echoes the same visual accents as its 1969 predecessor, the latter, at 6 o'clock, celebrates Zenith's partnership with the Rolling Stones with a bold overlay of the rock group's emblematic open-mouthed logo. The high-frequency wristwatch, which measures time to the tenth of a second, boasts an exhibition caseback through which the owner may admire its dynamic caliber as well as an engraving of the rock band's logo and "The Rolling Stones Edition" inscription on the sapphire crystal.

◀ **ACADEMY GEORGES FAVRE-JACOT**

A celebration of Zenith's 150th anniversary, this limited edition timepiece grants an unprec-edented view of the legendary fusée-and-chain system through a generous opening in the dial.

▲ **EL PRIMERO CHRONOMASTER 1969 TRIBUTE TO THE ROLLING STONES**

An iconic red tongue in the chronograph's 12-hour counter declares the rock-and-roll personality of this self-winding wristwatch.

The Swiss manufacture continues its birthday celebration with a tribute to another daring revolutionary, Felix Baumgartner, who on October 14, 2012, with Zenith on his wrist, leapt from the stratosphere on his way to history's most astonishing free fall. Breaking records for duration (four minutes and 20 seconds) altitude (38,969.4m) and velocity (1,357.6km/h), Baumgartner challenged the limits of human possibility. The Academy Christophe Colomb Tribute to Felix Baumgartner honors the achievement with a groundbreaking feat of its own—one poetically in line with the Austrian's fall from the skies. Though gravity propelled Baumgartner to unprecedented speeds, the force has been less of a friend to the world of mechanical watchmaking. Zenith demonstrates its the resourceful genius with an astounding miniature gyroscopic module inspired by the gimbal suspension systems of old marine chronometers. Counteracting the adverse effects of gravity on the mechanical movement, the timepiece's award-winning self-regulating gravity-control module, the first of its kind, ensures a perfect horizontal positioning of the escapement regardless of the wrist's countless possible positions. This resulting stability guarantees the widest possible amplitude of the balance wheel, and thus optimal precision. A 45mm platinum case with matte black DLC coating houses the mechanism. On the dial, the 10-piece limited edition complements the El Primero 8804 caliber's fascinating centerpiece, at 6 o'clock, with two clever nods to the inspiration for the timepiece. While a sculpted silhouette, representing Baumgartner in his space suit, adorns the power reserve indicator on the right of the dial's depiction of a turquoise Earth and aventurine Milky Way, a subtle white line at 12 o'clock in the principal subdial alludes to the adventurer's four-minute-and-20-second free-fall. An elaborate hand-engraved illustration on the caseback offers an homage to Baumgartner's journey from space.

▶ ACADEMY CHRISTOPHE COLOMB TRIBUTE TO FELIX BAUMGARTNER

This tribute to Felix Baumgartner's historic leap from the stratosphere counteracts the adverse effects of gravity with a groundbreaking gyroscopic module that maintains the horizontal positioning of the escapement.

Designed as part of Zenith's exciting partnership with the extraordinary Spindrift Racing team, whose conquering of the oceans aboard the Maxi Trimaran Spindrift 2 already boasts 10 world records, the El Primero Stratos Spindrift Racing timepiece takes to the seas. The DLC-coated steel wristwatch combines the El Primero's emblematic codes with a sporty character representative of its aquatic racing theme. Driven by the El Primero 4061 caliber with column-wheel chronograph, the 45mm timepiece juxtaposes the ruggedness of an authentic rotating bezel with the refinement of an exposed regulating organ at 10 o'clock. The use of non-magnetic silicon for the lever and escape wheel optimizes the watch's performance, thanks to the material's exceptional hardness, lightness and low friction coefficient. A carbon-fiber dial extends the all-black allure of the design while a telemetric scale inscribed with "Spindrift racing" allows the wearer to measure the distance or speed of a visible or audible phenomenon when cross-referenced with the chronograph's 36,000vph central seconds hand.

▲ EL PRIMERO STRATOS SPINDRIFT RACING

An aperture in the carbon-fiber dial of this nautical racing wristwatch reveals the beating heart of the legendary El Primero chronograph caliber.

ZENITH

ACADEMY CHRISTOPHE COLOMB PLANÈTE BLEUE   REF. 18.2211.8804/91.C713

Movement: manual-winding El Primero 8804 caliber, a unique gyroscopic system that ensures perfect horizontal positioning of the regulating organ; Ø 37mm, thickness: 5.85mm; 50-hour power reserve; 308 components, gyroscopic carriage contains 171 components; 45 jewels.
Functions: off-centered hours and minutes at 12; small seconds at 9; power reserve indicator at 3; self-regulating Gravity Control module at 6.
Case: 18K rose gold; Ø 45mm, thickness: 14.35mm (21.4mm with domed sapphire crystal); box-shaped antireflective sapphire with excrescent domes that cover Christophe Colomb module; water resistant to 3atm.
Dial: fine stone marquetry depicting European and American continents.
Strap: brown alligator leather with protective rubber lining; 18K gold triple folding clasp.
Note: limited edition of ten pieces; the gravity control module: a major milestone in mechanical watch making inspired by legendary marine chronometer instrument, a self-regulating gyroscopic module to guarantee horizontal positioning of regulating organ.
Also available: platinum with fine stone marquetry depicting European and Asian continents; black alligator leather strap; white-gold triple-folding clasp.

EL PRIMERO LIGHTWEIGHT   REF. 10.2260.400/69.R573

Movement: automatic-winding El Primero 400B Titanium caliber; Ø 30mm, thickness: 6.6mm; 50-hour power reserve; 328 components; 31 jewels; 36,000 vph; oscillating weight with Côtes de Genève pattern adorned with Spindrift racing logo; titanium main plate, barrel bridge, balance bridge, chronograph bridge, lever bridge and lever-wheel bridge; 5.2g lighter than regular El Primero caliber.
Functions: hours, minutes; small seconds at 9; date at 6; chronograph: 12-hour counter at 6, 30-minute counter at 3, central chronograph seconds hand.
Case: ceramized aluminum and carbon; Ø 45mm, thickness: 13.2mm; box-shaped antireflective sapphire crystal; water resistant to 10atm.
Dial: skeletonized; three colored counters.
Strap: black rubber; black PVD triple-folding clasp.
Note: limited edition of 250 pieces.

EL PRIMERO CHRONOMASTER GRANDE DATE   REF. 51.2161.4047/75.C713

Movement: automatic-winding El Primero 4047 caliber; Ø 30.5mm, thickness: 9.05mm; 50-hour power reserve; 332 components; 32 jewels; 36,000 vph; oscillating weight with Côtes de Genève pattern; silicon escapement wheel and lever.
Functions: hours, minutes; small seconds at 9; large date at 2; automatic column-wheel chronograph: 30-minute counter at 3, central chronograph seconds hand; sun and moonphase at 6; tachometer on flange.
Case: 18K rose gold and stainless steel; Ø 45mm, thickness: 15.6mm; box-shaped antireflective sapphire crystal; water resistant to 5atm.
Dial: brown-toned sunray; opening revealing heart of El Primero movement.

Strap: brown alligator leather strap with protective rubber lining; steel triple-folding clasp.
Also available: rose gold with silver-toned sunray dial, brown alligator leather strap, rose-gold pin buckle; rose gold and steel with silver-toned sunray dial, steel and gold bracelet or brown alligator leather strap, steel triple folding clasp; steel with silver-toned sunray dial; steel with silver-toned sunray dial; brown alligator leather or metal bracelet; steel triple-folding clasp; steel case with silver-toned sunray dial/brown alligator leather strap or metal bracelet/steel triple-folding clasp; steel case with black sunray dial/black alligator leather strap or metal bracelet/steel triple-folding clasp.

EL PRIMERO CHRONOMASTER 1969 TRIBUTE TO THE ROLLING STONES   REF. 03.2048.4061/77.C496

Movement: automatic-winding El Primero 4061 caliber; Ø 30mm, thickness: 6.6mm; 50-hour power reserve; 282 components; 31 jewels; 36,000 vph; oscillating weight with Côtes de Genève decoration; silicon escapement wheel and lever.
Functions: hours, minutes; small seconds at 9; automatic column-wheel El Primero chronograph: 12-hour counter at 6, 30-minute counter at 3, central chronograph seconds hand; tachometer on flange.
Case: stainless steel; Ø 42mm, thickness: 14.05mm; box-shaped antireflective sapphire crystal engraved with Rolling Stones tongue emblem, inscribed with "The Rolling Stones Edition"; water resistant to 10atm.
Dial: silver toned sunray; two colored counters, one bearing Rolling Stones tongue emblem.
Strap: black alligator leather with protective rubber lining; steel triple-folding clasp.
Note: limited edition of 250 pieces.
Also available: rose gold with silver-toned sunray dial and two colored counters, brown alligator leather strap, rose-gold pin buckle; steel with silver-toned sunray dial and two colored counters, brown alligator leather strap or metal bracelet, steel triple-folding clasp.

EL PRIMERO 36,000 VPH REF. 03.2040.400/69.C494

Movement: automatic-winding El Primero 400B caliber; Ø 30mm, thickness: 6.6mm; 50-hour power reserve; 326 components; 31 jewels; 36,000 vph; oscillating weight with Côtes de Genève decoration.
Functions: hours, minutes; small seconds at 9; date at 6; chronograph: 12-hour counter at 6, 30-minute counter at 3, central chronograph seconds hand; tachometer.
Case: stainless steel; Ø 42mm, thickness: 12.75mm; box-shaped antireflective sapphire crystal; water resistant to 10atm.
Dial: silver-toned sunray with 3 colored counters.
Strap: brown alligator leather with protective rubber lining; steel triple-folding clasp.
Also available: steel with black sunray dial, black alligator leather strap or metal bracelet, steel triple-folding clasp; steel with blue sunray dial, black alligator leather strap; steel triple-folding clasp.

EL PRIMERO STRATOS SPINDRIFT REF. 75.2060.4061/21.R573

Movement: automatic-winding El Primero 4061 caliber; Ø 30mm, thickness: 6.6mm; 50-hour power reserve; 282 components; 31 jewels; 36,000 vph; oscillating weight with Côtes de Genève decoration and Spindrift racing logo; opening on regulating organ.
Functions: hours, minutes; small seconds at 9; column-wheel chronograph: 12-hour counter at 6, 30-minute counter at 3, central chronograph seconds hand; telemeter on flange.
Case: stainless steel with DLC coating; Ø 45mm, thickness: 14.1mm; rotating bezel; box-shaped antireflective crystal; water resistant to 10atm.
Dial: genuine carbon fiber.
Strap: black rubber with Nomex fabric coating; black PVD triple-folding clasp.
Note: tribute to Zenith's partnership with Spindrift racing.
Also available: rose gold and titanium with black dial, black rubber with Nomex fabric coating, black PVD triple-folding clasp.

EL PRIMERO STRATOS FLYBACK RAINBOW REF. 03.2061.405/21.M2060

Movement: automatic-winding El Primero 405 B caliber; Ø 30mm, thickness: 6.6mm; 50 hour power reserve; 331 components; 31 jewels; 36,000 vph; oscillating weight with Côtes de Genève decoration.
Functions: hours, minutes; small seconds at 9; date at 6; flyback column-wheel chronograph: 12-hour counter at 6, 30-minute counter at 3, central chronograph seconds hand; telemeter on flange.
Case: stainless steel; Ø 45mm, thickness: 14.1mm; unidirectional rotating bezel with black aluminum disc; box-shaped antireflective sapphire crystal; water resistant to 10atm.
Dial: black with original colored 30-minute counter.
Bracelet: steel; steel triple-folding clasp.
Note: Zenith military chronograph legacy; tribute to Zenith Rainbow model from 1997.
Also available: Ti-Alum alloy with black dial, black rubber strap, black triple-folding clasp; boutiques and SIS exclusive model: limited edition of 250 pieces.

PILOT TYPE 20 ANNUAL CALENDAR REF. 03.2430.4054/21.C721

Movement: automatic-winding El Primero 4054 caliber; Ø 30mm, thickness: 8.3mm; 50-hour power reserve; 341 components; 29 jewels; oscillating weight with Côtes de Genève decoration; screwed plate with Swiss Civil aviation code: HB:-XXX.
Functions: hours, minutes; small seconds at 9; El Primero calendar chronograph: day and month at 3, date and 60-minute counter at 6, central chronograph seconds hand.
Case: titanium; Ø 48mm, thickness: 15.8mm; box-shaped antireflective sapphire crystal; caseback with Zenith flying instruments logo; water resistant to 10atm.
Dial: matte black; Arabic numerals with SuperLumiNova.
Strap: brown alligator leather strap with protective rubber lining; steel pin buckle.
Note: tribute to Zenith's aviation history.
Also available: titanium with rose-gold bezel, lugs, pushers and crown, black dial, brown alligator leather strap, titanium pin buckle.

ZENITH

PILOT DOUBLEMATIC
REF. 03.2400.4046/21.C721

Movement: automatic-winding El Primero 4046 caliber; 13¼ lines; Ø 30mm, thickness: 9.05mm; 50-hour power reserve; 439 components; 41 jewels; 36,000 vph; oscillating weight with Côtes de Genève pattern.
Functions: hours, minutes; chronograph: 30-minute counter at 3, central seconds hand; 24-hour time zones; large date at 2; alarm hour-hand in center; alarm ON/OFF between 8 and 9; alarm power reserve at 7.
Case: stainless steel; Ø 45mm, thickness: 15.6mm; box-shaped antireflective sapphire crystal on both sides; sapphire crystal caseback; water resistant to 5atm.

Dial: matte black; SuperLumiNova SLN C1 hour markers; black ruthenium hands.
Strap: brown alligator leather with protective leather lining.
Also available: 18K rose gold.

PILOT BIG DATE SPECIAL
REF. 03.2410.4010/21.C722

Movement: automatic-winding El Primero 4010 caliber; 13¼ lines; Ø 30mm, thickness: 7.65mm; 50-hour power reserve; 306 components; 31 jewels; 36,000 vph; oscillating weight with Côtes de Genève pattern.
Functions: hours, minutes; small seconds at 9; chronograph: 30-minute counter at 3, central seconds hand; large date at 6.
Case: brushed stainless steel; Ø 42mm, thickness: 13.5mm; box-shaped antireflective sapphire crystal on both sides; sapphire crystal caseback; water resistant to 5atm.
Dial: matte black; SuperLumiNova SLN C1 hour markers; black ruthenium satin-finished hands.

Strap: brown calfskin leather with protective rubber lining.
Also available: metal bracelet.

CAPTAIN MOONPHASE
REF. 03.2143.691/01.C498

Movement: automatic-winding Elite 691 caliber; Ø 25.6mm, thickness: 5.67mm; 50-hour power reserve; 228 components; 27 jewels; oscillating weight with Côtes de Genève decoration.
Functions: hours, minutes; small seconds at 9; large date at 1; moonphase at 6.
Case: stainless steel; Ø 40mm, thickness: 10.35mm; domed antireflective sapphire crystal; water resistant to 5atm.
Dial: silver-toned velvet finish; hour marker appliqués.
Strap: brown alligator leather strap with protective rubber lining; steel pin buckle.

Note: classic Zenith legacy watch.
Also available: rose gold with silver-toned velvet-finish dial, brown alligator leather strap, rose-gold pin buckle.

CAPTAIN POWER RESERVE
REF. 03.2122.685/21.C493

Movement: automatic-winding Elite 685 caliber; Ø 25.6mm, thickness: 4.67mm; 50-hour power reserve; 179 components; 38 jewels; 28,800 vph; oscillating weight with Côtes de Genève decoration.
Functions: hours, minutes; small seconds at 9; date at 6; power reserve indicator at 2.
Case: stainless steel; Ø 40mm, thickness: 9.25mm; domed antireflective sapphire crystal; water resistant to 5atm.
Dial: black-toned velvet finish; hour marker appliqués.
Strap: black alligator leather strap with protective rubber lining; steel pin buckle.

Note: classic Zenith legacy watch.
Also available: steel with silver-toned sunray dial, brown alligator leather strap, steel pin buckle.

CAPTAIN ULTRA THIN — REF. 18.2010.681/01.C498

Movement: automatic-winding Elite 681 caliber; Ø 25.6mm, thickness: 3.47mm; 50-hour power reserve; 128 components; 27 jewels; 28,800 vph; oscillating weight with Côtes de Genève decoration.
Functions: hours, minutes; small seconds at 9.
Case: 18K rose gold; Ø 40mm, thickness: 8.3mm; ultra-thin; domed antireflective sapphire crystal; water resistant to 5atm.
Dial: silver-toned sunray; hour marker appliqués.
Strap: brown alligator leather with protective rubber lining; rose-gold pin buckle.
Note: classic Zenith legacy watch.
Also available: rose gold with silver-toned sunray dial, rose-gold bracelet, rose-gold pin buckle; rose gold with white lacquered dial, rose-gold bracelet or brown alligator leather strap, rose-gold pin buckle; steel with silver-toned sunray dial or black sunray dial or white lacquered dial, black alligator leather strap, steel pin buckle.

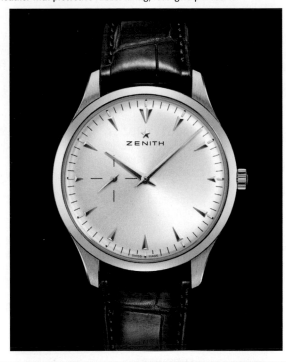

CAPTAIN ULTRA THIN — REF. 03.2010.681/11.C493

Movement: automatic-winding Elite 681 caliber; Ø 25.6mm, thickness: 3.47mm; 50-hour power reserve; 128 components; 27 jewels; 28,800 vph; oscillating weight with Côtes de Genève decoration.
Functions: hours, minutes; small seconds at 9.
Case: stainless steel; Ø 40mm, thickness: 8.3mm; ultra-thin; domed antireflective sapphire crystal; water resistant to 5atm.
Dial: white lacquer sunray; hour marker appliqués; Roman numerals.
Strap: black alligator leather with protective rubber lining; steel pin buckle.
Note: classic Zenith legacy watch.
Also available: rose gold with white lacquered dial or silver-toned sunray dial, rose-gold bracelet or brown alligator leather strap, rose-gold pin buckle; steel with silver-toned sunray dial or black sunray dial, black alligator leather strap, steel pin buckle.

CAPTAIN ULTRA THIN LADY MOONPHASE — REF. 16.2310.692/81.M2310

Movement: automatic-winding Elite 692 caliber; Ø 25.6mm, thickness: 3.97mm; 50-hour power reserve; 195 components; 27 jewels; 28,800 vph; oscillating weight with Côtes de Genève decoration.
Functions: hours, minutes; small seconds at 9; moonphase at 6.
Case: stainless steel; Ø 33mm, thickness: 8.65mm; set with diamonds; ultra-thin; moonphase adjusted via crown; domed antireflective sapphire crystal; water resistant to 3atm.
Dial: white mother-of-pearl; set with diamonds.
Bracelet: stainless steel; steel pin buckle.
Note: classic Zenith legacy watch; pair watch with Captain Men's collection.
Also available: rose gold with or without diamonds: white mother-of-pearl dial with diamonds, brown sunray dial, gold-toned sunray dial with diamonds, matte white dial with diamonds, silver-toned guilloché dial, rose-gold bracelet or brown alligator leather strap, rose-gold pin buckle; steel with or without diamonds, white mother-of-pearl dial with diamonds or silver toned guilloché dial, shiny gray alligator leather strap or metal bracelet, steel pin buckle; steel with diamonds, blue sunray dial, shiny blue alligator leather strap or metal bracelet, steel pin buckle.

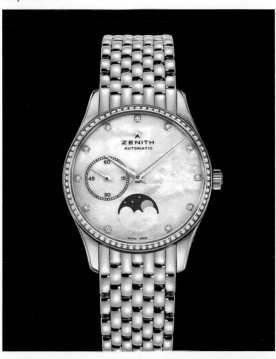

CAPTAIN PORT ROYAL — REF. 18.2020.3001/01.C498

Movement: automatic-winding Zenith 3001 caliber; Ø 25.6mm, thickness: 3.6mm; 42-hour power reserve; 25 jewels; oscillating weight with Côtes de Genève decoration.
Functions: hours, minutes, seconds; date at 6.
Case: 18K rose gold; Ø 40mm, thickness: 8.15mm; curved antireflective sapphire crystal; water resistant to 5atm.
Dial: silver.
Strap: brown alligator leather with protective rubber lining; rose-gold pin buckle.
Note: classical Zenith legacy watch.
Also available: rose gold with diamonds, silver dial, brown alligator leather strap, rose-gold pin buckle; rose gold and steel case, silver dial, brown alligator leather strap, steel pin buckle; steel, silver dial, steel pin buckle.

[Brand Directory]

ALPINA
8 Chemin de la Galaise
1228 Plan-les-Ouates
Switzerland
Tel: 41 22 860 04 40
USA: 877 619 2824

ARNOLD & SON
38 Boulevard des Eplatures
2300 La Chaux-de-Fonds
Switzerland
Tel: 41 32 967 97 97
USA: 213 622 1133

AUDEMARS PIGUET
1348 Le Brassus
Switzerland
Tel: 41 21 845 14 00
USA: 212 758 8400

BEDAT & CO.
45 Rue Agasse
1211 Geneva 17
Switzerland
Tel: 41 22 718 01 88
Canada: 514 418 8850

BLANCPAIN
6 Chemin de l'Etang
1094 Paudex
Switzerland
Tel: 41 21 796 36 36
USA: 877 520 1735

BOUCHERON
20, rue de la Paix
75002, Paris
France
Tel: 33 1 42 44 42 44

BREGUET
1344 L'Abbaye
Switzerland
Tel: 41 21 841 90 90
USA: 866 458 7488

BVLGARI
34 Rue de Monruz
2000 Neuchâtel
Switzerland
Tel: 41 32 722 78 78
USA: 212 315 9700

CARL F. BUCHERER
1805 South Metro Parkway
Dayton, OH 45459
USA: 800 395 4306
Switzerland: 41 41 369 74 80

CARTIER SA
8 Boulevard James-Fazy
1201 Geneva
Switzerland
Tel: 41 22 721 24 00
USA: 212 446 3400

CHANEL
25 Place du Marché St. Honoré
75001 Paris
France
Tel: 33 1 40 98 50 00
USA: 212 688 5055

CHAUMET
12 Place Vendôme
75001 Paris
France
Tel: 33 1 44 77 24 00

CHOPARD
6 Rue de Veyrot
1217 Meyrin Geneva 2
Switzerland
Tel: 41 22 719 3191
USA: 212 821 0300

CHRISTOPHE CLARET
2 Route du Soleil d'Or
2400 Le Locle
Switzerland
Tel: 41 32 933 80 80
USA: 954 610 2234

CORUM
Rue du Petit-Château 1
CH-2301 La Chaux-de-Fonds
Switzerland
Tel: 41 32 967 06 43
USA: 305 792 0884

DE BETHUNE
6 Granges-Jaccard
1454 La Chaux L'Auberson
Switzerland
Tel: 41 24 455 26 00
USA: 917 907 1127

DE GRISOGONO
39 Chemin du Champs des Filles
Bâtiment E
1228 Plan-les-Ouates
Switzerland
Tel: 41 22 817 81 00
USA: 212 439 4220

DIOR HORLOGERIE
44 Rue François 1er
75008 Paris
France
Tel: 33 1 40 73 59 84
USA: 212 931 2700

ERNST BENZ
Lake Geneva Business Park
7 Route de Crassier
CH-1262 Eysins
Switzerland
Tel: 41 22 595 19 07
USA: 248 203 2323

FREDERIQUE CONSTANT SA
32 Chemin du Champ des Filles
1228 Plan-les-Ouates
Switzerland
Tel: 41 22 860 04 40
USA: 877 619 2824

GIRARD-PERREGAUX
1 Place Girardet
2301 La Chaux-de-Fonds
Switzerland
Tel: 41 32 911 33 33
France: 33 1 72 25 65 43
USA: 201 355 4523

GLASHÜTTE ORIGINAL
1 Altenberger Strasse
01768 Glashütte/Sachsen
Germany
Tel: 49 3 50 53 460
France: 33 1 53 81 22 68
USA: 201 271 1400

GUY ELLIA
16 Place Vendôme
75001 Paris
France
Tel: 33 1 53 30 25 25
USA: 212 888 0505

HARRY WINSTON SA
8 Chemin du Tourbillon
1228 Plan-les-Ouates
Switzerland
Tel: 41 22 716 29 00
USA: 212 245 2000

HERMÈS
31A Erlenstrasse
2555 Brügg
Switzerland
Tel: 41 32 366 71 00
USA: 212 759 7585

HUBLOT
33 Chemin de la Vuarpillière
1260 Nyon 2
Switzerland
Tel: 41 22 990 90 00
USA: 800 536 0636

IWC
15 Baumgartenstrasse
8201 Schaffhausen
Switzerland
Tel: 41 52 635 65 65
USA: 800 492 6755

JACOB & CO.
1 Chemin de Plein-Vent
1228 Arare
Switzerland
Tel: 41 22 310 69 62
USA: 212 719 5887

JAEGER-LECOULTRE
Rue de la Golisse 8
1347 Le Sentier
Switzerland
Tel: 41 21 845 02 02
USA: 212 308 2525

JAQUET DROZ SA
2 Allée du Tourbillon
2300 La Chaux-de-Fonds
Switzerland
Tel: 41 32 924 28 88
France: 33 1 53 81 22 00
USA: 201 271 1400

JEANRICHARD
1 Place Girardet
2301 La Chaux-de-Fonds
Switzerland
Tel: 41 32 911 36 36
France: 33 1 72 25 65 43
USA: 201 804 1904

LONGINES
Saint-Imier 2610
Switzerland
Tel: 41 32 942 54 25
USA: 201 271 1400

LOUIS MOINET SA
1 Rue du Temple
2072 Saint-Blaise
Switzerland
Tel: 41 32 753 68 14
USA: 561 212 6812

PARMIGIANI
11 Rue du Temple
2114 Fleurier
Switzerland
Tel: 41 32 862 66 30
USA: 305 260 7770

PATEK PHILIPPE
141 Chemin du Pont du Centenaire
1228 Plan-les-Ouates
Switzerland
Tel: 41 22 884 20 20
USA: 212 218 1240

PERRELET
7 Rue Bubenberg
2502 Biel/Bienne
Switzerland
T: 41 32 346 26 26
USA: 954 575 7980

PIAGET
37 Chemin du Champ-des-Filles
1228 Plan-les-Ouates
Switzerland
Tel: 41 22 884 48 44
USA: 866 374 4430

POIRAY
8 Place Vendôme
75001, Paris
France
Tel: 33 1 42 97 99 05

RICHARD MILLE
11 rue du Jura
2345 Les Breuleux Jura
Switzerland
Tel: 41 32 959 43 53
USA: 310 205 5555

ROGER DUBUIS
1217 Meyrin 2 Geneva
Switzerland
Tel: 41 22 783 28 28
France: 33 1 58 18 14 67
USA: 888 738 2847

ROLEX
3-5-7 Rue François Dussaud
1211 Geneva 26
Switzerland
Tel: 41 22 302 22 00
USA: 212 758 7700

TAG HEUER
6A Louis-Joseph Chevrolet
2300 La Chaux-de-Fonds
Switzerland
Tel: 41 32 919 80 00
USA: 973 467 1890

VACHERON CONSTANTIN
10 Chemin du Tourbillon
1228 Plan-les-Ouates
Switzerland
Tel: 41 22 930 20 05
USA: 212 713 0707

VULCAIN SA
4 Chemin des Tourelles
2400 Le Locle
Switzerland
Tel: 41 32 930 80 10

ZENITH
2400 Le Locle
Switzerland
Tel: 41 32 930 62 62
USA: 973 467 1890